ASPEN COURSEBOOK SERIES

Your Client's Story

Persuasive Legal Writing

Ruth Anne Robbins

Clinical Professor of Law
Director of Lawyering Programs
Rutgers School of Law–Camden

Steve Johansen

Director of Legal Analysis and Writing
Professor of Law
Lewis & Clark Law School

Ken Chestek

Assistant Director, Legal Writing Program
Assistant Director, Center for the Study of Written Advocacy
Assistant Professor of Law
University of Wyoming College of Law

D1534364

To contact Customer Service, e-mail customer.service@wolterskluwer.com, call 1-800-234-1660, fax 1-800-901-9075, or mail correspondence to:

Wolters Kluwer Law & Business
Attn: Order Department
PO Box 990
Frederick, MD 21705

Printed in the United States of America.

1 2 3 4 5 6 7 8 9 0

ISBN 978-1-4548-0548-9

Library of Congress Cataloging-in-Publication Data

Robbins, Ruth Anne.
    Our client's story : persuasive legal writing / Ruth Anne Robbins, Steve Johansen, Ken Chestek.
       p. cm.—(Aspen coursebook series)
    Includes index.
    ISBN 978-1-4548-0548-9
    1. Legal composition. 2. Law—United States—Language. 3. Law—United States Methodology. I. Johansen, Steve. II. Chestek, Ken. III. Title.

    KF250.R625 2013
    808.06′634—dc23

2012041251

About Wolters Kluwer Law & Business

Wolters Kluwer Law & Business is a leading global provider of intelligent information and digital solutions for legal and business professionals in key specialty areas, and respected educational resources for professors and law students. Wolters Kluwer Law & Business connects legal and business professionals as well as those in the education market with timely, specialized authoritative content and information-enabled solutions to support success through productivity, accuracy and mobility.

Serving customers worldwide, Wolters Kluwer Law & Business products include those under the Aspen Publishers, CCH, Kluwer Law International, Loislaw, Best Case, ftwilliam. com and MediRegs family of products.

CCH products have been a trusted resource since 1913, and are highly regarded resources for legal, securities, antitrust and trade regulation, government contracting, banking, pension, payroll, employment and labor, and healthcare reimbursement and compliance professionals.

Aspen Publishers products provide essential information to attorneys, business professionals and law students. Written by preeminent authorities, the product line offers analytical and practical information in a range of specialty practice areas from securities law and intellectual property to mergers and acquisitions and pension/benefits. Aspen's trusted legal education resources provide professors and students with high-quality, up-to-date and effective resources for successful instruction and study in all areas of the law.

Kluwer Law International products provide the global business community with reliable international legal information in English. Legal practitioners, corporate counsel and business executives around the world rely on Kluwer Law journals, looseleafs, books, and electronic products for comprehensive information in many areas of international legal practice.

Loislaw is a comprehensive online legal research product providing legal content to law firm practitioners of various specializations. Loislaw provides attorneys with the ability to quickly and efficiently find the necessary legal information they need, when and where they need it, by facilitating access to primary law as well as state-specific law, records, forms and treatises.

Best Case Solutions is the leading bankruptcy software product to the bankruptcy industry. It provides software and workflow tools to flawlessly streamline petition preparation and the electronic filing process, while timely incorporating ever-changing court requirements.

ftwilliam.com offers employee benefits professionals the highest quality plan documents (retirement, welfare and non-qualified) and government forms (5500/PBGC, 1099 and IRS) software at highly competitive prices.

MediRegs products provide integrated health care compliance content and software solutions for professionals in healthcare, higher education and life sciences, including professionals in accounting, law and consulting.

Wolters Kluwer Law & Business, a division of Wolters Kluwer, is headquartered in New York. Wolters Kluwer is a market-leading global information services company focused on professionals.

Ruth Anne Robbins dedicates this book to her husband and daughters, who shared the writing journey with her: Steve, Shelby, and Gwen.

Steve Johansen dedicates this book to Lenore Honey Johansen. You are the hero of our story.

Ken Chestek dedicates this book to Robin Chestek, whose unfailing support and encouragement made this project possible. FFLA.

Summary of Contents

Contents

3 Story as a tool for persuasion 37

7 Representing your client, the protagonist   87

8 Telling the client's story: plot, conflict, and story types   103

Part IV: Revising, polishing, and finishing   211

14 Revising the Argument: finding your client's point of view   213

15 Revising the story: polishing the Statement of Facts   239

16 Making a first impression: the Preliminary Statement   251

17 Finishing up: the other parts of a brief   261

18 Creating ethos: tone and branding by good visual design   279

Part V: Oral argument   289

19 Persuading in person: oral argument   291

Epilogue   307

Acknowledgments

There are many people whom we need to thank, but the first are the three lawyers who wrote the appendices of this book while they were still in law school. They are Andrew Norcott Dodemaide (Rutgers–Camden), William F. Hanna (Rutgers–Camden), and Naima Solomon (Indiana University McKinney School of Law).

Others who contributed, materially or influentially, to this book include Toni Berres-Paul (Lewis & Clark), Victoria L. Chase (Rutgers–Camden), Brian J. Foley (Florida Coastal), David Thomson (Denver), and of course, Michael R. Smith (Wyoming).

There were many other people who provided immeasurable assistance, either by asking students to read early chapters or by supporting our work on the book. Those people include Sarah Adams (Touro), Bill Chin (Lewis & Clark), Alison Julien (Marquette), Derek Kiernan-Johnson (Colorado–Boulder), Allison Martin (Indiana University McKinney), Tracy McGaugh (Touro), Debby McGregor (Indiana University McKinney), Anne Villella (Lewis & Clark), Carol Wallinger (Rutgers–Camden), and Daryl Wilson (Lewis & Clark). We also offer thanks and gratitude to our deans, who encouraged and supported this project: Rayman Solomon (Rutgers–Camden), Bob Klonoff (Lewis & Clark), and Steve Easton (Wyoming). And special thanks to our administrative support at Rutgers–Camden, Marjorie Hemmings; and to our wonderful editor, Dana Wilson, and copyeditor, Lisa A. Wehrle, both of whom made the polishing process relatively painless.

Like all books, this one has been many years, many consumed Moonstruck chocolates, and many stories in the making. This book is also the result of several years spent studying and discussing Applied Legal Storytelling, and we thank the Legal Writing Institute and all of the people who have been involved with the conferences that brought us together. We are especially indebted to our U.K. colleagues Robert McPeake (City University, London) and Erika Rackley (Durham), and their efforts to bring Applied Legal Storytelling to an international audience. We also are indebted to those who have provided us feedback on our background articles—so many people in legal writing have provided us support and encouragement that we cannot hope to thank them all individually.

Finally, to our students over the years, we thank you for giving us the opportunity to teach persuasive legal writing in this manner.

Your Client's Story

Clients, persuasion, and storytelling

Topeka, Kansas, 1950. World War II had ended five years ago. The country was turning to happier times. The Baby Boom was underway. Factories were turning out cars and refrigerators and a new device called a television. Prosperity reigned.

But not everyone was pleased with the status quo of 1950.

> In September 1950, Linda Brown, an eight-year-old African-American child who lived in Topeka, Kansas, was ready to begin the third grade. Her first years of education had been spent at Monroe, an all-black school located about twenty-one blocks from the Brown home. In a modest neighborhood, the Monroe school building had been constructed in 1926. It was of brick in the Italian Renaissance style, well-cared for and . . . "a credit to the community" where it was located. The Brown's home was in a racially mixed neighborhood. The children of white and other nonblack families of the neighborhood attended Sumner School about seven blocks from the Brown residence. Named for abolitionist leader Charles Sumner, the first school on the Sumner site was initially for blacks only, but in 1885 it was designated for white students. The current building at Sumner was built in 1935. It was constructed of light-colored brick with a good deal of ornamentation. The testimony of the expert witness was that the Sumner classrooms were more spacious and the facilities more ample and in keeping with a good school situation. The academic programs at Monroe and Sumner were comparable.

> Bus transportation was provided for Linda and other Monroe students along a designated route. Linda boarded the bus at a pick-up station about seven blocks from her home. There was no shelter for waiting passengers, and to reach the pick-up station Linda and other black students had to walk through a railroad switchyard and cross Kansas Avenue, Topeka's main commercial street, where the motor traffic was heavy. No such hazards were encountered by students walking to Sumner.

> As the 1950–51 school term was about to begin Oliver Brown, Linda's father, was concerned about his daughter's safety and comfort, the inconvenience of her daily trip to and from Monroe School, and the quality of the educational opportunity afforded her by the Topeka school district. On the day appointed for her enrollment he led Linda to Sumner, the neighborhood school, and requested that she be admitted. The request was denied solely because the child was black and the rules of the board of education limited attendance at Sumner School to white, or approximately white, children. Linda continued to attend Monroe, but the events of that September morning commenced a series of happenings from which Linda Brown emerged as a celebrity and a folk heroine of the civil rights movement.[1]

We all know how this case turned out. In one of the most important decisions of the twentieth century, the United States Supreme Court ruled that separate schools for black and white children were "inherently unequal" and therefore unconstitutional.[2] But let's stop for a moment and consider the choices facing Linda Brown and her father Oliver in September 1950. The law of the land was, and had been for a long time, that separate facilities for black and white persons were permissible so long as the facilities were "equal."[3] To challenge that law meant that Linda and her family had to take on not only the entire city school system, but also a long-established line of precedents that originated in the United States Supreme Court. And the facts of her case were, overall, not shocking. At least one of the witnesses from her neighborhood described the blacks-only school as "a credit to the community," and the academic programs at the two schools were described by experts as "comparable."

Nevertheless, Linda and her family believed that enforced segregation was wrong, not only because of the inconvenience of having to travel to a much more distant school, but also because of how it made them feel. And by telling a compelling story about their experiences, they helped change our society in a dramatic way.

---

[1]Paul Wilson, *A Time to Lose: Representing Kansas in* Brown v. Board of Education 8–10 (U. Press of Kan. 1995) (footnotes omitted). The author of this book was an assistant attorney general for the state of Kansas in the 1950s. He wrote the briefs and represented the Topeka Board of Education in oral argument on the case before the United States Supreme Court. By the way, the reference in this passage to "approximately white children" is explained later in the book: Hispanic, Asian, and American Indian children were permitted to attend the Sumner school. Only black children were segregated at the Monroe school. *Id.* at 15. In Chapter 15, we return to this story, and particularly the interesting fact about the school's namesake.
[2]*Brown v. Bd. of Educ. of Topeka*, 347 U.S. 483 (1954).
[3]*Plessy v. Ferguson*, 163 U.S. 537 (1896).

Stories matter.

Lawyers are paid to advocate for their clients. Advocacy is a form of communication, designed to persuade someone. Legal advocacy, consequently, is a communication designed to persuade someone to take a position about the client's legal claim. And because human beings are hardwired to think and communicate in stories, one of the central premises for this book is that stories are a highly effective way to advocate on behalf of our clients. We tell each other stories all the time. Stories help us imagine what that other person senses or feels, something that we cannot know for certain, other than through empathy and conjecture. A story that "feels" true to the listener is a powerful tool for persuading that listener because that feeling comes from within the listener.

We call our approach to teaching "client-centered" because we believe the role of the lawyer is to show the court the client's story. But this text is more than just a theoretical discussion of how client stories work. We have organized this book around the central reality of a lawyer's life: handling a client's case, from start to finish. That process includes

- getting to know your client (his character, his goals, and the obstacles he faces in achieving his goals);
- investigating the law;
- formulating a strategy to tell your client's story within the confines of the law; and
- implementing the strategy through written and oral communication to the decision maker.

Notice that this organizational structure starts long before you actually place your fingertips on the keyboard to write something. While you might think that a book on legal writing would focus on the final product (the brief), the actual writing process begins long before you sit down to write. You need to know what to write about, which means getting to know your client's story intimately.

But before getting to that process, it's helpful to know about some basic principles of persuasion. The first few chapters introduce you to the fundamental principles of persuasive lawyering: understanding your client, understanding the process of persuasion, and understanding how legal stories are structured through legal argument. We will explore such questions as How do readers react to what you are saying? and How do you reach into the minds of readers and persuade them?

Think of the first chapters as creating the "setting" for the rest of the book. Our ultimate objective, of course, is to teach you how to produce writing that will persuade judges to rule in your clients' favor and how storytelling techniques can help you accomplish this.

The recursive process of writing

The writing process consists of four major stages:

1. Prewriting (research and planning)
2. Writing a first working draft (a "brain dump," or getting it all on paper)
3. Revising and rewriting (rethinking, reorganizing, improving)
4. Polishing (proofreading, formatting, editing for writing mechanics, word choices, concision, etc.)

As you probably know already, this is not a simple, step-by-step process. Not all of these steps need to occur in this exact sequence, although all of them have to occur at some point. The process of writing in any field is recursive, with the writer revisiting the different stages in a looping manner. A writer might have a document's organization initially set but then decide to completely reorganize the document. The same recursive process occurs in persuasive legal writing. The process begins when a client presents a problem. The lawyer may identify the likely legal means to resolve that problem and even have some ideas about how to connect the law to the facts of the client's story. However, before the lawyer can formulate a solution, she might need more information—more facts and more knowledge of the applicable law. That information will lead to a different understanding of the best legal argument for the client. The lawyer may begin writing an outline and a draft of a document. But the act of writing may also lead her to revise her understanding of the problem. Perhaps the lawyer will discard her initial legal theories and adopt new ones. Or perhaps she will maintain her same understanding but will deepen the analysis. Each of those outcomes will lead her, in turn, to search for new information.

All of this leads to a truism that you may have heard before: **writing is thinking**. Good lawyers begin to write even before they completely understand how to best solve their clients' problems. The act of writing leads the writer to have more ideas and to further refine her analysis. Indeed, some aspects of a persuasive argument become clear to the lawyer only after she has completed at least one—and often two or three—drafts. For example, it is sometimes difficult to determine the most effective theme of the client's case until later in the revising process.

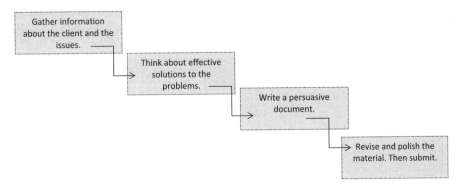

Figure P-1: Four stages of the writing process

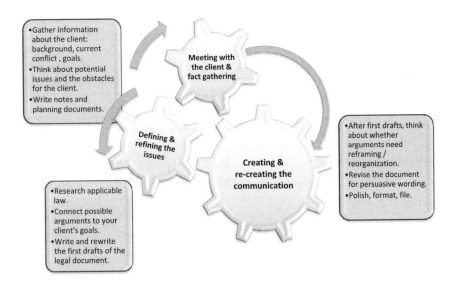

Figure P-2: Recursive writing process

The take-home point is this: because the writing process helps you to clarify your ideas, you will want to start the writing process early, creating preliminary documents that will help you begin to put together the client's story.

If writing were linear, we might identify the stages of the writing process as shown in Figure P-1.

This is, however, an oversimplification of how we really write. Though this is a useful *general* approach, in reality, we need to write, think, and gather information at each step of the process. Figure P-2, then, shows a more realistic approach to the process of effective writing.

This book has been structured to reflect this recursive process. The first chapter starts with the ultimate foundation of legal advocacy: the client. The second chapter then provides the foundational background about what persuades us, from classical rhetoric, to types of reader responses, to storytelling structures that deliver persuasive messages to the audience. The book next moves to the intermediate stages of researching the facts and bringing the law and facts together to form the outline and working drafts of the client's persuasive story. The third major part of the book discusses revising the working drafts for persuasion. The book concludes with the last steps: completing and, formatting the written persuasive document, and creating the oral argument that accompanies it.

The recursive nature of writing leads to what may be counterintuitive strategies. For example, the parts of a brief are not usually written in the same order that they will appear in the finished document. This book is written in the manner that a lawyer might approach a situation involving a brief: fact gathering, initial case planning, researching and drafting the legal arguments, and then revising the facts section of the document. Keep in mind the key idea that every stage of the writing process builds on what has come before. At each step, the lawyer gathers additional information, reflects on how that information fits with (or changes) what he has done before, and adds detail to the working drafts.

The sample scenarios and briefs

To demonstrate how these principles work in practice, this book uses two hypothetical cases that former law students worked on in prior legal writing courses. We chose these scenarios specifically because they are easy to imagine and represent understandable legal stories. One of the two scenarios involves a question of statutory interpretation about the phrase "dating relationship," as interpreted in an internet situation, and the other involves a question of common-law contract interpretation and enforcement in a situation involving unused hotel room reservations. From time to time throughout these chapters, we discuss how the lawyers representing clients in those cases might approach their various tasks. The appendices include sample briefs from these two simulation cases, and are the result of the processes we describe in this book. The sample briefs are largely based on briefs submitted by our former law students—and for their permission to use their work, we again thank those former students.

The first hypothetical case, *Hawthorne v. Beagle*, turns on the statutory interpretation of the phrase "dating relationship" and involves a domestic violence situation. The two parties meet at a speed-dating event, correspond online via video conferencing and Facebook, and then end that correspondence unhappily. We generally refer to this example as the "Internet dating case" or the "statutory construction case" throughout the book.

The second hypothetical case, *Gloucester Hotel v. Save Our Forest Trees, Inc.,* involves two parties in a dispute over hotel rooms. The defendant, SOFT, Inc., is a small nonprofit organization that plans a conference at a hypothetical chain hotel in Indiana. It signs a contract with the hotel to reserve a block of rooms for conference attendees, but does not attract enough registrants to fill the guaranteed block of rooms. The hotel sells those rooms to nonconference guests after the reservation deadline passes, but it still seeks to enforce a liquidated damages clause in the written contract to the tune of about $9000 (an amount larger than the profit SOFT actually earns from putting on the conference). We generally refer to this as the "hotel reservation case" or the "common law case" throughout the book.

Additional details about both of these cases appear in the various chapters as they become relevant. But for now, in the next chapter we see what happens when a lawyer first meets her client.

Part I

Introduction to storytelling and client-centered lawyering

Chapter 1

Meeting the client

In the beginning, there is the client. Lawyers exist because clients exist. Our job as lawyers is to act as a conduit between our client and the other parties necessary to resolving our client's problem. These include the opposing party, possible co-parties, and the court.

I. Client needs and goals in litigation

Clients have needs and goals, both within and outside the legal representation context. Clients who hire lawyers to represent them in transactions (such as writing a will or drafting a contract) may engage lawyers to protect their interests when things are going well. But things are rarely going well for clients who retain lawyers for litigation. Litigation usually disrupts clients' lives or businesses, sometimes in profound ways. It is the job of all lawyers to help their clients move toward those overarching needs and goals, be it through trial or appeal or through negotiation and settlement.

Effective legal advocates always act to further their clients' goals. It is easier to remember that when the client is a living, breathing person. But not all lawyers represent individuals. To give two simple examples: prosecutors represent the citizens of that jurisdiction, and corporate lawyers represent organizations. There are also times when a lawyer might not have met a client, even when that client is an individual—appellate brief writers, for example, might not have represented the client during the pretrial and trial proceedings but are working strictly from the record.

But even in those situations, the attorney must ask some real-world and fundamental questions about the client:

1. Does the client want to endure the financial and emotional expense of a trial or an appeal? These costs are significant when you add up the number of hours involved with preparing a case for trial or writing a brief including the fixed costs associated with ordering transcripts and copying and binding the briefs and record.

2. Is the client willing to settle the case? If so, under what conditions? A settlement might help the client meet the ultimate goals about her life, even if it means giving up something that she might be entitled to, legally. There's a premium on peace of mind, after all. The story-based question to ask here is what story resolution will be acceptable to the client.

3. Does the client understand how long it will take to resolve the case? Lawsuits takes months and sometimes years to resolve and an appeal takes several months at the very shortest. In some jurisdictions, an appeal may not be resolved until years after the initial verdict.

4. Do you and your client agree on the legal strategies you plan to use for the case?

These are the types of questions you should discuss with your client before beginning the appeals process.

II. Ethical considerations

You are undoubtedly aware that lawyers owe ethical obligations to their clients. On the surface at least, many of these obligations are fairly obvious: lawyers cannot steal clients' money; they must respect clients' confidentiality; lawyers cannot lie for their clients. However, the duties under even these fundamental concepts can become murky.

You will study these rules in detail in your professional responsibility course. For now, we highlight some of the most important ethical obligations that are likely to guide your role as advocates for your clients.

A. Providing competent service

A lawyer's first obligation to the client is to be competent.[1] This requires that the lawyer exercise the diligence, judgment, and care of a general practitioner. While this is a necessarily ambiguous standard, all lawyers are expected to understand applicable court rules, effectively research legal issues, adequately investigate factual issues, and clearly explain their client's claims through written and oral advocacy.

---

[1] *See* Model R. Prof. Conduct 1.1 (ABA 2012).

B. Being a zealous advocate

You are probably already familiar with the concept of the zealous advocate. This concept was famously explained by the English barrister Lord Brougham, who said, in explaining his defense of Queen Caroline against a charge of adultery, "A lawyer, in the discharge of his duty, knows but one person in all the world, and that person is his client."

Writing in 1820, Lord Brougham captured the strength of the lawyer's duty to his client that continues to this day. A lawyer's role is not to judge his client but to advocate on her behalf even when the whole world may seem to be against her. The story a lawyer tells in the discharge of that duty is the *client's* story told from her point of view.

Zealous representation has its limitations, however. Too often, lawyers hide behind a claim of zealous representation to excuse rude, boorish, or even deceitful conduct. Zealous representation means something very different than pushing for every advantage. Zealous representation and unprofessional conduct are two different concepts. A truly zealous advocate understands that part of zeal includes professional conduct toward the court and opposing counsel. A zealous advocate also respects the legal system. Nothing about being a zealous advocate permits a lawyer to lie, destroy evidence, or otherwise violate his ethical obligations to the court, opposing counsel, and the general public. Rather, the most successful lawyers are those who are able to advocate for their clients' positions while showing respect and courtesy to those who have a different story to tell.

C. Respecting client autonomy

Because lawyers recognize that the client's goals are the driving force of any legal action, the profession's ethical rules also recognize that the client controls the ends to a legal matter while the lawyer controls some, though not all, of the means.[2] For example, it is the client who decides whether to create a contract or file a lawsuit or accept a settlement offer. On the other hand, it is the lawyer who decides whether to object to the opposing counsel's question to a witness during a trial. Thus, at least in a general sense, it is the client who decides on the goals of the lawyer-client relationship, and it is the lawyer who decides how to best achieve those goals.

However, as you might expect, this dichotomy quickly blurs because many decisions fall somewhere in between the ends and means of representation.

---

[2] *See id.* at R. 1.2.

Those who take a client-centered approach to lawyering believe a lawyer's role is to advise his client as to her legal options. It is not the lawyer's role to substitute his preferences for those of his client. After all, it is the client's story, and the client will live with the consequences of how the story comes out. At the heart of the client-centered approach is a belief that a fully informed client is able to make the best decisions for herself. While the lawyer may have expertise in the law, the client necessarily has greater expertise as to what she wants. Thus, the lawyer is an advisor—he informs the client as to her options and then follows the client's direction as to which option to pursue.[3]

Sometimes client-centered lawyering is challenging. Imagine, for instance, that a client wants to accept a settlement that her lawyer believes is not in her best interest. The lawyer might believe that his client, a domestic violence victim, should obtain a restraining order and leave the batterer. But the client might ultimately decide to work out an arrangement with the batterer in which she moves back into the home. Although the lawyer might advise his client about his apprehensions, it is the client's decision to make.

In another example, suppose a client has suffered damages because of the other side's negligence. And suppose the insurance company for the defendant offers a quick settlement that the plaintiff's lawyer believes is a mistake for his client to accept. He is reasonably certain that the other side is almost certainly willing, or even expecting, to entertain a counteroffer from the plaintiff. Moreover, he believes the early settlement offer is grossly unfair for his client. The plaintiff's attorney also suspects that a few months from now, with time to gain some distance from the dispute, his client would likely regret accepting the offer. What can he do? Certainly he will discuss the downsides to accepting such an offer. He may ask her to take some time to reconsider. He might suggest she seek the advice of a trusted friend. But ultimately, if the client insists on making a poor decision (at least in her lawyer's judgment), counsel must remember that it is his client's lawsuit and acquiesce to her decision.

D. Keeping client secrets: client confidentiality

Perhaps a lawyer's most challenging ethical obligation is to keep her client's secrets. The attorney–client privilege bars a lawyer from disclosing client confidences in court. This ethical obligation is even greater, as

---

[3] *See* Steven J. Johansen, *This Is Not the Whole Truth: The Ethics of Telling Stories to Clients*, 38 Ariz. St. L.J. 961, 973–974 (2006) (citations omitted).

lawyers may not disclose virtually any information about their clients that their clients want kept secret. This nearly absolute duty to maintain client secrets has but few exceptions, such as when disclosure is necessary to prevent serious bodily injury or death. An illustration of the consequences of this duty is shown in the shadow box.

The Burden of Keeping Client Secrets

Sometimes, lawyers can have very compelling reasons to reveal a client's secrets. For example, in the early 1980's, Dale Coventry and Jamie Kunz were public defenders in Chicago. One of their clients, Andrew Wilson, confessed to Coventry and Kunz that he had shot and killed a man during a robbery of a McDonald's restaurant. However, Wilson refused to give his attorneys permission to disclose his admission even after he had been convicted of another murder and sentenced to life in prison.

For Coventry and Kunz, it was difficult enough to keep silent, knowing that their silence allowed a murderer to escape responsibility for his crime. However, the problem became even more difficult when another man, Alton Logan, was first arrested and then convicted of first degree murder for the killing that Wilson had admitted to. Logan was sentenced to life in prison, narrowly escaping the death penalty.

For decades, Coventry and Kunz protected Wilson's confidential confession. They had convinced Wilson to sign an affidavit confessing to the crime. Wilson agreed to allow them to disclose his secret upon his death. In 2008, Wilson died in prison. Coventry and Kunz then revealed his confession. Twenty-six years after he was convicted of a murder he didn't commit, Alton Logan was finally released from prison.

Many law students (and indeed, many lawyers) are troubled by this duty to keep silent even when that silence may lead to injustice. However, there are thoughtful and compelling reasons behind lawyers' duty to maintain their clients' confidences. First, clients must trust their legal counsel. Lawyers cannot competently advise their clients if the clients withhold information. Clients need to be assured that they can discuss their legal issues frankly with their lawyers without fearing breached confidences or other adverse consequences. Remember that the vast majority of clients want to comply with the law, and those frank discussions usually lead to securing justice rather than undermining it. For particularly troubling situations, it helps to remember that the lawyer likely only learned a client's secrets because that client came to her for advice. In essence, lawyers are privileged to know clients' secrets, and to ensure that clients will continue to trust lawyers, lawyers must respect that privilege.

Attorneys must also be careful not to breach their clients' confidences inadvertently. For example, they should never talk about their clients' cases in places where conversations may be overheard. Crowded restaurants, subways, and lobbies are not the place to discuss client matters—even on a cell phone. Likewise, it is imprudent for lawyers to talk to family and friends about their clients; once client information is disclosed, even to trusted sources, counsel loses all control over who else will hear that information.

Electronic communication has its own set of potential pitfalls. We have all had the experience of sending an e-mail to the wrong person. Most of the time, this is little more than embarrassing. However, if that e-mail contains client confidences and gets sent to the wrong person, it may be a cause for malpractice. All legal professionals, be they attorneys, paralegals, or support staff, should always check to make sure e-mails are going to their intended audience—before pressing the Send button. And Reply All should be used sparingly and with extra caution!

Other forms of electronic communication, like Facebook, Twitter, and blogs, are generally not appropriate forums for discussions about clients.

It may also be prudent to warn clients about keeping conversations private. Some clients are compelled to discuss their legal issues with almost anyone who will listen. Such conversations may help a client work through the stress of a legal issue. However, they can also have unintended consequences. For example, a federal judge reports that at a recent pretrial conference, the defense counsel informed the plaintiff's lawyer that the plaintiff had been blogging about the details of her lawsuit, including many of the confidential discussions between the plaintiff and her lawyer. As a result of her blogging, the plaintiff had waived the attorney–client privilege with respect to those conversations!

III. The client as a key audience

The first principle of legal writing is that audience matters. Everything we write must be crafted with our audience in mind. One audience for virtually all of our writing is our client. When we write *for* our client, we also necessarily write *to* our client. This means our writing should be accessible to our client so that she can understand the story we are telling others. It also means that the choices we make, both in telling the factual story and in creating the legal story, must be acceptable to our client. In literary terms, our client has final approval of our story arc, even though she may rely on us to craft the details of the story.

Throughout this book, you will learn ways to keep your persuasive document client-centered. The story you write in your Statement of Facts will be your client's story. The legal analysis in your Arguments will connect to your client's story. The word choices and details you weave into your analysis will further your client's story. The headings in your document will capture the essence of your client's story. Even choices about your document's font and format may be based on furthering your client's story. Simply put, the product you will create has one primary objective—to help your client achieve her goal. In the end, as at the beginning, there is always the client.

IV. Getting started: learning about your client

The first step of your project is learning about your client and her goals. How you do this will depend on where you enter the case. Often as a new lawyer (and even more so as a law student assigned to write a persuasive document), you will be assigned to work on a project well after your firm has accepted a client. If so, much of the preliminary work will have been done. Your senior partner will likely have briefed you on the details of the case and given you the case file. If you are working on an appellate brief, there will also be a record of the proceedings below; on appeal, the only facts that matter are those that are in the record. Furthermore, the only legal issues that matter are those that were preserved at the trial level. Thus, at the appeals stage of a problem, you are unlikely to do any original fact investigation. If you are dealing with an issue at trial, of course, fact investigation may be a critical part of your task.

Even though you are likely to be brought into the process well after the initial steps of representing a client, it is helpful to have some idea of how the client's problem landed on your desk. The usual first step of beginning a lawyer–client relationship is the client intake interview. This first interview is usually fairly limited. Before a lawyer accepts any client, he needs to consider several issues. Does the client have a plausible case? Can the client afford the cost of pursuing the case? Does this case create a conflict of interest with himself, his other clients, or the clients of anyone in his firm? Some of these questions cannot be answered during the initial meeting. Thus, the lawyer will gather just the information he needs from the client to decide whether he will accept the case. The intake form reproduced in Figure 1-1 shows the type of information gathered at an intake interview.

New Client Information Sheet

Today's date _____

Client's Full Name _____ SS# _____

Spouse's/Partner's Full Name _____ SS# _____

Street Address _____

City/State _____ Zip _____ E-mail Address _____

Telephone (Home)_____ Client Work _____

Spouse/Partner Work _____

Client's Employer _____ Spouse's/Partner's Employer _____

Emergency Contacts:

Name _____ Relationship _____ Telephone _____

Name _____ Relationship _____ Telephone _____

Why You Chose Our Office _____

Conference with Attorney Regarding:

For Office Use Only

| Fee arrangement: |
| Billing arrangement: |

Docket Control		Conflict Control	
Statute of Limitations Deadline		NAME	RELATIONSHIP
Tort Claims Act Notice Due			
First Appearance Due			
Other Deadlines			
File Review Frequency			
INSTRUCTIONS:			

File opened by: _____ Conflicts checked by: _____

Deadlines docketed by: _____ Engagement letter sent by: _____

Date: _____

Figure 1-1: Client intake form

If, after resolving any possible conflicts of interests and other potential obstacles to taking the case, the lawyer is willing to accept the client's case (and the client wants to hire the lawyer), then they will usually meet again so that the client can provide more details and the lawyer can begin planning the representation. Of course, the lead lawyer may do considerable work before bringing you onto the project. That said, whatever stage of the project you are asked to work on, you will need to begin your work with some initial planning. This planning begins with learning about the client and her legal issue. You will need to review the information you have to learn the following:

- What do you know about your client?
- What are the client's goals beyond winning the lawsuit?
- What are obstacles to the client meeting those goals?
- What are the tentative legal issues?
- What do you already know about the applicable law?
- What are your preliminary thoughts about theme or narrative arc?

We discuss how to address all of these questions throughout this book. As you progress through the writing process, you will revisit your preliminary thoughts about your client and her story. Undoubtedly, your final document will not be identical to your preliminary assessment of your client's story. But the planning document will get you started and will be useful to refer back to, especially in the early stages of research and reflection, where you are most susceptible to wandering away from your specific task.

In the next chapter, we begin to think about how the human mind works and suggest some ideas that can help you persuade your audience to your client's position.

Chapter 2

Understanding persuasion

Persuasion—what legal types like to call "advocacy"—is what lawyers do for a living. So it behooves us to familiarize ourselves with its key aspects. Persuasion is a rich and complex field of inquiry that cuts across many disciplines. Thousands of articles about it are written by psychologists alone. Other scholars and professionals who study persuasion include linguists, market analysts, graphic designers, neurobiologists, and sociologists. But we all use persuasion every day, even when we're not aware of it.

This chapter explores two fundamental principles of persuasion. First, it looks briefly at classical rhetoric and the concepts of logos, pathos, and ethos. Then it looks at audience responses to persuasive arguments and the most effective way to persuade an audience to respond positively to your client's position.

I. Classical rhetoric

The art of persuasion traces its roots back nearly 2,500 years ago to the ancient Greeks. Aristotle is widely recognized as the father of classical rhetoric. The principles that he developed remain just as relevant today as they were at the time he was writing. Aristotle recognized that persuasion occurs in three ways: through logic (in the ancient Greek, *logos*), through emotion (*pathos*), and through the reputation of the speaker (*ethos*). While logos, pathos, and ethos are distinct concepts, in practice, persuasion is most effective when you use all three to appeal to your audience. Logos makes your audience *think* you are right; pathos makes your audience *feel* you are right; and ethos makes your audience *trust* you are right.

Figure 2-1 will help you remember that all three of these concepts are interconnected and form the basis of persuasion. If you want to re-create one of these diagrams for yourself, consider using the three primary colors of yellow, blue, and red to represent the three elements.

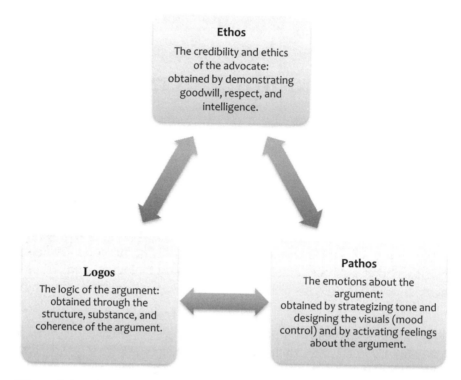

Figure 2-1: Ethos, logos, and pathos

Another way to remember the differences is with a cake metaphor.[1] Suppose someone bakes a birthday cake for you. The way we define the type of birthday cake it is captures the essence of logos. If we told you that it was a chocolate birthday cake, you would understand that the structure of the cake is chocolate flavored. A cake is not typically defined by its frosting but by the ingredients in the part made of flour.

And speaking of frosting, that is the pathos of the cake in our metaphor. Pathos is what helps keep the logos part from being too dry. If we offered you merely cake (logos) with nothing to break it up (nothing to drink either), you might thank us, but we are going to bet that you would probably prefer it with some frosting (pathos). People may have different preferences in the amount of frosting, naturally. Some people might even prefer to eat just the frosting without any cake. Those people might also feel a little ill afterward, as if they have overdosed on sweets.

Finally, to complete the metaphor, let's talk about the person who baked the chocolate birthday cake with frosting. That's the ethos of the cake.

---

[1]Thanks to Anne M. Mallgrave, Rutgers School of Law—Camden, for this metaphor.

You are much more likely to accept a piece of cake from someone you have reason to trust. If, however (and we're sorry to ruin the visual for you), the person who baked the cake washes her hands only once a month, you might not feel all that inclined to eat it.

A. Logos: the substance of the argument

Much of the reasoning that you are familiar with is really just variations of syllogistic reasoning. For example, when we apply case law through analogical reasoning, we use the syllogism. However, in most legal disputes, the power of the syllogism gets us only so far. Logic may provide a framework for thinking about a legal dispute, but it rarely resolves it completely.

To illustrate the power as well as the limits of logic, let's look at how we might approach a typical legal dispute. To keep things simple, let's assume that there is no dispute of facts.[2]

- Case A establishes that the law requires this result under these facts. (Rule Explanation = major premise)
- Our case has similar facts to Case A. (Rule Application = minor premise)
- Therefore, our case should get the same result as Case A. (Conclusion)

Similarly, statutory analysis often relies on syllogistic reasoning:

- Statute B prohibits specific conduct. (major premise)
- The defendant engaged in this specific conduct. (minor premise)
- Therefore, the defendant violated Statute B. (conclusion)

Of course, in the real world, legal reasoning is rarely this straightforward. Whether a problem is governed by case law, statutes, or both, there is often plenty of room for disagreement. Parties might disagree as to what the law requires (the major premise); or they may disagree about how the law applies to the issue in dispute (the minor premise). In either case, these disagreements are likely to lead to conflicting conclusions. The conflict does not arise because the parties disagree on the proper logical framework—both accept the syllogism. Rather, they disagree on what are the correct premises from which to create the syllogism. Persuading the court toward your client's view as to the "correct" premises usually requires going beyond logic to a more complete argument that draws on both pathos and ethos as well.

---

[2]This assumption is a convenience of law school that lawyers rarely experience in practice. Many legal disputes are centered on factual disputes.

Demonstrating the limits of syllogisms in legal analysis

Comedian Stephen Colbert provided a humorous example of the limits of syllogistic reasoning. In 2010, the Supreme Court held in *Citizens' United v. Federal Election Commission* that corporations had the right, under the First Amendment, to spend unlimited amounts of money to support political candidates. Colbert pointed out that this decision was based on several premises, all derived from Supreme Court precedents: (1) corporations are people; (2) people have the right of free speech under the First Amendment; and (3) money is a form of speech. If you accept all of those premises as true, the Supreme Court's decision is eminently logical. But a similar set of syllogisms could lead to a conclusion that corporations also have a right under the Second Amendment to bear arms.

To see the whole clip, visit http://www.colbertnation.com/the-colbert-report-videos/249055/september-15-2009/the-word---let-freedom-ka-ching.

So what does this mean for us? It means that as we start to think about building a persuasive argument, it is often helpful to start with the logic of our argument. As we outline, our overall framework should have a structure that is consistent with the logical framework that our audience expects. Although each step of our legal analysis must be logically sound, that is only our starting point.

B. Pathos: appealing to our audience's emotions

We use pathos effectively when we choose strategies that allow our audience to empathize with our client. We do that through story. Narrative structure has three elements: a character, the character's goals, and the obstacles that stand between the character and his goals. We establish empathy by showing how our client is like our audience, how his goals are familiar or understandable to our audience, and how the obstacles our client faces is like those our audience has faced—or perhaps will face in the future. The better we can develop empathy in our audience, the more effective our use of pathos will be.

Note that empathy is not based in logic. For example, no logical reason explains why a judge should rule in favor of a party because that party has similar goals to those of the judge. Nonetheless, judges, just like other people, are compelled to include these considerations in their decision-making calculus.

Empathy is also not synonymous with sympathy. Empathy conveys a sense of understanding about what a person is feeling or experiencing. Sympathy suggests a sense of sorrow or compassion for a person. Empathy does not require the audience to feel a person's emotion, but only to understand it.

Pathos is not limited to direct, substantive appeals to emotion. What Professor Michael Smith calls "medium mood control" is a secondary part of emotional persuasion.[3] (Here, the word "medium" means the mode of communication.) The tone or mood of the document is set in many different ways. Word choices convey a tone, certainly. A document that seems hostile rather than respectful can convey negative medium mood control. A document that uses polished language and is free from editing mistakes sets a positive tone. Likewise, the formatting of the document—the choice of fonts and layout—can affect readers' emotions. Things that you can't really control also contribute to the medium mood control of the document: where readers are sitting while reading the document, the lighting, the background noise, the time of day, and how readers are otherwise feeling.

Skepticism about emotional appeal is understandable. We have all been exposed to emotional appeals that are obviously bereft of logic. When pathos is overdone, it quickly loses its effectiveness. For example, Judge Richard Musmanno was a colorful judge on the Pennsylvania Supreme Court who became legendary for his strongly worded dissents. While Judge Musmanno was often keenly direct in his disagreements with his judicial colleagues, he sometimes seemed overwhelmed by the emotional basis of his objections. Consider his dissent in *Commonwealth v. Robin*. The issue in this case was whether banning Henry Miller's novel *Tropic of Cancer* violated the First Amendment. The United States Supreme Court had already ruled that it did. That didn't stop Musmanno from arguing otherwise. Here is his description of the novel:

> *Cancer* is not a book. It is a cesspool, an open sewer, a pit of putrefaction, a slimy gathering of all that is rotten in the debris of human depravity. And in the center of all this waste and stench, besmearing himself with its foulest defilement, splashes, leaps, cavorts and wallows a bifurcated specimen that responds to the name of Henry Miller. One wonders how the human species could have produced so lecherous, blasphemous, disgusting and amoral a human being as Henry Miller. One wonders why he is received in polite society.[4]

---

[3]Michael R. Smith, *Advanced Legal Writing: Theories and Strategies in Persuasive Writing* 11–13 (2d ed., Aspen L. & Bus. 2008).
[4]*Commonwealth v. Robin*, 218 A.2d 546, 556 (Pa. 1966).

While Musmanno may have been trying to appeal to his audience's emotions—anger, outrage, fear—his overwrought attack does little beyond undermining his own credibility.

C. Ethos: the credibility of the advocate

The final element of classical rhetoric is ethos, the reputation of the speaker (or, in our case, the writer). It would be grand if, on graduating from law school, you could begin your practice with a well-established reputation for professionalism, sound reasoning, and accurate and cogent writing. This, however, is not likely to happen. Rather, you are more likely to begin practice with a reputation as a new, inexperienced member of the legal community who still needs to learn a thing or two about how the world really works. And as one who still needs to establish her credibility with the courts, clients, and opposing counsel. This does not mean, however, that you will have to check your ethos at the door or will not have this tool at your disposal.

As a new lawyer, you can use ethos to persuade in several ways. First, remember that your written work says a lot about you. Your credibility is improved when your document looks professional and is free of typos, spelling errors, and similar distractions. When you are writing to a court, check the local rules for formatting and other expectations—and follow them to the letter. Design your document appropriately for your audience. (Chapter 18 looks in detail at document design.) The appearance of your writing is just as important as your own appearance. You wouldn't wear cutoffs and a dirty t-shirt to court; your document shouldn't look that sloppy or informal either.

Ethos is more than just looking good. Your document must also be substantively sound. This means that you must always remember the ABCs of legal writing: accuracy, brevity, and clarity. Your audience knows you are an advocate for a particular point of view. What you want them also to know is that you are reasonable and trustworthy. This requires that you describe the facts fairly, explain the law accurately, and recognize that there are counterarguments to even the strongest legal positions.

It may be tempting to omit troublesome facts or law from your argument. After all, it's not your job to make your opponent's argument. Resist this temptation. First, it is unlikely that opposing counsel will be so incompetent as to let your omission pass without comment. Your credibility will be damaged if your opponent points out obvious omissions or misstatements in your analysis—which she almost certainly will do. However, even if you are lucky enough to have an incompetent opponent, the judge is almost certainly not incompetent, and neither are his clerks—and they are likely to discover your efforts to paint an inaccurate picture. When that happens, you have lost your credibility—not just for the immediate case, but for a long time to come. All cases will have bad facts and bad law. Your job is not to hide them but to explain why they do not result in a bad outcome.

D. Putting it all together: persuasion requires logos, pathos, and ethos

Though we have discussed logos, pathos, and ethos as separate concepts, in practice, effective persuasion combines all three. The importance of blending these three forms of persuasion is sometimes lost in law school. One of the first lessons we learn in law school is that justice demands impartiality and that impartiality is best met through objective, rational thinking. Though we permit lawyers to appeal to a jury's emotions, to a degree, such appeals are tolerated, not praised. Furthermore, we expect judges, especially appellate judges, to not be persuaded by obvious emotional appeals; judges are expected to make decisions based solely on reason.[5] However, contemporary developments in cognitive science and neuropsychology suggest reason, without emotion, leads to poor decision making, particularly on important decisions about complex matters. Our brains are more likely to make wise decisions when the rational part of our brain—the frontal cortex—works in concert with the emotional part of our brain.

Neuroscientist Antonio Damasio tells a compelling story that illustrates the point.[6] Elliot, a patient, had a tumor removed from his frontal orbital cortex—that part of the brain that connects the rational frontal cortex to the emotional parts of the midbrain. As a result, Elliot suffered no loss of IQ. But he was no longer able to connect emotions to rational thought. His frontal cortex still functioned, but emotion no longer played a part in his decision making. One might expect that Elliot would become the perfect "judge," able to make decisions based solely on reason—a Spock-like judge, uninfluenced by emotional appeals. In fact, Elliot became unable to make even the simplest decisions. Dr. Damasio would ask him to choose a day for their next appointment, and Elliot would spend hours evaluating the reasons for choosing Tuesday over Thursday—but never be able to assess the choices and make a decision. Tragically, when Elliot

---

[5] *See, e.g.,* Antonin Scalia & Bryan A. Garner, *Making Your Case* 32 (Thomson West 2008) ("Good judges pride themselves on the rationality of their rulings and the suppression of their personal proclivities, including most especially their emotions").
[6] Antonio Damasio, *Descartes' Error: Emotion, Reason, and the Human Brain* (Putnam 1994).

was no longer able to connect his rational thought to his emotions, this previously very successful and happy man was no longer able to hold a steady job. His wife and children eventually left him. His life essentially fell apart.

The lesson to be learned from Elliot is not that we should reject reason. Rather, it is that, in the pursuit of wise decision making, we should embrace rather than fear emotions. In fact, our brains work best when we engage in "whole brain" thinking—when our rational frontal cortex works in concert with our emotional neural centers. This is what happens when we hear stories. Stories are more interesting, more memorable, and more persuasive than other narrative forms. They also engage our brain in a way that is more likely to lead to good decisions. When we make decisions based on a combination of reason and emotion, we reach better decisions than when we rely on reason or emotion alone.

So, how do we effectively combine the persuasive power of logos, pathos, and ethos? We spend the rest of this book exploring how these concepts intersect in a persuasive legal document. At the outset, though, here are a few strategies to keep in mind.

1. Start with the logos

In your first semester, you may have written an objective document that predicted the outcome of a legal issue. This type of predictive legal writing is largely logos based. For persuasive documents, we'll not stop here. But to be sure, we must first have a solid grounding of the facts, the law, and the connection between the two.

2. Build empathy for your client's position

When we persuade, we are asking our audience to make a choice between competing positions. Our audience is most likely to choose our client's position when we can show how that position is consistent with the audience's own understanding of the issue and its resolution. This is best done weaving the logos of traditional legal analysis with the pathos of your client's story.

3. Establish your own credibility along with your client's

You establish your client's credibility by effectively telling her story. You establish your own credibility less directly: by telling your client's story accurately, by scrupulously following all court rules, by maintaining a professional tone, by accurately explaining the law and facts, by thoroughly editing and proofreading your document. Such attention to detail establishes your reputation as a trustworthy advocate.

II. Audience responses to persuasion

The goal of persuasion is to give information and guide an audience's response to it. Broadly speaking, there are three types of responses, based on creating, maintaining, or changing the audience's beliefs with respect to your position.

As part of responding to persuasive messages, the audience calls on their memories and experiences—and they do so by forming mental images and by drawing immediate—and often subconscious—connections to a series of "stock structures" of common or everyday experiences. This section of the chapter details each of the possible responses to an attempt to persuade.

A. Response shaping

Response shaping happens when the audience has no prior knowledge or experience. Children are engaging in response-shaping reactions as they learn to speak, to use utensils, and to ride a bike. An adult might have that sort of response-shaping reaction when she immerses herself in a completely foreign culture. However, because adults tend to filter new information through a lens of comparisons to prior knowledge or experiences, there is less response-shaping happening naturally in adults. That's partly why the older we get, the harder it is to adapt to changing technology.

In law, unless you are dealing with a case of first impression, lawyers have little call to make a response-shaping argument.

B. Response reinforcing

Response reinforcing happens when the audience already has a known reaction to input and the writer strives to reinforce that reaction. Most of the messages we receive each day serve that purpose. For example, you probably know what time of day heavy traffic will slow your commute. Each time you get caught in that traffic your belief system is reinforced: "I should not have left at this time."

In law, response reinforcing is our primary mode of argumentation. The use of legal authority appeals to the judge's existing conceptions. The strongest legal arguments are the ones that allow judges to believe they are following an established precedent. Asking the judicial audience to merely reinforce their existing beliefs is the easiest way to persuade that audience.

C. Response changing

Response changing occurs when the audience is asked to overcome their existing beliefs and form new ones. This is the most difficult form of response for an audience and therefore is the hardest form of persuasion for the writer. It is, however, what most people think "being persuaded" means.

When we write a persuasive document, we should keep in mind the two primary ways we have to persuade. Response reinforcing will almost always be more successful than response changing. If we can convince our audience that our client's position is consistent with what the audience already believes, we have a much better chance of persuading our audience than if we have to change the audience's mind. One of the best ways to create a response-reinforcing argument is to create empathy for our client. If a judge can see a legal problem from our client's point of view, he is more likely to accept that point of view. Likewise, we want to show how our client's position is in line with what the judge already believes. For example, judges believe that they should follow existing precedent; we want to show that our client's position is consistent with existing precedent.

D. Imagery in persuasion

People think in pictures. The pictures are ones that have been created for them, through a writer's use of details and description. If there is no description, then the audience will simply fill in the descriptive gaps with pictures from their own experiences—actual or learned from other media.

In a study conducted in 2000, cognitive psychologists asked 50 students to recall a memory about certain random topics. The topics were provided in either single-word or short phrases. Afterward the researchers asked the participants to describe the memory and their way of accessing it. The students described how they had "relived" more than one-third of the memories that trigger words had conjured. In 98 percent of those relived memories, the students reported being able to see, hear, and feel the memory. They had activated many sensory parts of their brain. Although vision is our strongest sense, people use other senses as well when they think.

The real take-away is that readers will call on memories using their senses unless they are provided with a substitute description. This critical aspect of persuasion is vital to a good telling of the client's legal situation (Statement of Facts), as well as an explanation of how the governing rules of law have operated (Rule Explanation) or should operate (Application).

Sometimes it is important, as part of advocacy, to thoroughly describe information relevant to the lawsuit. Using a more detailed description causes readers to call on images that more closely match what the writer intends. The good lawyer understands which images are critical to the client's case and which ones can be left to readers' own images.

Your favorite pair of jeans

To help understand why imagery details matter in Rule Explanation, here is a short exercise that calls on autobiographical memories. For 15 to 20 seconds, think about your favorite jeans—the best pair you ever had.

- Did you see the jeans in the memory?
- Where were you? In your home? Out and about?
- Did you place yourself in time, even relative time: "it was sometime in my junior year of college"?
- What were you doing in your memory? Wearing them? Washing them? Pulling them out of the drawer or shelf where you stored them?
- Do you remember how they fit or used to fit or what size they were?
- Do you remember how you came to own them? Why you stopped wearing them?
- Do you remember what color they were?

This exercise is designed to prove the point that you also access memories through sensory perception. It's an important point to keep in mind when deciding what details to include when telling a story, whether it is the client's story or the story of case precedent.

E. Stock structures in persuasion

It's a decent bet that you recalled your favorite pair of jeans as blue denim. That's because the common understanding of "a pair of jeans" is an article of clothing that are full-length pants made of blue denim.

It's also a good guess that when you purchased this book for your class, you probably did not expect it to contain a science fiction novel inside.[7] Rather, you expected it to read like a textbook, providing information that supplements or anchors your professor's in-class discussions. Your expectations are based on previous experiences of "textbook" you have had in other academic courses and perhaps in other legal writing courses.

---

[7]Sorry, it doesn't.

Likewise, on your first day of this course, you entered an assigned classroom. If asked beforehand, you probably could have guessed approximately what the room's layout would look like: a number of chairs, a surface in front of those chairs designed as a place for students' computers or notebooks, and a place in the room where the professor can write or project images. You probably also would have guessed that the room would include at least one door and a lighting system. All of those guesses would have been based on your stock structure of the concept "classroom."

We all rely on certain "standardized" pieces of information, such as settings or encounters with the world, to help us get through our day. All new experiences are understood by means of comparison to a stereotypical model. These standardized pieces of information have different names in different disciplines. Linguists refer to them as "idealized cognitive models," but in literature they are called "schemas" or "scripts." Another popular name, and the one that we choose to use in this book, is "stock structures."[8]

Part of effective persuasion is understanding how and when readers' minds activate stock structures. Understanding this allows us to activate stock structures for readers or circumvent them by substituting with our own description. Stock structures show up in almost every aspect of legal writing—from the facts we provide about the client's legal situation, to the rules of law, to the material we include in the explanations of case precedents.

1. Types of stock structures

Stock structures can come from our personal experiences or from cultural, social, or historical norms. There are three different types of these scripts:

1. **Situational:** "Hailing a taxicab" is an example of a situational stock structure. Most of us have seen that process—either by experiencing it firsthand or by seeing it acted out in the media.
2. **Instrumental:** These are the ordinary action items within a situation that we don't think about very much. Examples of instrumental stock structures are "buttering a slice of toast," "answering the phone," or "brushing teeth."

---

[8]Gerald P. Lopez, *Lay Lawyering*, 32 UCLA L. Rev. 1 (1984) (describing stock structures and using the example of hailing a cab in New York City at 7:42 p.m. on a gray Friday evening); George Lakoff, *Women, Fire, and Dangerous Things: What Categories Reveal About the Mind* 68–76 (U. Chi. Press 1987); *Routledge Encyclopedia of Narrative* 520–521 (David Herman, Manfred Jahn & Marie-Laure Ryan eds., Routledge 2008).

3. **Character (sometimes called "personal scripts"):** These have signature roles that a character may take on at any given moment.
These are often useful for things like rule explanation, where they
can convey a quick visual image for readers, for example, "the
plaintiff's nephew" or "the employee." They can also be used
(for better or worse) to convey an ethos of that character: "the pre-
school teacher" and "the used car salesman" Both carry a stock
structure about the character's credibility—that is, ethos.

2. Be careful: stock structures are different to different people

A few words of caution. Stock structures do provide an extremely useful
tool for lawyers because of the shortcuts they provide. But because stock
structures call up visual images in the minds of the audience based on their
own knowledge and experience base, they are susceptible to differences
and assumptions. Take time to consider and recognize where differences
in experience may have occurred.

Recognizing these differences may make a critical difference. For
example, suppose one of the key elements in a lawsuit involved someone
who was "purchasing movie tickets." The act of purchasing a movie ticket
is a stock structure, but that stock structure could be different depending
on geographical or generational influences. In Utah, the stock structure of
purchasing a movie ticket may include selecting a seat (because some
Utah movie theaters have reserved seating). Someone else's stock
structure may include purchasing tickets online. Another stock structure
might be standing in line.

3. Many legal disputes are centered in a debate about competing stock structures

You should also recognize that just as you might be strategically employing the use of stock structures in your advocacy, so will opposing counsel.
Remember to stop and unpack the assumptions that can otherwise happen in the other side's descriptions.

Try to spot the stock structures involved in your client's case. In truth,
many lawsuits are grounded in disputes about the meaning of a phrase in a
statute, case precedent, or contract—in other words, conflicting stock
structures. The Internet dating case provides a perfect example of that.
The central dispute in those sample briefs turns not on whether there was
an act of domestic violence, but on whether the family court was permitted to hear the case in the first place (i.e., whether it had subject matter

jurisdiction). And the competing arguments all focus on the phrase "dating relationship." There are so many different stock structures of what it means to be "dating" that the statute is ripe for judicial interpretation. As one of the lead cases pointed out, a phrase like "dating" can mean different things to different groups of people.[9]

III. Calculating how much persuasion is needed

Trying to teach persuasion as a precise cooking recipe is something like trying to teach art as a paint-by-number activity. But lawyers can draw on some rough guidelines.

A. Persuasion compared to coercion

Why do we like to say "advocacy" instead of "persuasion"? The word "advocacy" sounds better and more professional somehow. That could be because persuasion feels like it is on the same continuum as coercion. In fact, that's true. Persuasion is on the same continuum. It doesn't make "persuasion" a bad word per se, however.

Persuasion—and yes, we know this next will startle or disturb you—involves indirect threats. It implies that an audience who rejects the persuader's argument may experience certain undesirable consequences. Coercion, on the other hand, involves direct and consequential threats.

Here is an easy hypothetical that illustrates the differences and similarities. Suppose a parent asks a child to clean up her bedroom and to pick up all the laundry scattered around the floor (the authors are wryly assuming that many of us were on both sides of the scenario at some points in their lives):

> *Persuasion statement*: Please clean your room and put all of your dirty clothes in one place. That would help me because then I won't have to go searching myself or have to do multiple loads as you discover more items under your bed. If you do this, then I will have time to spend with you doing fun things like the bike ride we have planned.

> *Coercion statement*: If you don't clean up your room, we aren't going to be going on that family bike ride.

---

[9]For more reading, see Michael R. Smith, *Linguistic Hooks: Overcoming Cognitive Stock Structures in Statutory Interpretation*, 8 Leg. Comm. & Rhetoric: JALWD 1 (2011).

If asked, the persuasion statement is where most parents in that situation would undoubtedly prefer to start. The coercion statement is something that would happen later in time, after the attempts at persuasion have failed. But the same potential consequence exists in both statements, the loss of the bike ride.

What response do the statements create in the child? It depends on the child's knowledge base and perspective.

B. Judge Posner's formula for persuasion

Of course, real-world problems are rarely as tidy as bike rides. Most of the time, our client's story requires some mix of response—reinforcing and response changing. The more response changing, the harder it is to persuade. One formula of persuasion has been stated this way:[10]

$$\begin{array}{ccc} \text{Distance of} & & \text{Resistance of} & & \text{Amount of} \\ \text{audience} & \times & \text{audience from} & = & \text{persuasion (or} \\ \text{from author's} & & \text{author's} & & \text{coercion)} \\ \text{position} & & \text{position} & & \text{needed} \end{array}$$

This formula suggests that two factors determine how hard it will be to persuade an audience.

1. Distance

First is how far apart the author's position is from what the audience already accepts. Obviously, when the author's position and the audience's beliefs are exactly aligned, the persuasion will be easy—indeed maybe even unnecessary. On the other hand, when the author is proposing something in direct conflict with the audience's beliefs, persuasion will be much more difficult.

2. Resistance

The second factor is the audience's resistance to the author's position. When the issue is something the audience cares deeply about, the resistance is likely to be high. Thus, it may be easier to change an audience's mind about something less important (where shall we eat dinner tonight?) than something more significant (what religion shall I practice?)

When a judge is our audience, his resistance may be rooted in a number of factors. Of course, the judge's worldview will affect his degree of

---

[10] *See* Richard Posner, *Overcoming Law* 500–501 (Harv. U. Press 1995).

resistance to arguments. So too, however, will the level of the court. A trial judge will be more resistant to arguments for a change in the law than an appellate judge because a trial judge is bound by precedent in ways that an appellate judge is not. In addition, a lawyer's ethos will affect a judge's resistance to the lawyer's argument. Judges are less resistant to lawyers they respect and trust.

Conclusion

Developing sophisticated legal arguments brings together logos, pathos, and ethos and takes into account the audience's likely responses to the lawyer's attempts to persuade. As we move on to creating persuasive arguments, keep in mind that the most persuasive argument combines logic, emotion, and reputation, and that the most persuasive arguments are those that create a reinforcing response in the audience. Also remember that as the audience is reading or hearing the material, mental images are forming, either based on the lawyer's use of description or based on readers' own experiences and understandings.

There is one more critical aspect to persuasive theory: the importance of delivering the persuasive message in a story structure. Chapter 3 will introduce the fundamentals of story.

Chapter 3

Story as a tool for persuasion

Just as we use persuasion every day, even when we are not aware of it, we also use storytelling in our everyday lives. Humans live through story. It should come as no surprise, then, that storytelling is essential to good advocacy. In this chapter, we introduce basic concepts about story and storytelling. We further explore those concepts throughout the rest of this book.

I. What is a word like "story" doing in a serious legal writing course?

You have probably used the word "story" at least half a dozen times this week, without even being aware of it. The word "story" and its derivative, "storytelling," are ubiquitous. And intuitively, we know that stories persuade. Stories are inherently interesting. We grow up listening to stories, and we learn to tell stories to each other. We are entertained by stories. Politicians and public speakers often use stories to make points and to teach, and often to persuade. Stories are methods of delivering information. Although stories are certainly used to affect an audience at a gut level, stories are more frequently used simply as the most effective way to have the audience remember the information.

> **Try this: counting stories**
>
> If you want to test for yourself how important stories are in human interactions, count how many stories you hear in a single day. Then try to count how many stories you tell during that same period.

Because humans are hardwired to remember information when it is delivered as part of a story, much of this book—including the sections on legal argument—reads in terms of storytelling. Before we get to the specific parts of stories, however, we need to pause for a moment and define exactly what we mean by the term "story." Here is our definition:

> **Story**: A character-based and descriptive telling of a character's efforts, over time, to overcome obstacles and achieve a goal.[1]

That the word "character" appears twice in this definition is intentional. It reflects a central tenet of cognitive science: that people relate and respond to characters' stories. That is, we often "picture" ourselves in the situation that is portrayed by the story, and relate the experience described in the story to how we would react in the same situation.[2] If the character in the story reacts in a way that we can imagine ourselves doing, it feels "real" and we are more likely to understand and accept the character's point of view.

Think of the "story" as the whole of the client's case. The client arrives in the lawyer's office with a dispute that needs to be resolved, either because he seeks redress against some other person or entity or because somebody has claimed the client has done something wrong. That dispute involves a character (the client), an obstacle (which can be the other side of the case, or the law, or other challenges), and a goal (the client wants the dispute resolved in a way that favors him). This story is told in court over time, often in pieces. The pleadings (the plaintiff's complaint, the defendant's answer) are preliminary tellings of the client's story. There may be preliminary motions (supported by briefs) that tell and resolve parts of the story. There may be a trial, or an appeal, that provides a more comprehensive (and refined) telling of the story. You might think of each step of the process as a chapter of the client's overall story. Because each chapter is part of the larger story, each chapter should keep the client's larger goals in mind, even if that chapter is only a single step toward that final goal.

The possible chapters of any legal story might be depicted graphically as shown in Figure 3-1.

---

[1] This definition is derived from a definition proposed by storyteller Kendall Haven. Kendall Haven, *Story Proof: the Science Behind the Startling Power of Story* 79 (Libraries Unltd. 2007). We recognize that there are many definitions of "story," some of which are too broad to be useful. For example, Aristotle described the "whole" of a story as a narrative with a beginning, a middle, and an end. Aristotle, *The Poetics* 31 (W. Hamilton Fyfe trans., Harv. U. Press 1973). We have chosen Haven's definition because it captures what we believe are the essential elements that make stories interesting and are present in all legal disputes: characters, conflicts, and resolutions.

[2] *See* Ruth Anne Robbins, *Harry Potter, Ruby Slippers and Merlin: Telling the Client's Story Using the Characters and Paradigm of the Archetypal Hero's Journey*, 29 Seattle L. Rev. 767, 774 (2006) ("We understand narrative because we join the story and see ourselves as part of it: we place ourselves into the story and walk with the characters."); *see also* Steven L. Winter, *The Cognitive Dimension of the Agony Between Legal Power and Narrative Meaning*, 87 Mich. L. Rev. 2225, 2272–2277 (1989) ("the audience lives the story-experience, and is brought personally to engage in the process of constructing meaning out of another's experience").

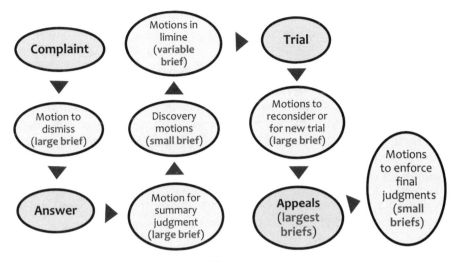

Figure 3-1: Possible chapters in a litigation story

II. Stories are persuasive, even to lawyers and judges

In legal education, the words "story" and "storytelling" are sometimes given a bum rap by people who believe that stories are not serious enough for legal discourse. One reason for this is that English has only one possible synonym for "story," and it's a debatable synonym at best: "narrative." A narrative is a holistic telling of a series of events, whereas a story has a more precise definition, as demonstrated above.

Narrative (including story) is one of the four methods of discourse (the others are description, exposition, and argumentation). But this hesitancy toward storytelling is not universal, not even on the United States Supreme Court. Justice Anthony Kennedy suggests that many judges begin with a "quick judgment[]" and then determine whether that judgment "makes sense, if it's logical, if it's fair, if it accords with the law, if it accords with the Constitution, if it accords with your own sense of ethics and morality."[3] Likewise, Judge Richard Posner of the United States Court of Appeals for the Seventh Circuit admits that "[i]ntuition plays a major role in judicial as in most decision making. . . ."[4]

It's really quite simple. We should tell stories in persuasive documents because stories persuade. One recent empirical study asked judges to

---

[3]Richard A. Posner, *How Judges Think* 257 (Harv. U. Press 2008).
[4]*Id.* at 107.

read two different versions of the same brief—one that confined itself to argumentation without storytelling, and one that included a strong story-based argument—and asked the judges to report which version was more persuasive. Briefs were written on both sides of the argument to simultaneously test or debunk the hypothesis that story is most useful when the case precedent leans against that party's position. In the simulation, the appellants had more than 130 years of precedent supporting their position, whereas the respondents had the better script for a made-for-television movie: trying to protect their picturesque small town feel from the nonaesthetics of a large has-everything store.

A majority of the study's participants chose the story-based brief, regardless of whether they read the appellant or respondent briefs.[5] The limited demographics of the study also revealed a preference for the story-based brief regardless of gender.[6] Interestingly, the story-based brief was preferred by most job groups with one exception: law clerks who were recent law school graduates. Figures 3-2 and 3-3 demonstrate the findings very succinctly.

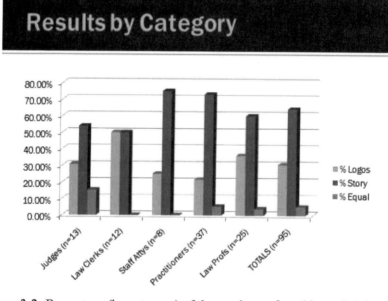

Figure 3-2: Percentage (by category) of those who preferred logos brief to story brief

---

[5]Kenneth D. Chestek, *Judging by the Numbers: An Empirical Study of the Power of Story*, 7 J. ALWD 1 (2010).
[6]The study was not designed to include other demographics, so there are no results based on race, religion, sexual orientation, or political ideology. The study participants came from many different geographical areas in the country.

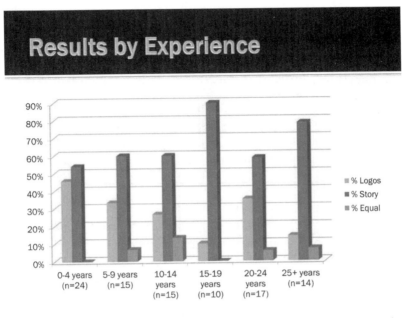

Figure 3-3: Percentage (by years of experience in current job) of those who preferred logos brief to story brief

Looking at these figures, the hypothesis that "story persuades" plays out with a legally trained audience. Judges, appellate attorneys, and staff attorneys (also known as career law clerks) are all persuaded by a story-based brief more than they are by a brief that relies heavily on pure logos. Only those participants who had recently graduated from law school were unsure.

III. The biology of storytelling

According to several branches of the biological sciences, the only results above that have a modicum of surprise are those of the new law graduates. The other participants were all responding to the biology of storytelling. Humans—and quite likely many other organisms—are programmed to accept and learn from stories, beginning at an early age. Babies, for example, focus on faces from as early as a few weeks after birth. Babies study how faces move and what emotions people are showing. They can smile in response to people's faces as early as six weeks, and they can cry if they are uncomfortable with a new person's face. By the time the baby becomes a toddler, he can understand a story and craves them. This is the bedtime story stage. By the age of six, most neurologically typical children can tell a full story from memory or imagination. That is the stage of dressing up as characters,

Stories are part of response-reinforcing in our audience

The biology and psychology studies of story confirm that our audience, be they clients, judges, or opposing counsel, will automatically use storytelling strategies to build understanding. The form of our argument, thus, is response reinforcing because our audience is predisposed to think in story. Moreover, when we present our client's argument in the form of a story, our audience is more likely to connect to our client and to be open to accepting our analysis.

To illustrate the power of our storytelling instinct, consider the following:

- He dropped the piece of paper into the goldfish bowl.
- Over the next six months, the company continued to make money at impressive rates.
- As the boat sped down the Columbia River, Hazel tried to forget.

These sentences have no connection to each other. In fact, they were randomly drawn from three different books.[1] Nonetheless, most of us naturally made connections between these sentences to form a story.[2] Did you make a connection between "he" and Hazel? What was Hazel trying to forget? Did she miss out on the money the company made?

If so, that's your mind logically creating a narrative to connect the three sentences. Imagine how a reader's mind will make connections when the author purposely develops the narrative! More important, imagine how reader will begin to relate, to understand the perspective of the characters in the story.

---

[1] Jasper Fforde, The Eyre Affair 101 (Penguin Books 2003); Michael Lewis, The Big Short 111 (Norton 2011); and Rick Riordan, The Son of Neptune 213 (Hyperion Books 2011), respectively.
[2] See Kendall Haven, Story Proof: The Science Behind the Startling Power of Story 34 (Greenwood Publishing 2007).

playing with dolls or action figures. These children are walking through stories and asking us to walk through with them.[7]

And that is how adults also experience a story. We go inside the story as observers. Silently, we shadow a character, experiencing muted versions of what she is experiencing. When we jump while watching a scary or suspenseful movie, we are experiencing a physical response that is related to what the character is feeling. Think about going to a movie theater to see a horror flick. Do you jump when a character

---

[7] Haven, *supra* n. 1, at 25.

is surprised by one of the antagonists? Do you feel yourself becoming anxious as the mood of the movie becomes ominous? Stop to consider that phenomenon. Intellectually, you know that you aren't in danger. It's only a 2-D (or 3-D or 4-D) performance. Yet you have an empathetic response. That is because we experience stories by living them or reliving them. When J.K. Rowling, author of the *Harry Potter* series, describes a pensieve—the magic bowl in which people visit other people's memories by becoming an invisible player inside of them—she gives a form and a name to what we automatically do with stories.

Cognitive psychologists also have recently studied the concept of "framing." A frame is a mental construct that helps readers think about or organize abstract concepts. One type, "surface frames," is narrow in scope, easily identified, and easy to counteract. For example, the characterization of the "activist judge" and "frivolous lawsuit" each use surface frames that attempt to deflect attention from the actual and deeper issue. "Deep frames," however, resonate with more deeply held values in the listener. Consequently, an argument that resonates with a person's deep frame is more likely to persuade him.

Cognitive scientist George Lakoff describes deep frames as ideas or values that structure how you view the world.[8] Deep frames can be stated in just

Surface versus deep frames: McDonald's coffee case

In *Liebeck v. McDonald's Restaurants*, the plaintiff sued for damages suffered when she spilled coffee in her lap, which burned that part of her body. As the case went to trial, the national media picked up the story and spun it with a surface frame argument, that it was an example of frivolous litigation that proved a need for tort reform. The jury, however, privy to the actual evidence, rejected this surface frame and awarded punitive and actual damages. Discovery revealed that McDonald's had made a conscious choice to serve superheated coffee that it knew was dangerous to drink on its purchase because the company derived an economic benefit from the higher temperatures—the coffee would cool and be at the right temperature for those drive-through commuters who waited until reaching work to drink it. The pictures of Liebeck's third-degree burns graphically showed the risks that McDonald's knowingly took, without adequate warnings to its customers. The deep frame of health and safety won the day.

---

[8]George Lakoff, *Whose Freedom? The Battle over America's Most Important Idea* 12 (Farrar, Straus & Giroux 2006).

a few words and should evoke a predictable response from the listener. For example, Lakoff describes the word "freedom" as a deep frame. At the heart of every deep frame is what he calls an "uncontested idea"; in this case, the idea is that "freedom" is good and is something all people long for.

This textbook returns to the concept of deep frames in Chapter 9 when we explore how to choose a theme in more detail. For now, it is simply important to recognize that everybody has deeply held values, and that persuasion is most effective when you craft your client's story so that it appeals to those deep frames.

IV. The storyteller's tool box

Storytelling has many components. We discuss many of them in this book, but we cannot hope to cover all of them. After all, this first course in written advocacy is just that: a first course.

Legal stories, though nonfiction, are still stories. Although fiction and nonfiction stories have obvious differences, they both use many of the same tools. There are two categories of tools that writers can use to accomplish their purpose: structural and stylistic (sometimes called aesthetic). Both types of tools are necessary. Imagine your piece of legal writing as a house construction project. A well-built house begins with a sound structure in the form of rough carpentry: a firm foundation; strong walls; watertight roof and windows; electrical, heating, and plumbing systems. The structure remains incomplete, however, until it includes floor and wall coverings, light fixtures, bathroom fixtures, cabinets, and appliances. A lawyer writing any sort of persuasive document (a brief, a demand letter, a proposal in a negotiation context) will use both the structural and aesthetic tools that fit the situation.

A. Structural tools for the legal writer

Recall the structural definition of story from a few pages ago: "a character-based and descriptive telling of a character's efforts, over time, to overcome obstacles and achieve a goal." Implicit to that structure are the following seven components.

1. Character

The "characters" are the participants in the story. They can be human or other. Characters who readers empathize with are "protagonists," while characters who oppose the protagonist are "antagonists." Characters who are neutral, but who may have important information to impart about the story, may be called "companion characters." Typically, your client is cast as the protagonist in the story, and the opposing parties are the antagonists. Witnesses with no stake in the outcome of the case may be companion characters.

2. Conflict

"Conflict" is the fuel that drives the action forward. In most stories, the protagonist (your client) seeks to resolve the conflict and return to a satisfactory condition. Conflict is usually characterized by using a metaphor: for example, "Person versus Nature." There can be multiple conflicts in a story if the story is tracking more than one character's pathway or if the protagonist's relationship to many characters is being explored. This is equally true in your client's legal story. The conflict might be primarily about

- the dispute with the opposing party or parties;
- a dispute about what the law is, or should be, or how it should be interpreted; or
- a dispute about the procedures used to resolve the case.

The chapters in Part IV discuss these three conflict types in more detail.

3. Theme

In literature, the "theme" is the "moral of the story," that is, the lesson that the author wants readers to take away from the story. In legal writing, the theme is the emotional center of the case. It is the essential reason that the writer advances to convince a judge or jury that a ruling in favor of your client is fair, just, and emotionally satisfying.

"Theory of the case" is a legal concept that differs from "theme," although the terms are sometimes mistakenly used interchangeably. The theory of the case describes the legal reason why your client should win. The theme gives the court a reason to want to rule in your client's favor. The theory is rationale based; the theme appeals more to values and to feelings. The differences between theory of the case and theme are explored in more detail in Chapters 9 and 16.

4. Setting

In standard story structure, "setting" refers to the physical and social characteristics of the time and place where the story occurs. Legal writers need to describe in appropriate detail the factual setting of the case: that is, the time, place, and background details about how the conflict arose. They also need to describe, in appropriate detail, the legal setting: the rules of law that form the legal basis for the court's ruling, as well as the facts of the precedential cases that provide context for those rules.

5. *Point of view*

"Point of view" refers to the perspective from which readers are invited to perceive the story. For example, some stories are told from the point of view of an "omniscient narrator," who knows everything or at least more than any single character knows. Other stories are told from the more limited point of view of an individual character in the story. In a legal document such as a brief, the lawyer should normally choose to write from the client's point of view, though not necessarily with the client's voice.

6. *Plot*

Many definitions of "plot" are available, but for our purposes, E.M. Forster's definition is the most useful: plot is the causal connections between individual events that constitute the chronology of the story.[9] The overall plot of a story is made up of story "beats" (or scenes) that connect through key causal words: "then . . . but . . . if . . . or . . . so . . . because . . . and . . ."

Note that plot and conflict are inextricably entwined. Without a conflict, there would be no need for anything else to happen in the story.

7. *Organization*

"Organization" is simply the sequence in which the events are told in the story. The narrative arc is the global organization of the story. In legal writing, the whole organization of the brief comprises the narrative arc. The parts of the arc are "order" (what happened before the conflict), "chaos" (the main incident), and "reorder" (what happened after the main incident, including the story's eventual resolution).

Not all stories are organized chronologically. In legal writing, stories are rarely told in exact chronological order, in fact. The facts section of the brief, for example, often establishes context by starting with the most recent events, such as the procedural history of the case, and then goes back in

---

[9]E.M. Forster, *Aspects of the Novel* 60 (Holmes & Meiers 1974).

time to talk about earlier events. The organization of the legal argument is not chronological either but is organized around the rules of law.

Other temporal ordering devices such as foreshadowing, flashback, and flash-forward are also organizational tools, though they are stylistic ones.

B. Stylistic tools for the legal writer

A writer of fiction has a much wider array of stylistic tools available than does a writer of nonfiction. Nonfiction writers, including legal writers, are bound by the existing facts and constrained by ethos considerations. For example, literary devices like suspense or humor are rarely appropriate for lawyers to use in persuasive legal writing. Their clients have engaged the services of a lawyer for serious reasons. The lawyer also must remember the audience—most legal readers have been trained to be skeptical readers and will assume that exaggerations or flamboyance is meant to cover up a lack of substance.[10]

Note that in our earlier house metaphor, the stylistic construction materials of light fixtures, bathroom fixtures, and so on were all very functional and necessary. The stylistic decisions of storytelling are the mood-controlling aspect of the all-important pathos needed for any persuasive communication. Professor Michael Smith calls this sort of pathos "medium mood control," where the word "medium" means the mode of communication (like the word's plural form, "media").[11]

1. Description and the selection of details

Writers also have a wide variety of ways to describe characters, objects, or settings. They can be described by name and category, sensory information, history, function, or comparison to other things. The selection of details from among the available descriptive material allows the writer significant control in creating a vivid or vague mental image for readers. These choices can greatly influence the mood the writer creates in the minds of readers.

---

[10] *See* Lance N. Long & William F. Christensen, *Clearly, Using Intensifiers Is Very Bad—Or Is It?*, 45 Idaho L. Rev. 171, 174–176 (2008).
[11] Michael R. Smith, *Advanced Legal Writing: Theories and Strategies in Persuasive Writing* 12 (2d ed., Aspen L. & Bus. 2008).

The difference between frames and stock structures

Stock structures, surface frames, and deep frames are related in the sense that they are all automatic, unconscious responses to stimuli and are based on how we view the world. But they are fundamentally different in that stock structures are value neutral, while frames are value driven.

Stock structures are neither inherently "good" nor "bad." They just are. They help us quickly understand what we see, read, and hear. They trigger mental images that help us make sense of the stimuli we perceive. Frames, in contrast, involve value judgments. They may or may not evoke mental images (what does "freedom" look like anyway?), but they do trigger emotional or normative responses, either positive or negative. For example, think of an "activist." You probably can imagine a person who passionately believes in some cause; that is an example of a stock structure. But if you called that person an "environmentalist" or an "eco-terrorist" (depending on whether you agree with what the activist believes in), you are using surface frames to express a value judgment about that person. A lawyer representing that person might call on the deep frame of justice or freedom by including details showing that client exercising his First Amendment rights in a peaceful manner.

2. Stock structures

Writers may also choose to tap into preexisting constructs in their readers' minds, which we called "stock structures" in Chapter 2. Recall that stock structures can be things, people, scenes, prototypes, or mini-events. For example, think of a law school textbook. The mental image you immediately called up is based on your own experience, but it is very likely that if you asked a student from another law school the same question, the two pictures would look roughly the same. "Textbook" is a stock structure, just as "combing one's hair" or "the annoying coworker."

3. Metaphor

Legal writers frequently use metaphors, both consciously and unconsciously, in persuasion because almost every conversation involves some metaphor.[12] Broadly speaking, this category of devices refers to ways of conveying multiple meanings or comparing ideas. Metaphor is

---

[12]On our short list of recommended readings is this article on the topic of metaphor in lawyering. Linda L. Berger, *The Lady, or the Tiger? A Field Guide to Metaphor and Narrative*, 50 Washburn L.J. 275 (2011).

a nonliteral comparison of two concepts or things; analogy is a literal comparison of concepts and things. We use metaphors in language in almost every conversation. As Professor Linda Berger points out, every time we check our e-mail, browse the web, or bookmark a website, we have used metaphoric language.[13]

4. Reference or allusion

Related to metaphor, an allusion or a reference uses a shorthand term to stand for a broader concept. These can be internal to the document itself or external, referencing an outside document or event. Think, "literary allusion" or "pop cultural reference." Allusions work at several levels in readers' minds and are powerful devices for engaging readers and invoking subliminal responses.

5. Tone

Writers have many stylistic devices to use, including word choices and placement, sentence length, and paragraph structure. By making careful choices in this category, the writer can create an almost infinite variety of moods, tones, and emotional responses in readers. In legal writing, those choices are somewhat more limited, but setting the proper tone is still very important. The legal writer needs to set a professional tone that conveys to readers that the writer is a serious person but respectful of the opposing side to the controversy. Doing so is one important way of establishing the writer's ethos, or credibility.

In the chapters that follow, you will learn more about how a lawyer can effectively use each of the structural tools shown in Table 3-1 to persuade readers.

But before we get specific about using these tools, we need to give some detailed thought about the story we want to tell about our client. That is the topic of Part II of this text. Chapter 4 begins that process by discussing the key audience for the story you will tell: trial and appellate judges.

---

[13]*Id.* at 279.

Table 3-1: Structural writing tools

Storytelling concept	Persuasive legal writing
Character	Clients (protagonists) and opposing parties (antagonists)
Conflict	(a) The factual dispute between the parties (b) The legal issue(s) in the case (c) The procedural issue(s) in the case
Setting or scene	(a) The factual setting (i.e., the facts of the case and the circumstances in which the dispute arose) (b) The legal setting (the rules of law and precedents) (c) The setting or scenes of case precedent, used in Rule Explanation
Point of view	The client's perspective
Theme	The central reason(s) that can reinforce or change readers' responses
Plot, Organization	Large-scale organization of the legal writing
Metaphor, reference/allusion/ stock structures	Often useful in extrapolating results from precedents or in explaining complicated or unfamiliar facts.
Tone	Very useful in legal writing. Legal authors often use persuasive word choices, sentence and paragraph structure, and selective use of active or passive voice to emphasize/deemphasize helpful or harmful facts.
Description	Useful to provide emphasis for helpful facts (more detail) or to deemphasize harmful facts (less detail). Careful use of stock structures can also create vivid images in the reader's subconscious, where persuasion is most effective.

Developing the client's story

The next several chapters discuss the lawyer's role in assisting a client achieve his goal. Part II is structured to follow the way that a practicing lawyer would approach a real case. Chapter 4 provides some background information about how different judicial audiences, whether trial judges or appellate, might view the client's story, which in turn helps the lawyer decide how to tell that story. Chapters 5 and 6 walk through the process of investigating both the facts (i.e., what happened to cause the client's problem) and the law. These two processes are closely related. Chapters 7 and 8 discuss ways to conceptualize the client's problem as a story and to make some preliminary choices about how to tell that story.

The process of writing a brief involves at least four steps:

1. **Prewriting:** research and planning
2. **Drafting:** getting the first rough draft down on paper
3. **Rewriting and revising:** reorganizing and filling out the material, and strategizing the word choices for persuasion
4. **Polishing:** formatting the final document so that it looks professional and readable

These Part II chapters are all about prewriting. Unclear writing is a result of unclear thinking. The prewriting phase allows you to clarify your thinking about the case. There are other skills courses as well as pro bono experiences in law school that deal exclusively with the prewriting phase: for example, courses that teach client interviewing and counseling, pretrial preparation, and discovery. These next chapters provide a brief glimpse of what those other important lawyering skills include. We recommend you take those sorts of courses and then hone what you study in them by participating in clinics, externships, and pro bono projects. The live-client experiences you will gain in those opportunities are invaluable.

Our ultimate goal in this part is to talk about the client's story. A lawyer cannot write a good story about the client until she has a clear sense of who the client is and what the client's goals are.

Chapter 4

Thinking about the audience

Legal documents have multiple audiences. Chief among them are the decider (typically, a judge or magistrate), the opposing party, and the client. In this chapter, we focus on the different roles that the deciders—the judges—play in writing the endings to legal stories. By understanding what the judges' roles may be, we can begin to design our client's narratives to best advantage.

Table 4-1 summarizes the differences between a trial court judge and an appellate judge. We explore these differences in further detail below.

Table 4-1: Differences between a trial and an appellate judge

Trial judge	Appellate judge
First neutral person to review the case	Builds on work of lower court judges
Strong incentive to make "right" decision for the parties before the court	"Error correction" only part of job; also needs to consider consequences of any decision on future litigants
Facts are often fluid; usually has discretion to "find" facts based on credibility of evidence	Facts are usually fixed by the lower court; credibility issues not reviewed
"Mentor" to the parties	"Mentor" to the lower court

When a lawyer writes a brief to the trial court, he is advising and assisting the court in writing the ending to the story of his client's case. Let's then think about writing a trial-level brief as part of "story creating." When one side appeals the final decision to an appellate court, that side is asking the appellate court to write a different ending to a previously completed story. There is an additional function to an appellate brief at that point. Because the appellate court knew nothing about the case until the completed record arrived in its office, the lawyer's role as advocate is to bring the appellate court up to speed on what the case story is about.

I. Trial judge: mentor to the client

When we view a client's legal dispute as a story, it is useful to assign roles to the participants in the lawsuit. The obvious role for the client is as the hero, or protagonist, of the story, while the opposing parties and witnesses are cast as other types of characters. We introduced this concept in Chapter 3 and will return to it in more depth in Chapter 7. The lawyer acts as a narrator, not as a direct character.

In a bench trial, the trial judge decides the case.[1] In that sense, the trial judge is more than just a passive "audience" who listens to the stories told by the competing attorney–narrators of the opposing sides. Rather, the trial judge must listen to the competing stories told, decide which of the competing protagonists is entitled to the court's assistance, and then implement the relief that provides what the court concludes is the appropriate "ending" to the story.

Understanding the trial judge's role as "mentor," or helper, to the client–protagonist of the story (if the client prevails, that is) helps an attorney to think about what the trial judge needs to hear. Essentially, the judge needs to find out how the law permits him to assist the client, but also why the assistance the client seeks is the right thing to do.

A. Judges want to "get it right"

The trial judge is a neutral person who evaluates a case and renders a decision, or series of decisions, resolving the dispute. The judge, therefore, must focus more intensely on the parties in front of her than an appellate court might. The contexts in which a trial judge encounters the client's story vary greatly. You might think that a trial judge only needs to concern herself with the story when she sits as a finder of fact at the final disposition of the case—that is, when parties either have no right or have waived their right to a jury trial. But in fact, trial judges need to think about a client's story from the very start of the case.

Table 4-2 lists just a few possible settings in which a judge needs to understand the client's character, obstacles, and goals.

---

[1]While in many cases juries decide the facts, this book is about writing to law-trained arbitrators, trial court judges, and appellate judges. So this book confines itself to a discussion of persuasion to those types of audiences. Many civil trials are bench trials because jury trials are extremely expensive and very often cause significant delays in case resolution.

Table 4-2: Possible procedural postures where a client's story becomes relevant

Case or procedural posture	What the judge needs to consider
Motion to dismiss civil case	Is the story told by the complaint plausible? Is the plaintiff's goal legally permissible?
Motion to compel discovery or for protective order	Is one character taking unfair advantage of another character in the unfolding story?
Motion for summary judgment	Is the evidence in the record (produced through discovery or otherwise) sufficiently credible that a jury might believe it?
Motion for temporary restraining order or preliminary injunction	Is the testimony at the hearing credible? Are the plaintiff's goals important enough to merit this extraordinary relief?
Trial or hearing on the merits (bench trial)	Which characters are telling the truth? Which ones are mistaken? How do all of the pieces of evidence fit together in a coherent story? Who should prevail?
Trial or hearing on the merits (jury trial)	Is one character trying to mislead the jury or take unfair advantage of other characters, or bring in inadmissible evidence?

The list could go on, virtually indefinitely. The main point here, of course, is that a trial judge needs to clearly grasp who the parties are in the cases she decides, not only to rule on the merits but also to make the numerous preliminary rulings she is called on to decide every day. A lawyer therefore must fully understand his client's story from the very first time he meets the client. Only then can he present the client's story persuasively, and in the correct context, to the trial judge.

B. Role of the trial court as fact finder

The client's story is inextricably bound up in the facts of what happened to cause the dispute. But the "facts" available to the trial court are different at various stages of the case, and much different from the facts available to any appellate court. Just as a professional photographer has many different lenses in his camera bag to use in different situations, the trial judge has many different lenses through which she will view the facts. The particular lens she uses depends on the context.

Consider Table 4-2. When the trial judge decides a motion to dismiss, for example, she must assume that every fact stated in the complaint is true, and she need not consider any alternative facts that are not stated in the complaint. However, when faced with a motion for summary judgment, the judge needs to look at facts advanced by all sides of the dispute, to determine (a) whether they conflict with each other, and (b) if they do, whether these conflicts make a difference legally. In still other situations (trials or hearings on the merits of a case or on some aspect of a case), the trial judge needs to evaluate the credibility of the evidence presented and render a decision as to what the facts really are. Thus, at different steps in the trial process, the facts available to tell a client's story may differ considerably.

Appellate judges have far less room to maneuver in evaluating facts. For the most part, appellate judges must defer to the trial court's resolution of all questions of fact. The burden on the appellant and the standard of review are so high because the trial judge was in a far better position to assess the context of the testimony in the overall story: the trial judge saw and heard the parties in person. Thus, the trial judge is in a better position than an appellate court to make credibility decisions based on the demeanor of witnesses and other nonverbal evidence as well as the words themselves. For example, trial transcripts make no note of whether witnesses testified in calm voices or whether they mumbled, shouted, or cried.

All of this means simply that in any proceeding in the trial court, the facts are more likely to be in play than they are on appeal. Arguments about what the facts really are, and what they mean, may be very important to the trial judge. The trial advocate therefore needs to understand how the trial judge must view the facts and then be fully prepared to reason with the facts at whatever level the trial court must do so.

C. Respect for higher authority

If the trial court is the "master of the facts" of the case, the appellate court is correspondingly the "master of the law." The deference that an appellate court has for a trial court's findings of fact does not extend to any holdings of law since the appellate court is in as good a position as (if not better than) the trial court to resolve questions of law.

Of course, a litigant who makes a novel claim or challenges a well-established legal rule must still make such arguments before the trial court to preserve a right to raise the issue on appeal. When presenting a claim that runs counter to existing legal rules or precedent, the advocate needs to rely much more heavily on the client's story.[2] To effect positive change, the

---

[2]Recall the story of Linda Brown, which led to the landmark decision of *Brown v. Board of Education*, discussed in the Prologue.

lawyer needs to show how the existing rule unfairly harms or limits the client or people like the client. Telling a compelling story about how that rule is harmful is the surest path to success in such cases.

II. Appellate judge: mentor to the trial judge?

If the role of the trial judge is to serve as a mentor to the hero–litigant who appears before her, the role of the appellate court is somewhat different. It may be helpful to think of the appellate court as a mentor to the trial court judge.

While the trial judge is primarily focused on "getting it right" so that the "correct" party wins, appellate judges must take a somewhat broader view. Certainly, a significant part of the function of the court is error correction (at least at the level of the intermediate appellate court or, in those few jurisdictions that have no intermediate appellate court, the state supreme court). Every litigant is entitled to at least one fresh set of judicial eyes to review the matter to make sure that the trial court did not make a mistake.

> **Appellate courts and facts**
>
> One appellate court described the role of factual record on appeal this way: "When practicing appellate law, there are at least three immutable rules: first, take great care to prepare a complete record; second, if it is not in the record, it did not happen; and third, when in doubt, refer back to rules one and two." Protect Our Water v. County of Merced, 1 Cal. Rptr.3d 726, 726 (App. 5th Dist. 2003).

But another function of any appellate court is law making. The principle of stare decisis requires the intermediate appellate court to look backward and forward at the same time. It looks backward to see whether the case before it was decided correctly—its error-correction function; it simultaneously looks forward to see what the consequences might be in future cases of any decision it renders in this case—its law-making function. And in the United States Supreme Court[3] (as well as in state supreme courts), the law-making function is the Court's primary focus.

This does not mean that client stories are not important in appellate courts; as Linda Brown's story illustrates, sometimes the stories are the

---

[3]The Supreme Court's website reports that its typical annual caseload (which would be primarily petitions for certiorari) is around 10,000 cases, but review is granted in only about 100 cases (or 1 percent of the petitions) per term. Supreme Court of the United States, *The Justices' Caseload*, http://www.supremecourt.gov/about/justicecaseload.aspx (accessed Sept. 7, 2012).

most important part of the brief. But it does suggest that since the appellate court's function is different from the trial court's, the story that a client tells at the appellate level may differ too.

The important points for any lawyer writing an appellate brief are these: first, an attorney has somewhat less flexibility in presenting the facts and telling his client's story since the facts on appeal are more rigid than at the trial level.

Second, even though the facts on appeal are more rigid, they are just as important. The story that begins in the fact section of the brief can resonate deep inside an appellate judge's mind and create an unconscious impulse to rule in the client's favor. The way the lawyer arranges and presents the available facts can go a long way to creating this impulse, as we explore in future chapters.

Third, a lawyer must take into consideration the appellate judge's larger role in law making when he writes an appellate brief. It may be sufficient at the trial level to show a trial judge how binding precedent requires a ruling in a particular way. But on appeal, the lawyer may need to go further and point out how a particular ruling is consistent with sound public policy, will be easy to implement in the future, or will have some other salutary effect on the law going forward. While such arguments may be made at the trial level too, they are likely to have more impact in the appellate court.

Finally, a lawyer writing an appellate brief must keep in mind that most appellate judges were once trial judges; and even if they weren't, they believe their trial court colleagues to be competent and thoughtful. As such, they are not likely to be persuaded by ad hominem attacks on the trial court or its ruling.

In the next chapter, we turn our attention to learning about the client's story, a job that occupies a large part of a lawyer's typical day at the office.

Chapter 5

Investigating the facts

You are in your office. Your client arrives with a problem, seeking your help. Maybe he wants compensation or other redress for an injury he believes another caused him; or maybe he has been sued but doesn't believe he caused the injury alleged. He seeks your legal advice about what to do.

Regardless of how knowledgeable you are about the law in any given field, all of that knowledge is of limited use until you learn what the client's problem is. Finding out what the problem is begins with interviewing the client—but it by no means ends there. The reality is that clients bring to the lawyer only their perception of some of the facts. Thus, after hearing the client's version of the story, the lawyer must do additional factual research and some targeted research into the law. Chapter 6 will help you think about the law and strategize about what legal theories to research and assert; for now, however, we want to focus on how to gather all of the facts that you need to effectively represent your client.

The facts that the client conveys to the lawyer during the initial client interview are usually insufficient in a number of ways:

- The client most likely does not know what facts are relevant to the governing law. Thus, he may withhold information because he doesn't believe it is relevant.
- The client may believe that he has done something wrong or embarrassing and may prefer not to disclose those adverse facts to the lawyer. This characteristic of human nature may operate despite reassurances that everything the client says is confidential and explanations that the lawyer needs to know everything so that she can prepare the best possible presentation of his case.
- The client may actually believe things that are not provable or even are not true. Clients are only human, after all. They can perceive only what they perceive. Other people may tell the client things that the client later recalls incorrectly or translates in his head using whatever filters and predispositions he may have. While the client may sincerely believe what he tells the lawyer, that version

of the facts will often include information that is unsupported by the other facts.

- And unfortunately, a few clients purposely lie to the lawyer to get the lawyer to do something she would not do if she knew the truth.

At least the first three problems are not only common, they are almost universal. In practice, a lawyer who does no fact investigation beyond what the client tells her is a lawyer who is probably committing malpractice. As a result, a typical day in the life of a practicing lawyer involves the lawyer engaged in the process of fact investigation. And, that is why fact investigation is one of the most important jobs a lawyer has. Regardless of the type of legal practice. A lawyer engaged in a business or transactional practice rather than litigation nevertheless needs to understand the business deal, or the family relations, or whatever kind of facts will determine how the client's rights might be affected in the future.

You can learn the critical skill of fact investigation in elective courses that include live-client clinics and externships, which allow you to

> **Why lawyers need to listen carefully to their client's stories**
>
> It is not always the bad facts that the client doesn't reveal at first. Sometimes there are helpful facts that the client doesn't realize are helpful.
>
> Julia (not her real name) sought help from a domestic violence pro bono project to get protection from her abusive domestic partner. She told her lawyer about some mild physical abuse that caused minor injuries. The lawyer prepared a motion for a protection from abuse order, although he worried that the evidence they would be able to present might not be enough to get the order.
>
> On the day set for hearing, as they waited in the coffee shop at the courthouse for the case to be called, Julia mentioned in casual conversation that it was sometimes difficult to manage her life since she was often unable to drive. Her lawyer asked her why she was unable to drive. "Well," she said, "most of the time when my boyfriend leaves for work, he takes the spark plugs out of my car so I can't go anywhere."
>
> Needless to say, the lawyer's plan for direct examination of his client changed immediately. The court granted the motion.

engage in actual fact investigation. Simulation courses such as interviewing and negotiations, trial strategy, pretrial discovery, and the like also teach fact investigation. Your legal writing courses cannot cover the topic in depth, and we encourage all law students to take courses that concentrate on fact investigation opportunities because the skill is so critical for your future careers. Our purpose in this section is merely to introduce you to the idea that facts are not always as they seem, and that you, even while in law school, need to think critically about what the facts appear to be, as well as what the opposing party may perceive them to be. Professor Brian Foley has described this condition as "factual indeterminacy": facts are never "fixed" and may be other than what the client would prefer.[1]

While very few *required* law school courses focus on fact investigation, the good news is that it is not hard to learn this. In fact, since you were a human being before you went to law school, you already know most of what you need: a healthy dose of common sense. You just need to practice using it in a legal context.

I. Facts require context to understand them

Imagine that a person in a uniform is walking toward you, holding a pad of paper and a pen.[2] What does she want?

Although your mind probably jumped to one conclusion, there are many possibilities, of course. To come up with the best answer, however, you need more context. Where are you as the person approaches? What are you doing? Do you know the person approaching, or is she a stranger?

Suppose you are sitting in a restaurant with a menu in your hand. Or you are in a coffeehouse, standing at a counter. The situation makes more sense now: the person approaching will be asking you what food or beverage you would like to order.

Suppose instead you are sitting in your car on the side of a road and you have just turned off your engine. You pulled over moments ago when a black and white car behind you flashed red and blue roof lights while closely following you. Obviously, the person approaching is a police officer who will be giving you a traffic ticket.

As Chapter 3 explains, you are able to fill in the details of these scenes because they are "stock structures," also sometimes called "stock stories," "idealized cognitive models," or "schema." Everybody recognizes thousands, maybe hundreds of thousands, of these stories. They help us make sense of the world around us. They represent patterns of normal human

---

[1]Brian Foley, *Applied Legal Storytelling, Politics, and Factual Realism*, 14 Leg. Writing 17, 38 (2008).
[2]This example was initially suggested in Steven Winter, *The Cognitive Dimension of the Agon Between Legal Power and Narrative Meaning*, 87 Mich. L. Rev. 2225, 2233 (1989), although we have expanded it for our purposes here.

behavior that we have all seen many times before. Stock stories help facilitate human interaction. For example, imagine that we had no stock structure for "police officer writing a ticket." To make sense of this interaction, we would need a much more explicit explanation. The officer might have to say something like this:

> Sir, please roll down your window. Thank you. I am a police officer. I have been appointed by the state to patrol this highway to be sure that motorists obey the speed limits. I have received training to do this. I use a radar gun that emits radio waves and measures the time it takes for them to echo back to determine the speed of passing vehicles. The state has given me authority to use this device to measure the speed of all vehicles traveling on this highway and to stop any vehicle that I determine to be traveling in excess of the speed limit that the state has posted on this road. I used this device on your car when you passed me just a moment ago . . .

And on and on. We couldn't get anything done if we always had to stop and analyze every interaction and every experience in our day. Stock structures allow us to make assumptions about a scenario and to proceed according to our understanding of what to do in analogous situations.

The lesson for legal writing, then, is this: in the absence of context, the audience will invent context, probably using stock structures that are already in their minds. Those contexts may be based on societal norms (such as what we expect when "being pulled over"), or they may be based on readers' personal experiences. But a writer cannot know for certain what stock structure his readers will use to invent the context. For that reason, the legal writer needs to provide readers with sufficient factual detail and context to trigger the stock structure that accurately reflects the actual situation he is describing.

This also means that the lawyer must have first identified, during the interviewing process, the lawyer's own assumptions about the stock structures that she is calling on while imagining the client's situation as the client described it. To use a simplistic example, if a client says to his lawyer "I fell on the rug," it might be worth investigating where the rug was and what it looked like. Falling on a bunched-up runner in a supermarket is very different from falling on wall-to-wall carpet in the client's own house. Likewise, the picture of "falling" could trigger images of someone ending up prone on the floor or someone ending with one knee on the floor but otherwise upright. Whether a lawyer is learning the story from her client or explaining the story to the court, she wants to be sure it contains enough detail to trigger the correct stock structures.

II. A four-step process to thinking about fact investigation

Unlike the law school casebook, in the real world, facts rarely present themselves in a tidy package. Once you're a practicing lawyer, you may learn the basics of your client's story from interviewing him, but as we saw in the example above, that could easily result in an incomplete, and possibly inaccurate, account of what actually happened. You will need to dig deeper.

A. First step: what facts are legally relevant?

Just as the facts don't magically appear on your desk, your client most likely won't walk into your office and say, "I have a question about the enforceability of a liquidated damages clause in a contract." The client's view is more like this: "This hotel that my organization had a conference at wants to charge us for rooms that they sold to other people! Can they do that?" Your job as the attorney is to elicit more of the facts from the client, to think about what the client may be overlooking, and to inquire further.

Once you have learned what you can from your client, the next place to look is into the substantive law that appears, at first glance, to govern the client's problem. Thus, in our hotel reservations example, you would need to learn more from the client about the dispute. Was the contract in your client's personal name or in the name of the organization? What was the purpose of the contract? When and where was it negotiated? Was there any prior dealing between the hotel and the client? Were the terms of the contract explained to the client? Did the client read the contract before signing it? How does the client know that the hotel sold rooms that the organization might have used? What explanation did the hotel give for seeking additional payment?

Many of these questions come from what you know about the law of contracts. You are looking to find who made an offer, whether it was accepted, whether the terms were sufficiently definite, and whether the contract was supported by adequate consideration. You would also ask some questions about whether a breach occurred and, if so, whether the hotel had been damaged by the breach.

All of these questions probably popped into your head based on what you learned in your course in contracts. But you may not know the law of the particular jurisdiction or the related relevant laws of discovery or evidence. More research might be in order. And the legal research is likely to suggest that there are more facts needed to help answer the legal questions. Thus, learning the facts helps you frame the scope of the research, but the two processes are recursive. The more you research, the more facts you may discover you need to determine. The first interview with the client is unlikely to be your only interview of her.

Your initial research into the law might suggest that there was no "meeting of the minds" between the hotel and your client, and that therefore no contract exists. Second, you might wonder whether the contract was imposed on your client by a party in a stronger bargaining position; this would make it a "contract of adhesion" that might be voidable at least in part by the weaker party (your client). Third, your research may suggest that the clause in the contract that calls for the payment of "liquidated damages" in the event of a breach might not be enforceable. Fourth, you may wonder whether, if the hotel was able to sell all of its rooms during the nights of your client's conference, it suffered any damages. Fifth, given your client's claim that some of her organization's members were turned away by the hotel because it was sold out on the nights of the conference, you may consider the defense of "impossibility of performance." All of these legal theories will likely suggest additional questions about the facts of the case that you need to seek answers to, either from your client or from some other source.

In addition to researching the substantive law, you may need to think about the law of evidence. Which of the relevant facts do you have admissible evidence for? Can you prove those facts in court? For example, returning to the hotel reservation example, your client claims that her organization was prevented from performing because the hotel was sold out on the night of the conference. How does your client know that? What admissible evidence do you have to prove that? If you have only hearsay evidence,[3] how can you go about obtaining direct evidence? All of these questions may lead you to additional fact investigation as well.

You will also want to investigate facts that technically may not be legally relevant. For example, you may want to find facts that explain your client's behavior or that of the opposing party. Background details might also be useful to humanize the client and to create visual imagery in the reader's mind. Selecting which details to use in the final written product is explored in Chapter 15; but during the fact investigation phase, you need to open your mind to a wide array of possibly relevant or helpful facts. You will sort out later on which ones actually to use.

---

[3]As you will learn in your course on evidence, hearsay is an out-of-court statement by somebody other than the witness, offered to prove that what the other person said is true. In our example, the fact that an unknown hotel clerk made a comment to a conference attendee that the hotel was sold out, which information was then relayed to Pat Freebird, contains multiple layers of hearsay and therefore might not be admissible at trial.

B. Second step: what is the chronology?

As we discuss in Chapter 3, we humans are hardwired to think in chronological terms; that's how we experience the world. When you hear a story out of sequence, you will struggle to rearrange it sequentially in your mind so that it makes sense to you. But given the way we gather facts and must present them at trial, it is likely that the facts of the case will come at you in random order. Your client will tell you certain things, often not chronologically. You will then fill in the gaps by talking to other witnesses, reading documents, or doing other investigation, discussed below.

At some point in your investigation, after you have gathered enough of the facts to have a sense of what is going on, but before you get too far into the investigation, you will need to prepare a chronology of what happened. It is often helpful to use a visual aid of some sort—a chart, spreadsheet, timeline, storyboard, sketch—to help you see the progression of events. Table 5-1 provides an example of a chart that you might compile based solely on what the client, Pat Freebird, explained during the initial

Table 5-1: Sample spreadsheet timeline for hotel reservations case

Date	Event	Proof
Early Jan. 2012	Freebird talks to reservation agent for Gloucester in Indianapolis; confirms dates for conference and room rate	Freebird testimony
About one week later	Proposed contract for room reservations arrives from Gloucester; Freebird looks it over briefly but does not read it carefully	Freebird
Jan. 24, 2012	Freebird signs contract and mails it back to Gloucester	Freebird; signed copy of contract
June 2012 (approx.)	Freebird gets calls from SOFT members reporting that the Gloucester block has sold out; Freebird suggests they book rooms in other nearby hotels	Freebird
July 19, 2012	Conference opens; many guests cannot get into rooms on time; some guests told that hotel was sold out	Freebird
July 30, 2012	Freebird receives invoice from Gloucester for $9480.38 for "attrition for unsold rooms"	Freebird; invoice

client interview about events leading up to a dispute between her organization and the hotel holding rooms for the organization's conference.

As you do additional fact investigation, you can insert additional rows to the chart. Using a spreadsheet allows you to sort information later, an advantage because many Statements of Facts are organized other than as straight chronologies. To create a visual image of how the facts can be organized, you may create a storyboard. Write each fact on an index card and lay them out in the order you want to tell them.[4] Storyboarding can help you visualize each fact and easily move facts to create a different sequence. You will discover which of these organizing tools works best for you. Whether you prefer charts, timelines, or spreadsheets is less important than whether the tool you use helps you visualize the facts in a way that leads to an effective story.

Ultimately, these tools will help you write a coherent story. But their initial purpose is to help you see some of the gaps that need to be filled. This step may also reveal some of the stock structures in your understanding of the facts. For example, Table 5-1 contains certain assumptions that will need some unpacking. What stock structure does the client mean when she says, "guests couldn't check in on time"? Was it fifteen minutes after the stated hotel check-in time? Two hours? And how many guests were told this? Two? Fifteen? Fifty? All of those facts might make a difference with regard to the issue of "substantial performance" and therefore might merit exploration. As you can see, this process of mapping the facts will help you see the gaps in your evidence. Filling in those gaps will change your map, and you will repeat the analysis again.

C. Third step: does it all make sense?

Once you think you have uncovered all of the legally relevant facts, as well as sufficient background details for the story to make sense, you should take a step back and look at what you have found. Think in story terms:

- Who are the characters?
- What are their goals?
- What obstacles do they face?

Then, do a thought experiment, trying to get inside the heads of each of the characters in the story. Do each character's actions make sense? Are

---

[4]Thank you to Professors Stefan Krieger and Reza Rezvani at Hofstra School of Law, for this idea. These professors teach the system to their clinic students as part of trial preparation.

they acting as one would expect a character to act in that situation? Would other people in the character's situation typically feel the same way the character feels? Try to perceive the situation from the perspective of every important character in the story. We discuss how to conceive the roles of the different characters in Chapter 7, but for this thought experiment, the precise role they play in the final story is less important than seeing the story from each character's point of view.

During the process, keep notes about whether the story makes sense. If there are gaps or problems, make notes about that as well. Those notes will lead to more fact investigation necessary to complete the picture.

D. Step four: have you made any assumptions that might suggest more fact investigation?

We want to stress, again, the importance of recognizing your own assumptions about the facts. Because of the way our minds operate, every story involves each listener filling in gaps with our own mental images or experiences.

Here are two simple examples to remind you:

- **Picture a parking lot**

What do you see? Is it an open, expansive lot such as one in front of malls or big-box stores? Or is it a small lot near your law school? Is it at ground level? In a multilevel structure? Is it the kind of parking lot one might find in a different country that is narrow and alley-like?[5]

- **Picture someone ripping the phone away from another person**

Again, what do you see? Who are the people? Where are they? Is the phone a cell phone? A cordless phone? A traditional landline phone? A wall-mounted phone in a person's house? Or at a large store as part of the intercom system? Was it just the receiver/speaker that was taken away or was a cord disconnected from the wall? Or, if it was the wall-mounted sort of phone, was the whole system pulled off a wall?

While these examples may seem pedestrian, they are taken from real cases where those particular facts were critical to the outcome of that case and where law students needed to conduct a thorough fact investigation to ascertain a clear picture of the events. Recognizing the assumptions we

---

[5]Thanks to Jason Eyster for this example from his excellent article. James Parry Eyster, *The Lawyer as Artist: Using Significant Moments and Obtuse Objects to Enhance Advocacy*, 14 Leg. Writing 87, 96 (2008).

make is an important lawyering skill. Many times, the facts that your client is visualizing will surprise you because you will be visualizing something very different.

Fact investigation is never a linear process. Lawyers typically learn things out of chronological sequence and often need to adjust, on the fly. That is part of what makes a lawyer's job interesting: using "people skills" to identify facts that will then help solve the client's problem.

III. Tools for fact investigation

The previous section suggested ways to think about what lawyers need to look for during fact investigation. In this section, we briefly suggest methods to go about looking for those facts.

A. Two types of facts: adjudicative and legislative

First, we need to define what we mean by "facts." While the word "facts" may seem clear and not requiring definition, most cases really deal with two different types of facts. The most common types of facts are what some scholars call "adjudicative facts."[6] These are the facts of the case before the court: essentially, the story of what happened between the parties that caused the dispute. Adjudicative facts must be proven through admissible evidence, unless stipulated or assumed as part of a motion standard—motions to dismiss or summary judgment are prime examples.

Less common, but still sometimes important, are "legislative facts." These are "outside world" facts that are not specific to the dispute before the court but that may shed some light on an issue that the court needs to decide. An example of a legislative fact is a census statistic, such as the fact that November 21, 2011, was a Monday or that July 2009 had some of the hottest days on record in Portland, Oregon. Lawyers may use legislative facts to argue for a specific interpretation of a statute, by offering those facts as context for the problem in society that the legislature attempted to address through legislation. Or legislative facts may describe a scientific principle that a lawyer may use to help the court understand what likely happened in the case. Legislative facts may also help describe the "setting" in which a dispute takes place—the demographics, zoning, weather

---

[6]Ellie Margolis, *Beyond Brandeis: Exploring the Uses of Non-Legal Materials in Appellate Briefs*, 34 U.S.F. L. Rev. 197 (2000). This is another one of the articles that we recommend reading, in full.

conditions, or the like, which could help explain why events unfolded as they did. We explain more about specifically writing about these types of facts in the context of making policy arguments in Chapter 11.

For the purposes of familiarizing yourself with the two different types of facts, keep in mind that adjudicative facts inform the court about the specific dispute it must resolve, while legislative facts are used primarily as background or supplemental explanation, often in the context of making a policy argument in a brief.

Second, the two types of facts require different types of proof. Adjudicative facts must be provided to the court through the tools provided by the applicable rules of civil procedure. Adjudicative facts are adduced through interrogatory answers; responses to requests for production of documents; admissions in the pleadings or through a request for admission, deposition, or trial testimony; exhibits identified during depositions or at trial; documents attached to affidavits; and in a myriad other ways. Collectively, all of these materials form the "record" of a case.

Legislative facts, on the other hand, do not require proof in the same way that adjudicative facts do, but they do require authentication. The authentication could be accomplished via the credibility of the source in which they are published. Statistics housed on websites that have a .gov extension carry the imprimatur of that government entity's ethos, and a court will likely take judicial notice of the fact. In other words, lawyers who use legislative facts research and cite to reliable authorities. Even when lawyers do not introduce legislative facts, judges regularly research legislative facts as a tool to help them decide cases.[7]

B. Tools for discovering facts beyond what the client knows

Most of the time, when lawyers think about how to discover the facts of the case, they focus on the formal tools of discovery provided by the rules of procedure for whatever court the case may be pending in. And certainly, these tools are very powerful and helpful; they may be the only way to determine facts that your opponent knows or believes. You have been introduced to—or will be introduced to—some of these tools in your

---

[7] *See* Coleen Barger, *On the Internet, Nobody Knows You're a Judge: Federal Appellate Courts' Use of Internet Sites*, 4 J. App. Prac. & Process 417 (2002) (providing often-cited standards for checking source accuracy and credibility); Ellie Margolis, *Surfin' Safari—Why Competent Lawyers Should Research on the Web*, 10 Yale J.L. & Tech. 82 (2007); *see also* Lee F. Peoples, *The Citation of Wikipedia in Judicial Opinions*, 12 Yale J.L. & Tech. 1 (2009) (providing guideline suggestions).

courses on civil and criminal procedure. We do not have the ability to talk about them in detail here other than to mention them by name: interrogatories, depositions, affidavits, subpoenas for testimony or documents, and motions to compel (a last-resort technique).

Beyond the formal methods for discovery, there are many informal tools for discovering facts, which lawyers use every day as part of deciding whether to use more formal means to bring the facts into the official record.

C. Client interview

The first and most obvious source of information is your client. During the initial interview with your client, you need to accomplish several things:

- Develop a trusting relationship with the client.
- Gather information about what happened, from your client's perspective. Start to identify sources for additional information (documents, other witnesses, etc.).
- Attempt to identify your client's goal.
- Differentiate roles. What is your client supposed to do to assist in developing the case, and what will you do as her lawyer?
- Establish your fee arrangement and other practical details relating to the representation.

D. Witness interviews

Often you will next talk to other people who were present or who otherwise have knowledge of the events leading to the lawsuit. Some

---

Some introductory ethos considerations during witness investigation

1. Your contact with these potential witnesses is not protected by attorney–client privilege. Assume the opposing counsel will learn that you contacted these people.

2. If you ask too many leading questions (questions that obviously suggest the answer), you risk planting false ideas or compromising the witness's recollection. Recollection is a fragile thing to begin with. The goal of interviewing a potential witness is to gather facts, not to educate the witness.

3. People are nervous to speak with lawyers, and the more a lawyer is able to put the person at ease, the more the person will probably be able to access their recollections. The worst thing a lawyer can do is to be pushy or unfriendly: that can turn a neutral witness hostile.

4. You may not directly contact people who are represented by counsel. You must go through their lawyer. (ABA Model R. Prof. Conduct 4.2)

5. If you contact people who are unrepresented by counsel, you must be clear that you do not represent their interests. (ABA Model R. Prof. Conduct 4.3)

of those witnesses may be known to the client, and some may be easily ascertained via common sense research. In the hotel example, a quick phone call to one of the organization members might help you learn how long the guests had to wait to get into their rooms.

E. Document review

Another important source of facts will be documents, many of which you will be able to obtain without formal discovery. For example, in a contract case like the hotel reservation example, the client should have a copy of the written agreement. In a personal injury action, a police report may describe the accident, and even though your client may not have a copy of it, a simple call or visit to the police station should be sufficient to get a copy.

F. Informal discussion with opposing counsel

Most states have adopted some version of the Model Rule of Professional Conduct 3.2, which states, "A lawyer shall make reasonable efforts to expedite litigation consistent with the interests of the client." Lawyers representing the plaintiff in an action might not know until initial demands or complaints are sent who opposing counsel is or whether there is opposing counsel. Assuming both sides to an action have retained lawyers, there is a good chance that the lawyers will be able to work together, without formal discovery requests, to help expedite litigation through candid exchanges of information without resort to demanding the information through motions to the court. Experienced lawyers know that it is in their client's interest to voluntarily provide such information if the court would ultimately demand that they do so anyway. This saves both clients time and money.

G. Electronic sources

Finally, in today's Information Age, electronic sources of information are readily accessible and can be highly useful. The events that are in dispute may have been reported in the news media, so there may be newspaper reports, television clips, or YouTube videos of the incident. The event may have been discussed in blogs. The possibilities here are potentially endless. You probably are also aware that lawyers—just like employers— regularly look at the websites, online bios, and Facebook or other social media pages of parties and witnesses. In some cases, a lawyer may even hire companies that specialize in unlocking the privacy controls of those pages.

Conclusion

As you gather facts, a picture of the case—and your client—begins to emerge. The next step in the process is to think about what all of this information means in the context of the law. What legal theories or remedies might be available to assist your client in achieving her goal? We take this topic up in Chapter 6.

Chapter 6

Understanding the client's problem in its legal context

None of the authors of this text have ever had a client come to our offices and tell us, "I've got a defamation per se case I'd like to talk to you about," or "I need to find out if this deed creates a fee simple determinable or a fee on condition subsequent," or "I need a restraining order against my ex-roommate, but I'm concerned about whether the family court will have subject matter jurisdiction." Rather, the clients arrive in our offices to tell us about a dispute, or to ask a general question about how to avoid a dispute by, for example, drafting a contract to protect the client's rights in the future. They tell us about the facts of their situations and then ask us to help them achieve some goal. It is up to us to figure out what all those seemingly random facts might mean, legally.

In the previous chapters, you learned about how to discover the facts of your client's situation and how to turn those facts into a coherent story about your client. But of course, that is just the beginning of your representation of the client. Now you need to apply your legal training to the problem and figure out how—and sometimes whether—the law can assist the client in achieving her goals. This is not a linear process.

For even a relatively simple legal problem, the research process can be quite daunting. In your first year of law school, your research assignments are likely to be quite narrow, and often the scope of the issues may be defined for you. In practice, of course, this is less often the case. Thus, it is good to start developing good research practices now—when the scope of your task is manageable. This chapter will explore some specific strategies for planning, organizing, and executing your research process. If you develop a sound research process, it will serve you well no matter how complex a future research task might be.

Typically, you will begin by stepping back and taking a high-altitude view of the situation, surveying all of your legal knowledge to think about any legal issue that might be involved. You will then need to conduct more specific research to determine which of those issues are viable. But as you conduct research, additional issues may present themselves, and you will need to circle back to investigate those new ideas. This chapter will help you navigate that process.

I. Identifying the legal issues

Imagine you are in an airplane, cruising at 35,000 feet en route to some distant city. Several hours into the flight, your traveling companion asks you to look out the window to find out where you are right now.

If you are not a frequent traveler or have little knowledge of geography, you probably won't be able to do much more than make a broad guess. But let's assume you travel this route often, and you do have a good idea of the local geography. You examine where the sun is in relation to the time of day and determine what direction you are looking. You look out the window for clues: you look for rivers, mountain ranges, highways, cities. You calculate how long you have been flying from the airport you took off from to get a general sense of how far you have flown. You compare what you see to your preexisting knowledge of geography. Based on this information, you can formulate an informed guess as to where you might currently be.

But this is still pretty much a guess. To pinpoint your location, you need more data. Perhaps your airline allows you to listen in to the air-traffic control frequency; as your pilot chats with various control centers, you can get a clearer sense of what city you are near. Or you may have a detailed map available to you, enabling you to look at the area where you think you probably are and then compare what you see on the ground to what is shown on the map. This lets you make a more accurate determination as to where you actually are.

Lawyers are frequent travelers; clients are our traveling companions. When a client asks, "Where are we?" she hopes that the lawyer can use his prior training and current research skills to come up with an accurate determination.

The process of thinking about a client's problem is very similar to how the frequent traveler tries to determine where the airplane is at any given moment. You begin by tapping into your background training: your knowledge of the broad areas of the law (torts, contracts, criminal law, etc.). Next, you start to think about more specific, narrow legal theories that might be involved; but then you realize how little you actually know about the specific area of the law. You need help! This suggests a three-step process for getting started.

A. Identify the domain

When you first start to think about your client's problem, thinking back to your first-year law school courses is a great place to start. Does my client's problem involve torts? Property? Contracts? A combination of these things? Be sure to leave your mind open to consider a very wide range of possibilities here; we'll start to narrow down the choices soon enough.

B. Identify possible issues within the domain

Now break it down further: if this appears to be a torts problem, what kind of tort might be involved? What kinds of property interests are affected? Make a list of the possibilities—but be prepared to expand your list when you get into the next step.

C. Research the issues

Before you can determine which of the issues may be involved, you will need to conduct specific research into each one of them. A few you may be able to dismiss quickly, based on your prior knowledge of what the law is; but many more will require you to do at least some preliminary, and maybe some highly detailed, research. Also, be attentive to what you find; the cases and statutes that you discover may suggest additional issues you had not considered before.

Let's see how this works by returning to our hotel reservations problem. Pat Freebird, the executive director of Save Our Forest Trees, Inc., has just left your office after describing the demand letter she received from the Gloucester Hotel chain. Where do you go from here? Your thought process might go like this.

1. Identify the domain

Since SOFT signed a contract with Gloucester, this is apparently a contract issue. But are there possible other theories as well? Did Gloucester misrepresent anything during the contract negotiations? Is there some potentially fraudulent conduct involved?

2. Spot the issues

The contracts questions are the most obvious, so let's start there. Was there even a contract to begin with? If so, are all of the terms clear? Can they be enforced? Did SOFT breach the contract? What are the damages?

3. Research

Was there a contract? Some contracts are considered contracts of adhesion. Unconscionable clauses in contracts of adhesion might not be enforced. Were the terms clear? The "attrition clause" that the Gloucester letter quotes claims to be a liquidated damages clause, but only some liquidated damages clauses are enforceable. What are the damages? A cause of action for breach of contract requires that the plaintiff prove that it has been damaged by the breach, but in our case, it looks like the hotel was sold out during the SOFT conference so it was not in fact damaged.

As you gain experience as a lawyer, this process will become easier. But even an experienced lawyer will sometimes encounter a client problem that stumps him. When he does, the best way to start is to get back into the airplane, gain some altitude, and look around.

II. Organizing your research

The best way of keeping track of your research is the method you are comfortable with. Experienced researchers develop their own preferred methods. However, if you are new to legal research, you might want to consider one of the methods we suggest here.

A. Commercial research programs

Both WestlawNext and Lexis Advance allow you to store research results in a set of folders and subfolders that you define. You can store cases, statutes, secondary authorities, or discrete quotations from any of those sources in any folder you create. While these tools are built into those services, they require you to be connected to WestlawNext or Lexis Advance to use them, and they are limited in what they do.

Several commercial products are available to help you organize research results on your computer. The best known of these, CaseMap by Lexis, helps you organize not only your research results but also your evidence. You can code both your research and your deposition transcripts or other evidence to specific issues that you define, so that you can retrieve both facts and law relevant to any issue at the click of a mouse. Other programs, such as MasterFile, provide similar services—for a fee, just like WestlawNext and Lexis Advance. All are database management systems, in which you enter "data" in the form of your notes regarding your research results. The program then helps you sort and retrieve your data in whatever form you need.

B. Create your own database

If you do not have access to CaseMap, MasterFile, or another case management program, it is relatively simple to create your own using a spreadsheet. The keys to effective use of such a system are

- identifying the key issues and sub-issues involved in the case (to help you sort and retrieve your results later); and
- carefully analyzing the cases, statutes, and other authorities you find and "coding" them to the issues in the case where they may be helpful.

This suggests you should create two spreadsheets. The first would be a simple listing of the issues and sub-issues that you may need to address; the second is a more complex listing of the cases, statutes, and other authorities that provide the legal rules that resolve those issues.

1. Creating the issues list

Let's return to the hotel reservations case to see how this works. In section I.C.2 above, you identified several major issues relating to the possible breach of contract case:

- Was there a contract at all?
- Were the terms of the contract clear?
- Are the terms enforceable?
- Did SOFT breach the contract?
- If SOFT breached, was that because Gloucester sold all the rooms before SOFT attendees could buy them?
- Was Gloucester damaged by the breach?

Note the logical progression of these issues, from broad to narrow, and in chronological order as the relationship between SOFT and Gloucester evolved. In this sense, the arrangement of the issues tells the legal story of the case.

In section I.C.3, you did some research to refine your issues list. You discovered some new concepts that provide some more specific legal rules. You might revise your original issues list to include these sub-issues, looking something like this:

- Is there a contract?
  - Offer?
  - Acceptance?
  - Consideration?

- Is it a contract of adhesion?
  - Is there a disparity in bargaining power?
  - Was the contract offered on a take-it-or-leave-it basis?
  - Is the attrition clause unconscionable?
  - Is the attrition clause a true liquidated damages provision?
- Are damages reasonably calculable?
  - Is amount of damages specified proportional to actual loss?
  - Is provision punitive?
- Breach of contract?
  - Did SOFT breach?
  - Did Gloucester suffer any damage?
- Was it even possible for SOFT to perform?

As you do more research into these issues, you may start to discern certain sub-issues, elements, or factors that courts employ in cases like this. You should constantly be revising and refining your list of issues and sub-issues; Figure 6-1 shows a somewhat more developed list of issues, which was developed by additional research. The main issues appear in boldface, with the bulleted sub-issues below.

Finally, to help you keep track of your research results and tie them to your issues, you should assign each issue and sub-issue some sort of code. To make it easy to sort your research results by issue, it is simplest to assign a number to each issue and sub-issue, something like the system shown in Figure 6-1.

Note that the issue numbers are not sequential. There are several reasons for this. First, identifying a main issue with a number divisible by 10 allows you to show the hierarchy of how the issues relate to each other: the first digit of each sub-issue is the same as the first digit of the main issue to which it is related. Second, leaving gaps between each major issue allows you to add more sub-issues as your research proceeds and you discover potential new sub-issues. And if you discover a new major issue, you can always add it to the bottom of your list as your research proceeds.

2. Creating the database of authorities

Next you need to create a comprehensive list of possible authorities and the relationship of each to the identified issues. This is where a standard spreadsheet program such as Excel or QuattroPro can be very useful. If you design your spreadsheet carefully, simply using the Sort feature will help you group all of your authorities according to the issue or issues that they address.

Issue #	Main issues & sub-issues
10	**Is there a contract?**
11	• Offer?
12	• Acceptance?
13	• Consideration?
20	**Is it a contract of adhesion?**
21	• Is there a disparity in bargaining power?
22	• Was contract offered on take-it-or-leave-it basis?
23	• Is the attrition clause unconscionable?
30	**Is the attrition clause a true liquidated damages provision?**
31	• Are damages reasonably calculable?
32	• Is amount of damages specified proportional to actual loss?
33	• Is provision punitive?
40	**Impossibility of performance?**
41	• Event beyond control of breaching party
42	• Absolute impossibility to perform results
50	**Breach of contract?**
51	• Did SOFT breach?
52	• Did Gloucester make SOFT's performance impossible by selling all available rooms?
53	• Did Gloucester suffer any damage?

Figure 6-1: Issue list for SOFT case

We suggest creating a spreadsheet with the following columns:

				Issue #				
Authority name	Citation	Court	Date	1	2	3	4	Notes

A template with these columns is available as an Excel spreadsheet at the website for this book.

Table 6-1: Raw database as cases are found

Authority name	Citation	Court	Date	Issue # 1	2	3	4	Notes
2625 Building Corporation v. Deutsch	385 N.E.2d 1189	Ind.Ct.App.	1979	33				Great case on facts! Involves hotel room reservations and failure to use rooms (but oral contract only); hotel not allowed to keep payment
Pigman v. Ameritech Publishing	641 N.E.2d 1026	Ind.Ct.App.	1998	20	22			Good case: exculpatory clause in contract unenforceable as unconscionable
Kincaid v. Lazar	405 N.E.2d 615	Ind.Ct.App.	1980	10				Interp. of contract up to court; will enforce on its face if unambiguous
Beck v. Mason	580 N.E.2d 290	Ind.Ct.App.	1991	30	12			Intent of parties controls whether clause is liquidated damages or other
Sanford v. Castleton Health Care Center	813 N.E.2d 411	Ind.Ct.App.	2004	12	21	20		Failure to read K before signing no excuse; defines adhesion contract
Collins v. McKinney	871 N.E.2d 363	Ind.Ct.App.	2007	50	53			List of elements of cause of action for breach of contract
Rogers v. Lockard	767 N.E.2d 982	Ind.Ct.App.	2002	30	12			Intent of parties controls whether clause is liquidated damages or other
Prather v. Latshaw	122 N.E. 721	Supreme	1919	41				Act of other party preventing performance excuses breach
General Bargain Ctr. v. American Alarm Co.	430 N.E.2d 407	Ind.Ct.App.	1982	30				Definition of liquidated damages clause (p. 993)
Grott v. Jim Barna Log Systems–Midwest, Inc.	794 N.E.2d 1098	Ind.Ct.App.	2003	10				Presumption of free bargaining
Trimble v. Ameritech Publishing	700 N.E.2d 1128	Supreme	1998	20	22			Disapproves of Pigman; maybe this is not a good issue for us

This list of headings, also known as a "header row," describes "fields" of a database. Each row beneath this header row should include a single authority: a case, a section of a statute, a court rule, and so on. In database terminology, these are "records." Not every cell needs to be filled out, of course. Statutes will not have an entry for "court," for example. The key to this spreadsheet is identifying which issue from your issue list the authority is relevant to. Each one may be relevant to more than one issue, of course, which is why there are four columns identified for "Issue #." Record the number(s) of the issue(s) that each authority helps with in those columns.

The final column, "Notes," is where you can record a very brief synopsis of the main point or points of the authorities. This will help you later on in selecting which authorities you need to study further.

As you encounter new authorities, just keep recording them in separate rows, going down the spreadsheet. It doesn't matter what order you put them in; you will use the Sort feature of your spreadsheet later on to put them in a more useful order.

A sample research spreadsheet for the SOFT case—based on Indiana law—might look something like Table 6-1. (Note that this is not intended to represent a complete database; yours will probably include many more cases and perhaps a few statutes or court rules, depending on the kind of issue you are researching.)

III. Selecting the issues to write about

Once you have finished the first round of your preliminary research, you can use your spreadsheet to help you organize your results. From there you can determine (a) whether additional research is needed, and (b) which issues appear to be viable.

A. Arranging your research results

The value in using a spreadsheet program to record research results is that you can use the built-in Sort feature to rearrange the data in any way you choose.

Sorting a database can occur at multiple levels. The top-level sort arranges each row of the spreadsheet according to the value in one of the columns (either alphabetically or numerically, depending on the kind of data contained in that column). But when more than one record (row) contains identical values in that field, all records with the same value are listed one after the other. You can then define second-, third-, and lower-level sorts to arrange the rows with those identical values according to the values in a different field.

This is easier to see by using an example. Take another look at Table 6-1. You can see that the researcher has listed eleven authorities. They are listed in the order in which the researcher found them (essentially, random order). But because the researcher carefully listed (or "coded") the issues that each authority related to, we can now sort the spreadsheet to gather together all of the cases that relate to the same issues.

Table 6-2 shows the same authorities as Table 6-1, but this time they have been sorted using the spreadsheet program's Sort feature. The top-level sort was on column E (which bears the heading "Issue 1"); this grouped all of the records according to the main issue that the authority addresses. But since three of the authorities involved issue 30 (defined on the issues list as "Is the attrition clause a true liquidated damages provision?"), a second-level sort on column D (the date of the authority) arranges all three of those authorities so that the most recent cases jump to the top of the list of cases related to that issue.

You can, of course, sort and resort the data on any of the fields you define in the header row.

B. Analyzing your results

Once you have sorted the data, you may notice some gaps in your research. Consider these examples:

- You may have no authority identified for some of the issues.
- You may have conflicting authorities for several of the issues (you can see that by looking at the "Notes" field for each authority listed as relating to a specific issue).
- You may have statutory authority but no interpretive case law for one or more issues.
- The authorities you have for any issue may be very old, or from nonbinding jurisdictions, or inadequate in some other way.

Any shortcoming you find in analyzing your results might suggest additional research that you should do to flesh out your legal analysis. You can just keep adding new authorities to the bottom of the spreadsheet, then resort the sheet periodically to see where you are.

Of course, some of the issues on your issues list may turn out to be based on well-settled principles of law and won't require a great deal of research or analysis. For example, in Figure 6-1, our list of issues for the SOFT case

Table 6-2: Database sorted by issue and date

Authority name	Citation	Court	Date	Issue # 1	2	3	4	Notes
Grott v. Jim Barna Log Systems–Midwest, Inc.	794 N.E.2d 1098	Ind.Ct.App.	2003	10				Presumption of free bargaining
Kincaid v. Lazar	405 N.E.2d 615	Ind.Ct.App.	1980	10				Interpretation of contract up to court; will enforce on its face if unambiguous
Sanford v. Castleton Health Care Center	813 N.E.2d 411	Ind.Ct.App.	2004	12	21	20		Failure to read K before signing no excuse; defines adhesion contract
Pigman v. Ameritech Publishing	641 N.E.2d 1026	Ind.Ct.App.	1998	20	22			Good case: exculpatory clause in contract unenforceable as unconscionable
Trimble v. Ameritech Publishing	700 N.E.2d 1128	Supreme	1998	20	22			Disapproves of Pigman; maybe this is not a good issue for us
Rogers v. Lockard	767 N.E.2d 982	Ind.Ct.App.	2002	30	12			Intent of parties controls whether clause is liquidated damages or other
Beck v. Mason	580 N.E.2d 290	Ind.Ct.App.	1991	30	12			Intent of parties controls whether clause is liquidated damages or other
General Bargain Ctr. v. American Alarm Co.	430 N.E.2d 407	Ind.Ct.App.	1982	30				Definition of liquidated damages clause (p. 993)
2625 Building Corporation v. Deutsch	385 N.E.2d 1189	Ind.Ct.App.	1979	33				Great case on facts! Involves hotel room reservations and failure to use rooms (but oral contract only); hotel not allowed to keep payment
Prather v. Latshaw	122 N.E. 721	Supreme	1919	41				Act of other party preventing performance excuses breach
Collins v. McKinney	871 N.E.2d 363	Ind.Ct.App.	2007	50	53			List of elements of cause of action for breach of contract

includes a series of issues (issues 10–13) involving questions of whether a contract was formed to begin with. The rules regarding offer, acceptance, and consideration are good examples of well-settled rules that have not changed much (or at all) for decades, and thus one or two cases setting those rules out may be all that you need.

C. Selecting the issues for deeper analysis

You started with a broad list of issues, just to make sure you didn't miss anything potentially important. But one of the most common mistakes made by new lawyers (and many older ones) is presenting too many issues to the court. This "scattergun" approach is generally ineffective for the following reasons:

> **Judgments, not wishes**
>
> As you are sorting through your potential issues, be sure that you make your decisions about which issue to include based on sound judgment rather than on wishful thinking. For example, do not decide to omit an issue just because it is troublesome for your client. Ignoring the weak points won't make them go away, and you can be sure your opponent will highlight your weaknesses. Rather, choose to eliminate the issues that are so insignificant that they do not affect the outcome of your case. Similarly, potential issues that turn out to be well-settled will warrant little or no discussion. Remember, judges are busy people; keep their attention focused on what really matters.

- It makes the advocate look indecisive or lazy. The judge may see a brief listing 14 different issues and think, "This lawyer doesn't have any good argument to make at all, so he'll try anything." Or worse yet, "This lawyer doesn't understand his case very well."
- If you have a page or word count limit, using those pages or words to discuss issues with little merit deprives you of the pages or words you could use more effectively to discuss issues that are more significant.
- It is distracting. You don't want to force the reader to wade through a lot of "iffy" arguments to get to the gems.

Of course, deciding what is an "iffy" argument and what is a gem is part of the art of being a lawyer.

Your research spreadsheet, if constructed well, can help you decide which issues are worth discussing and which you should abandon. After you sort your research results by issue, you can scan the "Notes" field for each issue group and get a good picture of what the rules are for each issue. This will help you understand whether the issue works for your client or whether it is not worth developing further.

Let's try this out on the research results for Pat Freebird and SOFT. Recall that in Figure 6-1, the first major issue (number 10) deals with whether a contract was formed in the first place. You may conclude, based on your knowledge of what Pat admits she did, that all of the elements for a valid contract (described in more detail in sub-issues 11–13) are present in the case and that this is not likely to be a very fertile ground for defending her organization. You could then rationally decide not to raise that issue at all in your brief, but to focus on other issues that are more likely to result in a favorable outcome.

The second major issue (number 20), whether the contract was one of adhesion, may be more promising. In looking over the cases you found through your research, you might conclude that Gloucester had a great deal more bargaining power than SOFT (sub-issue 21) and that Gloucester drafted the initial contract and presented it to SOFT on a take-it-or-leave-it basis, offering no real opportunity for bargaining (sub-issue 22). But that last sub-issue, number 23 on your list, may be problematic. Was the provision truly unconscionable? You may decide you need to study the cases you found on that sub-issue more closely to see what kinds of things have been found "unconscionable" in prior cases. Then you can determine from that closer analysis whether you should raise that issue.

The third and fourth major issues may both look very good, from SOFT's point of view. It seems likely that the damages are easily calculable (sub-issue 31) since the contract itself specifies the formula by which the damages may be calculated. Likewise, the damages (more than $9000) seem disproportionate to the actual loss (sub-issue 32) since the evidence suggests the hotel was sold out on the night in question and therefore suffered no damage at all. For the same reason, sub-issues 52 (impossibility of performance) and 53 (the requirement of damages as an element of a cause of action for breach of contract) look very promising, again because the hotel was sold out and couldn't have accommodated any more SOFT guests anyway.

From this analysis, you might now conclude that you have two viable major issues: whether the attrition clause is a valid liquidated damages provision (issue 30) and whether Gloucester may prove a breach of contract (issue 50). Both of those major issues have two sub-issues, which look pretty strong. Based on this analysis, you might reasonably forgo making any argument about whether this was a contract of adhesion (issue 20) since that seems weaker and more distracting to the judge.

IV. Next steps

Having tentatively identified the major issues you want to focus on, it is time to conduct more detailed research and analysis of the rules governing those issues. The next chapter will help you think about how to structure an argument in your client's favor for each of the issues you have chosen. In upcoming chapters, we will discuss how to write about these issues in the ways most favorable to your client.

Chapter 7

Representing your client, the protagonist

At the heart of every story is the central character or protagonist. In a legal story, the protagonist is usually our client. It is her story that we tell, and we will want to tell it from her point of view. The first step of creating that story is to develop our protagonist–client. This chapter draws on literary theory to explore the different types of protagonists that we may choose from to describe our client. In addition, it examines the role of other characters, including the opposing party and others who play less significant roles in our story.

This chapter also examines how we begin to think about the obstacles the client must overcome to reach her ultimate goal. When we have identified the client's character, goals, and obstacles to that goal, we have the underlying structure of our story. This structure forms the foundation of our persuasive document. Later we will build on this foundation by adding the stylistic or aesthetic refinements that complete our story.

Learning how best to tell a persuasive story on behalf of a client is a career-long journey. Even longtime professionals continue to study the art of storytelling. It thus follows that lawyers should likewise study the fundamentals. The good news is that storytelling can be taught.[1]

---

[1]Material in these paragraphs was adapted from Brian J. Foley & Ruth Anne Robbins, *Fiction 101: A Primer for Lawyers on How to Use Fiction Writing Techniques to Write Persuasive Facts Sections*, 32 Rutgers L.J. 459 (2001), *citing* Robert McKee, *STORY: Substance, Structure, Style and the Principles of Screenwriting* 15 (Regan Books 1997) (analogizing writing training to music training, saying that writers should think more like composers and recognize that they need formal training in the craft).

I. The client as a character in the legal story

Representing a client well, whether it be in litigation, a transaction, or any other context, requires you to understand the characters in the client's story, in both the context of the dispute and the client's overall life. The most important character, of course, is the client itself, even when the client is an organization such as a corporation.

No matter who the character, the same truism will exist: characters have *needs*, which are baseline survival fundamentals, and *goals*, which are aspirations. As a lawyer, you must consider both when representing a client because, after all, the client's needs and goals are what brought him to your office in the first place. Thus, your primary considerations are answers to these sorts of questions: What challenges does the client face before meeting her desired goal? How does the current legal action fit in—as a pathway to achieving the goal, or a roadblock that hinders the client from reaching the goal?

For example, negotiating a contract for the purchase of raw materials will help the client produce the finished product and reach the goal of selling that product. The contract is a pathway to help the client satisfy its need of the raw materials that are necessary to creating the finished product. Negotiating the contract moves the client forward toward the goal. In contrast, a defendant in a negligence action needs your help to get past the roadblock of litigation. Getting past that roadblock will allow the client to achieve her goal of getting back to her normal life that existed prior to being sued.

Lawsuits involve many characters: the client, the opposing party or parties, the various witnesses, and the fact finder. You may have noticed that "lawyer" was not on that list. That's because lawyers are the narrators of the story. They are not characters unless their actions have become part of the lawsuit itself (e.g., in a malpractice claim or in a case involving an argument about ineffective assistance of counsel). Remember, our legal story is not about us; it's about our client.

We already know that legally trained audiences tend to be skeptical. Judges and other lawyers all expect to learn of a client's story by the lawyer telling it from the client's perspective. However, they also expect lawyers to be reasonable. Efforts to paint the positive character of the client that are too extreme or overt make the story lose credibility. The story similarly loses credibility when the opposing party is portrayed as a villain. Therefore, lawyers must very carefully present the characters in the lawsuit as believably and reasonably as possible.

A. The client as hero

Usually, the client is portrayed as the protagonist of the legal story. But remember that the legal action is just one chapter in the client's overall story. The client is also the protagonist of a larger storyline or of multiple storylines.

When considering how to portray the client, keep in mind that people respond—instinctively and intuitively—to certain recurring story patterns and character archetypes.[2] According to the famous mythologist Joseph Campbell, human nature categorizes protagonists as one of several different categories of heroes. Each of the different types of heroes is defined by the challenge or obstacle that they must face and overcome.[3] Table 7-1 shows these different heroic archetypes.[4]

A person can be on more than one hero trajectory at a time. Most people are, depending on the situation. A client might be an every-person hero in the workplace, a caregiver hero at home, and a creator hero with his volunteerism. The question for you becomes which one of those heroic archetypes best portrays your client and meets her goals. Think about which hero type will be most effective in telling a particular client's story. Note that reasonable minds may differ on this point. This is not a question of finding the lone, objectively correct archetype. Rather, it is a process to make a conscious choice about how you want to portray your client in that particular situation.

Who are you?

In choosing the best heroic archetype for your client, you will likely have several viable options. Most of us play multiple roles on life's stage. Finding the best fit for your client will depend on the factual context, the legal issue, and the theme of your story. To see how varied our roles in life can be, put yourself in your client's shoes. Try this:

- List all the characters you regularly play in life: e.g., law student, child, parent, employee, civic volunteer.
- Match a heroic archetype to the various characters you play.

---

[2] According to a traditional definition, archetypes are the "primary form that governs the psyche." James Hillman, *Archetypal Psychology: A Brief Account* 1 (Spring Publications 1985).
[3] Joseph Campbell, *The Hero with a Thousand Faces* (Princeton U. Press 1990).
[4] A version of this chart originally appeared in a longer article on the same topic. Ruth Anne Robbins, *Harry Potter, Ruby Slippers and Merlin: Telling the Client's Story Using the Characters and Paradigm of the Archetypal Hero's Journey*, 29 Seattle L. Rev. 767 (2006).

Table 7-1: Heroic archetypes

Hero type	Task and challenge	Illustrative examples (cultural; legal)
Warrior	Fights for what really matters	Prototypical Hollywood big-action movie hero; sports champion or person trying to move past serious physical injury
Creator	Gains identity through creations	Writer or artist struggling to succeed, such as Harry Potter author, J.K. Rowling; small-business owner
Caregiver	Helps others without martyring self	Religious icon or leader such as Gandhi; parent taking care of family against odds; prosecutor taking care of society
Every person	Is able to live as everyone else can: with rights to life, liberty, and the pursuit of happiness	Rosa Parks; plaintiff in civil rights or discrimination lawsuit
Orphan	Finds way back into society after having been cut off from it	Harry Potter; domestic violence victim seeking restraining order
Outlaw	Changes what is not working in society	Robin Hood; whistleblower in corporate corruption case
Sage/ Scholar	Searches for better life through study or knowledge	Jane Goodall; student trying to do well in school
Explorer/ Wanderer/ Seeker	Searches for better life through exploration of the world	Early colonists and pioneers; explorers Meriwether Lewis & William Clark; advocacy groups trying to break new ground or call attention to societal issues
Magician	Understands and transforms the universe at a profound level	Merlin, Gandalf, Dumbledore transformed their worlds; Steve Jobs transformed ours
Ruler	Creates and maintains a thriving community	Queen Elizabeth I of England; prosecutors are ruler heroes, trying to maintain an ordered and safe society for the citizens
Lover	Gains bliss through relationships	Cinderella variations; loss of consortium plaintiff; wrongful death plaintiff
Jester/Fool	Changes society by exposing the absurd for what it is	Jon Stewart and Stephen Colbert; author of a satirical publication involved in a defamation suit such as Larry Flynt
Innocent	Remains in safety	Dorothy from The Wizard of Oz; someone who is incapacitated or is a child **Note:** This heroic archetype works well only for clients who are children or who are rendered in a childlike state by illness, age, or accident.

B. Using your client's back story: competing considerations

You will probably know things about your client that are not necessarily "legally relevant" and yet are facts that you might want the audience to know. These facts could include anything from age, gender, family, education, work experience, volunteer work, military service—anything in her background that could shine a positive light on your client. These facts may be very important in certain types of legal actions. For example, they may be necessary to show how your client is entitled to damages in a negligence or discrimination action.

Even when the relevance of the client's back story is not immediately apparent, it is important to investigate some facts of this nature because they might become legally relevant. Or, equally important, as you learned in Chapter 5, these facts will give a more complete picture of the protagonist of your story—your client. Chapter 9 talks more about ways to weave small bits of that back story into your persuasive document. At this point in the litigation process, it is enough to collect the facts and to begin a list of things that you know about your client as well as a list of follow-up questions that you need to ask.

Your client, the speeder

Your client wishes to challenge a speeding ticket. According to the summons, he was traveling at 70 mph in a 55 mph zone. The penalties for going 69 mph are much lower than going 70 mph. It is your task, therefore, to try and plead the ticket down to the lower offense. Which heroic archetype is more likely to work for the case?

1. Your client won a medal in the last Olympics (warrior hero).
2. Your client spends at least one day a month volunteering for a local charity (caregiver hero).
3. Your client is a 3L who was on his way to a judicial clerkship interview and didn't want to be late (scholar hero).
4. Your client wrote a thesis paper about the dangers of speeding and the error range of speed detector machines (scholar hero).

Hero type # 1 might be appropriate if the discussion was about a person giving a motivational speech. But here it smacks of looking like an argument that some people are above the law.

Hero type #2 calls on sympathies, but the facts are disconnected from the legal action so that the information looks like just an empty attempt to call on emotions without reason. This heroic archetype might become the appropriate choice in a different legal action, however.

Hero type #3 and #4 both fit the legal action and add some understanding to the defense. Either one could be chosen for the circumstances. Most lawyers would probably pick #3.

On the flip side, some aspects of your client's fuller story should not be used at all. At trial, certain facts cannot come into evidence for a variety of reasons. On appeal, litigants are always limited by the record developed in the trial court. Thus, you must choose an archetype that is consistent with the admissible evidence.

C. Your client's character will have weaknesses

Just as virtually every legal dispute has unfavorable facts (or unfavorable law), every hero has her weakness. In myth, the hero's flaws are a central obstacle that the hero must overcome to succeed on the journey. Those flaws symbolize the universal imperfection of being human. Likewise, in the real world, clients will have flaws. They may react to the opposing party in a way that makes you wince; they may arrive late to every appointment, including court appearances; or they may communicate poorly and therefore won't do well on the witness stand. The client's flaws may or may not be critical to the success of the lawsuit. They might influence decisions about the strategy of the case—anything from decisions about whether the client will testify to decisions about legal arguments. Chapter 12 talks about handling adverse materials, while Chapter 14 helps you decide which of these flaws you might need to address in your written advocacy.

D. The client's narrow and broad goals

Your client's most immediate goal is to win her lawsuit. However, that narrow goal is unlikely to build empathy with your audience—every litigant wants to win her lawsuit. That goal doesn't give your audience any reason to support your client over her opponent. The more persuasive tack is to see the favorable resolution of the lawsuit as a step toward a more universal goal. By taking a broader view of your client's goals, you provide a more compelling story that puts the immediate dispute in a context that will resonate with readers.

Your client's goal is also central to determining what kind of hero she is. Imagine the owner of a local restaurant who was sued for breach of contract when she canceled produce deliveries from the plaintiff, a local farmer, and entered into a new contract with another farmer. The restaurateur may have canceled the deliveries because she was having issues with quality or timing. She has a goal of bringing a valuable service to the community—by providing healthy food choices, creating jobs in the local community, and encouraging quality relaxation time for her patrons. This would fit with the creator heroic archetype or even the caregiver archetype. On the other hand, if we choose to portray her as an every-person hero, we would emphasize that she is working long hours to put food on her own table. Her small restaurant is her livelihood—and the trouble she is having with the food supplier is creating a problem in her ability to keep the restaurant in business. That, in turn, is preventing her from reaching the goal of stable support for herself and her family.

The above example demonstrates that these concepts work for defendants in a lawsuit just as they work for plaintiffs. It is often easier to see the goal of plaintiffs than of defendants. On the surface, the goal of most defendants is to make the lawsuit go away. But defendants have a broader story than just the legal dispute. The restaurant owner doesn't just want to get the farmer to go away. She wants to continue serving the community. If you can tell her story to show these larger goals, you help the judge understand your client's situation. And understanding is the first step toward building the empathy that will persuade the court to support your client's broader goals.

Hidden heroes

You probably weren't in law school very long before you realized that someday you might have to represent someone you don't like—someone who doesn't seem very heroic. You may also be wondering about other settings where your client does not fit the traditional protagonist role. For example, on occasion, you may be faced with a "pure question of law" where the real issue turns on the interpretation of a statute and the underlying facts of your client's case seem less important. While there are situations where your client will not be the protagonist, they are relatively rare. Thus, do not be too quick to abandon your client as hero or protagonist.

Let's take the obvious problematic case—a criminal defendant accused of a horrific crime. An axe murderer is not a hero. And if we were defending such an unsavory, indeed, thoroughly indefensible, person, we may feel hard pressed to make him a hero. However, even one accused of an axe murder is entitled to a defense. He can still demand that the prosecution proves its case. He is still entitled to the protections that all citizens are entitled to. Thus, we could tell his story as a citizen—the every-person hero entitled to the presumption of innocence and constitutional protections that are fundamental to our system. Our focus would not be on his conduct, but on his role as an accused citizen.

II. Other character roles in the legal action

Of course, your client is not the only character of the legal story. Certainly, the opposing party is an important character, and there may be other minor characters as well. While these characters will usually be less developed than the protagonist–client will be, they nevertheless play an important part in the client's story.

A. The opposing party: gatekeepers or shape-shifters rather than villains

Although your client is the protagonist, that doesn't necessarily make the opposing party the villain antagonist. In a lawsuit, the audience is rarely looking to help good prevail over evil. Rather, the judge or jury is looking to resolve a dispute between two parties who are presumed to both be acting in good faith. If you portray the opposing party as evil, you are more likely to undermine your own credibility or cast doubt on your judgment than you are to hurt the opposing party.[5]

Imagine again the small restaurant owner who has been sued for breaching a contract with a local farmer. Portraying either side as a villain would look a bit absurd. The farmer and the small business owner are both sympathetic characters.

Of course, there are exceptions to this principle, but they are rare, especially in a civil dispute.

A criminal dispute may offer more opportunities for a good versus evil story, but even then, very few defendants are all bad. In fact, casting the opposing party as the antagonist can backfire because one person's villain is another person's hero. Think of the character of the Wicked Witch of the West. Do you know her as the villain of *The Wizard of Oz* or as the heroine of *Wicked*?

Instead of portraying the opposing party as a villain, you could portray him as a "gatekeeper," sometimes also called a "threshold guardian." Gatekeepers are exactly what the word suggests: people who create roadblocks that could keep the hero from achieving her goals unless the hero rises to the challenge of getting past the obstacle of the gatekeeper. Gatekeepers might be unpleasant for their own reasons, but their own chief goals are about something other than simply thwarting the hero. In the

---

[5] *Id.* at 786–789 (exploring alternatives for the opposing party).

classic comedy *Monty Python and the Holy Grail*, both the Knights Who Say Ni, and the Black Knight are gatekeepers. Not evil villains, but merely defenders of their own turf.

When the lawyer sets up the opposing party in this gatekeeper role, the judge is simultaneously cast as a mentor who has the ability to guide the client past this gatekeeper challenge so that the client can achieve her goal.[6] This perspective also recognizes that the opposing party may have legitimate reasons for opposing the client, even though those reasons must ultimately give way to the client's pursuit of her goal. The judge then has an easier time with the client's proposed resolution because the decision is something other than a ruling that the opposing party is completely at fault. The judge is also given some leeway in fashioning a result that is acceptable to both sides of the dispute.

As an alternative to the gatekeeper, you may choose to portray the opposing party as a "shape-shifter," a character who morphs from one type of personality to another. In the restaurateur and farmer example, the farmer might portray the restaurant owner as a shape-shifter who has transformed from being a reliable and stabilizing business alliance to being a threat to the stability of the farmer's business. That's a very different—and very reasonable—spin on the story's characters.[7]

B. Judges, witnesses, and lawyers

That still leaves other people involved in the lawsuit. They too must be cast as characters in the story. The role of the witnesses is relatively straightforward. Witnesses who testify positively for your client are "companions," whose goals include helping the client–hero. Other companion characters could be expert witnesses since they travel with and help the hero with their own gifts. Even "neutral" fact witnesses called by the attorney are a type of companion character since they help the hero overcome some obstacle.

Other witnesses may be gatekeepers. An opposing counsel's expert witness who offers an opinion adverse to your client is a gatekeeper. So are hostile witnesses or neutral witnesses whose testimony impedes the hero in her journey to achieve her goal.

You, as legal advocate, should never play a role within the client's legal story, however. Instead, you should act as the story's narrator. Portraying

---

[6] *Id.* at 782–786 (exploring the judge as mentor and giving examples).
[7] For more reading about shape-shifters, *see id.* at 789.

yourself as the hero of the client is probably doing the client a disservice by putting the client in the precarious position of a victim, a party who needs to be saved. Most audiences are less understanding of a victim than they are of a hero. Because you want your audience to connect with the client's story and not your own, you should keep the client at the center of the story.

III. The client's obstacle: the conflict type of lawsuit

Finally, all stories need an obstacle or a conflict for the protagonist to struggle with and overcome before reaching the goal. This conflict engages readers by making the story interesting. (It also creates the need for a lawsuit in the first place!) If a character achieves a goal without struggle, the story is dull and your readers won't care. Thus, when you tell the client's story, do so by framing it around the obstacles your client is working to overcome. The immediate obstacle your client faces, of course, is the conflict with the opposing party. However, just as the client's goals go beyond the specifics of this case, so might her obstacles. Once again, you want to construct the story in a way that suggests that its significance is greater than only winning the immediate lawsuit.

Literary theory scholars identify the following conflict types:

- Person versus Self
- Person versus Nature
- Person versus Society
  - Or the flip, "Society versus Person"
- Person versus Machine
  - Also phrased as "Person versus Institution" or "Person versus Leader"
- Person versus God
- God versus Everybody
- Person versus Person

For example, you experience a "Person versus Machine" conflict every time you need to talk to a customer service representative but reach only a recorded voice telling you to "press one." (Here, you confront not just the machine that plays the recorded message, but the more daunting machine of the Big Corporation.) People trying to pick up their lives after a tornado destroys their property face a "Person versus Nature" conflict. Hamlet struggling with whether to be or not to be is a "Person versus Self" conflict.

These conflict types are often readily apparent in the legal story as well. For example, a prosecutor is working on a "Society versus Person" conflict type, where the prosecutor represents the citizens of that jurisdiction trying to keep an ordered and safe society. In the prosecutor's story, the defendant is the person who has done something adverse to the order or safety of the community. In the defendant's story, however, this may be a conflict of "Person versus Society," if the theory of the case is "SODDI" (Some Other Dude Did It). Or, if the defense's theory of the case is that the police or prosecutor committed some sort of violation of constitutionally protected rights, then the defendant will portray the case as "Person versus Machine" (i.e., that the government has acted as a machine). Or, the defendant may be pleading insanity, which would be a "Person versus Self" conflict type.

We have deliberately moved "Person versus Person" into the last position on our list of conflicts because it should probably be last on your list of optimal choices. Selecting "Person versus Person" as the conflict type ensures that Person wins. Which Person? Yes, that's the problem. It's unclear. It also sets up a situation where the opposing party is almost necessarily set up as a villain. One person's hero is another person's villain, and vice versa.[8]

The conflict of the lawsuit flows throughout the whole of the brief. The requested relief of the brief, in fact, is a request to the court to resolve the conflict in the client's favor. Thus, the conflict type is first seen in the Preliminary Statement or Question Presented section of the brief. It may also be spotlighted in the Statement of Facts, depending on whether the type of legal question is a factual question, a mixture of fact and law, or purely a question of law.

But no matter which type of legal issue, the Statement of Facts cannot end the legal story for readers. Remember that a story ends when readers discover—or, in the legal story, when readers decide—whether the protagonist overcame the obstacles to attain the goal.

> **Conflict types and themes**
>
> As noted in Chapter 3, conflict is one of the structural tools that a writer can use to tell an effective story. In the story arc, or plot, conflict causes the pre-existing order to fall into chaos, which is what drives the plot forward. "Conflict" differs from the "theme" of the brief, which we discuss in detail in Chapter 9. The "theme" of a brief is the emotional center of the case: the "moral of the story." It captures the essential reason why the court should want to rule in your client's favor.

In legal writing, the end of the story occurs after readers have considered the underlying facts and the obstacle-clearing elements of the legal

---

[8]Also discussed in Foley & Robbins, *supra* n. 1, at 472.

arguments. Thus, the Statement of Facts usually represents just the exposition of the story. It sets the stage for the rest of the story by identifying the characters, explaining the protagonist-client's goal, and showing the obstacles facing this protagonist-client. By the time readers have finished with the Statement of Facts, they may have formed an opinion about how this story *should* unfold, but they will look to the Argument section to see how it *does* unfold.

The difference between real and fictional characters: behavior

Fictional characters (since they don't really exist!) tend to act in ways that are more extreme than those of us who exist in the real world. We expect fictional characters to behave badly and to make poor choices. In fact, the story's conflict and ultimate climax depend on their acting this way. Real people, like their fictional counterparts, also act badly and make poor choices. But the difference is that audiences are less tolerant of such behavior in the real world. (You may have personal experience with this, yes?) Perhaps an even more important difference is that when a real person acts "out of character," it causes others to reassess the person's perceived character. What this means for us is that when we establish our client as, say, a creator hero, we need to look for facts that appear inconsistent with that character. Too many inconsistencies (or even a single but central inconsistency) can undermine our entire story. In fiction, inconsistent behavior adds depth to a character. In the real world, it undermines credibility.

IV. Finding your client's archetype

Your client may represent several archetypes. She may be a creator, an every person, or a scholar. To find the match that best tells your client's story, you will want to have a thorough understanding of the law and the facts. However, you may want to use the form shown in Figure 7-1 on page 100 to get started thinking critically about your client character.

A. Selecting a heroic archetype

Pick at least two or three heroic archetypes that you think might be appropriate for your client. Keep an open mind; more options may fit than you first imagined. You are going to want to do this little exercise several times so that you can see the options.

- What is a possible heroic archetype for my client?
- What is my client's goal that matches the archetype?
- What are the obstacles the client faces in reaching that goal (again, they should match the archetype)?
- What facts do I have that support the use of this archetype?
  - Use specific facts that can be cited in the record or evidentiary exhibits.
  - Leave out any opinion or judgment on the part of the narrator (i.e., your opinion).

Where in the brief are the client's overall goals discussed?

The short answer: "If you include them, keep them far away from the first paragraph of the Statement of Facts." Remember that you must be careful of how you tell the back story because your readers are trained to be skeptical of overt attempts to persuade with calls to sympathy.

The back story can certainly show up in your notes or checklists, however. And the client's overall life challenges might be woven into the legal story, but only in a careful and subtle way. The next chapter talks about writing "shadow documents," and later in the book, as you are working on revising language to fit your case theory, we revisit some techniques of how to best convey this type of back-story information.

B. Missing information and reasonable inferences

Developing archetype possibilities also allows you to see that some facts needed to complete the story are missing. If the lawsuit is still in the pre-trial phase, more conversation with the client or potential witnesses might be needed. Likewise, you might conduct additional discovery. At the appellate stage, the record is set, of course. But you might still look for nonadjudicative facts (statistical or other legislative facts, as discussed in Chapter 4). At the same time, this exercise in archetypes could help identify additional needed legal research.

Studying the facts through this sort of lens also might help you better visualize the incidents. Doing so could lead to reasonable inferences from the facts. That is different than interpreting the facts. Here's an example. Suppose someone describing a scene says something like "everyone in the hotel stopped what they were doing to watch the argument between the woman and the registration clerk." An inference you could draw is that the argument was loud enough to catch people's attention.

As you start to put together your list of facts, be sure to ask yourself these questions:

- What information do I still need about the following? (Remember that on appeal, you cannot add to the record.)
- What, if any, reasonable inferences about my client's character can I make from the evidence or record?

C. Repeating the steps

The first and most obvious heroic archetype that your client's story "fits" is not always the one that is the best for the lawsuit. Every domestic violence case involves a lover hero whose relationship with Prince(ss) Charming has turned out to be a harmful one. But the client might also be a creator hero. Suppose her start-up business is suffering because she has had to take time off because of the abuse. Or perhaps the client has cut off friendships and other family connections because of the abuse. Then the client is also potentially an orphan hero.

Another way to visualize this is by using a chart similar to Figure 7-1. That gives you the option to see several choices at once.

Archetype	Client's goal	Obstacle to that goal	Facts that could be used to demonstrate the particular archetype (cite to the record or evidence for every asserted fact)	Facts that are inconsistent with my client's heroic archetype (cite to the evidence or record for every asserted fact)	More information to investigate to round out this archetype consideration (if at appellate level, only nonadjudicative facts)	Inferences I can make about character based on the record (inferences are different than your own opinions)

Figure 7-1: Choosing your client's archetype

V. Identifying the central conflict your client faces

In the same manner, you will want to go through the conflict types that could be involved with your client's case. Keep an open mind—as you do the legal research and begin writing the legal argument, all of this can easily change.

- The central conflict of my client's story is _____ versus _____.
- The following facts establish this conflict: (cite to the evidence or record for every asserted fact):

  _____
  _____
  _____
  _____

Once you have decided how you will portray your protagonist-client, you are ready to develop the rest of her story. The next chapter explores how to develop the plot of the client's story.

Chapter 8

Telling the client's story: plot, conflict, and story types

The factual investigation is complete. You have started your research into the legal theories that might apply. You have thought about what kind of hero your client is and even done some preliminary writing about the facts of the case. This chapter discusses getting specific about how to present the case to the court.

I. Types of stories

In Chapter 3, you learned about the power of stories to persuade and some of the structural and stylistic tools that fiction writers use. Experienced and successful legal writers use similar tools. We explore one of those tools in this chapter: plot.

The plot line is the glue that holds all of the elements of a story together. It is the central organizational structure of a work, be it fiction or a legal brief. Plot carries the brief from its beginning, which Aristotle called "order," through the complications, also called "chaos," to the satisfying ending called "reorder." In this chapter, we examine how you, as a lawyer can think about a plot line for the entire brief. The plot is more than just the material in the Statement of the Case. It carries across the whole legal argument as well. By creating a strong plot line, the brief will read like a story and therefore will engage the reader's attention, for the same reasons that any other story does.

Works of fiction frequently have several interconnected plots. There is usually a main story line that is what the work is "about." But there may be subplots and parallel story lines that influence or interact with the main action in some fashion. Ultimately, all of the subplots provide some part of the ultimate resolution, or "denouement," of the story.

As we suggested in Chapter 3, the same is true of a legal case. In every story about your client's case, there are three possible choices for the main story line, or plot:

1. The story line might be principally about **the dispute between the parties**. The plaintiff claims that the defendant injured the plaintiff in a specific way, and the plaintiff wants to be restored to some satisfactory condition. This is what we usually think of when we think about a legal story and is often the most important story line.
2. The story line might be principally about **the law**. In such story lines, the conflict may not turn on the specific dispute between the parties, but rather on the meaning or validity of the particular law at the center of the dispute. This type of story line may have as much impact on future conduct as it does on the parties themselves. The landmark litigation over segregated schools that culminated in the landmark *Brown v. Board of Education*[1] decision is an example of this kind of story.
3. The key story line might be principally about **the process of resolving the case**. This kind of story is often about things like whether a particular court has jurisdiction to decide a case or whether a controversy really exists or is "ripe" enough for a court to consider it. Such stories are sometimes told by defendants seeking to have a case dismissed without a decision "on the merits" of the underlying controversy.

Another way of describing these three options is to think of them as three potential conflicts for the court to resolve: (1) Is the conflict principally between the parties? (2) Is the conflict principally about the law itself? Or (3) Is the conflict principally about the court's procedures for resolving disputes?

Of course, these options are not mutually exclusive. Any case might involve a combination of these options, or even all three of them. And the parties to the lawsuit might even disagree about which story line is the principal one. The plaintiff might tell a story focusing on the factual dispute between the parties, while the defendant might choose to tell a procedural story about why the court should not decide the merits of the dispute. And the story may change over the course of the lawsuit. The defendant may initially seek to dismiss the case on procedural grounds, choosing to focus on the story of the case; if that is unsuccessful,

---

[1] 347 U.S. 483 (1954); see discussion of this case in the Prologue.

A tale of two stories

One recent case shows the relationship between selecting the right story line and a successful outcome. In *Mohamed v. Palestinian Authority*, 132 S. Ct. 1702 (2012), plaintiffs, the widow and son of a U.S. citizen who was allegedly tortured and killed by Palestinian Authority (PA) intelligence officers, sued the PA under the Torture Victim Protection Act, 28 U.S.C. § 1350 [note 2(a)]. The Act created liability for individuals who committed acts of torture. The brief for the victim's family understandably focused on the harm: PA agents apparently kidnapped, tortured, and ultimately killed the victim, and the Authority should therefore be held responsible for the acts of its agents. But PA's counsel focused almost exclusively on the law: the interpretation of the word "individual" in the statute. The United States Supreme Court, in a unanimous opinion, held that the word "individual" could not be interpreted to include organizations such as the PA. By framing the issue as a conflict about the law rather than as a factual dispute between the parties, the attorneys for the PA won the case for their client.

the defendant may later shift to tell a story about the law or focus on the factual dispute itself.

All of which is to say that at some point, early in the development of your client's story, you need to decide what the central conflict is about and build your theme and theory of the case along that story line. If opposing counsel chooses to focus on a different conflict, you will then need to decide whether to engage on that issue or try to refocus the court on the conflict you think is most important. Your choice on this matter may change as the case moves forward. A single brief in the case may deal with two or all three of these conflicts, or different briefs at different stages of the case may focus on different conflicts. These are choices you need to carefully consider.

II. The arc of a plot

Literary critics have studied plots for years. Principles of literary criticism also work well by analogy in persuasive legal writing. The five stages of plot development are generally described as

1. introduction/exposition,
2. complicating incident/rising action,
3. climax,
4. falling action, and
5. resolution (or denouement).

This arc is visually represented in Figure 8-1.

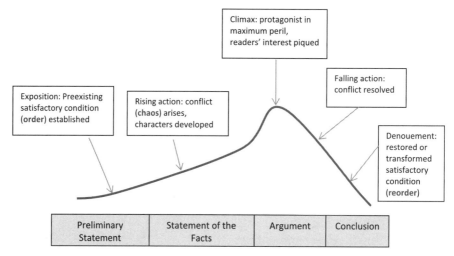

| Preliminary Statement | Statement of the Facts | Argument | Conclusion |

Figure 8-1: Arc of a plot

As shown in Figure 8-1, this trajectory loosely describes a well-organized legal brief. We discuss each of these components in more detail below.

Another way of thinking about the plot is to imagine the protagonist on his journey toward some worthy goal; he thinks of this condition as "order." When he is knocked off his hoped-for course by some outside person or force, "chaos" results. He then seeks the assistance of the court to put him back on his chosen course ("reorder"). This path is represented graphically in Figure 8-2.

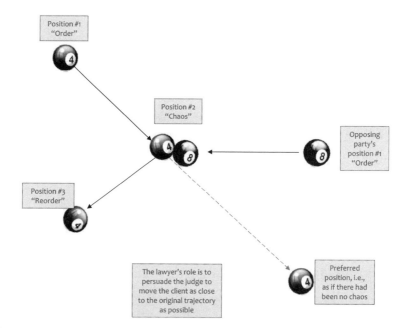

Figure 8-2: Schematic of the parties' interactions with each other

Note that since we are discussing brief writing in this chapter, we think of the readers as the judges who must decide the case. This creates an interesting opportunity for the writer because the "ending" of the story—the resolution of the plot—is ultimately in the hands of his readers. This situation gives readers even more incentive to be attentive to the details, of course, but it also means that the writer needs to think clearly about what details readers need to craft a satisfying ending to the legal story. For example, in our hotel room reservation case, SOFT's attorney wants readers to understand from the outset that SOFT is a small, nonprofit organization that had little or no opportunity to negotiate the precise language of the hotel's standard room reservation agreement. She needs to establish this plot point in the Statement of Facts and continue this aspect of the story line throughout the brief.

A. Introduction/exposition

Most works of fiction—which have more leeway and a different audience than readers of a legal brief—begin with the protagonist in a state of repose or peace. Here, readers learn enough context about the who, what, where, and why for the story to make sense. Physical objects or conditions may be described so that readers can visualize where the story takes place. Characters are introduced. Usually the story begins with everything in stasis. Calm prevails; the protagonist is happy.

The fact section of a plot-based legal brief should likewise begin with an introduction, in which the factual setting is revealed. Helpful background details that explain the protagonist's character can be included here as well. However, recall the lessons of Chapter 7. The legal writer needs to be careful about how much detail to include in this section because much of the detail needed for the reader to fully understand the characters' motivation may be legally irrelevant. Including too much background detail might be seen by judges either as wasting their time or (even worse) as an attempt to manipulate readers or to improperly play on their emotions.

B. Complicating incident/rising action

Once the stage is properly set, the action begins. Something happens. A conflict arises. The status quo is upset; something is no longer right.

The conflict, of course, drives the story and grabs readers' attention, and this is revealed through the complicating incident in any story. The incident may be a series of incidents, one building on another (rising action). Or it may be a single event that requires no further development.

This is all the stuff of a compelling fact section. A good Statement of Facts reveals not only the character of the protagonist (your client), the antagonist (a possible role for the opposing party), and any other characters who are not parties to the suit but who play some role in the story. The fact section also defines the factual conflict that brings the parties to the court, seeking redress.

But just like in fiction, the story need not be told in strict chronological order. A common device in fiction writing is to begin with the complicating incident (to grab the reader's attention) and then jump backward in time to show the events that have put the protagonist in peril. The "flashback" then reveals the condition of stasis that existed before the conflict arose; the setting in which the story takes place and the character of the protagonist are also developed.

SOFT's brief in the hotel reservation case, shown in Figure 8-3, includes an example of this flashback technique.

Once the setting and character are introduced, the events leading up to the controversy can be filled in. Readers know what the conflict is since it was introduced in the first few paragraphs; now the details about how the conflict arose can be filled in. This "rising action" can provide further insights into the protagonist's character, painting her in a positive light as somebody deserving of the court's assistance (see Figure 8-4).

At this point the rising action has begun and the factual conflict (the "chaos" at the heart of the story has been revealed. But this is about as far as the fact section can take us. The plot is far from fully developed yet. Readers are not ready for the climax; you cannot resolve any conflicts in the fact section. You need more.

Both the introduction and the rising action must be continued in the Argument section. The fact section describes only the factual setting and identifies the factual conflict. The *legal* setting (the fixed legal rules that must be applied by the court) must be described in the Argument section, and the *legal* conflict must be explained there as well. Thus, at the beginning of the Argument section, you need to complete the introduction by adequately describing the legal principles that are needed to resolve the conflict. And, if there is a dispute as to what those rules are, or should be, the legal conflict needs to be developed and explained sufficiently. This is a continuation of the rising action that began in the Statement of Facts.

Statement of Facts

Global climate change has been the subject of a great deal of scientific inquiry and discussion in recent years. Many scientists have explored possible causes of the phenomenon and possible steps that society might take to slow or reverse the trend. One theory is that deforestation contributes to the problem by removing large numbers of trees that could otherwise convert a notorious greenhouse gas, carbon dioxide, into oxygen. One nonprofit organization, Save Our Forest Trees, Inc. (SOFT), has devoted its existence to promoting an exchange of ideas and information among climate scientists working on this issue.

Preexisting satisfactory condition

In summer 2012, SOFT hosted a two-day conference at the Gloucester Hotel Indianapolis. However, because Gloucester had booked other events at the same time and sold out the entire hotel on the nights of the conference, SOFT conference attendees were not able to purchase the number of hotel rooms specified in the contract between SOFT and the Gloucester Hotel. Gloucester's attempt to charge SOFT for the rooms its members could not buy has led to this lawsuit.

Complicating incident sometimes referred to as the "chaos"

Foreshadowing of legal conflict

A. Save Our Forest Trees

Ms. Freebird, now thirty-two years old, formed SOFT shortly after being awarded a bachelor's degree in biology and volunteering her time with other nonprofits and environmental advocacy groups. While her title is Executive Director for SOFT, in fact she is the organization's only employee, working long hours to realize its mission of connecting scientists and environmentalists to share their research findings and discuss ways to bring awareness to the problem of deforestation and climate change. Freebird Dep. 2:14–3:9, Aug. 20, 2013.

Flashback to previous condition of order

SOFT's headquarters are in Ms. Freebird's home, although she charges no rent to SOFT. Operating costs are kept to a bare minimum by communicating and advertising primarily over the Internet and through e-mail. Ms. Freebird herself earns only $30,000 in income, although she is a full-time employee. *Id.*

Character development

B. The Indianapolis Conference at the Gloucester Hotel

In summer 2011, SOFT selected Indianapolis as the site for a conference. Ms. Freebird called the Hotel to inquire about conference dates in July 2012. She requested a block of 150 rooms to be held over for July 13 and 14, 2012 (approximately 75 per night). *Id.* at 7:13–8:9. Based upon that number and the dates requested, the reservation agent for Gloucester told Ms. Freebird that the Hotel could offer a rate of $159 per night, which represented a significant discount from the Hotel's normal rate of $189 per night. *Id.* at 8:1–6. Shortly after that phone call, a form contract arrived in the mail entitled "Group Contract," dated August 15, 2011 ("the Agreement"). Ms. Freebird checked the form to ensure that the room rate and block were accurate, and then signed it and returned it in the mail. *Id.* at 9:2–10:14.

Ms. Freebird did not read the contract in detail before signing it but testified at her deposition that "most of those contracts are all the same; just a bunch of legalese." Id. Based upon past arrangements with other hotels in the Gloucester chain and in the hotel industry generally, Ms. Freebird believed that the Agreement was meant to be simply a confirmation of the earlier conversation with the person she spoke to on the telephone. She believed that a signature was necessary to ensure that her group would get the discounted rate. *Id.*

In late June 2012, several SOFT members contacted Ms. Freebird to tell her that Gloucester was already sold out. *Id.* at 21:13–19. Ms. Freebird assumed from this information that the block of rooms under the Agreement had all been reserved by other members. She then recommended to the callers that they seek accommodations at another nearby hotel. *Id.* at 22:2–18.

> Legal setting established (these facts become legally relevant in Argument section)

Figure 8-3: Flashback technique, as used in SOFT's Statement of Facts

When Ms. Freebird and the other participants arrived at the Hotel for the July conference, many SOFT guests were unable to check in on time. *Id.* at 26:1–27:16. Guests Carla Johnson and Milton Jones were both told by a clerk at the registration desk that the Hotel was "completely sold out." Johnson Aff. ¶ 4, Aug. 7, 2013. Many conference attendees were told that their rooms were not ready for the 4:00 p.m. check-in time they were promised; in fact, many participants did not get into their rooms until after 6:00 p.m. Freebird Dep. 19:2–14. On account of the "chaos," many of the out-of-town guests staying there missed the conference's opening reception and the catered refreshments. *Id.*

Complicating incident

C. Pat Freebird Returns to Eureka

Attendance at the conference turned out to be lower than Ms. Freebird had expected. Instead of 200 registrations, there had been only 152; and several of those were Indiana residents who did not stay overnight at the Hotel. Because of the lower-than-expected attendance, the conference generated only $5,800 of income over expenses. Def.'s Answer Interrog. ¶ 11 and Ex. 2 thereto.

Rising action begins

A week or so after the Indianapolis event, SOFT received an invoice from the Hotel charging $9,480.38 for "attrition for unused guest rooms." The invoice claimed that there were 53 "unused" rooms. Freebird Dep. Ex. 3. Ms. Freebird was unsure how there could have been a shortfall if the Hotel was turning away guests and claiming that it had been full, so she called the Hotel for an explanation. Nobody provided her with any information. *Id.* at 29:14–30:2.

Ms. Freebird then spoke with some of the people who had registered for the conference and found that several of them had been charged $189 per night rather than the discounted conference rate for their rooms; she assumed this was because the reserved block had sold out and that the guests then bought rooms at the regular hotel rate. *Id.* at 31:15–23. She also discovered that at least a dozen SOFT members had been unable to book rooms at Gloucester during the conference and had to stay in other nearby hotels. *Id.* at 32:16–20.

Since she had not gotten a satisfactory answer on the phone, Ms. Freebird wrote a letter to the Hotel requesting a list of the participants who had reserved rooms, including how many were counted as part of the group. *Id.* Ex. 4. She hoped she would be able to determine from that list whether everybody who should have been counted toward the room block was in fact counted. *Id.* at 32:3–7. But instead of the guest list, about a month later, an attorney for the Hotel sent a letter insisting upon full payment of the entire amount within one week. *Id.* at 32:17–21 and Ex. 5. The attorney claimed that the amount sought represented liquidated damages for unused rooms ("attrition"), based on this clause in the contract:

[remainder of fact section omitted]

Figure 8-4: Rising action in the SOFT brief

C. Climax

In literature, the climax occurs when the protagonist is at the height of peril. Things are out of kilter, making readers uncomfortable and aching for things to get better, to return to a condition of stasis. Readers' attention is at its peak. How will the conflict be resolved? How does the story come out?

In a legal brief, this moment occurs at the point when readers (1) know the characters; (2) understand the factual dispute (what happened to drive the parties to the court for assistance); and (3) understand the legal dispute, including the legal principles needed to resolve the dispute. Readers wonder: How are these issues going be resolved? How is this going to turn out? And readers of the brief are even more interested because they are the persons who ultimately decide, or at least vote on, how the story "turns out."

Note that the climax *must* occur within the Argument section of the brief because only then is the legal setting and the rising action of the legal issue fully developed, arriving at the climax of the story.

D. Resolution/falling action

In fiction, the climax often happens very near the end of the story because it is more entertaining that way. Once the climax is reached, readers are usually brought back to stasis very quickly, as if riding a roller coaster. Things fall into place rapidly, and the story reaches a satisfactory conclusion.

In legal writing, this is not always true. In some situations, it might be: if the legal rule is hard to decipher or is a question of first impression, the writer may need to spend a great deal of time with the rising action to arrive at a sufficient description of the legal issue, explained clearly enough that the court can then take appropriate action. In such situations, once the difficult rule is synthesized, the application of that rule to the facts may be fairly straightforward, resulting in a very short section of falling action/resolution.

The more common situation, however, is the opposite: the rules are fairly straightforward, but the way in which they should be applied to the specific facts of the case at hand may be more difficult. In that situation, the falling action/resolution part of the plot is likely to be much more complex and lengthy.

E. Denouement

And then there is the conclusion.

Readers like happy endings. All of the conflicts are resolved in a plausible way and the characters return to a state of peace and calm. The resolution can be a return to the prior condition of stasis (a *restorative* resolution) or to a new, yet tranquil and satisfying, condition (a *transformative* resolution).[2]

Likewise, the plot-based legal brief needs to come to a plausible conclusion. The writer returns to the theme that has been developed throughout the plot and makes it explicit. All of the conflicts are resolved, and the court is led to a calm, rational, just conclusion: your client wins, either by being restored to status quo ante or by being placed in a new, satisfying condition, consistent with the theme of the story.

The next few chapters talk more specifically about the writing of the various parts of a brief to fit the plot line of a good legal story.

---

[2]Anthony G. Amsterdam & Jerome Bruner, *Minding the Law* 113–114 (Harvard U. Press 2000).

Part III

Creating the working draft

In every writing project, there comes a point when it is time to push the researcher aside and start writing. Once you have met the client, investigated the facts, and completed the initial research, you are ready to begin writing the Argument.[1] Starting to write is often the most difficult part of the writing process—moving the ideas that are loosely defined in your head to a workable written draft of an Argument.

Luckily, the first writing stage involves merely producing the workable draft. Getting to the finished draft will come later. The next five chapters are designed to get the ideas that are in your head onto paper. Once you have completed that draft, the next step is revising that draft into a persuasive story. Part IV of this book discusses revising.

I. Where we are now

Producing a good draft of a brief involves six steps:

1. Get to know the client and his goals.
2. Gather and assess the facts of the client's story.
3. Find and assess the law that applies to the client's story.
4. Identify the persuasive theme or themes.
5. Determine the facts and arguments that will best represent the client's interests.
6. Write and organize the working draft.

You have already worked through the first three steps—though it is likely that you will be returning to each of them since writing is recursive, not linear. Now it is time for the heavy lifting of putting pen to paper. Or, more likely, fingers to keyboards.

---

[1]There are, of course, other parts to a brief besides the Argument. Those other parts are discussed in Chapter 17. However, the heart of a brief is the Argument section, and that is what you will spend the most time creating.

Creating a working draft begins by sketching out the story you want the brief to tell. Chapter 9 gets this process started with a planning document called a "shadow story." It shows you how to use that document to visualize the case theme and turn it into a first draft of the facts section of the brief.

We then turn to the Argument section of the brief. But before you can determine what arguments to make for your client, it helps to know what kind of arguments are out there. Chapters 10 through 12 therefore explore three aspects of argument: interpreting statutes, exploring policy, and dealing with adverse material. There is another form of argument—synthesizing and applying case law. However, you most likely spent considerable time exploring case law analysis in your first legal writing course, so we do not address it in detail here. We return to case analysis in more detail in Part IV: revising the legal story—the Argument, the Statement of Facts, and the other parts of the brief—to make each section and the overall document more persuasive.

After looking at statutes, policy, and adverse materials, Chapter 13 explores how to organize the legal arguments into a coherent whole.

Writing is part of the thinking process. For some, our approach to brief writing may at first seem counterintuitive. Some people may prefer to outline the Argument before they get down to writing the actual substance. Outlining can certainly be a useful way to get started. However, even if you prefer to create an outline before you write, you should remember that writing is part of the thinking process. As you write your arguments, you may discover arguments that you had overlooked; you may discover holes in your research or reasoning; you may even discover whole new issues that change the very nature of your client's case. Consequently, after you have actually written out your arguments, you will want to revisit your planned organization. You will also need to create headings and other structural markers that will make the organization of the Argument clear to your reader. At that point, Chapter 13 will be very helpful.

We realize that not all writers can create an outline before they write. For many of us, we need to get our ideas down on paper first and then see how they best fit together. Our first drafts may look more like a stream of consciousness babble than a coherent document. That's fine too. Our goal is to create a well-organized, perfectly written *final* draft. If we need to write a messy, disorganized first draft before we get there, no worries. Organizing our thoughts is often easier once we have those thoughts on paper.

Whether you outline before or after you write your working draft, the time has come to start writing. As you work through the next chapters, you will come across many potential strategies for creating arguments. Some of them will fit perfectly with your brief problem while others may seem less relevant. Through the writing process, you will likely discover that some arguments fall away and new arguments take their place. That is as it should be. Remember, we are not yet writing the final, perfect Argument. Though we are putting pen to paper, we are still in the thinking stage of the brief writing process.

II. What happens next

We start writing.[2]

---

[2]Even if it's crap. Just get it on the page.

Chapter 9

Starting to write: shadow stories and working drafts of the Facts section

Recall that in the Prologue we described the four main phases of any writing project. The first phase is "prewriting," which consists of research and planning. Up to this point in the book, we have been talking about researching both the facts and the law that may help resolve the story. This chapter turns to the planning part of the prewriting phase before moving into the first working drafts.

I. The first parts of writing: sketching a "shadow" draft of the Facts section

Crafting an effective and final version of the Statement of Facts requires careful, deliberate planning that spans the whole of the document-writing adventure. The Statement of Facts is the section of a document that lawyers quite often sketch first and then rewrite last. The process of doing so allows legal writers to focus on the issues, hurdles, and possible avenues for a successful resolution.

These are the key steps in writing the facts section of a brief:

- Creating a separate "shadow story": essentially, what the lawyer wishes she could bluntly **tell** the court about her client, the opposing party, and the events. This is the prewriting, or planning, phase of the process.
- Taking the shadow story and turning it into a working draft of the facts section that blends the client's needs with the ethos of legal storytelling.
- Revising the draft so that the story is presented from the client's point of view and **shows** readers—without telling readers—the theme.

119

This draft will be much more subtle and carefully crafted than the working draft so that it conveys—but refrains from bluntly *telling*—the story and theme that the lawyer has selected as the most effective for the client.

• Polishing the section for precise word choices and to juxtapose fact placements to create key connections between facts.

A. What is the shadow story, and why do we need it?

The idea of the shadow story is to draft the version of your client's story that your client *wishes* you could tell. Your client may be angry, frustrated, even delusional about the opposing parties and his conflict with them. At the very least, he is likely to see the dispute from only one point of view— his! Most of the time, we would never actually write the Statement of Facts from such an obviously biased perspective because it would undermine our own credibility. However, for the shadow story, that is just what we will do: tell the story with all our client's anger, biases, and emotion. It is time to "let it all out."

A shadow story helps to plan and shape the client's story. While it may feel a little like the second phase, writing the first draft, this is still planning (on paper) what to later write about in the working draft. The shadow story is the anything-goes document—filled with all of your client's back story and your opinions and judgments. To be crystal clear: this isn't a draft of the document itself. It's a method for developing the theory of the case and the story that you will include in the "real" document.[1]

Typically, shadow stories are fairly short. That is because a shadow story is simply one of the other supporting documents that shadow the actual brief. You learned about another of type of shadow document in Chapter 6 (and you may have learned this last semester): the case charts that lawyers use to help themselves synthesize the rules of law from the various statutes, regulations, and cases. Just as case charts are separate documents that never touch, but only shadow, the actual legal argument sections of the brief, the shadow story likewise will only inform, but not appear in, the Statement of Facts. To ensure you don't make a potentially disastrous mistake, save the shadow story as a separate document—perhaps even

---

[1]Credit for the idea and initial teaching of the "shadow story" belongs to Victoria L. Chase, Clinical Associate Professor of Law, Rutgers School of Law–Camden, Podcast, *Using Corroborating Narratives in Cross-Examination—An Effective Alternative to Traditional Cross Examination Strategies and Telling the Client's Story Effectively* (2d Applied Legal Storytelling Conference, Lewis & Clark Law School, Portland, OR, July, 2009)(available at http://lawlib.lclark.edu/podcast/?p=2067).

shade the whole document with a gray background to remind yourself that this is merely a shadow of the real thing!

Case charts are useful to help us think about the legal analysis. And that is the same reason we create the shadow story or any shadow documents in legal writing. The shadow story is a type of checklist that allows thinking. The Statement of Facts needs to be persuasive and written in a client-centered way. So, just as a lawyer creates synthesis charts to help her organize her thoughts about the rules of law, writing the shadow story allows the lawyer to form ideas that will lead to the eventual finished product.

For example, consider the hotel room reservation example. Remember, after the reservation deadline had passed, the hotel sold rooms guaranteed to SOFT to other guests at a higher price. SOFT's lawyer may wish that she could simply tell the court, "It is real hubris for that big hotel to sue my client, the little nonprofit organization, for that ridiculous amount of liquidated damages when the hotel actually *made* money from the breach of contract!!! My client essentially did the hotel *a favor*." Of course, she can't include those two sentences in the Statement of Facts. But she can write them down in the shadow story. Later, the shadow story will be a framework for choosing the facts and the juxtaposition of the facts that will create the same feeling in readers without the obviously biased tone. For example, to show that the hotel actually profited from reselling the room, she would include in her Facts the dollar figure profit

> **Why is it called a shadow story?**
>
> The shadow story is named after the shadow cast by an object on a sunny day. It is not the object itself, but it is shaped by the object. You can learn something about the object by looking at its shadow, but the shadow is flatter than the actual object and is often misshapen. Just as you learn more by looking directly at the object and seeing all of its colors, dimensions, and other details, you will include in your brief the necessary details to allow the reader to see the actual story.

that the hotel would have made if the organization members had rented all of the rooms they were supposed to, versus the dollar figure profit the hotel actually made on those nights. These facts *show* the hubris of the hotel without *telling* readers that the hotel made an unfair profit.

The shadow story is the story you wish you could tell. It is the unfiltered version of the story, as seen by your client. It may be emotional, angry, one-sided, and clearly biased in favor of the client. It should reflect the intensity of emotion that your client is feeling about the legal dispute. At this point, don't worry about it if the story seems extreme or biased or one-sided—that's exactly what the shadow story should be. Although, in the filed brief, you can't ignore the evidence that goes against the client, in the shadow story, you can minimize or dismiss those facts that might offset the client's point of view.

Yes, you read that previous paragraph correctly. Go ahead and tell the most one-sided version of the story that you can. Include your own opinions or judgments if you think it helpful to remind yourself later to replace them with facts from the citable record. Put it in a dramatic font or use lots of exclamation points or boldface. Whatever you want. It doesn't even have to be written in prose. You can draw the shadow story if you prefer. Write it in bullet points. Set it to music. It doesn't matter because your intended readers will never see it. The trick, naturally, is that this document isn't a "draft," nor will it ever get near the document you are calling "the brief."

Sketching the shadow story is not only useful, it's fun. It is the place to let the passion come out, to show your client's sense of outrage. Remember that there's no need to worry about losing credibility because no one is going to see this version except you.

B. Identifying your theme via the shadow story

Besides being fun to write, the shadow story helps you plan your document in an important way: it can help you select the theme for your brief. Once you have written your shadow story, it should be easy for you to identify the theme or themes that your story tells.

Remember in Chapter 3 you learned the difference between a "theme" and a "theory of the case." The theory of the case is the legal theory (or theories) that provide the justification of why the court can legally rule in your client's favor; this is the logos of your case. The theme, on the other hand, refers to the value-based, emotional reason why the court should *want* to rule in your client's favor (the pathos of your argument). You want to give the court a reason to think that a ruling in your client's favor is fair and just, not merely legally permissible.[2]

Chapter 3 also introduced the concept of "deep frames," which cognitive scientist George Lakoff describes as ideas or values that structure how you view the world.[3] At the heart of every deep frame is what he calls an

---

[2]Professor Richard Neumann describes the theory as a "justifying argument" that shows the court how it is *possible* to rule in your client's favor, and the theme as a "motivating argument" that makes the court *want* to rule in your client's favor. Richard K. Neumann, Jr., *Legal Reasoning and Legal Writing: Structure, Strategy and Style* 309–310 (6th ed., Wolters Kluwer L. & Bus. 2009).

[3]George Lakoff, *Whose Freedom? The Battle over America's Most Important Idea* 12 (Farrar, Straus & Giroux 2006).

"uncontested idea": for example, the idea that freedom is good and is something all people long for.

Examples of other concepts that might be considered deep frames:

- Light (openness; transparency)
- Strength
- Health
- Fairness/justice
- Happiness
- Love
- Truth
- Opportunity
- Independence (autonomy, self-reliance)
- Community
- Charity (helping others; unselfishness)
- Obedience (respect for authority)
- Faith/spirituality
- Discipline (hard work; focus)
- Generosity

Each of these concepts, at its very center, is nearly universally accepted as "good." If the advocate can show the court how a ruling in favor of your client advances a deep frame, the court will be more motivated to rule in favor of your client.

Deep frames work at an unconscious level and therefore may trump facts. Lakoff believes that deep frames are how each of us defines common sense; they shape the way we view the world. A person who encounters a fact that is inconsistent with a deep frame is likely to reject the fact as untrue, irrelevant, or unimportant because the fact seems to defy common sense.[4] Suppose, for example, readers start with the deep frame that free enterprise is good and that businesses must therefore be free to create the jobs that provide workers with the means to support their families. Readers may then reject facts that show that environmental regulation is necessary to promote public health; such regulation costs money, which impairs businesses' ability to create jobs, which then conflicts with readers' deep frame.

The concept of a deep frame is closely related to that of theme. Since you want to find a theme that resonates with your audience (judges), you should search for a theme that is in harmony with a deep frame likely to be held by most people, including judges.

---

[4]*Id.* at 13.

To help you find your theme, look over your shadow story. Does it give readers a reason to care about what happens to your client? What deep frame is triggered by the shadow story? Look back over the suggested list of deep frames above, but remember that list is not comprehensive; there may be other deep frames that your story might resonate with. If you find that you cannot identify the deep frame that is triggered by your shadow story, you may need to rethink your story to find one or more deep frames that readers are likely to connect with.

A good way to whittle down to the theme of the case from the shadow story is to distill it into a simple phrase that is six words or fewer. For example, the defendant in the hotel reservations case might sum up the theme as "hotel getting paid twice isn't fair." The hotel might sum up the theme as "people should honor their guaranteed obligations."

More on six-word stories

The idea is borrowed from the famous but apocryphal tale about Ernest Hemingway being challenged to write a story in only six words. He won the challenge with the story, "For sale, baby shoes, never worn." Whole websites and books are devoted to six-word stories. It's a technique that provides a simple yet powerful way to test many things in your own brief writing, from theme, to theory of the case, to rule explanation.

C. The theme is not the theory but runs in parallel

The *theory* of the brief provides the logical basis for your argument. In contrast, the theme of a brief should evoke an emotional response from the reader. The *theme* should explain the motivations of the characters and give readers a reason to respect and "root for" those characters. Thus, in addition to the legal theories based on the rules of law, you should strive to include a strong, pathos-based theme. The theme is the emotional core that persuades a court that ruling in your client's favor is the right thing to do. But the theme should work together with the legal theory. They run in parallel.

For example, in our hotel reservation example, one of the legal theories for SOFT would be that the liquidated damages clause of the contract was unconscionable. The substantive law of contract for the jurisdiction where the dispute arose would then provide the factors, standards, and rules that the court would employ to determine whether the clause was, in fact, unconscionable. This is the stuff of the legal theory of the case.

But the lawyer also needs to develop a strong theme in parallel, so that the court can determine whether the clause of the contract is unconscionable. To develop that parallel theme to the theory of the case, the lawyer representing SOFT needs to argue that it is the weaker party in the transaction: it is a small, nonprofit organization trying to raise money to promote a worthy cause, while the hotel is part of a large nationwide chain of hotels trying to maximize its profit. We like to cheer for the little person. It's part of the deep frames of both independence and discipline or hard work. To tap into those frames, the lawyer representing SOFT should point out the fill-in-the-blank contract form that the hotel presented did not appear to leave room for negotiation, and that the hotel employee with whom Pat Freebird was speaking did not have the authority to change any of the form language. The lawyer would also point out that the clause of the contract could result in a windfall for the hotel. If it were able to resell any, or all, of the rooms the organization did not reserve by the reservation deadline, the hotel, in effect, would be getting paid twice: first by the organization and again by the actual occupant of the room. That results in an unfairness (a third deep frame), resulting in a larger profit for the hotel and less money available for the nonprofit organization to pursue its mission.

Of course, if the legal theory is "unconscionability," it is pretty easy to see how theme will necessarily play a large role in the persuasive process. Unconscionability is an equitable concept, and the entire body of equity law is based on principles of fairness and justice, which are inherently narrative based. But what if the legal theory is more solidly law based? Does narrative reasoning have anything to add? Yes, it still applies.

Here's an example of using theory and theme in parallel. Another possible line of defense for our lawyer to argue in our hotel reservation example is that the liquidated damages clause does not meet the legal requirements for such clauses. Assume that the law of the jurisdiction holds that liquidated damages clauses are enforceable only if they are a "reasonable estimate of actual damages" and are appropriate only in situations where actual damages are impossible or very difficult to prove. That test looks like a standard, elements-based legal rule, but there is ambiguity in

> **Try this: identifying theories and themes**
>
> Identify the theory of the case in the other sample simulation introduced in the Prologue: the Internet dating relationship case. Then identify two or more possible persuasive themes that are likely to resonate with most readers.
>
> You will want to do the same with the simulation or case file that you are currently working with. Remember that part of the exercise will be trying on different ways of framing.

two phrases, "reasonable estimate" and "difficult to prove." The lawyer arguing for the nonprofit organization will need to engage in some narrative reasoning about the relative expectations of the hotel and the organization at the time the contract was entered into. In that scenario, the theme becomes one of "fairness" by highlighting facts that show that actual damages were easy to calculate—indeed that the hotel didn't have *any* actual damages.

In short, the theme permeates the case and works together with the case theory.

John Lennon on ethos in storytelling

Back when the Beatles were in their heyday, John Lennon was known for his brash, outspoken personality. While his outlandish statements were often tongue in cheek, he occasionally created serious controversy. Perhaps the most dramatic example was when he said the Beatles were "bigger than Jesus Christ." That statement led thousands of young fans to protest, some even publicly burning their Beatles records. Later, Lennon created more controversy as an outspoken critic of the Vietnam War.

While Lennon continued to be outspoken, as he aged he took a somewhat less extreme approach in his public statements and consequently became a more effective social critic. A more mature Lennon acknowledged the limits of outrage as a tool of persuasion in his song Revolution:

> *You say you want a revolution*
> *Well you know, we all want*
> *to change the world . . .*
> *But if you go carrying pictures of Chairman Mao*
> *You ain't gonna make it with anyone anyhow.*

Lennon's caution—that the hypothetical of aligning one's political calls for change with one of the twentieth century's harshest critics of Western culture would likely be poorly received within the same Western culture that Mao criticized—has a parallel when it comes to persuasion in the law. When we represent a client, we often develop an understanding for his position. Lawyers are, after all, supposed to be zealous advocates. Thus, we tend to see the legal dispute from our client's perspective. This is a good thing. However, lawyers must also guard against being so zealous that our reader mistrusts us. So, as we show our client's story, both in the Statement of Facts and in the Argument, we must remember the Lennon Principle—avoid "carrying pictures of Chairman Mao." Instead, we need to tell the client's legal story in a way that fosters understanding in our reader without telling a story of extremist viewpoints.

D. Why the shadow story remains in the shadows

The next section of this chapter moves you into the process of writing the first draft of the fact section, by replacing all of the "tell" words in the shadow story with evidence and details that "show" the story you want your audience to hear. But first, it is important to understand why the shadow story remains in the shadows.

What the client wishes his lawyer to include in the legal storytelling might be different from what readers need or expect from the lawyer. Thus, there's a balancing act between the two main audiences of the lawyer's work product. For example, the client may want a "pit bull lawyer." Indeed, many clients have extreme, one-sided views of their legal story and want their lawyer to advocate from that perspective. At the same time, lawyers must be professional toward both the court and opposing counsel and parties. The lawyer's task becomes capturing the essence of her client's story without appearing to tell such a biased version as to lose credibility—for the lawyer and the client.

The shadow story is a key *tool* for understanding the client's point of view; it is an important means to an end—but only that. After capturing the client's passion in the shadow story, it's time to find ways to temper the story's presentation to maintain credibility. In revising, the lawyer looks for ways to *show* the client's passion without actually *telling* the court that the client is passionate.

II. Writing a working draft of the Statement of Facts

The Statement of Facts is a story waiting for its final ending. For a first working draft, it's fine to go ahead and return to all of the storytelling know-how acquired prior to law school, with a few primary caveats. First, this story is written on behalf of your client; it therefore should be written with the client's point of view and desired outcome firmly in mind and perhaps even placed up front in the opening paragraph as a framing concept.

Second, the story must be *shown* from the existing facts as opposed to *told* by means of the writer's speculation or judgment.

A. Incorporating the theme into your brief

After you decide on the theme for the case, you must look for ways to weave it subtly into your persuasive writing. Forgo using the word "theme" in a sentence because even a sentence that only hints at the word theme may sound phony and contrived. For example, omit sentences beginning with "The theme of this case is . . ." or "This case is about . . ." Both of those introductions lead to heavy-handed *telling* the reader what to think, rather than *showing* her. As previously explained, the more effective and persuasive strategy in the Statement of Facts is to show the reader something, through strategic use of concrete detail. Keeping your case theme in mind while writing the facts section will help you decide which details to include.

Both the theory of the case and your theme appear first in the Preliminary Statement, which we discuss in detail in Chapter 16. However, even though you want readers to understand both the theory and the theme from early in the brief, the Preliminary Statement usually one of the last sections that you'll write. The theory and the theme may be refined as you work through writing the Argument and the Statement of Facts. Thus, we revisit the theme and theory in the chapters ahead. For now, however, you want to select facts to write about that reveal your chosen theme or themes.

B. Use citable facts instead of unsupported opinions

The purpose of the Statement of Facts is to provide the reader with exactly that—the facts. A "fact" is something that either happened in the story between or among the parties, or something that exists in our everyday world. An easy way to remember the difference between a fact and something that isn't a fact is that facts are supportable by a citation to the record or by a credible source of information. An example of the latter might be historical weather records kept by a meteorological center. Cites to the record are important in Statements of Facts and are required by court rules in almost every jurisdiction in summary judgment, post-trial, and appellate briefs.

The absence of evidence may also be a "fact." For example, you might write in your Statement of Facts "at no point during the parties' argument did the plaintiff call the police." Including an absence of fact in the Statement of Facts is perfectly acceptable, so long as you refrain from making an unwarranted inferential leap. For example, adding that "therefore the plaintiff wasn't really afraid of the defendant," would be an inferential leap that is unsupportable by a citation to the record, and therefore must be omitted from the fact section. In your Argument, however, you could suggest that the court draw that inference.

Critically, there is a distinction between facts and opinions. In particular, the lawyer's opinion must stay outside of the Statement of the Facts. Lawyers are prohibited from testifying on behalf of their clients. It is the lawyer's role to be the storyteller rather than a character inside the story. In practical terms, that translates to a caution for legal writers to leave their own opinions and judgments out of the Statement of the Facts. The opinions and judgments of characters inside the story are certainly includable—as long as those opinions and judgments are in the record.

Opinion words typically make an appearance as adjectives or adverbs that attempt to tell rather than to show the reader what sorts of conclusions to make about the incident:

> The plaintiff obviously wasn't scared of the defendant.

That statement is someone's opinion. It might also be a conclusion of law if one of the legal elements involves fright on the part of the plaintiff. If there is no cite to testimony that the writer can provide for that statement, then the writer has included her own opinion.

A better way to show the same thing would be a sentence such as this:

> Although the plaintiff claimed at trial that she was afraid for her safety during her argument with the defendant, she admitted that she didn't call the police afterwards nor tell anyone about the incident until two days later when she was out socializing with friends at a happy hour.

Attorney testimony

Consider this example from a hypothetical brief:

> The three Bears came home, **absolutely shocked** to find that someone had entered their home, eaten their porridge, and broken Baby Bear's **favorite** chair. Papa Bear was **furious** and directed his **extreme** anger at the **poor** management of the secluded gated community.

All of the words in boldface are examples of the lawyer testifying, by opining about what the facts mean. Don't do that; write this instead:

> The three Bears came home to find that someone had entered their home, eaten their porridge, and broken Baby Bear's "favorite" chair. (R. at 3.) "That really pisses me off!" Papa Bear roared. (R. at 4.) "Why are we paying $1,000 per month for a neighborhood high-powered surveillance system when we can't even go for a walk without someone raiding our home?" (R. at 4.)

The facts contained in this version would all have record cites to support them, as does the second example in the shadow box. There's an inference that the writer is clearly trying to convey, but the writer has not testified herself.

C. Showing versus telling the story

In the above example, you may have noticed the increase in word count. But if the plaintiff's lack of fear is a key part of a legal story, then adding in extra description is worth those extra words. Those extra words allow the writer to guide what sort of mental images readers will be calling on, as they read and process the facts section of the document.

Recall our advice earlier in the chapter that you should *show* readers what is going on in the facts, rather than *tell* them. You do this by showing readers the facts in the case in enough detail that they see in their own minds what is going on and, from the words and mental images, arrive at the meanings and conclusions you hope to convey. Showing is very different from telling, which simply orders readers to think or feel a certain way about the story, based on the judgments or opinions of the writer.

1. Description of actions, settings, objects, and (sometimes) characters

To show a story, use description in key places. These four things are susceptible to description:

- Actions
- Settings
- Objects
- Characters

> **Avoid pitfalls when describing a character**
>
> Be particularly mindful of describing a character too fully all in one place in the Statement of Facts, especially in the opening paragraphs. Including too many details about a character may create skepticism in legal readers because it can look like a blatant appeal to emotion. Instead, spread those details out across the whole of the section.

Use strategic thinking to choose what to describe and how to describe it. **Increased detail emphasizes a point, whereas decreased detail deemphasizes a point.** Using more description in a particular part of the story will provide greater emphasis, as readers more carefully construct their mental images. As a corollary, decreasing the descriptive detail about actions, settings, objects, or characters will permit readers to either conjure any image that comes to mind or to form only fuzzy pictures before moving on to the next words in the section.

2. Selecting the specific details for the descriptions

Showing the precise image requires you to select details that will form the description. There are five types of details to choose from when describing objects, actions, settings, or characters.

- **The name**. A name can also include a category. For example, "national park" is a named category of settings.
- **The function**. For example, the first paragraph of the facts section of the SOFT brief in the hotel reservation example describes SOFT's function, concluding with the statement that the organization "has devoted its existence to promoting an exchange of ideas and information among climate scientists working on th[e] issue [of global warming]."
- **The history or development**. SOFT's brief in the hotel reservation example also provides a brief history of the organization, so that the court can get a mental image of the group as small but dedicated to a worthy cause.
- **Sensory information**. These are the details that specifically create visual images or that call on other senses. The look, sound, taste, smell, or texture of something are all sensory details.
- **Analogy to other objects, actions, settings, or characters**. An analogy detail describes something through comparison to other things—sometimes implicitly. In the hotel reservation example, the SOFT organization is described using both explicit and implicit analogy details:

    > SOFT's headquarters are in Ms. Freebird's home, although she charges no rent to SOFT. Operating costs are kept to a **bare minimum** by communicating and advertising primarily over the Internet and through e-mail.

    In that excerpt, the term "bare minimum" is an explicit analogy, while the other details create a vivid mental image of a small business run out of somebody's home. This plays into the writer's theme that SOFT is a small organization being unfairly taken advantage of by a multibillion dollar international hotel chain.

The fun—and the hard work—of the facts section is choosing which facts matter to both the legal theory of the case and your chosen theme, and to then select and place the details that best describe those facts.

III. Putting down the working draft of the Facts section

Once you have completed the first working draft, you'll want to set it aside for a while to get some distance from it. Keep an open mind; a significant amount of revision happens after you write the working drafts of the legal argument. When a lawyer is certain that the shadow story and first draft represent the *only* story of the dispute, that's when she's likely to get in trouble. Remember, there's another story out there. After all, the other party is not likely to go to the time and expense of opposing the client if the client's case is crystal clear. Now is the time to put the facts down and study the legal arguments. After writing them, you might decide that the archetype you thought was your second or third choice for your client has become the best and first choice. The theme might become more sharply in focus or it may change altogether. Chapter 15 returns to the Statement of Facts and discusses the last steps: shaping and polishing.

... we'll wait for you.

Chapter 10

Working with the law, part 1: interpreting statutes

Many legal issues begin with statutory analysis and interpretation. The foundation of statutory interpretation is quite simple: a court must interpret a statute so that the statute accomplishes what the legislature intended. It is not the court's role to determine whether a statute is effective or premised on good policy. It is the court's job to follow the legislature's intent, unless the statute is unconstitutional.

Finding the legislative intent, however, is not as easy as it might seem. Usually, the best evidence of legislative intent is the precise words that a legislature used in the statute. Courts begin with the premise that the legislature meant what it said, and if the meaning of a statute is clear on its face, the court will apply that plain meaning. However, meaning is a slippery thing, and lawyers often disagree about the plain meaning of a statute. Consequently, we often need to look beyond the plain meaning of a statute to determine the legislative intent.

We have several interpretive tools to aid us in this task. These tools can be either intrinsic or extrinsic. By "intrinsic tools," we mean those that we use to interpret the words of the statute itself. On the other hand, "extrinsic tools" look beyond the express words of the statute for clues as to the statute's meaning, for example, by examining legislative history.

Because the words of the statute are usually the best indicator of legislative intent, we begin with intrinsic tools that examine the text and context of our statute. The text-based tools, often called "canons of construction," are simply principles for interpreting language that assist us in determining the meaning of the specific words of a statute. In addition, we have canons that are context based. We use these tools to draw meaning from the language that surrounds the disputed term or phrase. This may include the surrounding sections of the statute or related statutes that use the same terms. Finally, there are canons of general construction, principles that do not aid in interpreting specific statutory language but provide broader concepts of interpretation. For example, we prefer constitutional interpretations to unconstitutional interpretations. (Courts will assume that the legislature does not intend to pass unconstitutional laws, so it makes sense that, when given a choice, courts will opt for an interpretation that does not violate the Constitution over one that does.)

When the intrinsic tools do not resolve statutory ambiguity, a court will look beyond the text of a statute to the extrinsic tool of legislative history. Legislative history is simply the various records of the process of enacting a statute. This includes testimony before legislative committees, committee reports, various versions of a bill, and other documents that were created while the legislature was deliberating on pending legislation. In addition, a court will sometimes look beyond the legislative history to the broader historical context in which legislation was enacted.

Finally, some courts will look to find the legislative purpose behind a statute. For example, a remedial statute, such as most environmental legislation, may be broadly interpreted to give effect to the goal the legislature had when it enacted the statute. Thus, the meaning of "navigable waters of the United States" is given a broad meaning under the Clean Water Act because courts interpret the legislative goal of the Act to protect as much of the waters of the United States as possible.

> **Legislative history versus legislative intent**
>
> Students sometimes use the terms "legislative history" and "legislative intent" interchangeably. This is a bit like confusing a hammer for a blueprint. Legislative history—the record of a statute's enactment—is one tool of statutory interpretation. Legislative intent, on the other hand, is the guiding principle of all statutory interpretation. We use all of our interpretive tools, including the plain meaning, contextual canons, legislative history, and the rest, to determine the legislative intent of a statute. The legislative intent is what the legislature meant a statute to do. The legislative history is one tool that helps us figure out that meaning.

This chapter provides an overview of the most common statutory interpretive tools. Some of these tools may be familiar to you already.

I. How to read a statute

Reading a statute requires precision. Remember that most statutory disputes are about the meaning of a single word or phrase. Thus, as we first read a statute, we must remember that every word counts. It is impossible, of course, to predict which words are likely to be disputed, but we can start with a framework that can help identify the likely scope, meaning, and potential ambiguities of most statutes. There are two initial steps to getting an understanding of a statute. First, read the statute in its entire context, not just the section you found. Second, begin reading the relevant sections of the statute critically.

Before we begin, it is important to understand the difference between statutes and codes. A "statute" is what the legislature votes on and is ultimately signed into law by the executive branch. Statutes generally are broken down into discrete "sections," which serve different functions (as we will describe in a moment). A "code" is a book that publishes most, but sometimes not all,[1] of the sections of the statute. Often the individual sections are sequentially numbered in the code; these numbers may or may not reflect the numbering sequence of the original statute passed by the legislature. But sometimes, different parts of the statute are placed in different "titles" or "chapters" of the code because the statute may be complex and may affect different parts of the law. For example, the Patient Protection and Affordable Care Act adopted by Congress in 2010 was codified in many different titles of the United States Code because some sections of the Act affected business and labor while other sections affected taxes.

When you research, either electronically or in books, the best and easiest way to research is in the code (either federal or state). That's because the code books (especially the electronic versions in commercial databases) are updated frequently as the legislature adopts amendments to previous statutes. But remember that when you find a section of a statute in a code, what you are looking at needs to be read in the context of related sections of the code. Sometimes those sections are part of a single statute adopted by a legislature, while other times they are a combination of statutes adopted over many years. The "legislative intent" must therefore be determined by looking at the entire context of the statute, not just the single section that your research found.

A. The statutory context

When researching statutes, you will generally find specific provisions, or sections, that satisfy your search criteria. Often, your search will lead to a section that appears to be highly relevant to the issue you are researching.

---

[1]For example, sections that have a temporary effect, such as budgetary provisions, will not appear in the permanent code.

But that section was probably not enacted by itself. It is most likely part of a larger statute, or several statutes, that contains multiple, related sections. For example, the statutory provision that prohibits the "taking" of endangered species[2] is part of the broader statute generally known as the Endangered Species Act.[3]

Thus, even when it looks like the section you found answers your research question, you must examine the entire statutory context to fully understand how the section you found relates to your legal question.

A typical statute adopted by a legislature often includes most or all of the following sections:

- Title
- Purpose or Preamble
- Definitions
- Scope (situations to which the statute does or does not apply)
- Operative (general rule; what's prohibited or required, etc.)
- Exceptions (if not included in operative sections, definitions, or scope)
- Enforcement (penalties or remedial provisions)
- Cross-references
- Severability or savings clause
- Effective date

B. Reading the statute critically

Once you have a sense of the overall statutory context, it is time to look more critically at the sections that are relevant to your issue. Ask the following questions for any statute you need to interpret:

- To whom does the statute apply? (The court? The state? "Any person"? Employers? Tenants?) Once you have figured out to whom the statute applies, you will need to figure out whether that includes the people involved in your dispute.
- Does the statute provide any express definitions of key terms? Many of the words used in the operative provisions may have special meanings assigned by the definitions section; these definitions may change your analysis of whether the statute

---

[2] 16 U.S.C. §1538 (2010).
[3] *Id.* §§1531–1544. Note that this single act of the legislature (the statute) is codified in numerous sections of the United States Code.

applies at all, to whom it applies, or any of the questions listed above.

- What does the statute require, permit, or prohibit? All statutes affect people's conduct. Is your statute demanding some action by someone? Granting rights to someone? Restricting someone's behavior? Be sure you can identify the specific conduct being regulated.
- Are there any exceptions to the general rule?
- What consequences attach to noncompliance? Does the statute provide some remedy for an offended party? Require some punishment or sanction? Does it allow someone to bring a claim in court? If so, what court?
- When does the statute apply? Always make sure you are reading the relevant version of the statute. Usually, the current version of a statute is the version that applies to your problem. However, if a code section was recently amended, an earlier version of the statute may apply. You will learn how to find out when a code section was amended in your research class.

By way of example, this is how it works in the Internet dating example. That case raises an issue about whether Ms. Hawthorne was a victim of domestic violence as defined by a New Jersey statute, *N.J.S.A.* 2C:25-19(d).[4] An experienced critical reader would first parse the statute to make it easier to see its component parts. Here's the relevant statutory section:

> d. "Victim of domestic violence" means a person protected under this act and shall include any person who is 18 years of age or older or who is an emancipated minor and who has been subjected to domestic violence by a spouse, former spouse, or any other person who is a present or former household member. "Victim of domestic violence" also includes any person, regardless of age, who has been subjected to domestic violence by a person with whom the victim has a child in common, or with whom the victim anticipates having a child in common, if one of the parties is pregnant. "Victim of domestic violence" also includes any person who has been subjected to domestic violence by a person with whom the victim has had a dating relationship.

---

[4]New Jersey citation form is being used here. Note that as a lawyer briefing to a New Jersey court, you would use local court citation rules, as shown here, rather than general ALWD or Bluebook format. *Compare* Assn. of Leg. Writing Directors & Darby Dickerson, *ALWD Citation Manual: A Professional System of Citation* app. 2 (4th ed., Wolters Kluwer L. & Bus. 2010), *with id.* app. 1.

Here's how we might break this down:

"Victim of domestic violence" means:

1. A person who is 18 or older OR an emancipated minor, AND

   who has been subjected to domestic violence by a:
   spouse; former spouse;
   OR
   A present or former household member.
   OR

2. Any person who has been subjected to domestic violence by a person with whom:
   The victim has a child in common;
   OR
   the victim anticipates having a child in common IF one of the parties is pregnant.
   OR

3. A person who has been subjected to domestic violence by a person with whom the victim has a dating relationship.

Once we have parsed the statute into its component parts, it becomes much easier to answer the questions we need to ask to understand the scope of legal issue:

1. To whom does the statute apply?

The statute identifies three potential ways to be a "victim of domestic violence." A person must suffer domestic violence by a spouse, former spouse, or household member (if the victim is at least 18); the parent of their child or potential parent if one party is pregnant; or someone in a dating relationship with the abused.

2. Does the statute provide any express definitions of key terms?

The statute defines "victim of domestic violence." However, we should also look within this definition to see if it uses any other terms that are defined by the statute. For example, "domestic violence," "household member," and "dating relationship" are all potentially ambiguous terms that may defined either within the statute itself or by case law.

3. What does the statute require, permit, or prohibit?

Because this statute is a definition, it does not create any obligation or right by itself. Once we understand the meaning of the definition, we would need to look elsewhere in the statutory scheme to determine how this definition fits within those parts of the statute that do create obligations or rights.

4. What are the exceptions to the general rule?

The definition does not create any explicit exceptions. If a person does not fit with the meaning of "victim of domestic violence," she is going to be excluded from the scope of the statute. Note that this conclusion is itself an application of the canon of construction *expression unius est exclusion alterius*, which means that the inclusion of items in a list implies that other things are excluded, which we will discuss in the next section.

5. What is the consequence of not complying?

Again, because this is a definition provision, it does not have any penalty or sanction for not complying with it. What rights are given to people who fall within the definition are specified in the operative sections of the overall statute, so you would need to look there.

6. When does the statute apply?

We will need to do a bit more research to find out when this definition was enacted and, more important, when was its effective date. If it was enacted after the incident giving rise to our dispute, it will most likely not apply to our case.

Once you have answered these questions, it is time to start looking for the terms that are likely to be at issue in your dispute. Of course, you already know that in the Internet dating example, the issue is the meaning of "dating relationship." However, the author of the brief could not have determined this without first carefully parsing the statute and analyzing all the potential issues. This is the heart of statutory interpretation. There are many interpretive tools at our disposal. The following sections provide an overview of the most common interpretive tools, beginning with the text of the statute and its plain meaning.

II. Text-based interpretive tools

The beginning of all statutory interpretation is the words of the statute itself. This section reviews some of the most common text-based tools of statutory interpretation. This is not an exhaustive review. The first step is to consider the plain meaning of the text. Of course, opposing lawyers often disagree on the plain meaning of the most common words in a statute. Thus, we need to look deeper into the text of the statute by relying on the canons of construction.

Note that this is not an exhaustive list of intrinsic interpretive tools. For a more thorough review, you may wish to consult a treatise on statutory interpretation.[5]

A. Plain meaning

Since the ultimate purpose of statutory interpretation is to determine the intent of the legislature, the starting point for all statutory interpretation is the "plain meaning" rule. That is, when the statute is clearly worded and susceptible to only one reasonable interpretation, that is the "plain meaning" and the court needs go no further in interpreting the statute. Stated another way, the plain meaning of a term is its ordinary and everyday usage. If a term's meaning is clear on its face, then there is no need to look beyond the plain meaning of its terms. That seems simple, but in practice is less so. For example, let's look at a simple dog bite statute:

> The owner of any dog is liable for the damages suffered by any person who is bitten by the dog. . . .

Cal. Civil Code §3342 (1997).

This statute would clearly include a situation involving a labradoodle. The plain meaning of "dog" would not be in question. On the other hand, the statutory term "bitten" might be arguably ambiguous. For example, if the labradoodle didn't attack but only ripped a person's jacket while playing in a dog park, was the person "bitten" per the statute? Does the statute require the dog actually to bite the person, or does biting the jacket also establish liability? What if the dog playfully put his jaws around somebody's arm, but did not break the skin?

To determine the meaning of "bitten," we might first look to the dictionary meaning. Often courts will use dictionaries as sources of finding the plain meaning of a term. However, if a dictionary gives us insufficient guidance, we may then look to other textual evidence of the legislature's intent.

---

[5]For a thorough examination of how one state's courts use textual canons, see *Interpreting Oregon Law* (Jack Landau et al. eds., Or. St. B. 2009).

B. Canons of construction

In addition to the plain meaning rule, there are many interpretive principles, or "canons of construction," that help us give meaning to the text of a statute. While "canon" may sound like an immutable and powerful tool, these canons really are just basic principles of how we interpret text. In other words, they are specific expressions of what most would consider common sense.

These canons can be very instructive. However, as Karl Llewellyn pointed out decades ago, for every canon, there is an "equal and opposite canon" that could suggest an alternate meaning.[6] The most persuasive canon is usually that which seems most consistent with other interpretive tools. One rule of thumb is that if your interpretation of a statute suggests a meaning that is contrary to common sense, you will most certainly lose, no matter how elegantly you apply the canons of construction.

Here are some of the most common canons of construction:

1. The plain meaning rule

Yes, the plain meaning rule is a canon of construction. It is where all statutory interpretation should start.

2. Canons regarding specific words

- "May" is permissive, that is, it gives discretion to someone.
- "Shall" and "must" are mandatory, that is, they create a legal duty or obligation to someone.[7]
- "Or" is a disjunctive connector, establishing alternatives.
- "And" is a conjunctive connector, establishing multiple requirements (e.g., the elements of a cause of action are always connected with an "and").

3. Canon regarding grammar

- Doctrine of the last antecedent: a referring phrase applies only to the last antecedent unless the referring phrase is separated by a comma or context suggests otherwise:

  I saw Juan and Mary **with a puppy**. (Only Mary was with a puppy.)

  I saw Juan and Mary, **with a puppy**. (Both Juan and Mary were with a puppy.)

---

[6]Karl N. Llewellyn, *The Common Law Tradition: Deciding Appeals* 521–535 (Little, Brown 1960).
[7]Note, however, that a number of cases have interpreted the word "shall" to mean "may."

4. Canons regarding lists of things

- *Noscitur a sociis:* Interpret ambiguous words in a list by the company they keep:

  > A city zoning ordinance of Michigan City, Indiana, established a height restriction of 30 feet in residential areas. A homeowner applied for, and was granted, a building permit to build a second-floor addition to his home and a 55-foot-tall tower, topped by a room enclosed in glass to provide scenic views of Lake Michigan. The homeowner claimed that his observation tower was a "tower" that could extend 25 feet above the normal 35-foot height restriction. The homeowner argued, and the city agreed, that the zoning ordinance's exception for "towers" permitted this structure to be built.

  > That controlling zoning ordinance's exception allowed "penthouses or roof structures for the housing of elevators, stairways, tanks, ventilating fans, or similar equipment required to operate or maintain the structure, and fire or parapet walls, skylights, towers, steeples, flagpoles, chimneys, smokestacks, radio and television aerials, wireless masts, electric and telephone service poles, water tanks, silos, storage hoppers, elevators or similar structures" to exceed the height restriction by no more than 25 feet. The Indiana Court of Appeals, applying the canon of *noscitur a sociis*, held that the word "tower" must be interpreted to be similar to the other words in the list: structures that are not habitable. Since the observation room atop the "tower" was habitable, the court decided that the room did not fit within the zoning ordinance's exception. *Ross v. Harris*, 860 N.E.2d 602 (Ind. Ct. App. 2006).

- *Ejusdem generis:* When a list of terms is followed by a general catchall phrase, that phrase should be interpreted to be consistent with the specific terms of the list:

  > The Motor Vehicle Theft Act defined "motor vehicle" to include "an automobile, automobile truck, automobile wagon, motorcycle or any other vehicle not designed for running on rails." 18 U.S.C. § 408 (1926). In *McBoyle v. U.S.*, 283 U.S. 25 (1931), the issue was whether an airplane was a "motor vehicle." Because all of the specific terms in the list were vehicles that moved on land, the Court held that "any other vehicle" applied only to vehicles that ran on land, not those that fly. *McBoyle*, 283 U.S. at 27.

- *Expressio unius est exclusio alterius:* The inclusion of one thing implies the exclusion of other things not included. When a statutory list includes several things and does not include a catchall phrase, the court will not include within its scope those things that are not expressly listed:

  > A statute that exempted from real estate taxes property owned by a municipal government for "streets, sewer lines, water lines, and

other municipal purposes" did not exempt a power plant and electric lines operated by a municipal government since those things were not included on the list of exempt purposes. *Town of Pine Bluffs v. St. Bd. of Equalization*, 333 P.2d 700 (Wyo. 1958).

5. *Other textual canons*

- *The court may not omit what has been included nor add what has been excluded.* If an interpretation of a statute requires adding language to the statute or ignoring words that are included in a statute, that interpretation is disfavored. This canon is premised on the principle that the legislature crafts statutes with care, and it is not the court's role to amend the express language of the legislature.
- *Construe terms consistently throughout a statute.* When the legislature uses the same term in different provisions of a statute, the court will give that term the same meaning in every provision.

C. Contextual canons

In addition to textual canons, a court also considers the context of the statutory term at issue. It is sometimes difficult to distinguish between "text" and "context." Text is the specific term at issue, and context is the text surrounding the specific term at issue. However, for most purposes, this distinction is not important. Rather, the key is to begin your statutory analysis with intrinsic interpretive tools, that is, the words of the statute—including both the specific terms and the context in which they are found. That said, there are two kinds of context interpretive tools: the surrounding statutory context and the historical context.

1. *The statutory context: definitions and* **in pari materia**

The statutory context includes looking at other sections of the same statutory scheme. The statutory scheme may include a list of specially defined terms as well as a statement of legislative purpose. These sections, and others as well, may shed light on the meaning of a particular term in a different section of the statute.

One section that you must always consult is the definitions section. Definitions can resolve potential ambiguity by giving a precise meaning to a statutory term. On the other hand, definitions sometimes *create* ambiguity when the plain meaning appears obvious from the text. Remember, definition sections are not a tiebreaker to resolve ambiguities arising from textual analysis. Definitions trump any other interpretive tool as they reflect the legislature's specific intent as to the meaning of the defined term. In addition, other statutes that govern the same subject or have a similar purpose are said to be *in pari materia*. In other words, the meaning we give a term in one statute should generally be given the same meaning in a related statute. The idea behind this principle is that the legislature is aware of all of its previous enactments and if it uses the same word in a statute with a similar purpose as

How to craft an *in para materia* argument

1. Widen the lens through which you are looking at the particular statute to come up with a broader category

One way to do this is to look at the overall indexing of the statute. Criminal statutes, for example, are often grouped together by type of crimes. If you obtained the statute electronically, you can still easily expand the search to see the broader categories (and sometimes they are just listed at the top of the page). Or, click the Table of Contents button at the top of the screen to see where this section appears in relation to other parts of the codified statute.

2. Once you have that broad lens, think of other statutes that fit into the same category

This may be a repetitive step if the statute's indexing system helps you. But otherwise you will have to think creatively in step one to get here. For example, if you need help answering a question about the Endangered Species Act, you might broaden your scope of research to include other statutes that protect animals. The Migratory Bird Act or the Bald Eagle Act might give you some clues. If they don't, then you might widen the scope even further to statutes that are also designed to protect natural resources. Is there something in the Clean Water Act that could help your argument?

3. Research those other items in the category and see whether they provide some interpretive answers

These answers may come from different sources. For example, a related statute may provide a specific definition for a particular term. Or a court may have interpreted the term in the context of the related statute. The more consistent interpretations you find, the stronger the in pari materia argument is likely to be.

4. Communicate to the reader that there are analogous interpretations to the statute you are dealing with

You are going to need to walk your reader through the steps that you just took to get to the analogy.

5. Recognize when it isn't working

It is important to note that not all statutes are appropriate for an in pari materia argument. For example, "residence" may have a different meaning in tax law than it does for immigration law.

an existing statute, the legislature probably intended that word to have the same meaning in both statutes.

2. Consider the historical context

Sometimes a court looks to the broader context in which a statute was enacted. For example, the PATRIOT Act was adopted shortly after the September 11, 2001, attacks on the World Trade Center and the Pentagon. At that time, there was widespread concern in the United States that law enforcement lacked the powers it needed to protect citizens from future terrorist attacks. Those concerns undoubtedly played a role in the drafting of the Act, and the historical context could be useful in interpreting the statute to be consistent with Congress's intent in passing it.

D. Substantive canons

In addition to text and context, there are some canons explaining general principles of interpretation. These substantive canons are not about how to interpret particular terms, but rather reflect broader, often policy-based, principles.

1. Punitive statutes are to be narrowly construed; remedial statutes are to be broadly construed

When a statute's primary effect is to punish, it will be narrowly construed. On the other hand, a statute that is primarily designed to remedy a problem (for example, an environmental protection statute) should be broadly construed to meet the legislative purpose.

2. Constitutional interpretations are favored over unconstitutional interpretations

When a court is faced with two possible interpretations of a statute, and one would make the statute unconstitutional, the court will favor the other interpretation. For example, when the Affordable Care Act was before the United States Supreme Court, one of the issues was whether the "penalty" imposed on individuals who did not purchase health insurance was a tax authorized under Congress's taxing power. If so, the statute would be constitutional; if not, the statute would not be constitutional. Chief Justice Roberts, in writing for the majority, held that because the penalty could reasonably be read as a tax, it was constitutionally valid.[8]

---

[8] *Natl. Fedn. of Indep. Bus. v. Sebelius*, 132 S. Ct. 2566 (2012).

3. The legislature does not intend absurd results

Similar to the constitutional preference canon, courts likewise disfavor interpretations that lead to absurd results. Thus, if the meaning of a statute appears clear on its face, but that meaning leads to a result that is clearly absurd, the court will reject that meaning in favor of one that is not absurd.

4. Statutes codifying the common law are to be broadly construed; statutes in derogation of the common law are to be narrowly construed

Many statutes simply mirror the existing common law. In essence the legislature enacts statutes to ensure the common law continues. In such cases, the statute is to be broadly construed to reflect the policies underlying the common law. On the other hand, when the legislature passes a law that changes (i.e., is "in derogation of") the common law, it is to be narrowly construed.

5. The rule of lenity

Similar to the rule that punitive statutes are to be narrowly construed, statutes that impose either criminal or civil sanctions (such as fines) are also to be read narrowly. Ambiguous terms in such statutes should be construed so as to impose the penalties in the fewest circumstances possible. This is premised on the need to ensure the law provides clear notice as to the scope of the law.

III. Purpose-based interpretation

Sometimes the express text of a statute remains ambiguous even after thorough application of the canons of construction and careful review of legislative history. On occasion, an apparently reasonable interpretation of a statutory term or phrase will lead to a result that seems contrary to a fundamental goal of the statute. In these situations, a court will expand its interpretation of the term or phrase to examine the underlying purpose of the statute. If faced with a choice between one interpretation that furthers the legislative purpose and one that does not, the court may adopt the one that furthers the purpose, even if a literal reading of the statute suggests a different result.

Keep in mind two important points about purpose-based arguments. First, you need some authority to establish what the legislative purpose of a statute is. For some statutes, the legislature will include a statement of purpose or similar provision at the beginning of the statute. Such statements tend to be aspirational and may set goals that are not realistic. Thus, even when the legislature has provided an explicit expression of purpose, a court may be unwilling to further that goal when the express language of the statute suggests a different result.

The respondent's brief in the Internet dating case provides a good example of how to use legislative purpose to give meaning to a statutory term:

> The pertinent section of the statute does not provide a definition of what constitutes a "dating relationship." Interpreting courts have rejected the notion of an absolute or plain meaning to the phrase. Instead, courts will interpret it in light of the policy set out by the New Jersey Supreme Court to look at the Act through a broad lens. *Cesare v. Cesare*, 154 *N.J.* 394 (1998). The New Jersey Supreme Court has stressed the importance of a liberal interpretation "to achieve its salutary purposes" so as to "'assure the victims of domestic violence the maximum protection from abuse the law can provide.'" *Id.* at 399.
>
> Because the legislature has called for a liberal construction, courts have developed and use an expansive and liberally construed factor test to determine when parties are in a dating relationship. . . .

In this example, the author has a particularly strong legislative purpose argument because the New Jersey Supreme Court has already relied on the statute's express "salutary purposes" to interpret the statute broadly. Because the *Cesare* court held that the statute should be interpreted broadly to meet the legislative purpose, this same principle should be applied here.

Another place that we may find evidence of legislative purpose is in the legislative history. Statements in the legislative history can be persuasive, but the usual cautions discussed above apply. Remember, unlike express statements of purpose, the legislative history is never expressly approved by the legislature as a whole.

The second point about legislative purpose is that we should not confuse it with legislative intent. Legislatures often pass a broadly worded aspirational Purpose section of a statute, as Congress did in the Endangered Species Act. However, that broad aspirational language will only get the lawyer so far when interpreting a specific section of a statute. Remember, all statutory interpretation is aimed at finding the legislative *intent* of the specific statutory language at issue. Understanding the stated purpose of the legislation can be a useful tool in finding that legislative intent. However, what a legislature states as its broad goal is not the same thing as the mechanism it establishes to achieve that goal. If, for example, a specific term seems to be more limiting than the broadly stated purpose, a court will often give that term its more natural, limited meaning rather than stretch its meaning to fit the wider scope suggested by the stated legislative purpose. Remember that the stated purpose of any legislation is simply an aid to the court in resolving ambiguities in the operative sections. If the court finds no ambiguity in the operative sections, it will never look at the Purpose section.

How legislative purpose saved the snail darter . . .

One of the best examples of how legislative purpose can reveal legislative intent of a particular statutory term is found in *Tennessee Valley Authority v. Hill*, 437 U.S. 153 (1978). In that case, plaintiffs sought to prevent the operation of the newly built Tellico Dam on the Little Tennessee River because the dam threatened the habitat of the endangered snail darter. The snail darter was a three-inch fish found only in this area of the Little Tennessee River. The TVA argued that Congress could not have intended the Endangered Species Act to prevent the operation of a fully built, federally funded dam just to save an obscure fish—especially considering that there were more than 130 different species of darter in the United States. However, the Court noted that the expressly stated purpose of the Endangered Species Act was the far-reaching protection of endangered species:

> As it was finally passed, the Endangered Species Act of 1973 represented the most comprehensive legislation for the preservation of endangered species ever enacted by any nation. Its stated purposes were "to provide a means whereby the ecosystems upon which endangered species and threatened species depend may be conserved," and "to provide a program for the conservation of such . . . species. . . ."

Id. at 180.

This expansive purpose of the Act reflected the congressional intent that the Act be broadly construed to protect endangered species habitat. Even though Congress had continued to fund the construction of the dam after the snail darter had been listed as an endangered species, the Court held that the stated purpose of the Endangered Species Act would prevail despite any potential economic losses resulting from not building the dam.

IV. Legislative history

Sometimes, application of the canons of construction and other tools of interpreting a statute based solely on the words of the statute do not yield a clear answer. In that situation, courts sometimes look to extrinsic evidence to determine what the legislature intended. One tool for this is to examine the "legislative history" of the statute, including testimony before committees that considered the bill, committee reports, amendments added or rejected during deliberations, and other documentation developed as the bill worked its way through the legislature.

Legislative history can be a slippery thing. For significant legislation, the history can be voluminous. It is often possible to find conflicting evidence of the legislature's intent within the history. A plaintiff may be able to find testimony before a committee that supports her position while the defendant can point to a floor debate that suggests just the opposite meaning. It is sometimes easy to pick and choose the selective legislative history that favors your position and discount that which does not. As Judge Harold Leventhal is credited with saying, "the trick is to look over the heads of the crowd and pick out your friends."[9] On the other hand, sometimes the legislative history is frustratingly silent. It is surprising how often a legislature simply didn't consider a situation that, in hindsight, seems to go to the heart of a statute. In those cases, legislative history cannot help us.

You should also remember that nobody votes on most forms of legislative history. That one witness testified as to the meaning of a particular phrase does not mean that the legislature collectively agreed with that witness. Justice Antonin Scalia, who has frequently criticized the usefulness of legislative history, notes that "resort to legislative history to determine legislative meaning is at best a shaky endeavor."[10]

Justice Scalia's cautionary admonition notwithstanding, there are a few guiding principles that can help us assess the persuasiveness of particular legislative history. As a starting point, remember that the purpose of legislative history is to show what the legislators were thinking when they enacted a particular law. From that starting point, we can draw a number of other principles.

A. The more the merrier

Legislative history is most illuminating when it reveals a consistent interpretation of a statute throughout the legislative process. If hearing witnesses, committee reports, sponsor statements, and floor debates all

---

[9]Antonin Scalia, *Common Law Courts in a Civil-Law System: The Role of United States Federal Courts in Interpreting the Constitution and Laws*, in *A Matter of Interpretation: Federal Courts and the Law* 36 (Amy Gutmann ed., Princeton U. Press 1997).
[10]*Nat. Resources Def. Fund v. EPA*, 948 F.2d 345, 350 (7th Cir. 1991).

consistently suggest a particular meaning, there's a good chance that the legislature as a whole agreed with that interpretation. On the other hand, a single remark in a committee hearing would have been heard only by committee members who were present for that testimony, and there's no guarantee that they even agreed with the statement. Thus, the more consistent the evidence you can find in the legislative history, the more likely that evidence will be seen as reliable.

B. Who's talking makes a difference

Throughout the legislative process, many people may comment on proposed legislation, including the bill's sponsors, other legislators, lobbyists (who may be representing an organization pushing for the legislation), agency administrators who may ultimately be charged with enforcing the law, and other interested people. A court will not view all of these people equally. Generally, those with the most expertise or interest in the bill will be accorded the most weight. Thus, bill sponsors tend to be given more deference than other legislators. Legislators are given more deference than nonlegislators. Administrative experts are given more deference than other interested citizens.

As with most legislative history principles, this general hierarchy is quite fluid and depends on the specific circumstances of the legislation. For example, nonlegislators generally have less sway than legislators do. However, a spokesperson for an organization that is promoting the legislation may be given considerable deference as one who likely had considerable influence with the enacting legislature. One way to consider how much weight to give a particular speaker's statements is to think about the ethos of the speaker. The more knowledgeable, respected, and powerful the speaker, the greater the deference will be given to her assertions.

C. Not all legislative history is created equal

Some forms of legislative history are more valuable than other forms. In most instances, committee reports are the most helpful. These reports reflect the consensus of the committees that recommended a bill to the larger legislative body. They are the careful considerations of the legislators who have spent the most time working through the details of the bill and have, at the very least, been approved by the majority of the committee. Furthermore, at least in theory, every member of the legislature at least had the opportunity to read the bill before voting on the proposed law.

Another powerful source of legislative history can be changes, amendments, and deletions to a bill that occur in the legislative process. These include things like floor amendments, though they are not always made on the floor. If "black" is in the original version of a bill and the legislature changes it to "white" in the final version, we have a strong indicator that this change was intentional and that the legislature did not mean "black" when it said "white."

As a general rule, the more likely that a piece of legislative history reflects the understanding of a broad base of legislators, the stronger it indicates the legislative intent.

D. Hindsight is not insight

Sometimes a legislator or an executive who signs the bill may comment on the meaning of a law after it is passed. Such comments, even by a bill's sponsor, are generally given little weight. It is true that such statements may reveal what that particular legislator thought about the meaning of the law. However, statements made after enactment necessarily could not have influenced the rest of the legislature at the time it voted on the bill. Because the purpose of legislative history is to reveal the collective thinking of the legislature at the time of enactment, post hoc explanations are generally not helpful.

E. No one voted on this stuff

Remember that legislative history is only an indicator of the meaning of a statute. It is not the statute itself. The legislature never expressly approves statements made in legislative history. Even a clear, persuasive explanation of a statutory provision is nothing more than the author's opinion. Thus, even a really helpful statement in the legislative history cannot trump the plain meaning of a statute. Legislative history can reveal legislative intent; it cannot create it out of whole cloth.

V. Case law

For many statutory issues, we have more than just the statute itself to guide us. If a court has interpreted a statute, that interpretation becomes binding precedent that should control similar cases in the future through the principle of stare decisis. Thus, if we have binding case law that interprets a specific term that is relevant to our dispute, our interpretive task may be quite simple—the statute means what the court says it means.

Of course, opposing parties may disagree as to how the court interpretation applies to a particular set of facts. In that case, our statutory issue becomes similar to a common law analysis in which comparing and contrasting precedent cases becomes important.

The Internet dating case provides a good example of how case law has refined the meaning of a statute. The statute itself does not define "dating relationship." However, through several cases, we know that the term should be broadly construed. We also know that courts have developed several factors to consider when determining whether a particular situation constituted a dating relationship. In cases like this, these court decisions effectively amend the statute and make it easier to determine its meaning.

Judicial interpretations can be useful even when they have not addressed our exact statutory question. For example, if a court addressed a related issue, perhaps interpreting a related term, or even our term in a different context, we can draw on its reasoning. If the court cited specific legislative history, that history should be persuasive in our case as well. Likewise, if the court cited the purpose section with approval, or relied on a particular canon of construction, those same interpretive tools should resonate again in our case.

Finally, it is important to remember that, at least in theory, if a court misconstrues the legislative intent of a statute, the legislature can amend the statute to correct the court.

Obviously, when the legislature effectively overrules a court decision, the original court decision is no longer good law. However, the legislature's failure to react to a court opinion can also be informative. If the legislature chooses not to correct a court decision, one may reasonably argue that the court must have interpreted the statute correctly. In essence, legislative silence implies agreement with the court's interpretation. This is particularly likely when the legislature amends other parts of a statute after a court has interpreted it, but leaves the section that the court interpreted unchanged.

> **. . . but amended legislation abandoned the snail darter once and for all**
>
> This is what happened after the snail darter case, *TVA v. Hill*. Two years after the decision in *TVA v. Hill*, Congress passed another statute expressly authorizing the completion of the dam, notwithstanding the snail darter. The dam was completed and brought online. The snail darter soon disappeared from the Little Tennessee River. Fortunately for the snail darter, small populations of it have been found in other rivers.

VI. Administrative interpretations

You may have had only limited experience with administrative law in your first year of law school. This is simply because of the time constraints of the 1L curriculum. Administrative law is a large and important source of law. Administrative agencies, at both the state and federal levels, have tremendous power. These powers include interpreting statutes. Indeed, many of the details of a statutory scheme are left to specific agencies to determine. For example, the subtleties of preserving specific endangered species is far too complicated for the U.S. Congress to sort out. Thus, when it enacted the Clean Air Act, it gave the Environmental Protection Agency the power to promulgate rules that establish most of the specific details of the Act. The EPA has expertise in environmental protection and thus is best equipped to develop rules that carry out the statutory purpose.

Lawyers, judges, and scholars debate just how much discretion a court should give an agency's interpretation of a statute. Courts recognize that agencies have greater expertise in their specific areas and will defer to that expertise. On the other hand, courts are experts in interpreting statutes. Just how willing a court is to defer to agencies will depend on the particular circumstances of each case. The somewhat complex principles regarding agency deference are beyond the scope of this book. You will study it in detail in administrative law classes. However, if you're working on a problem involving an administrative regulation, there's a good chance that the degree of deference a court gives to that regulation will be a central issue of your problem.

VII. How to craft a statutory interpretation argument

You are the West Dakota state prosecutor in a criminal mischief case: a woman defendant has been charged with criminal mischief. After finding out that her spouse was having an affair, she used a sledge hammer and sulfuric acid to destroy their jointly owned vintage 1957 Chevy Impala, formerly in mint condition. The spouse has pressed charges. The criminal mischief statute in this jurisdiction defines the crime as "the intentional destruction of the property of another." The defendant has filed a motion to dismiss the charges, arguing that the language of the statute precludes her prosecution because she was an owner of the car and therefore the property was not "of another." There is no case law interpreting the criminal mischief statute that addresses the issue. Can you make an argument that is supported by persuasive legal authority?

The first argument that you may make (and should always try to make, when plausible) is the plain meaning argument. For example, the argument may begin, "The language of the statute contains no exclusion to it. Nor is the common understanding of the phrase one of exclusion. Rather, the phrase 'property of another' is merely descriptive of one aspect of the property's ownership. As is within the average person's understanding, it is entirely possible for property simultaneously to be owned by multiple people."

This is a pretty good start. But adding a textual interpretive argument can really drive home the point. In this case, we might consider the following steps.

A. Look at the statute through a broader lens to come up with a category

One way to do this is to look at the overall indexing of the statute. Criminal statutes, for example, are often grouped together by type of crimes. If you obtained the statute electronically, you can still easily expand the search to see the broader categories or look at the table of contents to see the bigger picture. What kind of statute is similar to a criminal mischief statute? Does the indexing of the statute help? It turns out that criminal mischief is grouped under the chapter "crimes against property." That could be useful.

B. Look for other statutes that fit into the same category

This may be a repetitive step if the statute's indexing system helps you. But otherwise, you will have to think creatively in step one to get here. For example, the chapter that includes criminal mischief also includes other crimes against property: theft, burglary, larceny, and arson.

C. Research related statutes

These answers may come from different sources. For example, a related statute may provide a specific definition for a particular term. Or a court may have interpreted the term in the context of the related statute. The more consistent interpretations you find, the stronger an *in pari materia* argument is likely to be. For this example, imagine that our research came up with a case interpreting the arson statute. The arson statute defines arson as "the intentional destruction, by fire or firebombs, of the property of another." Hot dog![11] That statute is similar just on its face.

---

[11]Pun was so intended.

And now imagine we found one of the cases that interpreted the arson statute:

> *State v. Ranger* (W.D. Ct. App. 2013): Appellate court affirmed trial court's denial of defendant's motion to dismiss arson charges. The defendant allegedly set fire to a building owned by himself and business partners. Defense counsel argued that the arson statute did not apply because the building was not "property of another." Disagreeing with that narrow interpretation, the appellate court ruled, "the term 'property of another' in the arson statute does not automatically exclude situations in which the actor is a partial owner of property. Rather, if any other person holds an interest, then the property is both 'owned by another' as well as owned by the actor."

Research Tip

A good place to find other statutes or cases that have interpreted a word or phrase in a different context is the *Words and Phrases* volume of the relevant West Digest.

Good news! Since the court held that joint ownership can be interpreted to include "owned by another," the prosecution looks like it can now proceed.

D. Communicate to readers that there are analogous interpretations to the statute you are dealing with

Now you're going to need to walk your reader through the steps that you just took to get to the analogy.

Here's a sample way to start writing the above example

Although this jurisdiction has not yet interpreted the criminal mischief statute's language "property of another," our appellate court has broadly interpreted the same phrase in connection to another crime against property statute, the arson statute. *State v. Ranger*, 345 P.4th 543 (W.D. Ct. App. 2013). The appellate court in *Ranger* concluded that the phrase is inclusive rather than exclusive: "if any other person holds an interest, then the property is both 'owned by another' as well as owned by the actor." There is no functional difference between the destruction of property by fire and the destruction of property generally. If the wife in our situation had set fire to the car rather than used sulfuric acid, the court would be bound to allow the prosecution, per the interpretation of the same term in the arson statute. The method of destruction of the property makes no legal difference; thus, the phrase "property of another" should be interpreted to allow prosecution of a person who is accused of criminal mischief for the destruction of jointly owned property.

Conclusion

Effective reading and interpretation of statutes requires careful attention to detail. You may be surprised at how easy it is to misinterpret a provision or at how often you fail to spot potential ambiguity in your first reading. To improve your efficiency and accuracy, practice the following steps:

- Find the operative section of the statute that applies to your issue.
- Look at the entire statutory context to see where your section fits.
- Ask these questions for every statute:
  - To whom does the statute apply?
  - Does the statute provide any express definitions of key terms?
  - What does the statute require, permit, or prohibit?
  - What are the exceptions to the general rule?
  - What is the consequence of not complying?
  - When does the statute apply?

Answering these questions will get you started. From there, you will want to decide what interpretive tools will be most helpful. Start with the plain meaning of the statute. Remember that generally, the closer you stay to the text of the statute, the stronger your analysis will be. Finally, don't forget that even the most logically reasoned statutory interpretation will not succeed if it leads to a nonsensical conclusion.

Another special problem you may encounter in writing the Argument section of your brief is whether, and how, to include policy arguments. That is the topic of the next chapter.

Chapter 11

Working with the law, part 2: creating policy arguments

Policy arguments examine the possible future social consequences of a particular ruling. Because policy arguments look down the road at what the net effect of a decision might be, policy arguments are used to inject consideration of "real-world effects" into the arguments. It might be the policy argument that gives your argument that commonsense spice that it needs.

Policy arguments are good choices, for example, when the particular argument seeks to elicit a response-creating or response-changing effect in the audience. We know that we have the best chance of persuading an audience when we present an argument that reinforces that audience's existing position. When writing for a judge, this usually means our strongest argument will be based on existing, binding authority. However, sometimes this option is unavailable. Sometimes we want to argue for a change in the law, or we are dealing with an issue of first impression, where we have no existing law. In other cases, we may have binding authority to support us, but it may not be as clear-cut as we would like. In these circumstances, we may strengthen our connection to existing authority by showing how our position is consistent with the policy behind the existing law.

In the right circumstances, policy arguments can be powerful tools. When used inappropriately, however, they can undermine a lawyer's credibility.

This chapter explores the what, when, and how of making policy arguments.

I. Future world: the uniqueness of policy arguments

Policy arguments look to the future. That makes them different from other types of legal argument, all of which look backward in time at *what was*.

Policy arguments take a forward-looking approach to an argument, predicting what *will be*. Judges are interested in policy arguments because they want their decisions to make sense in the future and be a guide to others as precedent for future cases.

But it is the very nature of trying to predict the future that causes the trepidation with which lawyers and judges approach policy arguments. We have a hard enough time understanding our current world, much less anticipating what the future will bring. The same is true for the legislatures and judges who created our existing law. Thus, trying to convincingly argue the future consequences of competing interpretations of existing law is challenging indeed.

A common pitfall of policy arguments is that they tend to overstate the consequences of a particular decision. Think about stories set in the future. They often fall into two extreme categories: utopian (a world that approaches perfection compared to ours) or dystopian (a world that looks much worse than ours does or that is post-apocalyptic).

The reality is that the future is likely to look a lot like the present. Overstating the benefits or pitfalls of a particular ruling can undermine your credibility. Be wary of overstating consequences in policy arguments.

Though an unpredictable future can make policy arguments tricky, we need not fear them. Indeed, we make decisions every day based on what the future might hold. We choose our clothing based on what we expect the weather to be; we decide which politician to vote for based on what we think the candidate would do if elected to office. Because making decisions in the "now" based on what we think the future consequence of those decisions might be is so common, lawyers should not fear making a policy argument in the appropriate circumstance. The take-home lesson is more about wording and presentation than it is about the substance of the argument itself. The goal is to stay away from using words of hyperbole. A lawyer who tries to paint a picture of the apocalypse is a lawyer who is risking a lot of her ethos.

II. When to make policy arguments

Despite the cautions, policy arguments are an important part of presenting the substance or logos of an argument. Policy arguments help the reader understand how the lawyer's proposed outcome for the client fits into a bigger societal picture. Likewise, policy arguments appeal to pathos because they help round out the fairness factor of an argument.

They can be a good way to reinforce the theme you have chosen for your case by tapping into the reader's deep frames (recall the discussion of themes and frames from Chapters 3 and 9).

Think back to Chapter 2 and the Posner persuasion formula. Additional persuasion is needed if the court's distance either from the client's position or the court's resistance to the position has increased. Policy arguments are important when the court might have a greater-than-normal resistance to the client's preferred outcome. That typically happens in a response-creating or response-shaping situation.

Despite the potential risks, policy arguments are critical in certain situations. They are also useful in other situations too, of course. But these four situations should automatically alert a lawyer that it might be time to use a policy argument.

A. Arguments for a new rule in lieu of the existing rule (seeking response-changing result)

There are times when a lawyer must ask a court to change an existing interpretation of the law. In those situations, the argument must, out of necessity, talk about how society has changed and how, going forward, a new rule better reflects those societal goals. This type of policy argument is best offered as a supplement to more direct arguments as to the meaning of existing law rather than as a substitute. Even when we are arguing for a change in the law, we have a better chance of succeeding if we can show how the change is consistent with existing legal principles. It is very difficult to convince a court to abandon common law rules based solely on a policy argument.

The classic example of lawyers arguing for a change in the law based on changing societal goals and expectations is *Brown v. Board of Education*, discussed in the Prologue to this book.[1] In that case, Thurgood Marshall and the other lawyers representing the plaintiffs argued that express and unequivocal Supreme Court precedent (that "separate but equal" facilities are constitutionally permissible) should be overturned. Part of what makes *Brown* a landmark case is that the Court agreed. Such direct overruling of existing law is very rare.

---

[1]*Brown v. Bd. of Educ. of Topeka,* 347 U.S. 483 (1954).

B. Arguments for a new rule because there isn't a rule in place (seeking response-shaping result)

When a client's case raises a novel issue of law in that jurisdiction, the client's lawyer will need to both propose a rule and argue that the proposed rule "fits" with the existing fabric of that jurisdiction's law and society. Providing policy arguments to support that new solution will be a critical part of this argument. In this situation, a lawyer may rely on persuasive authority from another jurisdiction that has already addressed the issue. However, persuasive authority alone is not particularly effective. When relying on persuasive authority, a lawyer will want to show how the other jurisdiction's decision was consistent with policies valued by the courts in his own jurisdiction.

C. Arguments about the way to interpret a statutory word or phrase when the law is undeveloped or underdeveloped (seeking either a response-shaping or response-reinforcing result)

Statutory terms are rarely 100 percent clear. A lawyer attempting to help a court define a term will typically look at similar terms as used in that jurisdiction's statutory scheme. While the court will often seek answers in the legislative history or the purpose section of the particular act, there are times when that information is of only limited use or doesn't exist. But even when the usual tools of statutory interpretation don't provide an answer, the court must still decide the case. Policy arguments can help the court find a principled interpretation that addresses the harm that the statute was designed to redress.

For example, if arguing to define a "household pet" for the purposes of zoning law, a lawyer might look to that jurisdiction's administrative code to see how "household pet food" is defined. Likewise, an attorney might look at the definition of "household pet" in other jurisdiction's zoning laws. Which of those two definitions are most helpful in the context of this dispute will depend on which of the two statutory schemes best parallels the policy behind this jurisdiction's zoning law.

In the Internet dating example, the phrase "dating relationship" used in the New Jersey Prevention of Domestic Violence Act is vague and needs to be interpreted. One way of interpreting that language might be to look at how that term, or a similar one, is defined or used in other jurisdictions or in other statutes in New Jersey. Coupling those types of comparisons with a policy argument showing how those other interpretations advance the legislature's intent is more likely to persuade the court to adopt those other interpretations.

III. The nature and types of policy arguments

Before going further, it is important to think about the possible types of policy arguments. In any situation, more than one type of policy argument may work. It isn't a question of the "correct" versus "incorrect" policy argument. It's a matter of choosing the most persuasive policy argument for the particular client's situation or, more accurately, for those people who are or who will be situated like the client.

We discuss the more logos-like policy arguments first because most judges claim to be influenced primarily, or only, by logos. Thus, at least in a very general sense, these policies may be the most likely to persuade. However, although the more pathos-based social value policy arguments are presented last, lawyers rely on them as frequently as logic-based policy arguments.[2]

A. Judicial administration

This broad category of policy arguments focuses on the real-world pragmatics of a legal interpretation. The goal at the heart of this type of argument is typically "judicial economy" or a "fair and efficient judicial system." Notice how that last phrase builds in two concepts: fairness and efficiency. At times, these concepts work in harmony, but at other times, they are in apparent opposition to each other. In reality, such arguments actually appeal to both logos and pathos. Because they feel grounded in law, however, these policy arguments are among the most successful types of policy arguments.

There are several types of policy arguments that fit under this umbrella.

> **Policy arguments are for trial courts too!**
>
> In Chapter 4, we discussed the differences between trial and appellate cases. One of the ways we mentioned was that appellate courts tend to be more focused on the future consequences of their decisions (the precedential effects), while trial judges tend to be more focused on getting the "right" result for the litigants before her. But this does not mean that policy arguments are unimportant at the trial level; the trial judge can and will encounter all four of the situations described in this section.

---

[2]For more in-depth reading about making policy arguments, see the excellent work of Ellie Margolis, *Closing the Floodgates, Making Persuasive Policy Arguments in Appellate Briefs*, 62 Mont. L. Rev. 59 (2001); Ellie Margolis, *Teaching Students to Make Effective Policy Arguments in Appellate Briefs*, 9 Persp. 73 (2001).

1. The new rule should be firm (or flexible)

The very phrasing of the heading above demonstrates the yin/yang balance between two opposing policy arguments. Either one of those phrases could be used as the basis for an effective policy argument. They are presented together because they are so closely related. Notice how the underlying policies for firm rules parallel those of flexible rules:

Firm rules:

- A firm rule articulates a clear and predictable standard.
- Firm rules result in more consistent, predictable application, or equal justice for all. That makes them *fair*.
- Firm rules are also easier for laypersons to understand, which means that people can gauge their actions and know the consequences. That also makes the rules *fair*.
- The predictability of a firm rule makes it easy for a court to administer. Easy rules are *efficient* rules.

Flexible rules:

- A flexible rule allows courts to change and adapt the rule with new circumstances.
- Flexible rules make the system more responsive to the individual stories of a client. That makes the rule more *fair* in light of the circumstances.
- Flexible rules recognize that legislatures cannot anticipate every possible application of a statute. That makes the flexible rule more *fair*.
- People will have more confidence in a judge to interpret a flexible rule appropriately and will work within the system. That makes the rule more *fair*.
- Flexible rules do not require new legislative action for every unforeseen situation. That makes the rule more *efficient*.

2. The existing or proposed rule is too complex

Related to the firm versus flexible argument is this type of policy consideration. The argument, essentially, is that if lawyers and courts will have a difficult time understanding the rule, then the court will have trouble with both the efficient and fair delivery of justice.

3. Floodgates argument

This type of argument is based on the presumption that efficiency is very important in a particular situation, whereas the risk to fairness is not as great. In a floodgates argument, one party to the action argues that a statutory interpretation or new rule proposed by the other party creates a class of litigants entitled to relief that is so broad that the very number of cases will overwhelm the court system. That, in turn, will lead to a decrease for resources to "true" litigants.

4. Slippery slope argument

A slippery slope argument shares some traits with a floodgates argument: both predict an inevitable crowding of the court system. While a floodgates argument, however, typically talks about classes of people who will flood the courts with similar causes of action, a slippery slope argument predicts that the law itself will stretch to the point of no return. Courts won't be able to stop application to more and more cases, and that will lead to absurd results down the line. The net result will be something very different from what the court probably intends.

This makes a slippery slope argument one that focuses on fundamental fairness more than efficiency.

> **Floodgates versus fairness**
>
> Mr. Beagle's brief in the Internet dating example makes a floodgates argument. The defendant argues that interpreting the term "dating relationship" to include situations where the parties have not interacted romantically in person could lead to numerous restraining order applications being filed by people who have never met, except on the Internet. In that example, the defendant's attorney assumes that a court will value maintaining the efficiency of an already-crowded domestic violence court system over the loss of access to the courts by people who chat over the Internet.

B. Economic arguments

Just as with judicial efficiency arguments, economic arguments are also balancing the tensions between a fair and efficient legal system. An economic policy argument prioritizes financial concerns as a method of determining fairness for society at large. Of course, by prioritizing the good of the whole, an economics approach might compromise the fairness to a particular litigant or class of litigants.

Examples of economic policy arguments beyond judicial efficiencies include these:

- This proposed rule/interpretation represents a fair allocation of limited resources.
- The proposed rule is fair because it spreads the economic loss over a larger percent of the population.

- This rule is fair because it assigns the loss to the party who is best able to bear it without undue burden.
- This rule encourages the economic values of this country (e.g., "save the little Mom and Pop stores from big megastores").

C. Institutional competence arguments

An institutional competence policy argument evaluates which of the three branches of government is best equipped to deal with a particular issue. For example, when a court steps in to determine a legislative purpose, it acts as a judicial legislator. Thus, if one's opponent was arguing for an expansive reading of a statute, one might respond that a court is not competent to expand the scope of the statute expressed by the legislature and should therefore apply a narrower meaning in line with the express terms of the statute.

> ### Money might be the answer
>
> A wise person the authors know advises, "When you don't know the answer to why something is or should be, the answer is probably money."* Think of an economics argument for the project you are working on right now. What is the economic impact of your position? Of your opponent's? Does imagining the financial impact of a decision cause you to see the issues in different ways?
>
> *Steven C. Robbins, Esq.

D. Social values arguments

The last category of policy argument is based on society's values (sometimes also called normative or tradition-based arguments). Professor Michael R. Smith defines social values for this purpose as "[t]he enduring belief that a specific mode of conduct or state of existence is preferable to another."[3] A policy argument along these lines argues that the proposed rule promotes or undermines shared societal values.

The very words "values" and "beliefs" quickly signal that these policy arguments are based on pathos more than the other types of policy arguments. While that may or may not be true, the distinction is often irrelevant because, as we will soon see, social value policy arguments can be supported with logos-based authority just as much as the other types of policy arguments.

---

[3]Michael R. Smith, *Advanced Legal Writing: Theories and Strategies in Persuasive Writing* 89 (2d ed., Wolters Kluwer L. & Bus. 2008).

IV. How to make a policy argument

Policy arguments have three parts: a prediction, a judgment about the prediction, and support for the prediction and judgment.

A. Prediction

Because a policy argument looks toward the future, it must include a prediction about the way the world will look if the proposed rule of law is adopted. Of course, an attorney may also predict what the world will look like if his opposing party's proposed rule of law is adopted.

B. Judgment about the prediction

A lawyer must also include a judgment about the prediction. It is a policy argument, after all. Policy arguments are not meant to be neutral but are meant to persuade. Readers should be able to tell whether the lawyer, as the client's advocate, is predicting sunshine or gloom as part of the policy argument. Note how this differs from how you were taught to approach or present policy considerations in your predictive writing course or other academic writing settings. In predictive writing, it is perfectly reasonable to consider both the pros and the cons of a prediction and to study the countervailing policy considerations. In a brief, however, one side of a policy consideration must be argued as preferable. So, for example, an attorney might argue for the fairness of a flexible rule, even though there are potential arguments supporting a firm rule.

C. Support for the prediction and judgment

Finally, as with any legal argument, the lawyer should cite authority to support the predictions and judgments about the predictions.

1. Legal support

Many policy arguments are well supported by cites to legal authority. Those legal authorities range from legislative history to analogous rules and reasoning borrowed from other jurisdictions or other similar rules in the same jurisdiction. Other sources of legal support include statistical data collected by branches of the legal system, such as court filing statistics or uniform crime reports of that jurisdiction. Many of the statistical data is available online. As a general rule, most courts will accept, as verified, data that is published on a government website (i.e., with a .gov extension).

2. Nonlegal support

Many policy arguments rely on nonlegal data to support the predictions or the judgments about the predictions. For example, the United States Supreme Court cited social science research about the effects of segregation on African American schoolchildren in the seminal case *Brown v. Board of Education of Topeka*.[4]

Although nonlegal support most usually appears in appellate briefs and decisions, its use is not limited to just the highest courts.

Some regularly cited nonlegal materials include these:

- Statistical data collected in another discipline (e.g., census data, demographic data, or economic data)
- Generally accepted medical data ("generally accepted" means by others of stature in the field)
- Social science research results that are generally accepted as using sound methodologies and reasoning
- Other materials that a court might take judicial notice of, such as historical facts, weather data, and other similar sets of information

These types of materials are sometimes referred to as "legislative facts."

Terminology: judicial notice and legislative facts

The evidentiary term for a court accepting nonlegal material is "judicial notice." It is used in a sentence like this: "The court took judicial notice of the filing statistics compiled by the administrative office of the courts." Nonlegal research supporting a policy argument is also referred to as "legislative facts" (see Chapter 5) or "Brandeis briefing." The term Brandeis briefing refers to a brief written by Justice Louis Brandeis while he was in practice. *Muller v. Oregon*, 208 U.S. 412 (1908). In that brief, Justice Brandeis included statistics about the health effects on women who were subjected to long work hours.

In contrast, facts that are part of the parties' stories are sometimes called "adjudicative facts," presumably because those facts are under consideration by the court (i.e., subject to adjudication).

---

[4]347 U.S. 483, 494 n. 11 (1954).

Relying on nonlegal sources is perfectly acceptable in appellate practice. These sources might be nonlegal, but they are the product of research. When a court rule disallows facts "outside the record," it is limiting its analysis to facts about the parties' stories (sometimes referred to as "adjudicative facts"). Bringing in new parts of the story is disallowed because the opposing side lacks notice and an opportunity to cross-examine that evidence. But "going outside the record" of the parties' stories by bringing up unproven adjudicative facts is very different from citing factual data (legislative facts) supported by verifiable and independent sources. The authors of the Model Rules of Evidence specifically rejected a rule that would have limited judges from considering or researching outside pertinent data. Although a number of legal scholars have criticized the permissiveness, the reality is that judges are doing independent statistical research even when the lawyers have not included that data in their briefs. It behooves a lawyer to do that sort of research.[5]

The task therefore becomes finding sources that are verifiable within a particular discipline. If the lawyer finds this difficult to ascertain, a best bet is to consult a reference librarian, who will have more training and access to the materials or to people who will be able to assist.

The respondent's brief in the Internet dating example provides a good illustration of how to make a policy argument.

1. First, it makes a prediction about the future:

   > Courts must continue to broadly define "dating relationships" and recognize that technology will play an increasingly significant role in dating practices. To do otherwise will soon render the Act largely irrelevant to the modern world.

2. The author then argues that a broad definition will be a good thing because it will be consistent with the purpose of the Act:

   > This case is a perfect example of why the court must continue to construe "dating relationship" broadly. The presence of technology in this relationship is merely a sign of modern times. In every other way the bond looks like a traditional dating relationship. The Legislature, in leaving "dating relationship" undefined, purposely deferred to future courts to refine the contours of the term to reflect future understanding of dating.

---

[5]To repeat the resources from Chapter 5, see Coleen Barger, *On the Internet, Nobody Knows You're a Judge: Federal Appellate Courts' Use of Internet Sites*, 4 J. App. Prac. & Process 417 (2002) (providing often-cited standards for checking source accuracy and credibility); Ellie Margolis, *Surfin' Safari—Why Competent Lawyers Should Research on the Web*, 10 Yale J.L. & Tech. 82 (2007).

3. The author then supports that policy argument with authority, citing a prior case that is consistent with the policy:

> As the appellate court in *J.S.* has signaled, modern relationships should be understood and colored by "generational influences." Skype was just a vehicle to let the parties be in the same room with each other in real time.

> Even if these parties fall under the category of "online dating," that is still within the new boundaries of this era and this Court has plenty of discretion to include online dating as falling within the jurisdiction of the Act. That is why the sixth "catchall" factor in the *Andrews* case exists.

4. Finally, the author buttresses her argument with nonlegal authority that provides support for her factual assertions about the evolving concept of dating:

> Online dating is a growing trend that shapes the structure of dating relationships. The *New York Times* has reported,

> Since the current recession began, the popularity of online dating has surged—memberships are up and new matchmaking portals have emerged to take advantage of the demand—industry growth of up to 30 percent is expected in the next year or two, according to the tracking site DatingService.com.

> [Scott James, *In Calculations of Online Dating, Love Can Be Cruel*, N.Y. *Times*, Feb. 12, 2010, at A25A.]

> In 2007, the online dating industry was estimated to have generated $900 million in revenue.[6] This number is estimated to grow to over $1.9 billion by 2012.[7] The practice has become so common that to provide protection for online daters, the New Jersey Legislature passed the Internet Dating Safety Act in May 2007.[8] Just as the Legislature did, the Judiciary should act to provide protection for online daters.

This deliberate development of the argument combines several policy-based concepts. It expressly argues that broad interpretations are necessary to meet the purpose of the Act. It supports that assertion with existing authority. It also implicitly argues that a flexible rule is more fair than a fixed, narrow rule. Also implicit is the institutional competence policy argument: the judiciary needs to defer to the legislature's intent to have a

---

[6]Businesswire.com, *JupiterResearch Sees Steady Growth for Online Personals, Despite Explosion of Social Networking* (Feb. 11, 2008), http://www.businesswire.com/portal/site/home/permalink/?ndmViewId=news_view&newsId=20080211005037&newsLang=en.
[7]*Id.*
[8]The Internet Dating Safety Act requires that online dating sites tell customers whether they do background checks on their members.

flexible, evolving meaning of "dating relationship." Notice that it incorporated all these policy arguments without ever mentioning the word "policy"!

In the next chapter we conclude our discussion of special problems in writing the Argument section by thinking about how to deal with adverse material through counterargument.

Chapter 12

Working with the law, part 3: managing adverse material

May you have a lawsuit in which you know you are in the right.
—Old gypsy curse

Every legal dispute has at least two sides: your client's and your opponent's. And no matter how convincing your client's story is, your opponent's story, left unaddressed, may be just as compelling. In addition, your client's story will always include some adverse facts or law. If there were no adverse facts or law, then there'd be no lawsuit, just a settlement.

One of our tasks is to recognize our opponent's counterstory and provide our readers with a sound basis for rejecting it. Legal persuasion, as Kathy Stanchi notes, is not only about presenting favorable information, but about confronting and defusing adverse information as well.[1]

> ### Phrasing
>
> We use the phrase "adverse material" to denote information that could hurt a client's chances of successful resolution to the dispute. We believe that phrase is more descriptive than "negative material" because not all negative material is adverse or vice versa.

The process of confronting adverse information requires four steps:

1. Recognizing what material is adverse and harmful (be it factual or legal)
2. Choosing a structure for countering that material
3. Choosing when to counter adverse material
4. Conveying a rebuttal in the most effective manner possible

This chapter begins by exploring the types of adverse material a lawyer might face in the client's case, the psychology of why it is best to address

---

[1] Kathryn Stanchi, *Playing with Fire: The Science of Confronting Adverse Material in Legal Advocacy*, 60 Rutgers L. Rev. 381 (2008). Kathy Stanchi's scholarship in this area is significant for legal writing, and we recommend reading it when you can.

and defuse adverse material, and when it might be better to leave adverse material unaddressed unless and until the opposing party raises it. The chapter then explains how we can best address the arguments that should not be ignored.

I. What kind of adverse material is there?

The categories of information that might be adverse to a client's successful resolution of a legal dispute fall into a few broad categories, all of them easy enough to recognize.

A. Adverse aspects about the lawsuit procedures

The easiest way for a defendant to get a case to go away is to find a procedural flaw in the plaintiff's case. If the case is not properly in front of a tribunal, then there is no day in court for the defendant to worry about. For example, if the statute of limitations has passed, the plaintiff no longer has a claim—no matter how strong it may be on the merits. Likewise, on appeal, most claims must have been preserved in the court below. If a party did not preserve its claim of error by objecting at the trial, the appellate court will not consider the party's assertion of error on appeal.

B. Disputes about the relevant facts

Opposing parties will likely disagree about the underlying stories. First, they could disagree about what happened. This kind of dispute will be decided by the trier of fact, so in most cases, this kind of disagreement will not be at issue on appeal. On an appeal, of course, the facts are limited by what is in the record and what the trier of fact found at the trial. Even on appeal, though, there is likely to be a counterstory. Even if the underlying facts are not disputed, the parties will likely view the significance of particular facts differently. How the story is told—who is the protagonist, from what point of view is the story told, what is the protagonist's goal—will most certainly differ.

C. Disputes about the applicable law

The parties may disagree about what law applies to the legal problem. The plaintiff may argue that a precedent is "on all fours" while the defendant argues that the case is easily distinguishable. Even if the parties agree that a particular statute or case applies to the dispute, they very often will disagree as to *how* that law applies. Certainly, in cases of statutory interpretation, the parties will likely disagree over the legislature's intended meaning of the key terms in the statute. This disagreement should be apparent in how the parties explain the rule.

Related to that are disputes about applicable standards of review.[2] There may very well be an argument that the question in front of a court is one of law, even when the facts are very relevant to the outcome. An appellant wishing for a day in appellate court hopes for a de novo standard of review because that makes success more likely for the appellant client. A respondent, in contrast, looks forward to a high standard of review to protect the ruling at the trial court level. Sometimes—more often than you might suspect—the applicable standard of review is fuzzy and there are arguments both in favor of and adverse to the client's position.

Typically, that situation occurs when the parties have no meaningful dispute about how the events unfolded but are disputing only the interpretation of a statute or term. For example, if the Internet dating relationship case was on appeal rather than before the trial court, the lawyers could potentially argue different standards of review. The prevailing party's lawyer might argue, on appeal, that the trial court's ruling that the online-based relationship is enough to be "dating" is a factual determination, subject to a highly deferential standard of review on appeal such as a plain error standard. But, simultaneously, the appealing party could argue that the appellate court has de novo review of the question of Skype-as-dating because no one is disputing the facts of the relationship, but only whether Skyping alone can constitute "dating" as a matter of law. Neither brief presents a very different account of what actually happened, but rather each asks the court to interpret the term "dating relationship" as it does or does not apply to that story.

II. Structuring the counterargument: sidedness and refutation

Once recognized, there are different ways to handle adverse material. One way, of course, is to pretend that the adverse material doesn't exist. Another is to acknowledge that it exists, but to leave it unaddressed. Advocates of this "mentioning" approach, called the "sponsorship

---

[2]For a more detailed discussion of standard of review, see Chapter 17.

theory," believe that juries will attach special importance to an adverse fact if disclosed by the lawyer to whose client the material is adverse.[3] In other words, by addressing an argument, we give it credence, or sponsor it, even if we later refute it. The danger of this approach is readily apparent—we must rely on readers to refute the unchallenged argument on their own.

A third way—and the way that cognitive studies suggest is the most effective—acknowledges the existence of the adverse material and refutes it. The adverse material is "managed," in other words. Lawyers who support this theory argue that a good lawyer knows that zealous representation and one-sided representation are potentially inconsistent concepts—though not always. Knowing when and how to manage the adverse material is another advocacy strategy that depends on the material and the circumstances of the case.

Which ways are more persuasive? The best way to start that conversation might be visually. Figure 12-1 shows a chart that summarizes psychologists' conclusions.

When you are reasonably sure the other side will make arguments about facts/law:

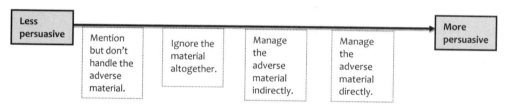

Figure 12-1: Continuum of choices about handling adverse arguments

There are more complicated terms in the psychological literature, but they boil down to these three: ignore, mention, manage.[4]

- Ignoring the adverse material offers only positive information that supports the client's position.
- Both mention and manage approaches acknowledge the adverse material. Each approach would acknowledge the existence of harmful material or arguments. Notice that mentioning without managing the adverse material is worse than simply ignoring it.

---

[3]Stanchi, *supra* n. 1, at 382.
[4]The terms used by the psychologists are "sidedness" (one-sided or two-sided) and "refutational" or "nonrefutational" responses. *Id.*

- A managing response is one that goes beyond acknowledging the harmful material or opposing arguments; it responds to that material by refuting it.
- There are two ways to manage: challenge the adverse material directly or challenge the adverse material indirectly through a more oblique attack. In legal argumentation, the indirect approach can be a strategically sounder choice if the tone of the indirect refutation demonstrates better ethos or respect by the advocate than a direct refutation. Ethos is always important.

> ### Examples of managing adverse material
>
> - "Some people say this economic policy will increase unemployment, but that isn't so because . . ." (direct managing of adverse assertion by providing counterevidence)
> - "It's true that my client was convicted of robberies in the past, but past convictions are not evidence of guilt in the current case." (indirect managing—does not challenge adverse facts but counters by raising legal issue of relevance)
>
> Examples are from Kathryn Stanchi, Playing with Fire: The Science of Confronting Adverse Material in Legal Advocacy, 60 Rutgers L. Rev. 381, 394–395 (2008).
>
> **Ethos bonus:** Notice how neither example openly criticizes the opposing party or the phrasing of their arguments.

Cognitive psychology studies have demonstrated that the most effective strategy involves managing adverse material. That approach is more effective because it causes sustained attitude change that is less vulnerable to opposing arguments. In other words, when readers are exposed to managed adverse material, they are more likely to be persuaded by the message and less likely to change their minds when confronted with an opposing viewpoint.[5]

On the other hand, just mentioning the adverse material is the least persuasive method—significantly less effective than ignoring the opposing viewpoints entirely! If the writer is not going to manage the adverse material or arguments, then it's better to ignore them completely.

These hypotheses have been tested in at least one legal setting using one set of briefs and law clerks' reactions to that set of briefs. The law clerks reported skepticism about the use of one-sided arguments contained in the brief because those arguments failed to take into account the value of opposing views.[6]

To manage a message about adverse material, a lawyer needs to directly or indirectly refute the opposing party's stance. That may be done by

---

[5]*Id.* at 393–397.
[6]*See* James F. Stratman, *Investigating Persuasive Processes in Legal Discourse in Real Time: Cognitive Biases and Rhetorical Strategy in Appeal Court Briefs*, 17 Discourse Processes 1, 7–13 (1994), cited in Stanchi, *supra* n. 1, at 409–414. Professor Stanchi offers some critiques of the study's assumptions and conclusions.

questioning or responding to the "'plausibility of opposing claims, criticizing the reasoning underlying opposing arguments, [or] offering evidence ... to undermine opposing claims.'"[7] These managing messages attempt to "remove" the adverse information either by denying the truth of the opposing claims or by arguing that the adverse information is irrelevant.

Later in this chapter we discuss some of the actual mechanics of how to make a managing argument.

III. Considerations when it is unclear whether the opposing party will use the adverse material

Figure 12-1 and the explanation in the previous section are premised on the theory that the opponent has made, or very likely will make the arguments that a lawyer is planning to counter. But when a lawyer is representing the moving party, whether at trial or on appeal, she must make a judgment call whether to address the adverse material.

A. Inoculation against adverse material

As you just learned, a lawyer shouldn't leave the adverse material unaddressed. On the other hand, a lawyer might not want to bring up an adverse fact or make the opponents' arguments for them when the lawyer is uncertain that her opponent will use those adverse facts or raise those arguments.

In those situations, the lawyer must decide whether to "steal the opponent's thunder"[8] by introducing the information—"inoculating the audience against the adverse material"—and then managing the information by refuting it. All of that happens before the opposing party is able to make the argument. Stealing the thunder works because it shows the audience that the adverse material is explainable. Implicitly, this shows that the adverse material is not as damaging as the audience might believe if first (or only) presented by an opposing party.

---

[7]Stanchi, *supra* n. 1, at 388–389, 399–402; quotation on 394 (quoting Daniel J. O'Keefe, *How to Handle Opposing Arguments in Persuasive Messages: A Meta-Analytic Review of the Effects of One-Sided and Two-Sided Messages*, 22 Commun. Y.B. 209, 211 (1999)).

[8]*Id.* at 415 (citing Kipling D. Williams et al., *The Effects of Stealing Thunder in Criminal and Civil Trials*, 17 L. & Hum. Behav. 597, 608 (1993)).

Imagine your study partner says, "You will soon hear some pretty awful things about me, and let me tell you why you are going to hear them and what actually happened." If the explanation she tells you is reasonable, you will probably think that she is giving you a logical explanation that counters whatever the "awful things" are. This will make you less likely to react negatively to the awful things when you later hear them from another source. Your study partner has inoculated you against the bad news. That's exactly how stealing the thunder works in a legal counterargument.

The phrase "inoculation against the adverse material" may remind you of vaccinations. A vaccine works by introducing a weakened form of a disease into your body. Your body produces antibodies and creates a memory for its immune system. That way, if the actual live and strong disease tries to infect you, your body's immune system remembers and produces a strong protective response.[9]

In the same way, social scientists recommend inoculating an audience to the adverse material. That's the best way to manage it. Thus, if a lawyer concludes that the opposing party is likely to bring up the adverse fact or legal argument, then it is better to bring it up first, in a weakened form, and to refute it. That way, when the opposing side brings up the adverse argument later, the audience is already prepared to see the logic of your answer, thereby blunting the effectiveness of the opposing argument.

> ### Example of inoculation
>
> An example of inoculation appears in the Gloucester Hotel brief in our hotel reservation example. In that case, the hotel can reasonably expect SOFT to argue that the attrition clause in the contract is unconscionable, an argument that is stronger if the party challenging the clause can show that it had no real opportunity to negotiate that term. The hotel, which filed its brief in support of its own motion for summary judgment before it knew what SOFT would actually argue, decided to inoculate the court against that argument by recasting it in terms of "failing to read the contract before signing it is no defense to the contract terms." See part A-1 of the Argument section of the Gloucester brief in Appendix C.

If, however, the lawyer concludes that the opponent is unlikely to bring up the material, then, the science tells us, the lawyer should not bring it up. If it comes up, he can always manage it after the fact. The opposite of stealing the thunder (with an inoculation) is called a "post hoc refutation." You can translate that into plain English as "managing the cat after it's let out of the bag." Figure 12-2 summarizes these strategies for bringing up adverse material.

---

[9]Yes, we know that the social scientists are mixing metaphors here between "inoculation" and "stealing the thunder."

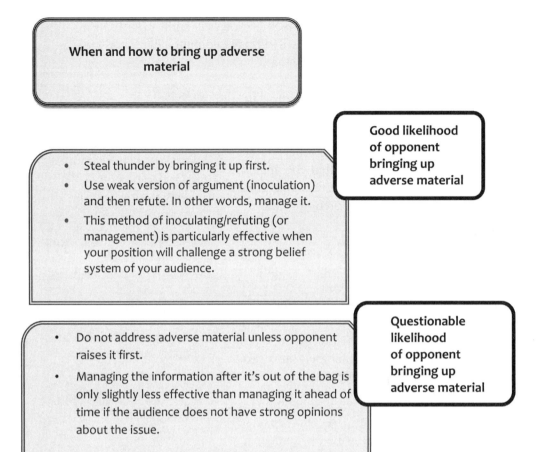

Figure 12-2: When and how to bring up adverse material

B. Deciding when to manage adverse material

So, how do you know when to assume that the opposing party will use the adverse material and that you need to manage the material by making a counterargument? That answer has a lot to do with experience in the particular area of law and in the particular practice setting. One overarching principle is to remember that the *less* you want to talk about the adverse material, the *more* you probably need to do so.

Making the correct call comes in knowing, or making an educated guess about what material your opponent will use. It is not always 100 percent clear that an opposing party will raise, or even knows, the adverse material that you have considered. While you can safely assume the same legal research competence (especially factoring in the duty as a lawyer to disclose controlling adverse authority), there are plenty of arguments that a lawyer may dream up that the opponent has not, or that the opponent has thought of but ultimately rejected for one strategic reason or another. That said, there are some principles to help you decide when to address adverse material.

1. Address adverse material that you are ethically obligated to raise

Of course, you always want to meet your ethical obligations. When it comes to counterarguments, one ethical duty is very clear: you must disclose binding, on-point adverse authority if your opponent fails to do so.[10] If there is a case or statute that is against your position, you have an ethical obligation to inform the court of that authority, even if it means you lose your case.

This may sound counterintuitive. After all, ours is an adversarial system; it should be up to opposing counsel to raise the authority that most helps his case. This is certainly true. And you can expect that most of the time, he will do so. But if your opponent doesn't find that key authority or somehow overlooks its importance, you cannot. In this circumstance, your duty as officer of the court outweighs your duty to advocate for your client.

Fortunately, while your obligation to disclose adverse authority is quite clear, its scope is also limited. You must disclose only binding authority. You are not required to disclose persuasive authority or authority that is not directly on point. However, as discussed below, you may *choose* to discuss adverse authority even if you are not ethically required to.

2. Address adverse facts that you know the opposing party will use

In almost every case, there are facts that you will wish did not exist. Sometimes your client acts badly. Often, the opposing party acts reasonably, at least from its point of view. And, unlike adverse authority, you have no ethical obligation to disclose adverse facts. If the opposing party overlooks facts that support his case, you are under no obligation to mention those facts. This may make it harder to decide when to steal the thunder of adverse facts.

You can be sure that when there's a fact that looks bad for your side, the other side is likely to raise it. You can steal their thunder by raising the fact

---

[10]"A lawyer shall not knowingly . . . fail to disclose to the tribunal legal authority in the controlling jurisdiction known to the lawyer to be directly adverse to the position of the client and not disclosed by opposing counsel. . . ." ABA Model R. Prof. Conduct 3.3(a)(2). Almost every jurisdiction has adopted some version of the Model Rules.

yourself and putting it into the context of your client's story. Show how the adverse facts look from your client's point of view. Remember that all heroes have flaws—no one is perfect, and no case is either. But imperfection differs from reasonability. What might look unreasonable from an objective viewpoint will be better understood when seen from your client's perspective.

> **Example of a direct refutation of an adverse fact**
>
> It is true that the plaintiff posted potentially insulting things about the defendant on her Facebook page. But that just tends to show that the parties indeed were more than just casual friends and that she was reacting to the end of a romantic relationship [from Appendix B].

If you do not know your opponent's theory of the case or are uncertain whether your opponent will incorporate specific, adverse facts, you need to exercise caution. You do not want to alert your audience to adverse facts that your opponent has overlooked or chosen to ignore. With these kinds of facts, you need to decide whether allowing your opponent to control the evidence outweighs the risk of introducing bad facts that might not have been introduced at all. How you decide this issue, of course, will depend on the specific circumstances of your case. However, a good rule of thumb is to remember that your opposing counsel is just as clever as you are. Avoid the easy, but wishful, thinking that if you ignore problematic facts, they will just go away.

3. Address and manage the opponent's strongest argument as soon as you bring it up

Sometimes, you will look at a legal dispute and not see any significant arguments for the other side. This may give you a sense of great confidence. That confidence is misplaced. Your opponent undoubtedly has facts and legal authority that supports his position. Your task is first to recognize what those facts and authority are. If you cannot do so, you should be worried about whether you fully understand the legal issue. Put yourself in the shoes of the opposing party—what facts and authority would justify continuing the time and expense of this litigation?

Of course, often you will see your opponent's arguments all too well. Usually, there are "bad" facts or authority that you wish did not exist. But wishful thinking rarely wins in court. Instead, you must recognize these counterarguments and manage the information by incorporating effective strategies to deal with them.

Table 12-1 will help you brainstorm responses to strong arguments.

Table 12-1: Common arguments and possible counterarguments.

Their argument	Your possible response
The plain meaning of the statute supports their client's preferred outcome.	There is no plain meaning because the term is subject to interpretation. *Or* The plain meaning is different and is favorable to your client's position because . . . (e.g., administrative regulations define the term differently or the jurisdictions' statutory scheme defines the term elsewhere in other related contexts)
Canons of statutory construction weigh in favor of their client's preferred outcome.	Either the canon is inapplicable to this situation because . . . *Or* A different canon of construction is more applicable because . . .
The legislative history supports an interpretation that favors their client.	The legislative history is unclear. *Or* The legislative history does not tell a complete story. *Or* The legislative history tells a story that contemplated a very different scenario. *Or* The legislative history is slight and contrary to the plain meaning of the statute.
Policy considerations support their client's preferred outcome.	More important policy reasons support your client's position because . . . *Or* The policy argument offered by opponent is inapplicable or would create a different ending to the story than what opponent suggested because . . .
Courts dealing with factually analogous situations have ruled in favor of the opposing party's position.	The facts of the reported cases are different in a crucial way because . . . *Or* There are other cases that are closer to the case in front of the court and that support your client's position because . . .
There is no binding law in this jurisdiction, but this court should adopt the law of *xzy* jurisdiction because . . .	The court should accept the law of *abc* jurisdiction because . . . (examples of arguments: trend of decisions, weight of authority, recency, number of highest courts, careful reasoning, policy considerations)

4. Avoid phantom counterarguments and look for the harder ones to manage

Novice legal advocates tend to make counterarguments that are easily rebutted. This is understandable. You have ready answers for weak arguments, and it is tempting to highlight your opponent's weaknesses as a way to bolster your own position. Unfortunately, this is rarely effective and often is counterproductive. If you represented the opposing party, what's the likelihood that you would raise those arguments? If you would not raise them, then likewise assume and expect that the opposing lawyer will also reject those arguments.

Instead, think of the best arguments for the opposing party and counter those. Remember your guiding principle here is *the more you want to avoid an argument, the more you need to address it.* The opposite is also true. The counterargument that is obviously flawed is usually not worth rebutting—at least there's no need for an anticipatory rebuttal. If our opponent brings it up, you will have the opportunity to deal with it at that time.

On being wrong

Kathryn Schulz is a journalist and self-described "wrongologist." She notes that when we encounter someone who disagrees with us, we tend to conclude one of three things:

1. *They are ignorant.* If we just give that person the information that we have, they will agree with us.
2. *They are idiots.* If they have the same information that we have, they must not understand that information. Apparently, they are too stupid to get it.
3. *They are evil.* If they have the same information and understand it, then they must be acting for their own, self-centered evil purposes.

As Schultz explains, while any of these conclusions could be correct, they are not the only possible explanations for someone disagreeing with us. There are some issues where reasonable minds can simply differ. Sometimes, when viewed through a different prism of experience, circumstances will lead to different conclusions. Perhaps most frightening of all, we might be wrong! As lawyers, we serve our clients best when we remember that the opposing party is likely informed, intelligent, and well intended.

From Kathryn Schulz, *Being Wrong: Adventures in the Margin of Error* (HarperCollins 2010).

IV. Where to manage the adverse material

Like most things in legal writing, there is no single right or wrong answer to the question of where to manage the adverse material, other than this: put it where it needs to go. What you want to remember are the principles: inoculate and manage that adverse material.

Suppose, for example, that the dispute you face is about what the legal rule, or the scope of that rule, is. You would need to address that in the Rule or Rule Explanation section of the relevant issue. It is better practice to lead with your argument before addressing the counterargument. Often, your argument will indirectly counter the other side's position, even if not does not do so explicitly. On the other hand, once you have made your argument, you may have an explicit sentence that provides a weakened form of the opposing argument before addressing the other side's possible (or probable) counterinterpretation. This is especially helpful when you determine that you need a more overt form of inoculating the reader. In either situation, you will still have preserved the emphasis position of the paragraph for your own client's point of view.

Likewise, if the rule is fairly clear but there is a dispute as to how that rule applies to the facts of the case you are arguing, the counteranalysis logically fits within the Application section of your CREAC[11] for that issue. Again, it is usually best to present your own application first, before discussing why your opponent's proposed application is not in keeping with the letter or spirit of the law, or the comparable facts, or whatever your argument is as to why your application leads to a better result.

Just remember that the adverse material needs to be *managed*. Managing requires more than merely saying words to this effect: "This is my argument. This is the other side's argument. But they're wrong." Rather, you manage the adverse material by explaining *why* the other side's argument is less satisfactory. To do so, you will need to carefully select details and present them logically.

V. Writing counterarguments

Once you have recognized the adverse material and the way in which the opposing party will most likely use that material, you need to plan how to write a counterargument—how, actually, to manage the adverse material.

---

[11]You probably learned CREAC, or IRAC, or some variation of this organizational tool in your first-semester legal writing course. We discuss this tool in more detail in Chapter 13.

A. Know when you have already made the counterargument

If your argument in chief already fully rebuts an argument likely to be raised by your opponent, there is no need to go any further. It is usually better to cut off an argument with a strong argument that is part of your overall story than it is to rebut the argument independently.

B. Avoid defensive phrasing of counterarguments

You now know that raising adverse material can help your audience resist the opposing party's efforts to use that adverse material. But you can easily work against yourself with the very wording of your managing. It is tempting, but less effective advocacy, to introduce a counterargument with a phrase like "opposing counsel will argue . . ." That creates a defensive posture that may work against your advocacy rather than for it.

Here's why it works against you. That kind of wording defuses your own advocacy by creating a visual image of the opponent making a strong argument. That sort of phrasing immediately puts you—rather than your opponent—on the defensive. Consider these examples:

> **Version 1.** Defendant will undoubtedly argue that this oral agreement is unenforceable because it violates the Statute of Frauds. But that argument has no merit. The agreement is governed by the Statute of Frauds because of an exception.

> **Version 2.** This oral agreement falls within an exception to the Statute of Frauds and is therefore governed by it.

The first version highlights that the defendant has an argument that needs rebutting. It gives readers a visual image of the defendant (or defendant's lawyer) standing up and making an eloquent argument. That kind of visual image works against your client's case. The second version does the rebutting with an affirmative statement, and the visual image is about something better for your client. The statement anticipates the argument without explicitly making the argument. Because it asserts an affirmative legal argument rather than a rebutting one, it is less defensive and hence more persuasive.

C. Put the weakest link in the middle

When writing about adverse arguments, remember to think about the organization of a paragraph and section, and be willing to use those positions of emphasis and deemphasis to help your argumentation. Some advocates like to set up each of their opponents' arguments and then knock them over one by one like bowling pins. The incorrect theory here is that managing the adverse material in one fell swoop will give the appearance of strength because it shows how every counterargument can be rebutted. However, that system also puts the weakest part of the argument in the most powerful position of the text—the beginning.

The better odds are going to be a different set-up to the counterargument than a bowling game. You should always put the strongest points in a position of strength in your text. The "prime real estate" in writing is the beginning and end of sections and paragraphs. Thus, when you have troubling points you must address, like the opponent's strongest arguments, introduce the strongest argument in the first paragraph or two, and then discuss the counterarguments after that.

This principle applies at every level of your organization—from the overall structure of the Argument, to each paragraph of each section, though not of each sentence (the ends of sentences are the emphasis points).[12] Always strive to put the most powerful text in positions of strength—in the prime real estate locations of the document—and put the lesser material in the middle, where it will carry the least clout.[13] Figure 12-3 shows these principles in graphic form.

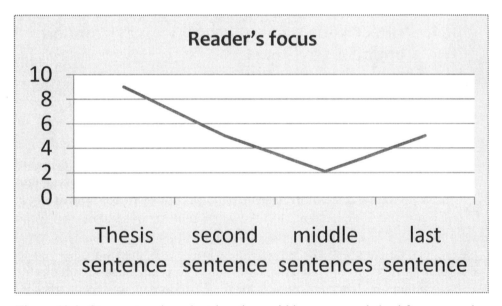

Figure 12-3: Strongest and weakest locations within a paragraph (and for paragraphs within a section of the brief)

---

[12]*See* Laurel Currie Oates & Anne Enquist, *The Legal Writing Handbook* 633–635 (4th ed., Aspen Publishers 2006).

[13]Thanks to Professor Carol L. Wallinger for the prime real estate language. See whether this Monopoly game metaphor helps: the beginnings of sections and paragraphs are the Boardwalk/ Park Place of a section, whereas the middles of sections and paragraphs are the Baltic Avenues. (How many metaphors can we throw into this chapter? Apparently, quite a few.)

The power of placement is apparent when you draft a counterargument that manages the adverse material. You must balance the need to inoculate with the countervailing consideration of making sure each paragraph is firmly written from the client's point of view. Thus the first sentence of a paragraph should place the client in a positive light. Next, you should confront the adverse material. In this way, you have put the adverse information in the middle—the weakest position. Finally, you should finish the paragraph with a direct or indirect refutation of the adverse material—putting the refutation in a position of strength.

One decision you must make is whether to directly or indirectly refute the adverse material. Usually, it is best to face the adverse information directly. But, of course, in law, the questions of professional demeanor and respect may require you to be a bit more discreet in managing an argument. So, although it appears that directly confronting the adverse material is the best option, Professor Stanchi outlines some reasons and explains some examples from advertising that show how material may be refuted with indirect arguments.[14]

D. Protect your own ethos: stay away from ad hominem anythings

Notice that the above options make no references to attacking or criticizing the opponent or opposing counsel. To do that would invite a rebound effect on your own ethos because it would show a lack of goodwill or respect.

In terms of editing, eliminate every instance of phrases such as "the other side's arguments are meritless." Those sentences tend to have little persuasive effect and are more likely to damage your own professional ethos. Even worse is descending into the world of ad hominem attacks. If the opposing party is presenting absurd, offensive, mean-spirited, dangerous, or just downright stupid arguments, it will not be necessary for you to point that out to the judge. She will surely recognize bad arguments for what they are. It is not necessary for you to undermine your own ethos by attacking the opposing party or its lawyer.

One way to think about this is to consider how you want to cast the opposing party in your client's story. It is almost always a bad idea to cast the

---

[14]Stanchi, *supra* n. 1, at 394–395.

opposing party as the villain. Judges, as impartial readers, assume both sides are acting in good faith. When you resort to ad hominem attacks, you implicitly suggest your opponents are evil villains. Readers, however, are likely to dismiss such attacks as unwarranted posturing and are likely to question the credibility of your client's story.

E. Make the adverse material consistent with your client's story

The same writing maxims apply regardless of whether the adverse material are bad facts in the story between your client and the opposing party or the adverse material is part of reported precedent that will be cited in the legal arguments. In all situations, the best advocacy strategy is showing that a seemingly bad fact or bad legal principle is not fatal to your client's position.

Particularly when addressing analogous cases, it is quite possible to find ways to present those cases as supportive of the client's desired outcome. The best way to find the support for your client's story is to refrain from engaging in one "myopic vision" of the facts.[15] There might be one factual distinction that is more importantly different than appeared at first blush. It might be that there were different policy reasons to decide the case in a different way than your client wishes. When you address the weaknesses in your client's case directly, you not only lessen the impact of those weaknesses, you implicitly add to your own credibility by acknowledging the opposing party's strengths.

F. Make the word choices of the counter-argument match and become part of your overarching story

Select the language of your argument with your goal in mind. Strategizing at the micro, or word-choice, level is a key part of any countering strategy. In the next chapters, we will talk about the importance of word choices.

---

[15] *Id.* at 412–413 (citing Kristen K. Tiscione-Robbins, *Paradigm Lost: Recapturing Classical Rhetoric to Validate Legal Reasoning*, 27 Vt. L. Rev. 483, 516–522 (2003)).

An example of management

The sample below is based on the Internet dating hypothetical. It could be part of Mr. Beagle's brief in support of a motion for reconsideration.

Although the Act is remedial in nature, and otherwise carries broad interpretations, those broad remedies exist for people who qualify as victims under the definitions section, *N.J.S.A.* 2C:25-19(d). Its protections extend only to people who qualify as victims of "domestic" violence; the word "domestic" is a key threshold that first must be met before there is a broad construction of the Act's terms. The statute was never intended to protect against all violence in all contexts; it addresses violence only in a domestic setting. The Appellate Division has cautioned trial courts against stretching the jurisdictional limits to the point of absurdity. *Smith*, 298 *N.J. Super.* 121 (holding that two former renters of a summer shore house were not household members under the Act). Accordingly, the statute's ambit goes no further than the violence that takes place in a "family-like" domestic context. *N.J.S.A.* 2C:25-18. Those relationships covered under the Act might take on unusual forms in the case law, but courts will still avoid a construction that might "torture the English language" by extending the statute beyond its rational limits. *M.A. v. E.A.*, 388 *N.J. Super.* 612, 618 (App. Div. 2006) (holding that it was impossible to construe a stepfather's sexually abusive conduct as creating a "dating relationship" with his stepdaughter because there must be limits to the phrase "dating").

Instead, when discussing dating relationships in particular, the Chancery Division has established a number of factors that a plaintiff must demonstrate before a court can establish jurisdiction based on a "dating relationship" under the statute. *Andrews v. Rutherford*, 363 *N.J. Super.* 252 (Ch. Div. 2003). In addition, the appellate courts have refused to grant jurisdiction when the circumstances indicated that there was no potential for future abuse between the parties. *Tribuzio*, 356 *N.J. Super.* 590.

Margin annotations:

Inoculation with weakened version of the plaintiff's argument.

Managing the fact that the statute is otherwise given a broad reading.

More managing and support. The author is framing the language of the Rule.

Acknowledge that cases have found "unusual forms," but immediately counters with authority that shows limits of scope of dating relationship.

Finish with strong restatement of client's position—that there are limits to scope of dating relationship.

VI. Wrap-up: this isn't easy, we know

Your goal with any counterargument is reassuring readers that you recognize the strengths of your opponent's position, but that those positions must ultimately fail. You want to ease readers' potential concerns about your position. You do not want your opponent's arguments to control your legal story. Instead, you want readers to see the legal dispute from your client's point of view. The opponent's arguments are mere obstacles to be overcome; they are not the central story itself. This means that while you will address the opponent's arguments, you will keep them in a secondary role.

Counterargument requires careful strategy. There are no precise formulas, only competing considerations. This chapter is perhaps one of the most difficult in the entire book. We aren't kidding when we tell you that it is hard for any legal writer. Counterargument, as with any aspect of persuasion, is a series of factor balancing. Knowing that, however, demystifies some of the strategizing process for the legal writer.

Now that we have addressed some of the common special problems you will frequently encounter in writing the Argument section, the next chapter will help you put it all together and get it on paper.

Chapter 13

Writing and organizing the working draft of the argument

The previous three chapters examined the types of arguments you will use in a persuasive brief.[1] As you worked through those types of arguments, you may have written the first draft of your argument section. On the other hand, you might prefer to outline your ideas before you actually start writing the text of your argument. No matter which approach you prefer, getting a working draft of your argument requires both getting your ideas down on paper and organizing those ideas into a coherent whole. This chapter will provide the foundation for completing that working draft.

Because the writing process is recursive, you may find yourself going back to the substantive discussions of the previous chapters and rethinking your initial arguments. Writing is more than expressing crystallized thoughts. Writing is thinking itself. You write to understand what it is you are thinking. Ergo, write! It doesn't matter what your argument's first draft looks like; it matters only that it is written. For most of us, it is easier to organize our thoughts once we have a first draft of those thoughts down on paper.

You have already learned that writing a legal argument is a form of technical writing. It is based on highly structured norms. Readers of legal briefs, in particular, have common expectations about how a legal argument should be structured. But while readers expect to see this logical structure, it takes you only so far when talking about advocacy on behalf of a client.

---

[1] As noted in Part III's introduction, there are other types of arguments as well, such as rule-based reasoning, and analogical reasoning. Since these types of arguments are typically covered thoroughly in your predictive writing or legal reasoning course, we do not repeat them in this text. But of course, you will need to understand how to use these types of arguments to best advantage in your brief writing.

Organizing an argument section of a brief occurs on at least two levels, large-scale and small-scale organization. Large-scale organization refers to the order that discuss the major issues and sub-issues. Small-scale organization, in contrast, refers to the structure of the discussion of any single issue or sub-issue. This is where the CREAC structure you learned last semester is important.

Think of the large-scale organization as an outline, with hierarchal headings and subheadings:

I. First Major Issue
[Arguments relating to the first issue, structured in CREAC form]

II. Second Major Issue
[Roadmap of one or more paragraphs, setting out any threshold information and then explaining to the reader how the sub-issues relate to one another]
  A. First sub-issue
  [Arguments relating to the first sub-issue, also structured in CREAC form]
  B. Second sub-issue
  [Arguments relating to the second sub-issue, also structured in CREAC form]

In addition to choosing your large- and small-scale organizational structures, you should also distinguish in your mind between "issues" and "arguments." An "issue" (or sub-issue) is a specific legal question that a lawyer asks the court to resolve. An "argument" is a reason the lawyer advances as to why the court should resolve the issue one way or the other. This is similar to the difference between a "strategy," which refers to a person's overall objective, and a "tactic," which is a way of achieving that objective.

Another way to think about this is to recognize that "arguing" is what you are *doing*. "Issues" are what you are arguing *about*. Since arguments relate to specific issues, they are tools for thinking about small-scale organization.

For example, in our hotel room reservation example, the sample brief for the nonprofit organization identifies the first *issue* this way:

> Is Gloucester's claim for additional payment from SOFT a penalty, and therefore not a valid liquidated damages clause?

When the author addresses this issue, the author makes two distinct *arguments* as to why the clause is an unenforceable penalty: (a) that actual damages for any breach would be readily ascertainable, and (b) that the amount specified as damages is grossly disproportionate to the actual damages that could be suffered.

I. Choosing your large-scale organization

In choosing the order in which you discuss your main points, always think independently about what structure best suits your client's needs and her story's strengths. Avoid automatically adopting the large-scale organization of an opponent's brief, for example, even when tempted to make such a point-by-point rebuttal. If you do, you are letting your opponent define the playing field. Ultimately you may end up with a structure that is similar to your opponent's (especially if there is an obvious logical flow to the issues), but that's okay so long as you make that choice after due consideration of your options.

A. "Logical flow" structure

A "logical flow" structure arranges the issues by one or more of the controlling legal issues. There may be a threshold issue, for example, that must come first. Often a court will resolve procedural issues before addressing the merits. If one of your issues is whether the court has jurisdiction (e.g., questions of ripeness, standing, personal jurisdiction over the defendant, or subject-matter jurisdiction), then logic suggests that you address that issue first. The court will certainly turn its attention to that question first, under the premise that it need not rule on the merits if it has no power to decide the case at all.

You would also use a logical flow structure when the substantive law calls for a sequential analysis. For example, in our Internet dating scenario, the substantive law calls explicitly for a sequenced analysis: first, the court must decide whether a dating relationship exists. If no such relationship exists, the case is over; but if one does exist, the court proceeds to the next step of determining whether the incident complained of fits one of the criminal categories defined by the statute as a violent act. When the substantive law directs the court to follow such a sequenced analysis, your brief should follow the same sequence.

Yet another example of a logical flow derives from how your court addresses certain types of issues. For example, some legal disputes raise both statutory and constitutional issues. Many courts will first attempt to resolve the dispute through statutory analysis. These courts will address the constitutional issue only if it cannot resolve the issue through the statutory analysis. In such a case, you should address the statutory issue first.

B. Argument chains

Many times, however, there is no obvious logical sequence to the issues. You then need to find another way to arrange the issues. In that situation, you may decide to use one of two types of argument "chains" to organize around. The first option is organizing from small to large requests. This is called a "foot-in-the-door" argument. The other option is to reverse the order and start with the largest request. This is a "door-in-the-face" approach.[2] The idea with either approach is that humans really do prefer to say yes to some sort of request. The first scenario starts a "bobble head" rhythm of saying yes to things. The second scenario starts with a pie-in-the-sky desired result and backs down so that it looks like the requester is negotiating toward something reasonable.

The difference between the two types of argument chains is very easily seen in a simple example of a child asking her parent for a pet. The child's desired result is either a dog or a cat.

Foot-in-door approach	Door-in-face approach
1. May I please have a fish?	1. May I please have a horse?
2. If you will say yes to a fish, then how about a gerbil? They are about the same amount of care in terms of daily feeding and habitat cleaning. And I can't really play with a fish.	2. If you won't say yes to a horse because of the expense and care, then how about a dog?
3. If you will say yes to a gerbil, then how about a cat? A cat isn't really all that much more work than a gerbil, and it lives longer and also is a lot more affectionate.	3. If you won't say yes to a dog because of the level of care involved with walking it, then how about a cat? A cat doesn't require anyone to walk it.

Another way to think of these types of structure is to think about the plot line for your brief. Your client, the protagonist, has a goal. Several routes may lead

---

[2]Kathryn M. Stanchi, *The Science of Persuasion: An Initial Exploration*, 2006 Mich. St. L. Rev. 411.

to his goal. In fiction, for example, the protagonist–hero may first choose the "safest" route that provides a successful start. After that, the hero will take a bit more of a risk on the next step, and then slowly increase the risk along the path to the final and largest hurdle. The foot-in-the-door may not lead to immediate success, but it provides a safer, more deliberate path to ultimate success.

Alternatively, our fictional hero could reverse the order. He could go for the big prize—the riskier one first, with the safer routes to be saved as a later alternative—a fallback position. If the bold but risky move fails, the hero still has the safer alternatives to pursue. This structure could be used to demonstrate to readers the seriousness of the peril the protagonist is in. This door-in-the-face approach is high risk, but it carries high rewards—success may come quickly.

The hotel room reservation case takes the foot-in-the-door approach. The attorney for SOFT starts with the safer issue, whether the contract clause is unenforceable because it is a penalty. The brief examines the case law that defines what a "penalty" is and then applies those rules to the facts of the case. Next, the attorney makes the argument that the hotel has failed to prove any damages, one of the elements of a cause of action for breach of contract. But in fact, this issue provides a smooth transition into the riskier issue: impossibility of performance. In that section, the attorney for SOFT points out that the hotel sold all of the rooms to other guests on the nights in question, making it impossible for SOFT guests to purchase the required number of rooms. The message just below the surface of this issue is that the hotel is being unfair to SOFT. It should not be allowed to be paid twice for the same rooms. While there may be some favorable facts here, the law is more difficult on this issue. Thus the author builds to this issue by first addressing the easier issue regarding the meaning of penalty.

But note that the author could have reversed the order of these arguments and led with the impossibility argument. This would have the strategic benefit of highlighting for readers the theme of fairness. By showing readers how the hotel would be paid twice for the same rooms, they may be more receptive to the arguments set forth on the other two issues, even if the impossibility argument does not, by itself, persuade the court.

Either of these patterns could work, though in law most briefs approach the arguments with a foot-in-the-door organization.

C. "Lead with strength" is the default choice

Now suppose there is no obvious logical sequencing to the issues, and no clear argument chain appears. The traditional advice of "lead with your best argument" is good advice to follow. Of course, leading with your strongest argument will often be consistent with other approaches to argument organization. Ultimately, how you arrange your issues depends on your reading of what will be most likely to persuade the potential audience, the court. Choices like this make the practice of legal writing and advocacy more art than science.

II. Roadmaps and headings: signaling the bottom line, up front

Once you have chosen your large-scale organization, it is a good idea to let readers in on the choices you have made. Your job as a writer is to make readers' lives easier. This is another important way that legal writing differs from other forms of writing.

Judges or clerks reading legal briefs want information, and want it quickly. Judges have very specific roles: they must learn both the applicable legal principles and the facts to which those principles will be applied, and then make a decision as to who wins. Since judges (and clerks) at all levels tend to be overworked, it is very important that you provide them with exactly the information they need to do their jobs. Anything you can do as a brief writer to assist your judicial audience in quickly locating and understanding that information will enhance your ethos—your personal credibility—with judges and their support staff.

Explicitly showing readers your chosen organization of the legal argument is one good way to assist judges in quickly locating the information they need to do their jobs. There are two ways in which good legal argument sections of briefs demonstrate organization: roadmaps and headings.

Educational psychologists have studied how headings and summary or roadmap paragraphs help readers to comprehend and retain information. Those studies have concluded that both headings and roadmaps help provide readers with the hierarchical structure of the material. Ultimately, this contributes to better recall because readers better understand the relationships among subtopics.[3]

---

[3]Robert F. Lorch et al., *Effects of Signaling Topic Structure on Text Recall*, 85 J. Educ. Psychol. 281, 287 (1993).

A. Roadmaps lay the groundwork for memory

Roadmaps, or summaries, create a knowledge base that readers can call on when later introduced to the material in more depth.[4] The information is learned the first time in the roadmap and placed into working (short-term) memory when the related text is read immediately afterward.

These studies have practical implications in legal documents, be they briefs, memos, letters, or any other document designed to persuade. A summary of the argument section or a roadmap paragraph between hierarchical sections of the legal discussion can provide a knowledge base for the later subsection containing more detail.

The roadmaps you include in a brief serve at least two functions. First, they provide readers with a brief overview of how the law governing any particular issue is structured. Second, they provide readers with some uncontroversial, foundational legal principles that influence the rest of the law in that section.

1. Describing the legal structure

One way to visualize the structure of your brief is to think of a road trip. Your audience (the judge) is in, say, Indianapolis. For your client to achieve his goal, the judge must get to Chicago. There are many different ways to get there: airplane, train, automobile, long-distance running. Your job is to choose the best mode of transportation depending on the circumstances and then explain the choice to your audience.

Most travelers need state-scale and city-scale roadmaps to get from where they are to an unfamiliar destination. They start with the larger and move to the local roadmap as they progress through the journey. Likewise, if you want the judge in your case to make the mental trip from wherever she starts to where you want her to end up, you need to provide the appropriate roadmap at the appropriate time. A global roadmap of an argument consists of the large-scale roadmaps in the brief, showing the relationship between major point headings. A local roadmap indicates the sub-elements in a particular sub-issue.

Take a look at the structure of this chapter, for example. Our objective as authors is to take you, the reader, on a journey that teaches you how to organize the argument section of your brief. Immediately at the beginning of this chapter, we provide you with an overview of what the chapter is about and where we want you to go. That represents the global roadmap

---

[4]John A. Glover et al., *Advance Organizers: Delay Hypotheses*, 82 J. Educ. Psychol. 291 (1990).

for this chapter. Now look between the A and 1 headings of this section; you see here an example of a local roadmap.

Note that both the global roadmap and the local roadmaps are fairly short. The roadmaps are not the place to provide specific detail about what the rules of law are nor how they work; they are designed simply to let readers know what to look for in the discussion that immediately follows. A driver who knows what landmarks to look for when following directions in an unfamiliar location is more likely to follow the directions correctly. And that driver is more likely to arrive at her destination less frustrated than one who has no idea where the route is taking her.

> ### IV. Argument
>
> The attrition clause in the contract is a penalty rather than a liquidated damages clause; it is therefore unenforceable. Payment of the invoice by SOFT would be grossly disproportionate to the damages (if any) suffered by the Hotel as a result of the shortfall in bookings by SOFT and result in a windfall to the Hotel. Moreover, the Hotel was not damaged because it was able to resell any rooms not reserved by SOFT guests, presumably at a higher price, and was therefore likely put in a better position than it would have been if SOFT's guests had filled the 53 "unused" guest rooms at the contract rate. In addition, by selling all of the rooms not reserved by SOFT, the Hotel made it impossible for SOFT to perform the contract.

The shadow box shows an example of a global roadmap from SOFT's brief in the hotel reservation case. It describes the three main issues to be addressed and introduces the key concepts that will form the basis for the argument. But notice one more important thing about this sample roadmap: it includes both SOFT (the protagonist) and the hotel (the antagonist). It makes the story of the brief more visual and therefore more accessible to readers.

One of the most common mistakes seen in legal briefs is a roadmap that focuses exclusively on the legal rule and forgets to mention the possible impact of different choices on the client. This is an easy mistake to make; after all, this is the Argument section of the brief, where the law is explained and applied. And indeed, perhaps the most important function of the roadmap paragraph(s) is to help readers navigate the sometimes complex and unfamiliar rules of law. But by definition roadmap paragraphs come at the beginning of a new section of the brief. Every time you change direction or topic (such as at the beginning of a new section), readers become alert: "This is new! I'm making progress here!" That means you have readers' attention—which is the best time to make a persuasive point. Thus, for example, you can show the possible impact on your client (either positive or negative) of the court's ruling one way or the other. By keeping the client front and center, judges will be reminded of why the points you are discussing in the body of each section are important.

2. Setting up foundational law

The second function of a roadmap is to lay out some foundational legal principles that help readers work with the concepts that follow. For example, if you are filing a brief in support of, or in opposition to, a motion for summary judgment, you will need to briefly recite the standard the court will need to apply to make its ruling. In a situation like that, since the standard applies to all of the sections of the brief, you would include this statement in the global roadmap.

Another example might be where you are arguing about a well-known elements type of test such as common law negligence. In that situation, you might wish to state the uncontroversial elements of the tort in the appropriate global roadmap paragraph and then use that structure to advise readers of which elements the parties dispute and which elements are undisputed.

One example of "foundational law" is shown in the roadmap at the beginning of this chapter. After introducing the three main sections of this chapter, we discuss the distinction between "issues" and "arguments," a basic principle that has meaning for several of the sections to be discussed.

This is also demonstrated in the first local roadmap of the SOFT brief, shown here in the shadow box. The ultimate issue in that section of the brief is whether the contract provision was a valid liquidated damages clause or an unenforceable penalty. Before the court can address that issue, however, the author needs to situate the issue in the wider domain of contract law. Thus, the author begins this argument with a global

A. The Hotel seeks to enforce a penalty because the amount claimed is disproportionate to the actual damages and is easily calculable

To recover for a breach of contract, a plaintiff must prove that (1) a contract existed, (2) the defendant breached the contract, and (3) the plaintiff suffered damage as a result of the defendant's breach. *Collins v. McKinney*, 871 N.E.2d 363 (Ind. Ct. App. 2007). The plaintiff bears the burden of proof as to the amount of loss resulting from a defendant's breach. The parties to a contract, however, may stipulate a sum in advance to be recoverable for a breach of contract where the loss suffered would be uncertain or difficult to ascertain. A liquidated damages provision "provides for the forfeiture of a stated sum of money without proof of damages." *Harbours Condo. Ass'n v. Hudson*, 852 N.E.2d 985, 993 (Ind. Ct. App. 2006).

description of the legal landscape (essentially, the uncontested and familiar elements of a cause of action for breach of contract). The road-map then quickly shifts to the specific legal issue: the law of liquidated damages provisions.

B. Headings chunk the information

Headings help readers search effectively for answers to questions about the text. They also provide the superstructure of the document, which leads to better concept recall.[5] Breaking up the information into "chunks" under headings also makes sense from a memory standpoint. Cognitive psychologists have long known that "chunking" information—grouping related information—raises memory retention rates.[6]

Here's an easy example that you might have heard before. Research has shown that most people can remember up to seven random numbers (plus or minus two) in their short-term memory.[7] However, it is easiest to remember seven numbers if they are chunked in groups of three and four numbers. This explains why phone numbers are broken down into "chunks" of three and four, rather than a list of seven numbers. The chunking makes them easier to remember.[8] Similarly, headings help readers identify chunks of related text, thus improving their recall of the information within each chunk.

The use of headings should be old hat to you from your course in predictive legal writing. Almost all briefs, and certainly briefs that are more than a few pages long, use headings to help readers follow the argument by chunking the information. In the first shadow box of this chapter, each of the lettered and numbered point headings serve that function.

C. The visual design of headings

For headings to fulfill their principal function, they must jump out at readers, visually. They must also attract readers' attention rather than cause them to look away. Thus, you should create visually distinctive point

---

[5]Stephen C. Wilhite, *Headings as Memory Facilitators: The Importance of Prior Knowledge*, 81 J. Educ. Psychol. 115 (1989).

[6]George A. Miller, *The Magical Number Seven, Plus or Minus Two: Some Limits on Our Capacity for Processing Information*, 63 Psychol. Rev. 81(1956); also made available online by Stephen Malinowski with the author's permission at http://www.musanim.com/miller1956/ (last accessed Sept. 5, 2012).

[7]*Id.; see also* Linda L. Lohr, *Creating Graphics for Learning and Performance: Lessons in Visual Literacy* 206 (Merrill Prentice Hall 2003).

[8]Alas, the advent of cell phones has required most of us to now remember area codes as well. Fortunately, the same technology has made *remembering* phone numbers less important.

How many headings do we need?

Once we recognize that headings serve to chunk information in a way that reveals our large-scale organization, we must decide how many chunks we need to have. As a general rule, we should have a main heading for each cause of action or issue on appeal and a subheading for each CREAC within that issue. If, for example, our brief has two issues—whether the court has jurisdiction and whether the defendant was negligent as a matter of law, we would have two main headings. The negligence issue would likely have sub-issues addressing each of the elements of negligence in dispute. Each of those sub-issues would require its own CREAC, so we would have a subheading for each sub-issue. Thus, as a general guideline, we should have one subheading per CREAC as that best reflects our large-scale organization.

Sometimes we may prefer to vary from the "one heading per CREAC" guideline. Sometimes a single CREAC requires a lot of explanation and may go on for several pages. In that situation, your readers will appreciate breaking the CREAC into smaller chunks. If your CREAC is longer than two or three pages, you should consider how you might break it up into smaller chunks to make it easier for readers to digest your analysis.

headings. But consider that formatting choices such as ALLCAPS and <u>underlining</u> will distract or confuse readers. *Even italic type has its limitations.* The better choices involve the use of light and dark (i.e., boldface). You can also vary the size of headings to show hierarchy.

At the same time, headings must serve the important function of chunking the information. To do that, keep headings in proximity to the text that they modify. That means close up some of the space between headings and text. You don't need as much space between headings and the text that follows as the space you have between paragraphs. For example, in this book, the space between our headings and our text is half of the space between paragraphs. Creating proximity between headings and the modified text can end up saving you several lines in a document. That's important when you must measure length in terms of the number of pages.

Last, make sure your point headings make a point. That is, they should make some persuasive statement instead of serving simply as a bland label denoting what the next section is about. Although there are many maxims that textbooks might provide you in terms of the content of headings, the truth is that the substance of your heading will depend on the brief, the writer, and the purpose. We have seen effective headings that serve as the "C" of CREAC (thus leading the writer to omit the actual C of

CREAC in the body of the text). We have also seen just as effective headings that are more akin to a rule statement.

Take a look at the headings in this chapter to see how they use boldface, size, and proximity to demonstrate the hierarchy and the chunking of information. Take a look also at the headings as used in the sample briefs in the appendices.

Remember that, in an appellate brief (and maybe in a longer trial court brief, if the court rules allow) your point headings will all appear, without any supporting text, in your table of contents. If the point headings make persuasive points, then the table of contents becomes a summary of your argument: one more opportunity to persuade.

Design tips for effective headings

1. Headings should be as short as possible and still convey the point.
2. Use boldface type so that headings stand out visually from the surrounding text.
3. Boldface shows contrast without altering the readability or legibility of the letters. Underlining, on the other hand, reduces readability and legibility because the underlining interferes with the tops and bottoms of letters.
4. Italics are less problematic than underlining, but they aren't all that great, either. At least, not a lot of them at one time.
5. HERE IS THE WORST OPTION. WHY WOULD YOU EVER TYPE A POINT HEADING IN ALL CAPITAL LETTERS? ALL CAPS ASSAULT READERS' EYE, DRAMTICALLY AFFECT READABILITY, AND MAKE IT ALMOST CERTAIN THAT READERS WILL SKIP THE POINT HEADING. WE DOUBT YOU HAVE EVEN READ THIS FAR INTO THIS TIP! IF YOU HAVE, SEE WHETHER YOU NOTICED THE TYPOGRAPHICAL ERRORS IN HERE.
6. Headings can be single spaced to maintain the contrast and since you won't use more than a few lines at most.
7. Headings should be numbered or lettered in outline style so that readers can see how the headings relate to one another.

    a. Subtopics need not be indented but can be in a smaller font size. If you must indent, be careful of how far you go because line length changes can throw off reading rhythms.
    b. Remember that when you have an "a," you must have a "b."

8. Check your headings for symmetry with one another. If you boldface or change typeface for headings, then every heading must be boldfaced and in that same typeface. Don't suddenly switch in the middle or at a particular sub-sublevel. That will throw off readers' understanding of the heading hierarchy.

III. Small-scale organization

Once you have chosen the large-scale organization for your issues, it's time to fill in the content underneath each of the major point headings and subpoint headings. This is where you begin organizing the body of your Argument section.

Like any other task, it's best to have a plan before you begin. Most writers start with the big-picture concepts and then choose a structure that serves their purpose. You have seen much of this material before, in your predictive writing course. But because client-centered persuasion must always take precedence over any formulas, there might be variations on the small-scale organizational structures you have previously learned.

A. Local roadmaps

The "local roadmap" is generally the very first thing readers encounter after the point heading introducing each section of a brief. However, you may write those roadmaps last since you may change your mind during the writing process about how you want to organize each section.

Because we discuss the difference between global roadmaps and local roadmaps above, we don't need to spend a lot of time here reviewing the function of the local roadmap. It will be helpful to remember, however, that there may be some foundational law that you need to bring in at the very beginning of any section, before you get into the detailed discussion of the legal principles involved.

One last note. As you gain more experience working on persuasive writing documents, you may (and should) start to question the existence of too many local roadmaps. Consider this organizational structure:

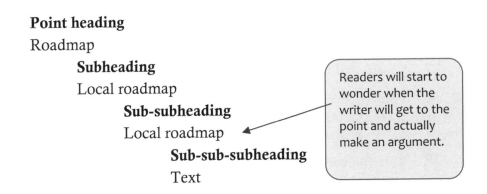

Point heading
Roadmap
    Subheading
    Local roadmap
        Sub-subheading
        Local roadmap
            Sub-sub-subheading
            Text

Readers will start to wonder when the writer will get to the point and actually make an argument.

Rather than having too many local roadmaps clutter up the actual argument itself, you may want to forgo some of the local roadmaps at the lower levels. Or you may want to reduce the amount of "mapping" information in the global roadmap, in lieu of doing more "mapping" in one or more of the local roadmaps. Readers will have a hard time remembering the sub-subcategories of information if you explain all of them on page 1 of the legal argument, even though they won't actually see those sub-sub-headings until page 6 of the argument.

B. Traditional structure: CREAC

The logical structure of each section of the brief is defined, of course, by the substantive law that you are discussing. This is the function of CREAC. We use the CREAC formulation for persuasive writing because it reminds us that the Explanation of the Rule is just as important as stating the Rule. The final C is a strategic choice: useful in certain writing situations but merely repetitive in others.

Novice legal writers sometimes latch onto the CREAC structure as the only way to organize the entire brief. In fact, a full-CREAC brief is likely only when you are working with an elements test. If the issue involves factor tests, you might find that the CREAC structure is too limiting. (Factor and elements tests are discussed in section E below.)

What is probably most important to remember about CREAC is that it sets up a method for providing readers with context before detail. The initial C provides the opening context and should be client centered. "My client wins this sub-issue . . ." The next thing that readers need is to understand the law of the sub-issue: both the overarching rule as well as illustrations of other stories (i.e., cases) where the rule was used in roughly similar situations. Only after that context can readers truly understand where your client's story fits.

The chart below summarizes the structure of an argument organized on the CREAC model.

1. Small-scale organization of legal analysis

C   **Fact-based, contextual conclusion sentence**. This should refer to your client's desired outcome for this issue or sub-issue. The C may appear as the heading itself instead of in the text—that's a strategy call.

R   **Rule Statement:** Sentences that summarizes and synthesizes the particular rule that is either controlling or that you want to become controlling. Write the Rule Statement from your client's point of view, as explained in Chapter 14.

E **Explanation (sometimes called Rule Explanation):** The supporting material that explains and illustrates your Rule. Without the context of the Rule Explanation the Rule might be too abstract or ambiguous.

A proper Explanation tells stories about how courts have applied the Rule in other situations. It answers readers' questions about the Rule:

- What is the goal or purpose of the Rule?
- In what kinds of other stories did courts use this Rule? What were the key facts of those stories?
- Are there examples in the cases that show how the Rule can be stretched or when it should be limited?
- If a statute, are there intrinsic, textual clues that support your formulation of the rule? Are there supporting statutory sections that support your formulation of the Rule?
- What equities or policies does the Rule serve?

Use in-text explanations when the Explanation is central to the client's outcome or when parentheticals do not otherwise suffice.

Use parentheticals to provide information that is not crucial to the argument or when you can provide the relevant information in one sentence.

A **Application:** The argument of how and why this court should use the Rule in your client's situation.

- Use analogical reasoning to show similarities and differences between the Explanation and the client's situation.
- Because the Rule and Explanation provide the context before the detail of the Application, generally the Application does not start until the subsection's Rule and Explanation are fully developed.

C **Conclusion:** A wrap-up sentence that completes the legal discussion of this section. Sometimes, you may omit an express statement of the conclusion if it just adds unnecessary repetition.

C. Variations on a theme of CREAC

Earlier in this chapter, we discuss options for large-scale arranging of issues. But even within the confines of any CREAC unit, you have choices in the arguments you raise. You also have choices on when to present counterarguments and which arguments to raise at all; these topics were discussed in Chapter 12.

CREAC is an effective method for organizing many legal arguments. However, a persuasive argument need not always follow a lock-step, pre-formed organizational structure. A judge who *wants* to rule in your client's favor is more likely to do so than a judge who feels she is merely *permitted* to do so. Sometimes, we may vary our CREAC structure to strengthen our persuasive punch.

The most common variations on CREAC are these:

c**R**EAC   This variation happens when the rule of law itself is in question and the facts are largely undisputed. This situation can arise where the "story of the law" is predominant, as described in Chapter 8. Although many moot court simulations focus on these pure questions of law, in practice, they are relatively rare.

If you are facing a situation in which you must argue for the rule of law itself, your brief may include several subsections (or sub-subsections) of Rule Explanation and a fairly short application of the law to your client's facts. In this situation, you may subtly weave your client's story into your rule explanation—this keeps your client in the story.

CRE**A**   This variation happens when the rule of law is fairly straightforward, but the application requires more explanation (typically when the "story of the client" is predominant).

RCEAC   This variation happens when the writer chooses to start with the Rule or part of the Rule itself (sometimes in the heading). Note, however, that the Rule, Rule Explanation, and Application still remain distinct.

C P R A   In this variation, the writer follows the Conclusion with a paragraph designed to prime the reader, emotively. This might be a story about our client or an explanation of public policy. The goal is to motivate the judge so that she wants to find a reason to rule in your client's favor on that particular issue. Although it is tempting to think about varying CREAC this way in every subsection, the impact diminishes with multiple uses. Save this one for a time when you really need it.

D. An outlined argument using the most common CR<small>EAC</small> variation

The box below shows an example of an argument structure, when the rule itself is at issue.

The defendant committed criminal mischief when he destroyed the marital dining room table because "property of another" includes jointly owned property that is destroyed by only one owner

A global roadmap here would outline the

- precise wording of the relevant parts of the controlling statute (criminal mischief statute);
- conundrum (statute mentions destruction of property of another, but is jointly owned property included?);
- overview or snapshot of the different legal reasons why the law should be resolved in the way you suggest

  1. **Criminal mischief is analogous to arson and theft, as part of the "offenses against property" crimes.**

     - Follow the normal statutory interpretation chain by looking at the cases interpreting the arson and theft statutes to determine whether those cases answer the "joint property" question for the analogous statutes.

  2. **The legislative history indicates that the legislators intended to include jointly owned property in the scope of the law because the law is supposed to act as a deterrent against destruction of property.**

  3. **Other states considering this precise issue have concluded that a defendant may be convicted for criminal mischief when he destroys jointly owned property.**

  4. **Because this court should read the criminal mischief statute to include jointly owned property in the definition of "property of another," this court must deny the defendant's motion to dismiss the charges.**

     - Apply rule principles developed above to client's facts.

Margin annotations:

Global roadmap

Rule heading
*The particular ordering of the Rules in this example was strategic only for this brief.

Rule heading

Rule heading

Application
This section is often comparatively short because there is no real analogical reasoning with the facts.

E. Handling factor tests

A factors test requires considering several, often competing, factors rather than the more straightforward analysis of an elements-based legal issue.

An element test is easier to organize. In an element test, the moving party must show something like:

Simplified example of a conjunctive test	Simplified example of a disjunctive test
1st element **And** 2nd element	1st element **Or** 2nd element

A factor test, on the other hand, looks something like this:

Factor test to determine if parties are dating in New Jersey domestic violence law	Courts' explanations of how to use that factor test
1. Was there a minimal social interpersonal bonding of the parties over and above mere casual fraternization?	Courts use, but should not be limited to, these factors and should consider other factors such as generational norms. *(the synthesized rule)*
2. How long did the alleged dating activities continue prior to the acts of domestic violence alleged?	Each factor carries some weight, but no factor is dispositive. And there might even be other factors to consider in a particular situation.
3. What were the nature and frequency of the parties' interactions?	
4. What were the parties' ongoing expectations with respect to the relationship, either individually or jointly?	
5. Did the parties demonstrate an affirmation of their relationship before others by statement or conduct?	
6. Are there any other reasons unique to the case that support or detract from a finding that a "dating relationship" exists?	
Andrews v. Rutherford, 363 N.J. Super. 252 (Ch. Div. 2003)	

There are two ways to approach the organization of a factors test. How you organize the argument will depend on how interdependent and inter-related those factors are to each other.

1. Interrelated factors

When the factors are intertwined with each other, as they are in the above Internet dating example, you may find yourself repeating the same facts from cases as you move through each factor's individual analysis. If that is happening, stop and think about reorganizing the explanation around the holistic stories involved in those cases. In Appendix B, Ms. Hawthorne's brief is organized in that fashion. The Application's paragraphs start with thesis sentences that relate to the various factors, but the structure is much more fluid or blended than six individual CREACs.

If there are relatively few cases that you are able to use, you may also choose an alternative organization. Rather than create individualized headings for each factor with miniature CREAC argument structures, you may opt to have no headings, but just paragraphs of explanation. Likewise, you might also choose to group some of the factors together and treat them as a group to show how courts have balanced the factors in prior cases. This is how the author organized Ms. Hawthorne's argument in the Internet dating brief.

2. Individualized factors

Another choice is to handle each element separately, with a CREAC structure for each factor. That choice makes sense when the factors are very distinct. In a negligence case, the court may consider distinct factors to determine whether the element of "failure to adhere to a standard of care" has been proven:

- Industry standards of reasonable care
- Local standards of reasonable care
- The usual protocols of the defendant and whether they were in use at the time of the incident
- The external factors that might have affected the defendant's ability to react to a dangerous situation (e.g., time of day, day of the week, time of the year)

> **If a court sets out a factor test in a particular order, do I have to discuss them in that order?**
>
> No. You are bound only by what makes the most sense to you in advocating for your client. If you are creating a list of factors based on your own research and synthesis, then create whatever list works best for your client. If you are using a list created by a court, then you may nevertheless change the order of discussion, provided you include a sentence or two about why you are addressing the factors in an order different from what you just led readers to expect.

In this type of a situation, it might make sense to set out each factor individually and to separately explain and apply the law related to each factor. The structure might look quite a lot like CREAC. However, unlike an elements-based analysis, in most cases, you will not analyze every potential factor individually. Usually, you will show how the factors fit together. Of course, in many cases, there will be some factors that simply do not apply to your situation.

3. Factor tests pop up everywhere

Even when you have an elements test, factors frequently play an important role. For one thing, many times the presence or absence of one of the elements may itself depend on a factors analysis. For example, one of the elements of a cause of action for negligence is a failure of the defendant to adhere to a particular standard of care. Determining whether that element is met depends, of course, on how one defines the applicable standard of care, which is often a fuzzy concept that depends on a number of factors.

At this point in the writing process, you should have a complete working draft of the main parts of your brief: the Statement of Facts and the Argument section. In Part IV and the chapters to follow, we will begin to work through these drafts and turn them into polished writing that you will be proud to file with the court.

Part IV

Revising, polishing, and finishing

Supreme Court Justice Louis Brandeis, himself an outstanding writer, is often quoted as having said, "There is no great writing, only great rewriting."[1]

For many writers, getting that first draft done is the hardest part of writing. But as Justice Brandeis admonishes, that is just the beginning of the process. To turn writing into "great writing," the writer must engage in the lengthy process of revising and polishing that first working draft. Part IV takes on the next two phases of writing: revising and polishing.

Chapters 14 and 15 discuss the revising stage. Although all sections of the brief must go through that stage, the longest time is spent on revising the Argument and Statement of Facts. Lawyers organize and shape the wording during the revising stage by focusing on the client's point of view.

Chapters 16 and 17 focus on other formal sections of the brief. Chapter 16 describes how to write an Introduction, or "Preliminary Statement," and Chapter 17 discusses the other formal sections required by most courts' rules of appellate procedure.

Finally, Chapter 18 focuses on the polishing phase of the writing process by providing some basic principles of document design and formatting.

---

[1] Many well-known, accomplished writers have described the pain of writing and rewriting. Author John Irving, for example, has said, "More than a half, maybe as much as two-thirds of my life as a writer is rewriting. I wouldn't say I have a talent that's special. It strikes me that I have an unusual kind of stamina." One of the textbook author's favorite writing quotations is this one by Nathaniel Hawthorne: "Easy reading is damned hard writing."

Chapter 14

Revising the Argument: finding your client's point of view

At this point, you should have a working draft of your Argument section. You should be reasonably confident in the strength of your analysis, and the organization should be clear. The next step is making the working draft as persuasive as it can be. That is done by carefully revising the working draft to make sure that the client's point of view is evident throughout the Argument.

The precise wording of legal arguments matters a great deal. The language must convey the argument from your client's point of view. That point of view perspective guides the language choices across the whole of the legal argument: the headings, the rule statements, the rule explanation, and the application. This critical concept, if kept front and center in each section of the Argument, will make the legal argument that much easier to revise. And doing so will make the Argument client centered and therefore more persuasive.

I. Cognitively priming your readers

Readers who are prepared to hear what you have to say are more likely to accept your message. (This is why most headline acts have "warm-up" performers play before they take the stage.) This psychological concept is known as "cognitive priming."[1] Readers process new information by forming constructs that they base on whatever context is most recently provided to them.[2] If no context is given, readers automatically fill in the gaps in the new information with their prior experiences, which fall outside the control of the writer. Strong legal writers use priming techniques to steer readers away from making guesses or assumptions based on the

---

[1]Michael J. Higdon, *Something Judicious This Way Comes: The Use of Foreshadowing as Persuasive Technique in Judicial Narrative*, 44 U. Rich. L. Rev. 1213, 1218 (2010).
[2]*Id.* at 1220–1221.

readers' own experiences, and to instead fill in gaps with concepts consistent with the client's story.

This well-known example demonstrates the point. What is the central figure in this diagram?

	12	
A	B	C
	14	

Is it the letter B or the number 13? It's arguably either one. If, before looking at that diagram, however, the text had included something about the graphic design of numbers, you might be more inclined to see this as the number 13 rather than as the letter B.[3]

Cognitive priming occurs when the audience draws on previously learned material to form an analytical response to new material. By priming early on in a section of writing, you may predispose readers to reach the desired answer.

In legal writing, strategically choosing precise words primes readers toward your client's point of view. Certain places in the legal argument lend themselves especially well to creating these types of **persuasion pressure points**:

- Headings
- Rule statements
- Rule explanation thesis sentences
- Application thesis sentences

In this chapter, we look at each of these persuasion pressure points to explore how to revise an Argument to make it more persuasive. Notice that each of these pressure points is a beginning: headings begin CREACs, Rule statements begin the explanation of the law, and thesis sentences, in either the Rule Explanation or Application, begin paragraphs. This makes them prime candidates for priming!

II. Persuading through headings and introductions

Priming can work for the client at the beginning of each subdivision of the argument.

---

[3]*Id.* (citing the example and explanation of Ian E. Gordon, *Theories of Visual Perception* (Psychology Press 2004)).

A. Writing persuasive point headings

Headings provide contextual clues for readers, the "you are here" signals. They also stand out, visually. That means readers' eye will naturally be drawn to headings. Headings are thus perfect opportunities to persuade readers toward your client's position. Your working draft should already have headings that accurately reflect your organization. Now is when those headings are revised to better prime readers for your client's story.

Headings require careful attention. Choose the language strategically to lead readers toward the desired response: the finished and polished headings will be client centered and will provide answers up front. The design and length also need to draw readers in rather than intimidate them. You want the audience to read your headings, not skip over them.

To start working on a persuasive heading, think about boiling the essence or purpose of that argument section down to a six-word story. Focus on exactly what that section needs to demonstrate for your client to move ahead in the argument.

To illustrate how to use the six-word story to revise a heading, consider opposing lawyers writing on the Internet dating case. Assume Mr. Beagle wants the court to focus on the limitation of the meaning of "dating relationship"— a question of law. On the other hand, Ms. Hawthorne wants to focus on the broad discretion of the trial court to determine whether a dating relationship exists—a question of procedure.

> **Try this: writing six-word headings**
>
> Come up with a six-word story for each of the major subsections of your working document. When you are satisfied with it, write it on a sticky note and put it on your computer screen as you write that subsection.

Here is what the six-word stories might look like for the headings on this point. Remember that six-word stories can be extremely informal. They exist simply as vehicles to boil down ideas to their essence.

> Mr. Beagle: "Skype kissing isn't dating relationship-y enough."
> *versus*
> Ms. Hawthorne: "Statute, trial judge discretion, both broad."

Now, compare these two headings from two student-authored briefs from the same case and about the same issue, but from opposing parties:

> Mr. Beagle: The parties' online-only interactions never created a relationship beyond a mere friendship.
> *versus*
> Ms. Hawthorne: The court has properly interpreted the expansive scope of "dating relationship" when it took jurisdiction over the case.

Notice how these headings, while each pointing toward opposite outcomes, aren't framed as mirror opposites of each other. They work toward opposite outcomes using different story lines. The first heading promises a fact analysis that will show how absurd it is for courts to allow online communication to form the basis of a "relationship" in a domestic violence scenario. The second heading, on the other hand, is centered on the procedural posture, that this case and issue was already properly decided by the trial judge, who was there to assess credibility and nonverbal behaviors. Although these two headings do not mirror each other, they both set up their argument from the perspective that best supports their clients' position.

> **Try this: rehearsing the skill of headings**
>
> Go back to an earlier document you wrote in your legal writing course: one of your memos. Imagine you now represent that client and are writing a persuasive brief. Re-write the heading so that it points toward a particular outcome and is presented from your client's point of view.

Keep in mind that, in the end, both of these subsections will discuss the same law. It is the frameworks that are presented differently. Both writers seek to prime readers toward a different conclusion because each writer has a different client who seeks a particular outcome. All of this comes across simply by wording the point heading to reflect the client's point of view.

It is certainly possible that both authors could have constructed client-centered headings without first drafting a six-word story. However, that intermediate step—of forcing oneself to boil an argument down to its essence—can bring even the most complex analysis into crisp focus. It is a simple but effective tool for crafting persuasive headings.

The main point to keep in mind here is that headings should be told from the client's point of view. But the way in which they are presented matters too. The format and style of headings depends to some degree on writer or reader preferences or customary practices in your jurisdiction. For example, a major point heading might merit a full sentence, complete with a "because" clause that explains, succinctly, the basic reason for the outcome. Other writers might prefer shorter headings that are phrases rather than complete sentences. For subheadings and sub-subheadings, shorter phrases probably make more sense for both visual and content purposes. (Refer to the shadow box in Chapter 13 for a discussion of some of the stylistic considerations for point headings.)

B. Setting a persuasive context up front (is there still a C in CREAC?)

Good legal writers will all tell novices that it is critical to put the bottom line up front in the argument section. Too often, the drafting process ends before the writer moves the bottom line from—well—the bottom to up front where it is does the work of cognitive priming. An easy acronym to use as an editing checklist reminder is "BLUF" or "bottom line up front."

The only debate among legal writers is what to include in that bottom line. Many writers start the section of an argument with a contextual client-centered sentence stating the conclusion (the C of CRAC/CREAC paradigm). Other readers leave the conclusion in the headings and begin the textual discussion with a statement of the governing rule.

Is it necessary to have a C sentence in the text of the section? The answer, of course, is: it depends! Many times, the heading of an argument's section is already a contextual and client-centered conclusion. In those instances, there's no need to repeat the information. You may lose readers' attention and interest if you do.

There's also a very pragmatic reason to skip the C in the text if the heading already does that work: it saves space. That can make a critical difference if the document is subject to a rule about maximum pages, length, lines per page, or maximum word count.

> ### Cutting and pasting cautions
>
> If you cut and paste text straight from the heading or from the roadmap into that opening context of the argument section, you are almost guaranteed to lose credibility with your reader. Cutting and pasting is obvious and conveys a tone of disrespect—a reader assumes that the writer did not trust the reader to have read the material the first time.

The catch is that readers have to see the heading and the text as one unit—that's often a function of formatting the heading so that it is in close-enough proximity to the text to be read with the text. (For more on formatting tips, see Chapter 18.)

Although the above paragraphs suggest that you stay away from including a separate C statement in the text of the argument section, there are times when it makes perfect sense to start the section with the conclusion:

- When the heading is simplified for length/readability purposes, thus suggesting a need for a longer textual sentence up front. The goal here is one of readability in the heading. Headings are so important, and so easy to throw off balance with their font size and boldface that if you see a heading that is extending too many lines, opt for a shorter one and a longer first textual sentence.

- When the writer chooses to make the heading a statement of law rather than a client-centered statement. That's an acceptable use of headings and a common variation on the traditional CREAC paradigm (look back at Chapter 13 for those variations on CREAC).
- When the person supervising your work prefers the repetition. Some readers do read headings separately from text, even when headings are visually close to the text. Thus some writers prefer to repeat their conclusions in the first sentence of text to make sure that readers who skim over the headings still have the context of the argument. But even then, don't repeat the conclusions word for word. Instead, rephrase the same idea.

III. Persuasively wording the rules

Like headings, rule statements will do a lot of the heavy lifting for your persuasion if you write them in a way that is client centered in tone and context. The goal of your rule statement drafting should be a clear, pro-client formulation of the governing rule of law, so that a court need change only a very few words to adopt it as a holding.

When drafting rule statements, imagine the holding you want the court to write. If the holding looks very much like your own formulations of the rules, then you have written it in a client-centered way. If, however, the court has to completely rewrite or "turn around" your rule statement for your client to prevail, then you need to revisit your approach. To formulate a client-centered rule that easily translates into a holding, begin by thinking about the visual images your rules create.

A. Client-centered imagery

Why does a persuasive rule statement strategy work? For the same reasons stated earlier in this chapter: rule statements prime readers for the examples you will illustrate during the rule explanation of the legal argument. Writing in a client-centered way also puts your readers into your client's frame of thinking. Finally, a client-centered statement will likely use some sort of imagery or metaphors that will help anchor the information in readers' minds.

Consider these two statements, both describing the same time of year:

> It was almost spring. The sun was shining, and the trees were budding. The whites and pinks of blooming trees were only a few weeks away.
>
> *versus*

> Winter appeared to be ending. The snow had melted and the trees were no longer bare.

Different images are formed in readers' minds for each of these descriptions. In the first, readers will likely visualize a sunny day in a season that looks something like the stock structure of "spring." (Stock structures are described in Chapter 3.) Readers are left with an impression of the season that is to come—trees in bud and about to bloom.

In contrast, readers of the second statement have a much harder time coming up with that same picture. Even though the writer's statement talks about the same period, the second statement will likely imprint an image of winter. Although the second statement talks about winter in the past tense, to get to a picture of almost-spring versus ending-winter, readers must do a great deal of original visualization work to imagine the almost-spring images contained in the first statement. Readers of that second statement will instead visualize winter, with snow and bare trees. Did you? Notice that the second sentence states the snow had *melted* and the tree were *no longer* bare! To get from there to an image of spring, there's much more effort involved. On the other hand, if the writer wants readers to visualize the end of winter instead of the beginning of spring, the second example will be more effective.

The same potentials exist when discussing the governing rule in an argument section. A writer can write the rule of law in a way that makes it easy for readers to imagine the writer's client prevailing. Or the writer can leave it to chance, risking a rule statement that leaves readers in a position of having to work harder to reach a conclusion that favors the writer's client. Obviously, we recommend writing the rule statement in a way that favors setting the context in a way that makes it easiest for the client to succeed. We will walk through examples in the next section.

B. Statutes and common law rules: the same advocacy principles apply

A lawyer's role—to analyze the governing law and to advocate for a client based on the situation—clearly extends into the communication of the governing rule of law. If the governing legal rule was so absolute as to defy advocacy, there would be no dispute. The parties would settle, since the very fact that there is a dispute must mean that the rules of law (or at least the application of the law to the facts of the case) are subject to interpretation. And thus, you must write rule statements with care. They are much too important to leave to a mechanistic formula of cutting and pasting from authority or, even worse, to leave to the opposing party to formulate.

This is true even when the rule you are formulating involves the interpretation of a statutory or regulatory term. While the applicable part of the statute or regulation itself must be quoted precisely, there would be no dispute unless the interpretation was somehow at issue. And it is that interpretation that allows the writer to create a persuasive formulation of the rule statement.

Likewise, as you learned in the introductory semester of legal writing, if the governing rule comes from common law, the lawyer's job involves more than just quoting from the case language. A lawyer is paid to explain the analysis. In persuasive writing, that might mean generating a rule statement that is told from a different point of view than the one used by courts in that case precedent.

Here are a series of examples that demonstrate how you can revise your rule statement to reflect the client's point of view. After each example is a table explaining what certain word choices were designed to do.

1. Statutory law

Even when the rule derives from a statute, lawyers still prime readers with advocacy in the way that the statute is introduced. Here is one example from a student brief on the Internet dating case:

> The New Jersey Legislature specifically called for a broad interpretation of the state's Prevention of Domestic Violence Act because of its protective purpose. Thus, courts interpreting the definition of "dating relationship" in Section 19(d) will take jurisdiction over a case such as this one, when the parties are in the type of relationship that is either family or family-like.

Trigger words	Priming purpose
broad interpretation	The theory of the case, "broad reading," is up front and center to prioritize the statutory analysis tools and to show the discretion of the trial court.
protective purpose	Provides a reminder of the plaintiff's need for help.
"dating relationship" in Section 19(d)	Exactly quote the key phrase from the statute. We must include this in our rule statement.

Trigger words	Priming purpose
take jurisdiction over a case such as this one, when the parties . . .	Wording makes it seem like taking jurisdiction is pro forma—like a permit or license. Notice too that the writer's client makes a brief appearance in this rule statement. That's perfectly acceptable in a brief in which the document exists to advocate.
. . . are in the type of relationship that is either family or family-like.	The phrase "type of relationship" stakes a pretty broad tent. The "either family or family-like" phrasing is also designed to show how large a tent jurisdiction is. Parties don't have to be family, just "family-like." Again, as a carryover, notice how the writer's statement suggests the outcome of the client's case.

An easy conversion into a judicial decision:

By carefully crafting the argument from her client's point of view, the writer has made it easier for the court to rule in her favor. First, of course, readers will look at the dispute from the client's point of view—and be more likely to adopt that same point of view. However, there is a second way that point-of-view writing helps readers—the precise word choices give judges a framework for their own work. With this kind of rule statement, readers can easily turn this into a holding with very little editing. "We interpret the definition of 'victim' in Section 19(d) to allow jurisdiction over a case such as this one, when the parties are in the type of relationship that is family-like." There are very few changes in wording between the writer's rule and the court's decision.

The other party's formulation of the same rule:

The other party to this dispute could likewise write a persuasive rule statement. That writer, however, would develop a different theory of the case and therefore would tell a different story, even while introducing the same statutory language. Here is an example, showing the opposing story to the first example:

> Because the New Jersey Prevention of Domestic Violence Act is expansive in the scope of its relief, the appellate courts are increasingly cautious about the overstretching of the jurisdictional boundaries in Section 19(d) of the Act by expanding the scope of "dating relationship." The most recent decisions have limited the types of people who may bring an action. Trial judges must dismiss a case such as this one when the parties have only a mere casual relationship that is outside the scope of close and family, or family-like, interactions.

Trigger words	Priming purpose
Because . . .	Readers are primed for a policy rationale for the interpretation the writer is about to offer.
increasingly cautious . . . overstretching	Suggesting this court likewise be cautious and consider the particulars of a given situation (as opposed to a liberal, broad application). Notice too, the use of visual imagery here. "Overstretching" feels like a rubber band that has stretched too far and is weakened as a result—perhaps about to break.
expanding the scope of "dating relationship"	Again, exactly quote the key statutory phrase.
The most recent decisions . . .	"Most recent" is a powerful way to synthesize a decision or a series of decisions.
limited outside the scope a mere casual relationship	Using the terms "limited" and "outside the scope" as counterwords to the opposing party's use of "broad" is much more effective than using the antonym "narrow"—particularly if the word "broad" appears in the case law and "narrow" doesn't. It's very important, when seeking to counter a particular phrase, to find words that are supported by the case law rather than simply choosing the antonym; "limited" as the antidote to "broad" is a good example of that lesson on efficacy. The antidote words to "family or family-like" were chosen the same way: the writer avoided using a direct antonym or using the word "not" to counter.
Trial judges must dismiss a case such as this one when . . .	Notice how the rule statement builds in the preferred outcome for this particular client.

An easy conversion into a judicial decision:

As with the first example, this writer's presentation of the rule statement provides persuasive priming for the outcome. And the writer has made it very easy for readers to convert the writer's words into a judicial decision: "The case is dismissed because the parties have only a mere casual relationship that is outside the scope of close and routine family or family-like interactions."

2. Common law

Similarly, in a common law context, the writer can state the applicable rule of law in several ways. Here are some examples, taken from the two opposing briefs in our hotel reservation example, showing how writers for the two parties made different persuasive choices in stating the same rule of law:

From the brief for the nonprofit organization:

> [A] contract provision that claims to be a liquidated damages clause will not be enforced if it is in reality a penalty for nonperformance. This determination is made on a case-by-case basis, without the benefit of strict guidelines, but using a number of factors. *Gershin v. Demming*, 685 N.E.2d 1125, 1127–28 (Ind. Ct. App. 1997).

Trigger words	Priming purpose
claims to be a liquidated damages clause	The word "claims" focuses readers' attention on the possibility (which the writer advocates) that the clause really is not a liquidated damages clause, but a penalty.
will not be enforced	This language leans in the direction that the advocate wants: do not enforce this clause.
in reality a penalty	Another direct suggestion of the conclusion the writer wants the court to make.
case-by-case basis, without the benefit of strict guidelines	The writer knows that the reasoning of this case tilts against his client; the contractual provision, on its face, seems to obligate his client to pay the claimed damages. But the facts of the client's particular situation create a strong argument in its favor. A nonprofit organization can ill afford to lose the money, while the hotel would barely notice whether it were paid or not. This sentence lets the court know that facts matter and that it has some freedom to decide the case in whatever manner seems just.

From the brief for the hotel:

Whether a contractual provision stipulating damages in the event of a breach is a valid liquidated damages clause or a penalty is a question of law for the court. *Mandle v. Owens*, 164 Ind. App. 607, 610–11, 330 N.E.2d 362, 364 (1975). In determining whether a stipulated sum payable on breach of a contract constitutes liquidated damages or a penalty, the court will consider the facts, the intention of the parties and the reasonableness of the stipulation under the circumstances of the case. *Nylen v. Park Doral Apts.*, 535 N.E.2d 178, 184 (Ind. Ct. App. 1989).

Trigger words	Priming purpose
a contractual provision stipulating damages in the event of a breach	The writer wants the court to focus on the fact that this is a contract and that it has been breached. Also, since "liquidated damages" sounds a little too much like a powerful party is taking advantage of a weaker party, the writer has described the clause as an agreement to "stipulate[e] damages," which sounds more like two equals reaching an agreement.
valid liquidated damages clause or a penalty	Here, the writer could not avoid the term "liquidated damages" since that is a term of art used by all of the court decisions. However, the writer has primed the court for a favorable ruling by placing the adjective "valid" before "liquidated damages."
In determining whether a stipulated sum payable on breach of a contract constitutes liquidated damages or a penalty	Similar to first point, but the repetition of the language "stipulated sum" and "breach of a contract" serves to reinforce the idea that there is an agreement between the parties that the nonprofit breached.
the court will consider	Here the writer chooses active voice to describe the role that the court must play in deciding the case. In the SOFT brief, the writer had recited this same standard in a direct quote from a case, using the passive construction "are to be considered." This suggests that the writer of the hotel brief is recruiting the court to agree with the hotel, by directly acknowledging the court's role in the dispute.

All of these choices are subtle, but important. And just as in the statutory examples above, both rule statements are worded so that it would be easy for a court to lift the statement right out of the lawyer's brief and drop it into the court's opinion.

IV. Rule explanation: illustrating the rule with precise details and stock structures

The same visual imagery and cognitive priming principles apply when providing readers with concrete illustrations of the rule's usage or development.

These two principles combine when a legal writer provides illustrations from case law or the like. Specifically, the purpose of providing those illustrations is to allow readers to create visual images, using either the specific details provided by the writer or stock stories or schemas. Recall from Chapter 3 that a writer uses stock stories to shape the way that the audience draws on their existing experiences, memories, or shared community understandings.

A. The storytelling of the rule explanation

Although it's critical in each argument section to provide a statement of the governing rule or section of the rule, that alone will be too abstract for readers. The analogies that the legal writer draws on for the heart of a legal argument must draw on readers' concrete concepts of the actual workings of that governing rule.

This is where story comes in again. Because humans learn best from information delivered in story form, the rule explanation part of a legal argument is best communicated as pure storytelling. Tell readers stories of what happened in other scenarios when the courts used that governing rule or subpart of the rule. That is called a case illustration or, if it helps remind you of what you are trying to do, a "case story." Stories of the legislative intent and process can also form part of the overall rule's explanation when you have a statutory issue.

To keep the client's point of view front and center, the legal writer must choose carefully which details to focus on and, most important, to have readers focus on. Think back to Chapter 9's discussion of description and the four things that can be described:

- Actions
- Settings

Avoid pitfalls when describing a character

Be particularly mindful of including too much description about a character all in one place in the Statement of Facts, especially in the opening paragraphs of the facts section. Including too many details about a character is one of the things that will create skepticism in the legal reader because it can look like a blatant appeal to emotion. Instead, spread those details out across the whole of the section.

- Objects
- People

Readers will want to know a general sense of where or when the key events took place and who or what was involved. The whole story of the case need not appear in the rule explanation, but parts of it will.

Because the legal writer typically needs to convey the illustration in a relatively few number of words, using stock structures to convey meaning takes on a special significance. The reader wants to know, *generally*, the types of characters or objects involved, the setting, and events, but the writer will want to rely on common understandings of many of those things. That permits him to guide readers toward only those specific details that really matter to understand that particular subsection's rule.

This means that the careful writer needs to strike a balance. On the one hand, the writer can't skimp on the information because that will leave readers with the need to read the authority for themselves to understand the writer's reliance on it. But, at the same time, the writer has to take care to avoid overloading readers with information that might clutter or distract them from the unique facts that are important to that particular subsection's argument.

This generally translates into providing three pieces of information to readers with each cited case: the basic story of the conflict, the holding

Deciding what to include in a case illustration

- What details and stock structures can you use that will put an indelible image in readers' minds?
- What unique facts of a case story did the court rely on to decide this part of the governing rule?
- Did the court comment on the importance of those unique facts or signal their importance through the use of detail?
- Did the court imply importance or imply a lack of importance through the use or omission of detail?
- How do those unique facts (or lack of unique facts) ultimately measure up to those of your client's situation?

of the case and any important reasoning, and the outcome of the case (meaning who won).

For example, in the Internet dating case, the respondent relies on the case *J.S. v. J.F.* One way of doing a case illustration for that case would be this:

In J.S. v. J.F., 410 *N.J. Super.* 611, 612 (App. Div. 2009), the defendant claimed that the parties were not dating because he allegedly paid for the plaintiff to accompany him to his family's Thanksgiving dinner. But testimony demonstrated that the parties had multiple dates, dinners, and evenings together and other regular interactions as a couple. The state appellate court found that, even if the defendant had, in fact, paid for the plaintiff's company, the evidence also described multiple other dates, dinners, and evenings together. And the court held that arrangements to pay for the "dating" do not necessarily end the dating inquiry. The appellate court affirmed the trial court's denial of the defendant's motion to dismiss the action.	**Basic facts** **Court's holding and reasoning** **Outcome of the case**

While that case illustration is completely accurate, it is fairly neutral in tone. A more persuasive way of illustrating this case would be something like this:

In one recent case with a relationship much more traditional than the one in front of the court today, the court ruled that the parties in that case were in a common form of a dating relationship. *J.S. v. J.F.*, 410 *N.J. Super.* 611, 612 (App. Div. 2009). In that case, although the defendant claimed that the plaintiff was merely someone whom he had paid to accompany him to his family's Thanksgiving dinner, the testimony at the final restraining order hearing demonstrated a typical relationship involving multiple dates and evenings in each other's company. Even if the defendant had, in fact, paid for the plaintiff's company, the court held that fact did not preclude further inquiry into the nature of the relationship.	**Bottom line (who won) up front** **Basic facts** **Holding and reasoning**

Notice that the court found a dating relationship based on the multiple dates the parties had. The Thanksgiving dinner details were really beside the point. The author chose to emphasize these details to show that even peculiar relationships (who pays for someone to go to Thanksgiving dinner?) can be part of dating. Perhaps more important, it makes the story of this case memorable.

Of course, how a writer puts these elements together is a strategy decision and will depend on how much reliance or weight the lawyer wants the reviewing court to give the case.

B. Write about cases by putting the bottom line up front

As with all persuasive writing, the thesis sentence that introduces the case illustration will likewise focus readers on those details that matter. For that reason, it is much more persuasive to start the rule explanation with the bottom line up front rather than with the case name and citation.

Based on the "bottom line up front" introduction in the example above, it should be easy to ascertain whether this case will ultimately be analogized or distinguished from in the Application. Notice how the case name and citation appeared at the end of the first sentence rather than serving as the lead off. Placing the case name and citation in the position of emphasis in a paragraph is a waste of the prime persuasion real estate of that paragraph.

C. Choosing the length of the rule explanation: in-text versus parentheticals

A writer has choices about how much space to use for writing about a particular case's story. Those choices range from a clause (a parenthetical) to in-text sentences, paragraphs, or pages. In some situations, only a brief statement of what the case stands for, followed by a citation, is necessary (typically where the rule stated is well settled, easy to apply, and uncontroversial). In other cases, some context about the facts of the case is necessary to help readers understand how the rule works. That context might be as little as a parenthetical explanation following the case citation or as much as one or more paragraphs, or even pages, providing a great deal of background and discussion about the case (a case illustration). These choices lie along a continuum; different situations call for different choices along that continuum.

There's no need to allot a full paragraph to each case discussed in an argument section. In fact, it's often a much stronger arguing technique to discuss several cases together in a single paragraph that starts with an overarching thesis sentence.

Deciding whether to use parentheticals or in-text explanations really depends on how much information readers need to understand about that case and how important the case is to the outcome of that subsection of argument. There are no hard and fast formulas but only competing strategy considerations. For that reasons, a good brief will have a mix of case explanation lengths.

At some point, the length of the document starts to become an important consideration. There's also a limit to how much a writer wants to include from a particular case in any one subsection. Only part of the case story is important for that subsection. It's at that point that the writer has a choice between in-text or parenthetical presentation of the case information.

1. *Will an illustration help readers at all?*

A great deal of the time, the answer to this question is yes. Only in the simplest of situations can a writer allow stock structures to carry the day. One test is how debatable the point being offered is. As noted earlier in this textbook, there's generally not a lot of debate, for example, about whether a labradoodle is a dog for the purposes of interpreting a dog bite statute. If you were citing a case for that point, a parenthetical is all you would need. On the other hand, the writer might need to use more detailed case explanations to talk about whether a dog licking some-one falls under the definition of "bite."

An example of an effective use of a parenthetical instead of a full case illustration is found in the hotel's brief in our hotel room reservation case:

> In some cases, a dispute has arisen as to whether a liquidated damages provision is the exclusive remedy or whether a nonbreaching party may seek relief in addition to liquidated damages. *See, e.g., Beck v. Mason*, 580 N.E.2d 290, 293 (Ind. Ct. App. 1991) (holding that describing an earnest money deposit in a real estate sales contract as "liquidated damages" was sufficient proof that the parties intended to limit their remedies to that clause).

2. *How important is the case to the argument?*

If the case is central to the dispositive argument, then it is better to opt for a more detailed illustration for that case. If the case illustration is not dis-positive but is merely supportive of the argument, then it is possible that a single sentence or a parenthetical clause may suffice.

3. How complicated are the facts of the case?

Even if a case is not dispositive, the context of the facts may still take a few sentences to explain to readers. In that situation, opt for better writing: choose to use in-text sentences. Remember that the choice can still be one sentence, two sentences, three sentences, or more. A writer is never committed to a full paragraph about a case unless she wishes to commit that much space.

D. Drafting parentheticals

Parentheticals appear at end of a citation sentence. They are typically clauses or phrases, as opposed to full sentences. Parentheticals might use single words or single descriptors. They might also borrow a quotation from a case that helps explain the rule further.

There are common pitfalls to parentheticals, the most prevalent of which is using a parenthetical to restate the abstract rule rather than using a story or a piece of a story to illustrate an example of the rule's use. Because this is such a common error, it's a good idea to check parentheticals for their content.

There are three different ways to use parentheticals. Some are more common than others. The bottom line for any legal writer is to choose among these and to draft accordingly.

1. Narrative parentheticals

Narrative parentheticals are the most common type. These substitute for an in-text rule explanation and provide enough detail about the story of the case to give readers a sense of what happened as it pertains to the subsections' rule statement. Often, but not always, this is the parenthetical that begins with present participles: the *-ing* words. For example, the brief of the Gloucester Hotel in our hotel reservation case includes this citation:

> *See, e.g., Beck v. Mason,* 580 N.E.2d 290, 293 (Ind. Ct. App. 1991) (holding that describing an earnest money deposit in a real estate sales contract as "liquidated damages" was sufficient proof that the parties intended to limit their remedies to that clause).

2. List parentheticals

List parentheticals are shorter forms of narrative parentheticals. These parentheticals can provide the relevant case information in just a word or two. Something like this:

> Oregon courts cast a wide net when contemplating what can be considered a pavement hazard that gives rise to a commercial owner's duty. *Gardener v. Portland Nursery,* 321 P.3d 622 (Or. 2004) (overgrown

rosebushes); *MacTarnahan v. MeMenamin,* 814 P.2d 802 (Or. 1982) (beer keg); *Blumenauer v. Wyden,* 409 P.3d 112 (Or. App. 2010) (spilled recycling can); *Beard v. Ringside Restaurant, Inc.,* 248 P.3d 624 (Or. App. 2002) (bag of root vegetables).[4]

3. Quote parentheticals

This last type borrows exact language from a decision. Quotes used in this last—and rarest—type of parenthetical often are where a writer mistakenly restates the legal rule. Instead, quote parentheticals should show a particular turn of phrase that adds concreteness to an otherwise abstract rule. One situation where it makes sense to use a quote in a parenthetical is where a metaphor has become central to a legal principle, like this:

> *Reynolds v. U.S.,* 98 U.S. 145, 164 (1878) (recognizing Jefferson's metaphor of the "wall of separation between church and state").

When your authority provides precise language like a metaphor or term of art, it is appropriate to quote that precise language in a parenthetical. Still, be careful that you are quoting language that helps explain the asserted legal principle rather than merely restating the principle itself.

Consider this passage from the hotel's brief in our hotel reservation example. In discussing when liquidated damages provisions in contracts are appropriate, the author notes the rule that such clauses are valid when the specified damages are not grossly disproportionate to the damages that would likely result from a breach. The brief goes on:

> [I]t is important to remember that this determination is evaluated as of the time of the signing of the contract, not at the time of breach. *Rogers,* 767 N.E.2d at 991 (liquidated damages clauses are unenforceable where the payment specified "is grossly disproportionate to the loss *which may result* from breach") (emphasis supplied); *Gershin,* 685 N.E.2d at 1128 (liquidated damages clauses are enforceable where the payment specified "is not greatly disproportionate to the loss *likely to occur*") (emphasis supplied).

The writer chose to cite two cases to emphasize the point that the determination is viewed from the point of view of the parties at the time they signed the contract. Since different courts expressed that concept in different language, the writer chose two different formulations of the rule to show that it is well settled and uncontroversial.

---

[4]Do not rely on these cases as authority. We made them up!

V. Application

So now you have written all of your rule statements and rule explanations so that they favor your client's position. Now it is time to apply those rules to your client's case to show why the law supports a ruling in favor of your client. Many of the same principles discussed above about drafting a persuasive rule statement also apply to drafting a persuasive application.

Just as writing a case illustration as a "case story" helps readers retain information about the case, including vivid details of the client's story helps readers see how a ruling in favor of the client will assist that client in achieving his worthy goal, whatever it may be. The application section of any CREAC is a golden opportunity to retell the client's story, or at least some important part of the story.

Application can be straightforward, such as where there is a clear statute directly on point or a nearly identical case. Or it can be more complicated, such as where the applicable authority is unclear or novel. But regardless of the situation, the writer's primary goal in application is to connect the client's case to the authorities used in the rule explanation.

To illustrate this point, here is a visual exercise. Create a single enclosed space by connecting all four of these dots:

•   •

•   •

Which answer is correct?

All of them!

Most people would connect the dots in the most obvious way—by drawing a square. However, nothing in the instruction required this. In fact, there are an endless number of ways to connect the dots that would be consistent with the instruction. Sometimes, looking to connect the dots in a different way can reveal new and persuasive insights. That's also the take-home message about connecting dots in legal analysis: sometimes you need to look beyond the obvious or superficial connections between your authorities and your case.

Remember back to Chapter 2 and the idea that response reinforcing is the easiest way to persuade somebody because the audience will be predisposed toward accepting the argument. Craft your writing to be as response reinforcing as possible, rather than response changing. The more you can show how your client's position is consistent with the judge's likely perceptions (or "frames") about what is fair and just, the easier it will be to persuade the judge that the client is right. This, of course, invites the question: how do we build a response-reinforcing argument? Following are situations you may find yourself in, including how to find response-reinforcing ways to apply the law to your facts.

A. Show how your legal position is consistent with existing precedent (arguing by analogy)

If the rule of law you are applying is a common law rule, it is obviously easiest to persuade a court when the facts of your client's case are materially identical with the facts of binding cases that were decided in a way that favors your client's position. When you have such a case (which lawyers describe as a case being "on all fours" with your case), writing the application is easy: you just show how the facts of your case are materially identical and argue that the same result should apply.

However, clients are rarely that lucky. More often, a dispute exists because there is more than one way to interpret and apply existing law and reasonable minds may differ on the most appropriate interpretation of existing law. Where novice legal writers sometimes fail is that they are unable to get beyond the surface of the precedent cases to reach a deeper

> **A time to tell**
>
> Throughout this text, we suggest that you should "show" your client's story to readers by using strong visual details rather than "tell" readers what the story is (or how to feel about it). In writing the Application, however, we make a bit of an exception. If you have previously shown the court what the case is about, in applying the law to the facts you can do a bit of telling.
>
> Thus, it would be perfectly okay to write something like "our case is just like the *Jones* case because, like Jones, the plaintiff in our case was similarly desperate to find the right shade of auburn hair."

understanding of what the existing law really means. Often a lawyer can find a more persuasive application of the law by looking for different ways to explain how the client's case is similar to the case law than might appear at first blush. Consider this passage from the rule explanation in the brief of the nonprofit organization in our hotel reservation example:

> In one case, a hotel was required to refund the plaintiff's deposit because of the otherwise disproportionate loss that the plaintiff would have suffered. *2625 Bldg. Corp. v. Deutsch*, 179 Ind. App. 425, 385 N.E.2d 1189 (1979). In that case, the plaintiff reserved six hotel rooms during the weekend of the Indianapolis 500 race and, upon doing so, paid $1,008.00 to the hotel, representing the full cost of the rooms. Two months prior to the reservation dates, the plaintiff cancelled the reservations and requested a refund. The hotel refused to return any of the advance payment. *Id.* at 1190.
>
> Although the contract in that case was oral and thus included no express liquidated damages clause, the court held that allowing the hotel "to retain damages representing payment for use of all the rooms, regardless of the fact that damages could be ascertained, would be to enforce a penalty or forfeiture." *Id.* at 1192. Moreover, "assessing Deutsch for the full amount of his room payments would cause him to suffer a loss which was wholly disproportionate to any injury sustained by [the hotel]." *Id.* at 1193. The court therefore ruled that the defendant hotel was required to refund the plaintiff's deposit.

Recall that the issue in our case is whether a liquidated damages clause in a written contract should be enforced or held to be an unenforceable penalty. At first glance, the case of *2625 Building Corp. v. Deutsch* appears to be unhelpful because the hotel reservation in that case was made orally and there was therefore no written liquidated damages clause to interpret. But look at the reasoning of the court: "retain[ing] damages representing payment for use of all the rooms, regardless of the fact that damages could be ascertained, would be to enforce a penalty or forfeiture." And doing so "would cause him to suffer a loss which was wholly disproportionate to any injury sustained" by the hotel. This sure sounds like the same rationale used by courts in interpreting written liquidated damages clauses. So, the author of the SOFT brief chose to include this case, along with other cases that did involve written contracts, and thereby managed to connect a case with very similar facts (i.e., a hotel getting paid for rooms not used by the party reserving them) to the facts of her own case, hoping that the case would reinforce the response the judge likely shares: it isn't fair for the hotel to keep somebody's money when it can resell those rooms to somebody else. Then, in the application part of the CREAC, the author applied the lesson of *2624 Building Corp.* to the facts of her case like this:

> Just as the court in *2625 Building Corp.* found that damages in the event of a breach were easily ascertainable, damages in this case are easily

ascertainable: the Hotel sent an invoice to SOFT for exactly 53 unused guest rooms. Freebird Dep. Ex. 3. More important, however, just as the court in *2625 Building Corp.* held that charging the patron who reserved the rooms but did not use them for the full value of those rooms was wholly disproportionate to any injury sustained by the hotel, charging SOFT with the full value of the rooms its members did not use is grossly disproportionate to any loss the Hotel might suffer. This is because the Hotel admittedly resold the rooms not reserved by members of SOFT. Pl.'s Answer to Req. for Produc. of Doc. ¶ 6.

B. Show how your position is materially different from precedent, and therefore should have the opposite result (arguing by distinction)

The opposite of a case "on all fours," of course, is a case that appears to reach a result contrary to what your client wants, on similar but not identical facts. In this situation, your application takes this form: "The case precedent says *x*, but the following dispositive facts are different. Since those facts were so important to the court's reasoning, and our case lacks those facts, the result in our case should be negative *x*." This is called "reasoning by distinction."

Here is an example of reasoning by distinction based on (but for the purposes of brevity, altered from) a description in Mr. Beagle's brief in the Internet dating example. Recall that in that case, Mr. Beagle was trying to prove that he was not in a "dating relationship" with Ms. Hawthorne. One of the applicable cases could be illustrated like this:

> In *Andrews,* the plaintiff and defendant were in a relationship for five months while the woman defendant had another boyfriend. 363 *N.J. Super.* 252 (Law. Div. 2003). The parties held themselves out as a couple in front of the plaintiff's family, but because of the defendant's other boyfriend, they hid their relationship from the defendant's family. *Id.* at 260. They were seen kissing, hugging, and being affectionate, and they went out at least 15 times over the course of a few months. *Id.* They would spend nights together, and they attended a number of social gatherings together. *Id.* at 261–62. The defendant argued that because she was in another relationship at the time, she could not be held to be in a dating relationship with the plaintiff. *Id.* Nevertheless, the court found that the sum of the circumstances sufficiently established that a dating relationship existed. *Id.* at 265.

Later in the brief, in applying that case to his own facts, Mr. Beagle writes:

> Previous cases have shown that there is usually a significant period of time, and frequent contact between the parties, before a dating

relationship can be found. In *Andrews,* the parties dated for four months, went out on at least 15 dates, were seen hugging and kissing, and on occasion spent nights together. 363 *N.J. Super.* 252 . . . . Since Mr. Beagle and Ms. Hawthorne met briefly in person only twice (once at a speed dating event and a second time by chance at a New Years' Eve party a few weeks later) and were never physically intimate, Ms. Hawthorne is unable to establish that the parties were in a dating relationship.

The most important thing to remember here is that, for reasoning by distinction to work, the distinction must be material. Thus, you would most likely never win by saying "The plaintiff in that case had red hair. Since my client has black hair, that case does not apply." Make sure that there is something in the reasoning of the court that suggests that the facts you are distinguishing made a difference, and be sure to quote that reasoning in the case illustration so that you can refer to it in the application. The petitioner in the example above did this by reporting the facts that the court in *Andrews* apparently found persuasive in determining that the parties were in a dating relationship, and then contrasting the facts of his own case with the facts reported in *Andrews.*

C. Show how the plain meaning of a statute directly supports the result your client wants

When instead of a common law rule you are dealing with a statutory rule, if possible, show the court how the statute unambiguously requires the court to rule in your client's favor.

In rare situations, that requires little more than reporting the facts of the case and showing the court how the express and unambiguous language of the statute requires the result the client seeks. This is rare because, if true, the parties would likely settle instead of bring suit. But if there is some ambiguity as to whether the statute applies or what it means, then the writer must examine and explain the rule more fully through statutory interpretation techniques, as described in Chapter 10. Once that is complete, the application is simply a matter of connecting the explanation of what the rule is to the specific facts of your case, similar to the manner of comparing precedent cases to the facts of your case.

D. If a statute appears to contradict the result your client wants, show how the statute does not apply

This is the corollary to "arguing by distinction" where the governing law is a common law rule. The only difference here is that you need to look for definitions within the statute, or previous court interpretations of the statute, that show why the statute does not cover your client's situation. The same caveat also applies here: make sure the difference between your case and what the statute covers is material.

After polishing the Argument section of your brief, it is time to rework the Statement of Facts in similar fashion.

Chapter 15

Revising the story: polishing the Statement of Facts

The working draft is now complete. The persuasion pressure points are in place. The brief looks like . . . a brief. It is time to start revising the working draft. Revising, in the latter stages, focuses on word choice and precision. Start with sections you wrote first so that you can account for any drift in the theme or the theory of the case that occurred during the later stages of writing the working draft.

The Prologue of this book began with the truism that **writing is thinking**. So many "A-ha!" moments happen while composing at the keyboard, that it is quite natural for legal writers to shift the original theory of the case or theme during the writing and revising stages. Now is the time to go back to the parts of the brief you wrote early on and conform them to the later-written sections. Budget a few days to do some additional work on the Statement of Facts. Doing that work will make it much easier to see what revising needs to be done in the Argument section. At the end of this process, and as the last major step, the other sections are added to the brief—the Preliminary Statement and any other parts required by the governing court rules.

I. A sequence for revising across the major parts of the document

Although there is no set order to revising and conforming the various sections of your brief, this chapter models one method of walking through the process. The sequence, shown in Figure 15-1, may appeal to you or you may decide to create your own. The real lesson here is to create and use a method of some sort that makes sure you ultimately have a completed document that is a coherent whole.

Figure 15-1: Late revising sequence

- Start by revisiting the **Facts section** of the brief.
- Afterward, go back and revisit the narrative explanations of the cited cases in the **Rule Explanation**. Because you have just read the Facts section again, new ideas may jump out about what the critical or relevant facts are from those cited cases that can be and should be used. Remember that the facts of the cited cases are there to provide concrete examples that illustrate stories about the synthesized Rule statements; they are also there to be compared to your client's facts in the **Application** portion of the legal Argument section.
- As you are revising the **Rule Explanation**, the wording of the synthesized Rule statements might also need some revising. Similarly, the wording of the **headings** might need some touching up. Look carefully at the language of both the Rule statements and the headings to assess whether it is presented affirmatively, from your client's point of view.

Last, because the whole legal argument may have shifted since the last reworking of the global and local **roadmaps**, reread those and check for consistency with the headings and the rule statements. Also read the roadmaps for repetition—if the Rule statement in an Argument section also appears verbatim or close to verbatim in the roadmap, decide the appropriate locale, and eliminate or condense the wording in the other locale.

II. Revising the facts

Because some time has probably elapsed since your last rereading of the Statement of Facts (or equivalent), the section may seem a bit stale, in need of a makeover. That section should now—hopefully—read as almost unfamiliar, as if someone else wrote it. This disconnection phenomenon is a useful asset to the writer in the late revising stage of the writing process. Because the writer's connection to the material has been broken, it's now possible to more accurately read the material as a first-time reader would. Critically assess: will the reader understand whose story is being told and what the goal of the storytelling is? What are the takeaway moments of the story? Are they pro-client?

A. Reworking any last telling versus showing statements

In the early working drafts of the facts section of the brief, you replaced the "tell" words in the shadow story with evidence and detail that "show" the story. Use this later revising process to look at any remaining judgment or opinion words, other than those that have cites to the record or those that are quotations of the parties. Should they be modified? Figure 15-2 illustrates the difference between words that tell and words that show. Remember, we show by adding specific details that illustrate what our conclusions tell.

"Tell" phrase that shows judgment		Revised to "show" phrases, showing description
a perfect day	⟹	a crisp late-October day with a breeze and temperatures in the mid-50s
a huge, heavy piece of furniture	⟹	a 5-foot-high china cabinet of solid oak, fitted with brass handles, and filled with two sets of dishes
She is a sweet little old lady who has been sued by an evil neighbor who claims that her house addition has disturbed their right to quiet enjoyment of their own property.	⟹	She is 83 years old and has lived in the same house that she and her husband bought together 50 years ago. She added a 10' x 10' screened porch to her home, with the money she saved from decades of making jams and jellies and selling them at local farm stands. On that porch her several dogs like to sleep at night.
This also works in the Rule Explanation		
The opposing counsel's reliance on that case is wholly without merit.	⟹	Although it may first appear that the case is similar, the facts are actually very different from this situation . . . [fill in details about the differences].

Figure 15-2: Words that tell vs. words that show

B. Organizational revising: headings as a possible strategy to create new beginning points

Recall that the beginnings and ends of sections and paragraphs are emphasis points. They are the places to highlight key and helpful material. Show the facts with detail and use other emphasis techniques such as active voice. The middle of sections and paragraphs, in contrast, are the deemphasis places. In those places you should minimize your use of detail. Other deemphasis techniques include the strategic use of passive voice, dependent clauses, and longer, more complex sentences and paragraphs.

To create more beginnings and ends within the Statement of Facts, consider whether to include headings. Headings in the Statement of Facts are optional. They may help show a transition, if the story is told topically as well as chronologically. Headings will also add more beginning points, which in turn creates more possibilities for emphasis. And, of course, headings themselves provide pressure points in persuasion because they are visually distinct from the text. Note that in the hotel reservation case sample briefs, the two parties made opposite choices here. The nonprofit organization SOFT included headings in its Statement of Facts (Appendix D), while the Gloucester Hotel did not (Appendix C). This is probably because SOFT arranged the story topically and used headings to introduce each new topic; the hotel chose to tell its story chronologically.

On the other hand, headings might detract from the section by interrupting the story's flow. And there's another caution to heed. Headings in the Statement of Facts must be factual, just as the text. Unlike the headings in the legal argument section, this section's headings should use descriptive "show" wording rather than the conclusory "tell" phrases that are more appropriate in the legal argument section of the brief.

III. Revising across the brief

These next several revising steps are useful for both the Statement of Facts and the Argument sections of the brief.

A. Visual impact moments in the Statement of Facts

Professor James P. Eyster recommends that, while revising, legal writers think about what visual images from the client's story linger the longest in the mind.[1] These might be images that were created because the writer described certain events, settings, objects, or characters in the most detail.

---

[1]James Parry Eyster, *The Lawyer as Artist: Using Significant Moments and Obtuse Objects to Enhance Advocacy*, 14 Leg. Writing 87 (2008) (an excellent discussion of visual impact moments and unexpected visual objects).

Or they might be images that the writer deliberately created by including unique, incongruous, or unexpected facts.

Each party in a case wants readers to have a different take-home visual image about the facts of the case—those memorable moments that crystallize the case and perhaps influence the outcome. These are called "visual impact moments." Think carefully about what your client wants the visual impact moments to be. Revise accordingly. Also think carefully about what the opposing attorney may set up as the visual impact moment for her client.

Consider this example from the brief of the Gloucester Hotel in the hotel reservation example. The following brief passage is taken from the Statement of Facts section:

> [The hotel manager] prepared the standard hotel contract for a group reservation and mailed it to SOFT's headquarters in Eureka, California. *Id.* at 11:10–14. It was returned by mail about ten days later, and the reserved block was entered into the hotel's reservation system. *Id.* at 12:3–6.

Nothing at first seems remarkable about that passage. But if you got the image that Eureka is located in a particularly scenic part of the country, near giant redwood trees, and that SOFT was not in a major hurry to get the contract in place (since it took ten days to sign and return the contract), then the writer has accomplished her visual purpose.

The details are there to help create a visual impact moment. In the Argument section, the hotel lawyer's choice to use detail in the Statement of Facts becomes apparent when she mirrors the amount of detail in a case illustration. There, the author discusses the case *Sanford v. Castleton Health Care Center*. Her case illustration for that case includes this description:

> In *Sanford v. Castleton Health Care Center*, 813 N.E.2d 411 (Ind. Ct. App. 2004), the plaintiff sought to avoid enforcement of an unambiguous provision of a contract with a health care institution for the care of her mother. The plaintiff brought her mother to the Castleton Health Care Center for treatment. During the admission process, her mother, who suffered from Alzheimer's, became agitated and aggressive; in addition, the plaintiff had to care for her own children who were with her as she completed the form. As a result, she signed the health care contract without reading it, although she admitted that nobody at the care facility prevented her from doing so.

The incongruous in Linda Brown's story

Reread the story of Linda Brown excerpted in the Prologue. Note that the whites-only school that was closest to Linda's house was named the Sumner School. Its namesake was Charles Sumner, an abolitionist leader. The irony that the school was later designated for whites only is an incongruous but unforgettable detail that sticks with readers. That is an example of a writer's deliberate use of an unexpected visual object, meant to create a visual memory for the reader.

The plaintiff in *Sanford* unsuccessfully attempted to argue that because of the chaos during the admission process, she should be excused from enforcement of an onerous provision of the contract because she hadn't had time to read the contract before she signed it. But the court enforced the contract anyway. This sets up a wonderful *a fortiori* type of argument for the Gloucester Hotel:

> Here, SOFT has even less reason to avoid the unambiguous contract language than did the plaintiff in *Sanford*. Ms. Pat Freebird, the SOFT Executive Director, testified that she received the contract in the mail in her office in Eureka, California, and that she had enough time to review its provisions to be sure they conformed to her understanding of the reservation she wanted to make. Freebird Dep. at 9:2–10:14. There was no chaos or confusion, or really any sort of time pressure; the contract was returned to the hotel ten days after it was sent. Mason Dep. at 12:3–6. Accordingly, the contract is enforceable on its own terms.

Readers are treated to two contrasting visual impact moments: the chaos of admitting an agitated, mentally impaired woman in need of immediate care to a nursing home, compared to the calm and tranquility of reviewing a contract in the comfort of one's own office, nestled amongst giant trees. If the first situation was not a reason to avoid a contract term, certainly the second could not succeed either.

SOFT, of course, wants readers to have a completely different mental image about the moment when the contract was formed. SOFT's theme is something of a David vs. Goliath story: a huge, multibillion-dollar international corporation that would never miss $9,000, against a small organization of people passionate about environmental causes, to whom $9,000 is a very large amount of money. One of the legal theories SOFT advances in its defense is that the amount stated as liquidated damages is really an unenforceable penalty. One of the factors a court considers in determining whether the stated amount is a penalty is whether the amount stated is "grossly disproportionate" to the amount of anticipated damages. So, SOFT describes itself in its Statement of the Facts this way:

> Ms. Pat Freebird, now thirty-two years old, formed Save Our Forest Trees (SOFT) shortly after being awarded a bachelor's degree in biology and volunteering her time with other nonprofits and environmental advocacy groups. While her title is Executive Director for SOFT, in fact she is the organization's only employee, working long hours to realize its mission of connecting scientists and environmentalists to share their research findings and discuss ways to bring awareness to the problem of deforestation and climate change. Freebird Dep. 2:14–3:9, Aug. 20, 2013.

> SOFT's headquarters are in Ms. Freebird's home, although she charges no rent to SOFT. Operating costs are kept to a bare minimum by

communicating and advertising primarily over the Internet and through e-mail. Ms. Freebird herself earns only $30,000 in income, although she is a full-time employee. *Id.*

This creates a very different visual image than the one that Gloucester tries to paint, and sets up SOFT's theme that it is being taken advantage of by a much larger and far more powerful organization.

B. Consistency using the facts

One purpose of the Statement of Facts is to set up the theme that makes readers *want* to rule in your client's favor. On the other hand, the Argument provides the denouement to the story; it gives the legal justification for readers to rule for your client. The two major sections must work in tandem. Now is the time to test that. Check to see whether each fact that the legal argument relies on is included in the Statement of Facts. If there are pieces missing in the Statement of Facts—introduced for the first time only in the legal argument's application material—they must be added to the Statement of Facts.

The priming function of the Statement of Facts works only when all of those critical facts are introduced to readers before they are used in the legal Argument section.

C. Choosing the way to refer to the characters

As the theme and theory of the case evolve, so might the way you refer to different characters in the legal story. Although the characters have already been named in the Statement of Facts, those names or descriptive designations could change throughout the drafting process.

Humanizing characters allows readers to connect more easily with them. Readers are more likely to identify with named persons than they are with characters who use only party designations. Balanced against that, however, is the relatively common inability people have to remember too many proper names. For this reason, it is important to rely on stock structures for many of the supporting characters. For example, a witness might be referred to in terms of her relationship to one of the litigants: "The Gloucester Hotel's business manager" or "Plaintiff's sister."

There are no formulas for determining how to refer to characters, including the opposing party or even one's own client. Lawyers must consider what each option conveys in terms of the tone or stock structure or visual

> ### Character names in Rule Explanation
>
> In Rule Explanation, it's almost always better to choose a party designation or a descriptive stock structure. The use of proper names is far too unwieldy. Which descriptor to use is a strategy decision for the lawyer. There are times when "Plaintiff" might be the best option to use in Rule Explanation. Or it might be useful to include something that conveys a stock structure. "Plaintiff, a law student . . ." would certainly catch your attention, wouldn't it?

image. A first name might convey a sense of familiarity, as if the person should be viewed in a casual manner. That may be appropriate in a particular type of case. It is common in family law cases, for example. Using someone's title might convey more formality—which might be the appropriate tone for a client in a business dispute.

Similarly, the choice of nomenclature for the opposing party is a careful strategy decision that depends on the theory of the case. That is why it is a late decision. The phrase "defendant" carries certain stock structures in our culture—ones that are not necessarily positive. Thus, if your client is a defendant, you might want to use different nomenclature.

One last caution about party nomenclature—you should be consistent in your approach. It might be tempting to refer to your client as "Widow Jones" and to the opposing party as "the defendant." After all, this approach humanizes your client and dehumanizes her opponent. However, this is also a rather transparent ploy that readers will quickly recognize. If you choose to refer to your client by her name, it's best to refer to the opposing party by name as well. And Widow Jones still looks pretty empathetic against, say, "Acme Loan Sharks."

D. Strategizing word choices

Certain types of words create especially vivid mental images for readers. The English language is filled with nuanced meanings that a writer can call on to create mental images. The more precise an image the writer needs to create, the more precise the word needed.

Broad	Narrow	Precise
telephone	cell phone	iPhone
he fell	he plunged	he plummeted
busy customer agreeing to hotel contract	distracted customer agreeing to hotel contract	harried customer agreeing to hotel contract

Of course, different word choices convey different levels of precision. Which one you choose depends on the circumstances. Sometimes, for example, the most precise word is critical. At other times, a very precise word might be too distracting. But most words fall on a continuum of broad to more precise, for example:

Here are some general guidelines:

> **How to tell active from passive voice**
>
> In general, active voice focuses on who is doing the action ("The judge overruled the objection."). Passive voice focuses on the action ("The objection was overruled."). Passive voice is okay when the action is more important than the actor, but much of the time you will want to create the mental image of an actor doing something.

- Verbs often create powerful images, especially when used in the active voice. "The storm **raged** around the farm, **obliterating** the wheat crop." To deemphasize, consider using a less specific word and passive voice for verbs, but use the latter strategy judiciously. Every legal writer is taught this technique, which means that every legal reader (such as a judge) knows how to spot it, too. An example is "the wheat crop was lost" (leaving open the questions by whom? how?).

- Nouns, especially precise ones, also aid mental imagery. Reread the previous example but omit the nouns. It won't make sense, and your mind will fill in something—it's unclear what. By way of another example, what image does this sentence evoke?

> Nora felt she could trust the man at her door.

Now consider this similar sentence:

> Nora felt she could trust the police officer at her door.

The second sentence, which uses a much more specific noun, creates a very different mental image. Nouns create the specificity.

- Adjectives and adverbs can describe or can convey opinion or judgment. Although these sorts of descriptor words are problematic in the Statement of Facts (unless used as part of a quotation from the record), they can be acceptable in the Argument when used within the bounds of respect and professionalism.

- Pronouns are useful shortcuts but can be confusing if they do not refer to the most recently used noun. For example, consider the following sentence: "Rob told Jason that as soon as his ship came in, all his troubles would disappear." Whose ship is coming? Whose troubles will disappear?

That shape-shifter word, "not"

The word "not" will probably appear dozens of times in early drafts of your persuasive document. It's a very hard word to avoid using. (But then, cold and flu viruses are numerous too, and nobody thinks they're an advantage.) Take note: it's bad strategy to balance the weight of your persuasion on the word "not." This small word is easily forgotten or misplaced, and it may actually give your opponent's argument an unintended boost. "Why?" you ask.
Picture this: **It did not rain today.**

Do you first picture rain? Many people do. This response is common because readers' minds easily let go or omit the word "not." Other more memorable words in a sentence make "not" less significant—forgettable even.

Compounding the issue is the length of the word. It's easily omitted or inserted accidentally. Many writers discover this type of error only after they have finalized their document (that is, if they discover it at all). Whether "not" is mistakenly omitted or inserted, readers understand the sentence to mean exactly the opposite of what the writer intends. The spoken "not" carries less of this risk because tonal emphasis can make it a memorable word that stands out. But in writing, it is both impractical and unprofessional to boldface, underline, or italicize every appearance of "not" in a document.

And then, there's the tone to the word "not" as a counter to the opposing party's point of view. Writing a story that is merely the opposite of your opponent's is much less persuasive than telling a different and competing story. The better strategy is to change sentences to affirmative ones whenever possible. Doing so almost guarantees that the story or the rule is told from your client's point of view.

These revisions of our original sentence tell more affirmative stories:

- It was sunny today.
- It failed to rain today.
- The drought continued today.

Keep in mind, though, that sometimes a writer deliberately chooses to use the word "not" (e.g., when she *wants* you to think about rain).

A writer cannot entirely eradicate the word "not" from a document of any length. It's too prevalent in our language. But it's important to keep an eye on the usage overall and to substitute as often as possible. The most critical places to substitute something else for "not" are in the **headings** and **thesis sentences** of the legal argument. The student-authored sample briefs in the appendices offer strong examples.

It's worth spending a few extra words (and minutes) to make arguments affirmative.

IV. What happens next in the writing process?

After these sections and major persuasion pressure points are reread and revised, the legal writer typically adds in the last sections of the brief. The whole document is then formatted—visually designed for persuasion—and then polished.

Chief among those last sections is the Preliminary Statement, which provides readers with an opening contextual frame for the writer's case theory. The next chapter discusses Preliminary Statements in more detail.

Chapter 16

Making a first impression: the Preliminary Statement

Think about the movie trailer. In two and half minutes, a trailer has to convey to the audience enough information about a movie to convince them that they want to see it. From a typical trailer, we learn the movie's genre, the central characters, the location both in time and space, and the essence of the plot. More important, we get a "feel" for the movie—and know whether it's likely to be a movie we want to see. A good movie trailer is itself a mini-story, designed to sell the much bigger story of the movie.

In a brief, the Preliminary Statement (sometimes called an Introduction) is similar to a movie trailer. It is an opportunity to introduce the essential elements of the argument in a condensed form. It is not, however, merely a summary of the extended analysis of the Argument section. Rather, it is a carefully crafted, free-standing version of a client's story. Like a good trailer, it may reveal some of the essential scenes of the upcoming story, but more important, it will introduce the central characters, the context for the story, and the theme that will carry through the rest of the brief.

There is another parallel between movie trailers and Preliminary Statements. Both can be critical to the success of the larger project. First impressions matter. Just as a movie trailer creates expectations in the viewer about the upcoming movie, a Preliminary Statement prepares the reader for what is coming in the remainder of the brief. In other words, a good

> **Speaking of trailers . . .**
>
> Have you ever wondered why they're called movie "trailers"? Back in the early days of the movie industry, the promotions for the upcoming attractions were shown *after* the feature film; that is, they trailed the movie. However, the movie moguls quickly realized that most of the audience didn't stick around to see the trailers. Soon, they began showing the trailers before the movie, when they had a captive audience.
>
> Though for different reasons, a legal writer should recognize that, like movie trailers, the Preliminary Statement is best placed before the feature-length version of the client's story!

Preliminary Statement primes readers to agree with the arguments that follow (see discussion of priming in Chapter 14). Consequently, the Preliminary Statement should be crafted with care, specifically designed to show the audience the strength of the client's cause.

Preliminary Statements in briefs are a relatively new phenomenon. Many briefs filed in both state and federal courts now include these statements. We discuss the formal parts of the brief, as required by various rules of courts, in the next chapter. We should note that many court rules, especially appellate court rules, neither require Preliminary Statements, nor even mention them as a typical part of any brief. The Federal Rules of Appellate Procedure have no such reference, for example. But that does not mean that the rules prohibit them; indeed, an increasing number of federal appellate briefs now include them as a first section. The persuasive value of making a strong impression with the first substantive thing readers will see suggests that you should always include a Preliminary Statement as an opening section of your brief, unless your local court rules specifically prohibit you from doing so.

I. Planning the Preliminary Statement

The first step toward creating a successful Preliminary Statement is to identify the central theme of the case. By the time you are ready to write the Preliminary Statement, that central theme should be well defined (*see* Chapter 9). The next step is to determine how to best convey that theme in a short statement. To do so, think about the many moving parts that make up your persuasive Argument section. You know that the structure of every story consists of a leading character, that character's goals, and the obstacles between the character and her goals. Usually, that leading character, or hero, is going to be your client.

Every story also has conflict, and that conflict drives one or more plots and subplots (*see* Chapters 7 and 8). However, as we learned in Chapter 8, every lawsuit has potentially three intertwining conflicts or plots: the conflict giving rise to the client's story line, the conflict in the law's story line, and the conflict within the lawsuit's story line, i.e., a procedural conflict.

Though you may think that your client's conflict is the most important, that may not always be the case. Thus, it is useful to think about all three possible story lines when developing a Preliminary Statement. One way to do this is to chart the three story lines of your case and then decide which one is the most important at the current phase of the lawsuit:

	Character	Goal	Obstacle
Client's story line			
Law's story line			
Lawsuit's story line			

Complete the chart with the specific elements of each story line. You should already be very familiar with your client's story—that is the whole reason for the brief, after all—and the obstacles that are hindering the client from reaching his goal. However, to help achieve that goal, you may also need to explore and resolve conflict within the law. What was the legislature's goal in passing a statute? What was the court's goal in establishing precedent? Likewise, the particular lawsuit may be at a point of procedural conflict. How have the parties progressed to this point in the litigation? Is the complaint sufficiently pleaded? Has a statute of limitations expired? What other procedural obstacles might be relevant at this stage?

Not every case will present all three story lines, at least not at the same time; but some cases will involve two or all three story lines. Which of these story lines is most important depends on the specifics of the particular case. But for the Preliminary Statement, select the theme for the brief by focusing on the key elements of the conflicts presented.

For example, consider the respondent's Preliminary Statement from the Internet dating case. Here's how you might build the story chart in this case:

	Character	Goal	Obstacle
Client's story line	Ms. Hawthorne	Getting on with her life safely	Threats of abuse from Mr. Beagle
Law's story line	Legislature, appellate judges	Protecting victims of domestic violence	Anticipating potential domestic relationships warranting protection
Lawsuit's story line	Trial judge	Properly apply statute	Appellant's misunderstanding of judge's discretion

As this chart shows, the author of this brief has three story lines—the conflict arising out of the parties' relationship, the conflict about the scope of the law, and the conflict about the trial court's discretion in interpreting the law (a procedural question). It is possible that all three story lines will appear throughout the brief. However, for the Preliminary Statement, the author will want to focus on the story line that is most important to the case, usually the story line the author judges most likely to lead to success for the client.

At first blush, it may seem that the relationship between the parties is the most powerful story line. After all, the respondent, Ms. Hawthorne, is an empathetic character, and the petitioner, Mr. Beagle, is an abuser. However, we also know that the characterizing of their interactions as a "dating relationship" is the weak link in this case. Focusing on the parties' relationship could be problematic. On the other hand, the respondent, Ms. Hawthorne, has already won in the trial court. The trial judge has broad discretion to interpret this statute that should be broadly construed. In fact, it looks like the procedural story line—emphasizing the judge's discretion—may be the best story line for Ms. Hawthorne. Here is how the author translated that story line into the Preliminary Statement:

Preliminary Statement

Plaintiff-Respondent, Ms. Elaina Hawthorne, began this domestic violence case in January 2010, seeking a Temporary Restraining Order (TRO) against Defendant-Petitioner, Arthur Beagle. The TRO was granted, and, per standard procedures, the date for a full hearing on the merits of a Final Restraining Order (FRO) was set for two weeks later. Ms. Hawthorne sought this protection based on Defendant-Petitioner Arthur Beagle's threatening and harassing conduct toward her just after the parties' breakup. Prior to the scheduled FRO hearing date, Defendant-Petitioner filed a motion to dismiss, challenging this Court's jurisdiction to hear the matter. This Court held a hearing on the sole issue of whether the parties' relationship falls under the jurisdictional category of "dating." At the end of that proceeding, and after hearing testimony from the parties, plus two other witnesses, this Court issued a written opinion, concluding that the parties did, in fact, have the requisite dating relationship, pursuant to N.J.S.A. 2C:25-19(d), and that Ms. Hawthorne was entitled to a hearing on the merits of a Final Restraining Order.

Nevertheless, Defendant-Petitioner has filed, also at the family, trial level, this Motion for Reconsideration of this Court's written opinion finding jurisdiction. This response brief, thus, is filed on behalf of Plaintiff-Respondent, Elaina Hawthorne, in opposition to that Motion for Reconsideration. By liberally construing the Prevention of Domestic Violence Act, this Court's opinion properly gave effect to the Legislature's intent and followed the guidance of prior appellate case law. Accordingly, Ms. Hawthorne respectfully requests that this Court deny Defendant-Petitioner's Motion for Reconsideration and move forward with the scheduled hearing on the merits of her application for a FRO.

Notice that the first paragraph goes into considerable detail about the procedure leading to the FRO. This detail suggests that the court has followed all the steps necessary to issue the FRO. Mr. Beagle has had the opportunity to make his case and lost. The trial court did its job. Without going into extensive detail, the Preliminary Statement established the theme of the case: this appeal should be dismissed on procedural grounds.

Notice also what is missing in the Preliminary Statement. There is very little mention of the relationship between the parties. Ms. Hawthorne's lawyer mentions Mr. Beagle's harassing conduct, but provides no insight into the parties' dating relationship. Surely, the lawyer for Ms. Hawthorne will need to address this story line in the Argument, but she wisely chose not to mention that at the outset. Having primed the audience for the strongest part of her Argument, the author has set the stage for the rest of the brief.

The Preliminary Statement doesn't need to explain every part of all three potential story lines. Rather, it needs only to bring out the core theme of the broader story. Here, that was the trial court's properly exercising discretion—the procedural story line. In a different dispute, the core theme may depend on understanding the client herself or the conflict underlying the substantive legal issues. By charting out the intertwined storylines, it is easier to identify the core of the story that you want to use to build the Preliminary Statement.

II. Expressing the theme of your Argument

Once you have decided on what story lines you want to introduce in your Preliminary Statement, you need to decide on how you will tell your client's story to effectively reveal the theme of your Argument. Remember, the purpose of the Preliminary Statement is to make a strong first impression—to get readers thinking about the legal issues from your client's point of view.

Usually, the most important part of a story is the central character. The identity of that character depends on the conflict you are describing, however. Thus, whether your primary focus is the conflict between the parties, the conflict within the law, or the conflict within the lawsuit, your Preliminary Statement should be sure to introduce the leading character.

A. Developing the character in a Preliminary Statement

If the chosen theme focuses on the conflict between the parties, the leading character is most likely your client. Thus, introduce your client in a way that makes the first impression you want readers to have about the client. For example, here is how one lawyer introduced the client in a case before the United States Supreme Court:[1]

> Petitioner Michael Turner was incarcerated for 12 months after a South Carolina family court held him in civil contempt of a court order to pay child support for respondent Rebecca Price's (now Rogers's) minor child. The contempt order provided that Turner could purge his contempt and gain release from jail if he paid his arrearage in full (nearly $6,000), but Turner, who is indigent, was unable to pay, and he served the full sentence.
>
> Turner was not represented by counsel at the contempt hearing, nor did the court advise him of his right to counsel. Had counsel been appointed, Turner could have made the evidentiary demonstration and legal arguments necessary to establish that he could not pay the thousands of dollars he owed, which, under South Carolina law and this Court's decisions addressing civil contempt, would have been a complete defense precluding his incarceration. Instead, Turner was left to defend himself (to no avail) and was jailed, in effect, for being too poor to pay.
>
> This 12-month sentence was neither the first time nor the last that Turner has been incarcerated for failure to pay child support without the aid of counsel. Because Price had received public assistance benefits, she assigned her right to child support to the South Carolina Department of Social Services (DSS), and the child-support enforcement proceedings against Turner became subject to automatic procedures carried out by DSS and the family court. Each time Turner's account fell into arrears, the court was required by law automatically to issue a rule to show cause why Turner should not be held in contempt. Turner has been incarcerated in this manner several times, and so long as he continues to owe unpaid child support, he will continue to face automatic contempt proceedings and the threat of incarceration. Indeed, Turner is presently in jail again for failure to pay child support.
>
> In the decision below, the Supreme Court of South Carolina rejected Turner's argument that he was constitutionally entitled to appointment of counsel at the contempt hearing. Notwithstanding this Court's decisions that have found a right to counsel in both criminal and civil proceedings that carry with them the "awesome prospect of incarceration," *In re Gault*, 387 U.S. 1, 36–37 (1967), the court held that the right to counsel applies only in criminal contempt proceedings.

---

[1] *Turner v. Rogers*, 131 S. Ct. 2507 (2011).

In reaching that conclusion, the court relied on the assumption that a civil contempt sanction is "conditional" and may be avoided through compliance with the underlying court order. But whether Turner in fact had the ability to avoid incarceration by complying with the child support order—and thus whether he could be sentenced to jail for coercive purposes in a civil proceeding at all—was the precise question before the family court. As a matter of fundamental fairness, Turner should have been afforded the assistance of counsel to show that he could not. The state court's contrary decision cannot be reconciled with this Court's teachings on the right to counsel, the special character and purpose of civil contempt, or the requirements of due process. This Court should reverse the judgment below.[2]

The short opening paragraph quickly tells us important facts about the client: he was incarcerated for a year for contempt of court; he is indigent. The next two paragraphs reinforce these facts: the petitioner is indigent and the only reason he was repeatedly incarcerated was that he was too poor to pay his child support and too poor to hire legal counsel. In three paragraphs, the writer has established the central character of this story and developed empathy for him; readers can put themselves in his shoes—the government has disrupted his life because of his poverty.

This example illustrates techniques for developing the character of the story. First, the central character, the petitioner, is the first character introduced—indeed, his introduction is where the author begins. In most stories, the central character is the first party we meet. By introducing the petitioner at the outset, readers are quickly oriented and know who this story is about.

Look at the words used to describe the petitioner and his challenge. He is "indigent." He was "incarcerated" for being "too poor to pay." The author has not chosen words that are obvious appeals to emotion. Instead, this appears to be an objective, matter-of-fact description of the client. This not only creates empathy for the client, but it also builds the author's ethos because she is not presenting an overtly biased description of the central character. She does not oversell her client's story.

The final paragraph then briefly connects the story of the client to the legal and procedural conflicts within the case. Notice that there is only a brief mention of the underlying legal analysis. Instead, the central theme of this case is one of fundamental fairness: the government should not be putting indigent people in jail merely because they are too poor to pay their child support. While the writer needs to show how that theme is consistent with

---

[2]Petrs.' Br., Michael Turner, *Turner v. Rogers*, 2011 WL 49898 at *2–*4.

the law, she need not make that connection in the Preliminary Statement. The writer has set the stage—revealed the essence of the case—and now readers are primed for the Argument that follows.

B. Developing the conflict and the goal of the story

If you have chosen to focus on the legal story line instead of the parties' story line, you may not need to develop the character as much.

For example, if the key story line is the conflict about the meaning of a statute, the central character (e.g., the legislature) may not be the most important aspect of the story line. If you have a statutory interpretation issue where both sides agree on the underlying facts but disagree as to the meaning of the statute, you may want to write your Preliminary Statement to highlight the legislature's *goal* in enacting the statute. Of course, you may also choose to focus on the conflict about the law plot line when your client is not particularly empathetic but has a strong legal position.

If you are trying to resolve a conflict within the law, it is likely that the main character will be the legislature that enacted the statute or the courts that have developed the law through cases. Statutory issues require determining the legislature's intent. In other words, you must find the goal of the legislative body that is the central character of the story. Consider this opening paragraph from a case before the United States Supreme Court:[3]

> The Torture Victim Protection Act of 1991 ("TVPA" or the "Act") provides that "[a]n individual who . . . subjects an individual" to torture or extrajudicial killing under color of foreign law shall be liable "to that individual" or "to that individual's legal representative, or to any person who may be a claimant in an action for wrongful death." 28 U.S.C. §1350 note §2(a). The question in this case is whether the term "individual" in that statute means what it almost invariably means in ordinary and legal usage—a natural person or human being. That question all but answers itself. While "person" often encompasses corporations and similar entities, "individual" does not. Indeed, Congress replaced the word "person" in an earlier draft of the statute with "individual" precisely to exclude organizations from liability.[4]

This opening paragraph simply identifies the relevant statute and states the question before the court. But in doing so, the author primes readers to assume the answer to that question. The issue is posed as one of whether

---

[3] *Mohamad v. Palestinian Auth.*, 132 S. Ct. 1702 (2012).
[4] Respt.'s Br., Palestinian Auth., *Mohamad v. Palestinian Auth.*, 2012 WL 293720 at *1–*2.

"individual" means what "it almost invariably means in ordinary and legal usage. . . ." Legal readers will likely intuitively extract the author's primary argument: Congress intends statutory words to be given their plain meaning. This point is reinforced in the last two sentences of the paragraph that provide further explicit details that reinforce the goal Congress had in enacting this statute.

In his first paragraph, the author identifies Congress's goal as to the meaning of "individual" in the statute. The rest of the Preliminary Statement goes on to develop this idea:

> The TVPA brings certain international human rights violations within the civil jurisdiction of U.S. courts. Mindful that it was creating a private cause of action with extraordinary extraterritorial reach, Congress proceeded carefully, tailoring the statute to achieve a limited but important purpose. By imposing liability on the responsible "individual," the Act prevents human rights violators from seeking safe haven in the United States. But by precluding suit against organizations alleged to be responsible for the individual's conduct (often the state itself), Congress limited the risk of international discord and potential interference with the Executive's conduct of foreign policy. Giving "individual" its ordinary meaning respects the careful balance Congress struck. The judgment of the court of appeals should accordingly be affirmed.

In this final paragraph, the author keeps his focus on the goal of Congress. And it appears to be a very thoughtful Congress indeed. It was "mindful" and "proceeded carefully" to create a statute that "limited the risk" of international discord and in doing so struck a "careful balance" that demands interpreting "individual" as the author proposes. The author has established his theme by telling the story of the law. The central character of that story is Congress. More important, the goal of that character—to find a balanced approach to regulating human rights violations—demands that the court resolve this conflict in favor of the author's client.

Conclusion

The Preliminary Statement should capture the theme of your brief. Think about the three potential story lines in your lawsuit: conflict between the parties, conflict about the law, and conflict about the procedure. Within each of those story lines are characters, conflicts, and goals. One story line is likely to lie at the heart of your argument. That is what your Preliminary Statement should express.

A Preliminary Statement sets the stage for your entire brief. It needs to identify the central theme of your argument and prime readers for what follows. It does not need to tell the entire story, however. That will come later. In fact, a Preliminary Statement that is too long may undermine its force. Like a good movie trailer, a good Preliminary Statement will leave your audience wanting to know more about your client's story. It should not leave your audience thinking that it has already seen the entire story.

We are nearing completion of the brief-writing process! The next chapter helps you with the more formal parts of the brief, including tables, issue statements, and other sections that may be required by the applicable rules of procedure (either appellate or trial level).

Chapter 17

Finishing up: the other parts of a brief

Certainly by this point in your legal career, you know the importance of rules—seemingly the law is nothing but! However, many law students, and surprisingly even some lawyers, overlook an important set of rules—those governing the documents submitted to courts. But since you are reading this chapter, this certainly won't be you.

I. Overview: the contents of a brief depend on the rules of the court

The large-scale requirements of a brief are governed by a jurisdiction's court rules. These rules typically differ, depending on whether the brief is trial level or appellate.

Looking at the governing court rules is a critical step. The wise lawyer looks at those requirements early rather than just before filing the brief. Courts are sticklers for those rules, and for that reason, lawyers must also be sticklers. A lawyer we know told us this story about an appeal he worked on early in his career:

> Back in the days when virtually all court documents were only available in hard copy, I had a case before the United States Federal Circuit Court of Appeals. This was the first time our firm had appeared before this court. Naturally, we were very careful to follow the court rules for how to prepare briefs and records. As it turned out, the court rules required that the page numbers of the record appear at the bottom center of the page. The transcript of the hearing below had the pages on the top right-hand corner. Accordingly, we very carefully added a second set of page numbers to the bottom center of each page. Shortly after we attempted to file the brief, the court administrator notified us that our brief was rejected because it had page numbers in two places. We had to reprint and resubmit all 50 copies of the briefs after whiting out the page numbers in the corner.

As should be apparent from this story, when you file documents with a court, you should pay strict attention to the rules governing those documents.

Each jurisdiction has its own unique set of rules. The rules for a trial-level brief in Oregon will require different things than the rules for a trial-level brief in New Jersey. And the rules for a trial-level brief in Wyoming will require different things than the rules for an appellate brief in Wyoming.

In addition to looking at rules governing the type of brief (i.e., trial level, summary judgment, appellate, etc.), there are also often two sets of rules that apply to court documents: those rules that apply across the applicable legal system (for example, the Federal Rules of Appellate Procedure) and those that apply only to the specific court, colloquially referred to as "local rules" (e.g., the Rules of the Seventh Circuit Court of Appeals). Within these sets of rules are two types of rules: those that govern the substance of a document and those that cover the form of the document.

This chapter deals primarily with the rules for appellate briefs since those rules are typically more specific than rules for trial level briefs. In fact, many trial courts have no rules, or only very minimal rules, for what should go into a brief. Our best advice is to look at the local rules for the court where you will be filing your brief, and follow them. And don't be surprised if you can't find rules for the substance of a trial-level brief.

II. Requirements of the Federal Rules of Appellate Procedure

Important reminder

There is no need to write the individual sections of your motions or briefs in the same order that they appear in the documents. In writing appellate briefs, for example, you begin your research and writing by focusing on the Statement of Facts and the Argument section. The Argument section, however, is preceded by other, mostly introductory and procedural sections. Nevertheless, you should wait to write these sections until the Statement of Facts and Argument sections are nearly complete.

To illustrate what you are likely to find in the court rules, this section walks through the Federal Rules of Appellate Procedure (FRAP). Of course, the rules that apply to your particular legal issue will depend on your jurisdiction. Most states have fairly specific rules of appellate procedure, some of them modeled after the FRAP. Before you begin to write, you should find and review the applicable rules for your jurisdiction. Plan to return to the rules several times through the drafting process.

In the federal system, the content of an appellate brief is governed by FRAP 28. Rule 28 identifies 11 sections that must be included in an appellant's brief. These include rules that address procedural issues as well as the ultimate legal issues. Obviously, you will spend the most time on the Argument section. However, do not underestimate the importance of the other sections. Sometimes, the most significant legal issue is rendered moot because of procedural problems. The text that follows reviews the required sections of both the appellant's brief and the respondent's brief.

A. Appellant's brief

1. Corporate Disclosure Statement

If a party is a corporation, it must include this disclosure statement that identifies any parent corporation or corporation that owns more than 10 percent of its stock.

2. Table of Contents

Every brief includes three versions of the argument on appeal—the brief version, the briefer version, and the briefest version. The Table of Contents is the briefest version.

The Table of Contents lists all parts of the brief and their beginning page numbers. In this respect, it is like every other Table of Contents you have seen. However, in an appellate brief, the Table of Contents also presents an opportunity to begin persuading your audience. The Table of Contents includes the point headings for each of the arguments on appeal. If the point headings are well done, readers will understand the brief's theme just from reading the Table of Contents. Many judges consider this to be the most important part of the brief because it establishes the essence of the appellant's argument. While the Argument section will fill in the details of those arguments, this is the place that you can begin persuading by effectively capturing both the logos and pathos of the arguments on appeal.

The Table of Contents is also likely to be the first place to establish your ethos. If the point headings are concise and clearly written, readers will begin to trust you. If they are poorly written or uninformative, that too sends a message to readers—but not the one you want. The Table of Contents is the place where your writing makes its first impression. You'll want to make sure that impression is a positive one.

The Table of Contents not only reveals the essence of your argument, it also reveals your organization. The headings and subheadings appear there in outline form.

Although the words themselves need to precisely match the headings in the body of the brief, the formatting does not need to match. Nor should it.

For example, within the brief itself, headings might differ in size and many or all of them will be boldfaced. If the entire Table of Contents appeared in boldface, however, it would be practically unreadable. The best choice is to make sure that each level of the outline is visually distinct, but that the page still uses plenty of white space. For example:

I. **Major headings may still be in bold** unless your brief contains no subpoints. (Remember, your table of contents should never appear in all bold type.)

 A. *If the question presented is divided into subparts, those subparts could be in italics instead of in bold.*
  1. If the subparts are further divided into sections, those sub-subparts could appear as regular, unbolded, unitalicized type, and sized down a little bit.
  2. Don't forget the basic rule of outlining: at any level of your outline you must have at least two sections. (If you have "Section A," you must have "Section B.")

 B. *The subparts may identify the different elements of a cause of action that are disputed on appeal.*

 C. *Creating the table in this way does two things:*
  1. It creates an appearance of an organized argument.
  2. It shows readers the specifics of that organization.

All of the major word processing programs include a feature to help you automatically create a Table of Contents, although you may find it necessary to reformat the table after it is created. For that reason, you may find it easier to create the table manually, after completing the final revisions to the brief (when the page numbers and point headings are finalized).

3. Table of Authorities

The Table of Authorities sets out all the authorities that the brief cites with references to the pages of the brief where they are cited. This is a helpful resource to readers who are looking for a particular case or statute within the brief. Both the judges who read the brief and their clerks who check your research will look closely at the Table of Authorities.

Frankly, putting together a Table of Authorities can be tedious. While all major word processing programs can automate the process of generating the table, you must still decide what needs to be included in the table and enter the correct computer codes so that the table is accurate. All the authorities must be properly cited, according to the citation rules of the jurisdiction. (Yes, citation rules vary from court to court—make sure you know the citation rules for your particular court!) While the Table of Authorities may not advance your substantive arguments, it does affect your ethos. A carefully compiled table reveals your attention to detail, increasing your credibility with readers.

In most jurisdictions, the rules do not require a specific, detailed format for the Table of Authorities. For example, FRAP 28 requires the table to include only cited "cases (alphabetically arranged), statutes, and other authorities—with references to the pages in the brief where they are cited." The rules leave the formatting details to the discretion of the author. Two principles should guide your formatting decisions:

- Make it easy for readers to understand
- Be consistent

Although you have considerable discretion in formatting your Table of Authorities, a few pointers may make this task easier:

- Many authors prefer to separate the cases by level: Supreme Court cases; Court of Appeals cases; and District Court cases. Though not required by Rule 28, it may be helpful, particularly when the brief includes citation to many cases.
- It is not necessary to include subsequent history in your case citations. It is inappropriate to include pinpoint cites in your table.
- If your brief cites extensively to regulations or to legislative history, you may include separate sections for those authorities. Otherwise, they may be included in the "Other Authorities" section.
- "Other Authorities" includes secondary sources such as law review articles, dictionaries, and treatises. If your brief does not include cites to such sources, it is not necessary to add them just to have this section in your table. Include "Other Authorities" only when your brief requires them!

4. Jurisdictional Statement

The Jurisdictional Statement is a concise statement that identifies the basis for the court hearing the appeal. It requires four specific statements:

- The basis for the trial court's jurisdiction
- The basis for the appellate court's jurisdiction
- The filing dates showing that the appeal is timely

• An assertion that the appeal is of a final order or judgment, or that the court has jurisdiction on some other basis

5. *Statement of the Issues*

This section identifies the specific issues on appeal. In some jurisdictions, this is known as the "Questions Presented." This is a critical section, as whoever asks the questions gains significant control over the answers. You may have learned about writing Questions Presented for objective, predictive writing in your first-semester legal writing course. Questions Presented in persuasive writing are similar to those used in predictive writing, with one important difference: in persuasive writing, the Question Presented is an opportunity to *persuade*. The way a question is phrased can have a lot of significance in how it is answered. Thus, you want to craft a question that leans favorably toward your client's position without tilting so far as to mislead the court or misstate the actual issue. In writing an effective Question Presented, you need to consider three factors: an appropriate form, an accurate and specific phrasing of the issue, and detailed and persuasive word choices.

Well, when you put it that way . . .

For an example of how appellants and appellees can present very different versions of the issue on appeal, consider *Hishon v. King & Spalding*, 467 U.S. 69 (1984), where the issue concerned whether federal sex discrimination laws applied to law firms' decisions with regard to promoting associates to partners. Here is how the plaintiffs framed the issue:

Whether large institutional law firms that are organized as partnerships are, for that reason alone, exempt from Title VII of the Civil Rights Act of 1964, and are free (a) to discriminate in the promotion of associate lawyers to partnership on the basis of sex, race or religion; and (b) to discharge those associates whom they do not admit to partnership based on reasons of sex, race or religion under an established "up-or-out" policy.

On the other hand, the law firm framed the issues from a different perspective:

1. Whether law partners organized for advocacy are entitled to constitutionally protected freedom of association.
2. Whether Congress intended through Title VII of the Civil Rights Act of 1964 to give the Equal Employment Opportunity Commission, a politically appointed advocacy agency engaged in litigation, jurisdiction over invitations to join law firm partnerships.

a) Formatting the Question Presented

Traditionally, a Question Presented is written as a single sentence that includes the specific legal question, the applicable law, and the specific facts of the case that establish the narrow issue before the court. This is a lot of information to fit into one sentence and can easily result in a very long, structurally complex sentence. To make this approach manageable, many experts recommend the "under, does, when" structure. This is a structure that works for virtually any Question Presented and ensures that, even when the sentence is long, it will be readable (and actually a sentence!). As you might expect, this structure has three parts:

> *Under* [state the applicable law],
>
> > *does* [pose the specific legal question]
> >
> > > *when* [incorporate the key relevant facts]?

For example, in the hotel room reservations case, the hotel might pose the Question Presented like this:

> Under Indiana law, is a liquidated damages clause enforceable in a contract for the reservation of 150 hotel rooms when both parties were free to negotiate its terms and where, at the time it was signed, the hotel could expect to spend an undetermined amount of money on advertising and discounted room rates if the other party did not fulfill its obligation to use the rooms?

This question identifies the applicable law, specific issue, and the important facts that suggest the liquidated damages clause should be enforced.

Now strictly speaking, this would not be the narrow question before the court of appeals. The court of appeals is reviewing the decision of the trial court. Thus, some attorneys would state the question in terms of what the trial court did:

> Did the trial court correctly rule that a liquidated damages clause is enforceable in a contract for the reservation of 150 hotel rooms when both parties were free to negotiate its terms and where, at the time it was signed, the hotel could expect to spend an undetermined amount of money on advertising and discounted room rates if the other party did not fulfill its obligation to use the rooms?

Though this deviates slightly from the "under, does, when" format, it retains its general structure and still results in a readable, persuasive sentence.

How's the whether?

Some attorneys prefer to begin a Question Presented with the word "Whether." For example:

> Whether a floating structure that is indefinitely moored, receives power and other utilities from shore, and is not intended to be used in maritime transportation or commerce, constitutes a "vessel" under 1 U.S.C. § 3, thus triggering federal maritime jurisdiction.

Petitioner's Brief in *Lozman v. City of Riviera Beach* (May 8 2012) (available at 2012 WL 1651366).

Although this is a common practice, many writing experts advise against it. One of the most common complaints about this format is that beginning a sentence with "whether" necessarily means that whatever you write will not be a question. Indeed, it is not even a complete sentence. To make sure the Question Presented is a sentence, some writers begin with "The Question Presented is whether . . ." This, of course, still doesn't put the Question Presented in the form of a question.

Despite the protests of these experts, the use of "whether" persists. If you prefer to avoid sentence fragments and like to pose Questions Presented as questions, you should feel free to avoid this structure. If you find such objections pedantic and tiresome, you will be in good company (and present a more traditional and formal style) if you adopt "whether" as your Question Presented starting point.

Some attorneys find this traditional format a bit clumsy, especially when the question on appeal involves a complicated legal or factual context. Consequently, they abandon the single-sentence format. Instead, they introduce the question with one to three declarative sentences, followed by a shorter statement of the legal issue. This "statement, statement, question" format allows for greater flexibility in crafting the Question Presented. Still, under this approach, one would incorporate the applicable law, specific legal issue, and key facts. For example:

> Indiana courts will enforce liquidated damages clauses where the potential damages resulting from a breach of contract are uncertain at the time the contract is bargained. At the time the Gloucester Hotel entered into its contract with SOFT, the hotel was unaware of what it would cost in advertising and reduced room rates should SOFT fail to use all the rooms it contracted to use. Is the liquidated damages clause the parties negotiated enforceable?

Either format for the Question Presented is acceptable. More important than which format you use is that you make sure your Question Presented is readable and persuasive.

b) Stating the legal issue

Of course, the most important purpose of the Question Presented is to inform the court of what issue you are asking it to decide. The issue must be stated accurately and precisely. To begin, think about what you want the court to do. If you are the appellant, you want the court to reverse the lower court on a particular legal issue. This usually means you are asking the court to correct a misapplication of the law to the facts of your case—as those facts were found at trial. In the rare case where the issue is a pure question of law, you are asking the court to correct a misinterpretation of the law itself, so that it can then correctly apply that law to your facts.

If you are the respondent, you are not asking the court to correct anything. You are merely asking the court to affirm the lower court. This usually means you are in a position of strength (appellate courts affirm lower courts much more often than they reverse them). Typically, the respondent will state the issue to suggest that the court need do little more than recognize the lower court resolved the issue correctly. Like the appellant, the respondent must also state the question accurately and precisely. Of course, the respondent has less flexibility because it is the appellant who decides what issues to raise on appeal.

Whether you are the appellant or the respondent, you usually will state the legal issue in terms of the existing law. If the issue is statutory, include the key word or phrase of the statute in the question. For example:

> Under N.J.S.A. 2C:25-19(d), are two people in a "dating relationship" when . . .

Or, if using the "statement, statement, question" form:

> The New Jersey Domestic Violence statute, N.J.S.A. 2C:25-19(d), defines "victim of domestic violence" to include a person who is in a "dating relationship" with someone who abuses that person . . .

Sometimes the parties will disagree as to what is the legal issue on appeal. Often, however, this part of the Question Presented is undisputed. Where the persuasion opportunity usually lies is in how you frame the legal issue by putting it in context. Putting the legal issue in context usually means incorporating key facts that refine the issue. In some cases, it may mean incorporating key policy considerations, especially where the issue is a pure question of law.

c) Framing the Issue by adding informational context

Framing the Question Presented is best done by carefully choosing the key facts that will narrow the focus of the question. Even though the facts are not in dispute on appeal, how you characterize those facts or which facts you emphasize can affect how the court perceives the issue before it. For example, consider how you might describe your client if you were appealing the conviction of an environmental sciences graduate student who was convicted of trespassing while protesting a proposed clearcut on federal forest lands. Is she a "student"? a "scientist"? an "environmentalist"? an "environmental activist"? Each of these words may accurately describe your client, but they also carry different connotations and you would choose the term that best fit your theme and theory of the case. (You probably wouldn't call her an "eco-terrorist," but the prosecutor might.)

The goal of framing the question is to establish the theme of your Argument in a concise and readable way. The ideal response of your readers is "if this is the question, I know what the answer *should* be." To capture your theme, use concrete, specific terms that direct readers to the answer you want without being so strident that they believe you have overstated your case.

Let's look at a few examples from our sample briefs:

Example one:

> Under Indiana law, is a liquidated damages clause enforceable in a contract for the reservation hotel rooms?

This example asks the correct legal question, but it includes no context. Not only does it fail to state the question narrowly, it misses the opportunity to persuade by putting the question in a context favorable to the author's client. One measure of persuasion is whether we can tell, just from reading the question, which party wrote the question. Either party could have written this example.

Example two:

> The Gloucester Hotel is part of a huge multinational conglomerate with untold millions of dollars at its disposal. SOFT is a small band of scientists dedicated to solving the most pressing problem facing the all inhabitants of our planet, global warming. Is the Gloucester Hotel entitled to demand SOFT pay it thousands of dollars in so-called "damages" even though it profited mightily as a result of the contract between it and SOFT?

This is pretty clearly a Question Presented that goes well past the line of effective advocacy. While you want to include persuasive facts, if you overstate your case, the court is likely to reject your framing of the question or, worse, conclude that you are so biased that you cannot be trusted to speak reasonably in the rest of the brief.

Surely we can do better than these examples. Consider a better framing of the issue from SOFT's point of view:

> Under Indiana law, is a liquidated damages clause in a contract an unenforceable penalty when the actual amount of damages is easily calculable according to the formula specified in the contract, the hotel was not damaged because it was able to resell all of the rooms not used by SOFT to other guests, and the damages claimed in the amount of $9,480.38 are grossly disproportionate to the actual damages of zero?

This example incorporates specific facts without resorting to vitriol. It includes facts that point toward the elements of an unenforceable liquidated damages clause without merely stating legal conclusions:

Legal element	Supporting fact
damages easily calculable	"formula specified in contract"
no actual damage	"hotel resold all rooms to others"
grossly disproportionate	$9,480.38 is way bigger than zero

By showing the relevant facts, in a rational tone, the author establishes her credibility and primes the judge to view the issue from the hotel's perspective.

As you draft and edit your Question Presented, keep in mind the following questions:

- What is the precise legal issue before the court?
- What story is most important to that issue?
- What characters are central to that story?
- What word choices will best capture my client's perspective?

6. Statement of the Case

Under the federal rules, this is essentially the procedural posture of the case. It explains the nature of the case, the course of proceedings leading to the appeal, and the disposition of the court below. This section covers the procedural bases, but it is not a place for argument. It should be a precise, accurate, and objective explanation of how the case has gotten to this point.

In some jurisdictions, the Statement of the Case includes many of the sections that stand independently under the federal rules. For example, in Oregon, the Statement of the Case includes the following subsections: the procedural posture, the jurisdictional statement, the judgment of the trial court, the Questions Presented, the Summary of the Argument, and the Statement of Facts.[1] In other jurisdictions, the Statement of the Case may include just the Statement of Facts. Or it may be called something else such as "Procedural History." As always, you need to check the local rules of the applicable jurisdiction to make sure you have all the preliminary pieces in the right place.

7. Statement of Facts

If you have told the client's story effectively, readers should have empathy for your client and her cause by the time they have finished reading the facts statement.

In addition to telling a compelling story, there are a couple of other things to keep in mind when writing the Facts section. First, on appeal, the facts usually are no longer at issue. You must accept the facts as they were found by the trier of fact below. Thus, every assertion must be in the record established at trial and be cited to the record. Second, the Facts section, while a great place to persuade, is not a place to argue. This is the place to tell the story. The legal significance of that story will come in later sections. Developing the factual record is discussed in Chapter 5. Writing the Fact Statement is discussed in Chapters 8, 9, and 15.

8. Summary of the Argument

This is the *briefer* version of the argument. It is considerably more fleshed out than the point headings or the Preliminary Statement, but far less than the full discussion that is the Argument section.

Many students struggle with finding the right level of detail for the Summary of the Argument. If it is too detailed, it seems redundant to include a summary that is essentially the same as the full Argument that immediately follows it. On the other hand, if it is too brief, it seems to be little more than unsupported legal conclusions that only leave readers

---

[1] Or. R. App. P. 5.

demanding more. There are a few principles that may help you find the right middle ground.

First, leave behind any expectations that readers will read the brief from front to back as if it were a novel. Rather, the different sections serve different functions. When readers want to understand the specifics of your argument (such as when they are reading it for the first time), they will look to the detailed Argument section. However, when they are looking to merely refresh their memories of the case

> **Advice from law clerks**
>
> Some judicial clerks we know tell us that the Summary of the Argument is the first section of the brief that they read. For at least those types of readers, then, the Summary of the Argument section is your chance to make a first impression on readers. Make sure it is a good one.

(perhaps when preparing for oral argument), they may need to read only the Summary that highlights the key issues and authorities. This means that a good Summary will follow the same organization and make the same key arguments as the Argument section.

The level of detail to aim for in the Summary is similar to the detail you would put in the global roadmap section of your Argument. You definitely want to address every issue raised in your point headings. You may reference the key statutes and cases, but do not provide an extended explanation of them. As a general rule, you can omit counterarguments from the Summary. In this section, readers are looking for a clear statement of your conclusions, but are not expecting all the underlying analysis that will support those conclusions.

9. The Argument

You have now reached the heart of the brief. Here, you explain the details of each of your contentions, complete with citations to authority and the record. How you do that is, of course, the focus of most of the rest of this book.

In addition, for each issue, you must include a statement of the applicable standard of review.[2] Rule 28 allows you to do this either as part of your discussion of the issue or under a separate heading placed before the discussion of the issues. Because the standard of review is often misstated—and sometimes mistaken for the substantive legal standard—it should usually be explained under its own heading.[3]

---

[2]In this context, we are talking about standards for *appellate* review. There are different standards for motions at the trial court level.

[3]Some appellate courts have rules that require a separate section explaining what the proper standard of review is. *See, e.g.*, Pa. R. App. P. 2111(a)(3).

As you have probably discussed in your civil procedure course, the standard of review defines the degree of deference the appellate court must give to the trial court. While different jurisdictions may use different terminology, there are generally three categories of standards of review: de novo, clearly erroneous, and abuse of discretion.

When an appellate court has "de novo" review, it reviews the issue on its own, giving no deference to the trial court's decision. The most common de novo review situation is when the appellate court is interpreting a pure question of law, such as the meaning of a statute. In that case, the court will interpret the statute as if it were the first court to review it. The appellate court would not defer at all to the trial court interpretation.

The "clearly erroneous" standard usually applies when the appellate court is reviewing findings of fact of the trial court. The appellate court will defer to the trial court on these findings unless findings are clearly inconsistent with the record. Generally, if there is any evidence to support a finding, the appellate court will defer to the trial court, even if, taking the evidence as a whole, the appellate court might have found differently.

The most deferential standard is "abuse of discretion." This standard is applied to administrative decisions of the trial court. For example, if the trial court refused to grant a request for an extension of time, that decision would be reviewed under the abuse of discretion standard. The abuse of discretion standard may also be applied to trial court decisions that involve balancing tests or a mix of facts and law. For example, in a child custody case, the court will consider several factors in determining what is in the "best interest of the child." Generally, the appellate court will not second-guess the trial court as to the proper balance of those factors and will look only for an abuse of discretion. This is a very difficult standard for an appellant to overcome. It is not enough that the appellate court might have reached a different result from that of the trial court. The appellate court recognizes that reasonable minds might differ, and it will not substitute its judgment for the trial court's unless there is essentially no basis to support the trial court decision.

In many cases, the standard of review is central to the appellate court's ultimate decision. Obviously, an appellant wants the appellate court to apply the de novo standard—giving no deference to the court below. On the other hand, the respondent would much prefer a deferential standard of abuse of discretion. Thus, to the extent possible, an appellant will frame issues on appeal as questions of law while a respondent will frame issues as questions of the trial court's exercise of judgment, limiting the appellate court's review to an abuse of discretion standard. Whether appellant or respondent, you want to make sure to identify the correct standard of review and keep it in mind as you fashion your argument.

10. Conclusion

The Conclusion is a short statement stating the precise relief sought. It is not a summary of the argument (you provided that earlier). Rather, simply tell the court what you want it to do, for example:

> The Court should reject the State's arguments, reverse the decision of the District Court in this matter, and grant the relief requested by the Tribe in its Complaint.

11. Signature

Though not required by Rule 28, all documents filed with the court must include the lawyer's signature. By signing the brief, you attest that, to the best of your knowledge, everything included within the brief is accurate. Thus, before you put your name to the page, be sure to review the entire brief one more time to correct any errors that might have escaped your previous reviews.

12. Certificate of Compliance

If you use a modern typeface (and unless you are using a typewriter, you do), you will need to include a brief statement that affirms that you complied with the word or line count limits. Generally, an appellant's brief is limited to 14,000 words or 1,300 lines of text, although many states have different rules. As always, check the applicable rules!

B. Appellee's brief

FRAP 28 requires the appellee's brief[4] to include most of the same sections as the appellant's brief. However, it permits the appellee to omit some sections unless the appellee is dissatisfied with the appellant's statement. These sections include

- the Jurisdictional Statement;
- the Statement of the Issues;
- the Statement of the Case;

---

[4]The federal rules refer to the appealing party as the "appellant" and the responding party as "appellee." To avoid confusion, we have generally used the terms "appellant" and "respondent" in this text. The proper terminology varies from jurisdiction to jurisdiction.

- the Statement of Facts; and
- the Statement of the Standard of Review.

Although the rule permits the appellee to accept the appellant's version of these sections, it is almost always unwise to do so. The appellant will certainly frame the issues and describe the facts in a light most favorable to his position. By conceding to this version of the story, the appellee loses a significant opportunity to tell her version of the story. It is far more likely that the appellee will want to reframe the issues and almost certainly will want to provide a different perspective of the facts.

III. Formatting rules

For appeals in federal court, FRAP 32 governs the form of briefs. In addition, each circuit court has its own local rules. You will need to check the local rules for your jurisdiction, as local rules are, well, local! The details vary, and each court has its own idiosyncratic expectations. Even if you are familiar with the practices of a particular court, you will need to review the current local rules as minor changes occur routinely.

In many jurisdictions, there are different rules governing a midlevel appellate court and the jurisdiction's highest court. The United States Supreme Court Rule 33.1 governing briefs is different from FRAP 32. But in state courts, the rules of appellate procedure may be the same for both appellate levels. The point, as should be clear by now—check the rules for your court!

Following formatting rules is a bit like cleaning your house before a party. If you do a good job, no one is likely to notice. If, on the other hand, you neglect to dust the furniture or vacuum the floors, that will get your guests' attention—and not in a good way. Similarly, if you follow the formatting rules carefully, readers may not notice how carefully you have cleaned and polished your brief, but they will focus their attention on the substance of the brief instead of the formatting details. On the other hand, a brief that does not comply with the formatting rules will, at the very least, distract readers and undermine your credibility on more significant aspects of your brief. More problematic, it will sometimes get your brief bounced out of court, costing someone a great deal of extra time and money to reformat and refile the brief.

Rule 32 has seven subsections that cover a variety of formatting issues, including the following:

- Reproduction: how the brief is printed, paper stock.
- Cover, including the content of the cover and the color for each type of brief.
- Binding: briefs must be able to lie flat when open.
- Paper size, spacing, margin size: briefs are to be printed on $8\frac{1}{2}''$ × $11''$ paper, double spaced, and with $1''$ margins.
- Typeface: briefs may be either monospaced or proportional spaced. A proportionally spaced text must use a font with serifs. (For more details about choosing an effective font, see Chapter 18.)
- Typestyle: briefs must use a plain roman-style type. Italics or bold may be used for emphasis. Case names must be in italics or underlined.
- Length: this rule is complicated by the various acceptable typefaces. A brief is limited to 30 pages, although the rules include alternative word count or line count options: a brief using proportionally spaced fonts is limited to 14,000 words, while a brief using a monospaced font (which we strongly recommend against) is limited to 1,300 lines of text. In addition, the author must certify that a brief using either of these alternatives complies with this rule.

In addition to Rule 32, each federal court has its own rules regarding briefs. For example, the Seventh Circuit has rules regarding the number of copies to be filed, electronic filing, and citation to unpublished opinion. In addition, it requires the appellant to include an appendix with a copy of the lower court decision. On the other hand, the Supreme Court requires that briefs use a font from the Century family.

Whatever court you are submitting to, be sure to check for all the rules that apply to that court. In the federal system, that could include the Federal Rules of Civil Procedure, the Federal Rules of Appellate Procedure, and the local rules of the particular court to which you will submit your document.

Within the rules, there are many ways that you can make your document more reader friendly. Of course, whatever formatting decisions you make must comply with the court's local rules. Those rules can cover everything from page limits to font size to how to fasten the papers of your document. The local rules are available on the court's website. Chapter 18 discusses formatting strategies in detail.

Comparing court rules

Court rules for briefs vary widely between jurisdictions and from trial to appellate courts. To illustrate that variety, the following table lists the required elements for a typical state trial court, a typical state appellate court, and a federal appellate court.

New Jersey trial court	Oregon Court of Appeals, Rule 5	U.S. Circuit Court, Rule 28

Motion for Summary Judgment: Statement of Material Facts	Indexes:
	    Index of Contents
	    Index of Appendices
	    Index of Authorities
		Corporate Disclosure Statement

	Statement of the Case	Table of Contents
Other motions: No content specified	Statement of the Nature of Proceeding to Be Reviewed	Table of Authorities
	Judgment Sought to Be Reviewed	Jurisdictional Statement
	Date of Judgment Below	Statement of the Issues
	Date Appeal Filed	Statement of the Case
	Question Presented	Statement of Facts
	Summary of Argument	Summary of the Argument
	Statement of Facts	Argument
	Assignment of Error	Standard of Review
	Preservation of Error	Conclusion
	Standard of Review	Signature
	Argument	Certificate of Compliance
	Conclusion	
	Signature	
	Proof of Service	

Chapter 18

Creating ethos: tone and branding by good visual design

One important way that lawyers demonstrate their ethos in legal writing is by paying attention to detail. Most judges believe they are good legal writers and thinkers. (And indeed, most of them are!) Consequently, lawyers who want to persuade these types of readers take the time to write well. They edit carefully and proofread carefully, ideally after stepping away from their documents for at least 24 hours. They check, recheck, and meticulously follow the local court rules pertaining to filed documents. They make final checks of the more tedious but nevertheless key elements such as tables of contents and authorities.

Likewise, you should plan to follow these steps to ensure your brief contains no technical errors. You don't want a judge thinking, "If she can't even run this through a spell checker, how can I trust her reasoning?" Just as you do not want to have to change the judge's mind about the substance of the argument, you don't want to have to change the judge's mind about the quality of your work. A well-written, well-formatted document allows readers to focus on the merits of your argument rather than be distracted by a poorly executed document.

The first semester of legal writing courses often covers the importance of polishing documents for grammar, citation, rules, and typographical accuracy. For that reason, we have omitted discussion of those critical aspects to writing. Rather, we devote our attention to the design or the "beauty factor" in persuasive legal writing documents. That is, we discuss what the document actually looks like. Courts and practitioners care about document design a great deal more than you might suspect.

To be read, documents must be readable. This chapter briefly discusses readability in documents that, like briefs, are all or nearly all text (as opposed to documents with lots of pictures, graphs, charts and other nontext material). The idea of this chapter is to explore a few fundamentals of good document design when you are managing a lot of text on the page.

This chapter also include tips for a few general techniques in word processing that, once learned, will save you time and improve your document design. Most of these word processing techniques can be learned in just a few minutes.

I. Document design principles

Making a textual document visually effective means making the document as readable as possible. The more readable the document, the more likely readers are to remember the content. Fortunately, there are many scientific studies that support the textual design concepts we discuss next.[1] Graphic design experts incorporate the findings into four principles for all-text documents: contrast, proximity, alignment, and repetition.

A. Contrast with size and weight

As we have written in previous chapters, headings are a key part of written persuasion. They need to stand out in a legal document, and that means that headings should visually contrast. Providing visual contrast goes a long way to further that principle. You have probably already incorporated contrast into your legal writing documents by making headings look different from text. And, within levels of hierarchy—sections and subsections—you probably varied something about the way the headings were presented.

To present a hierarchy in the information, graphic designers choose deliberate contrast, either with typeface or with size, weight, or color.

Notice what wasn't mentioned. *Italicizing*, underlining, and ALLCAPS. In ascending order, each of those emphasis choices makes it harder to read at our normal rate. Using all capitalization is the worst thing you can do if you want your headings to be legible and easy to read. Oregon and South Dakota have recognized this phenomenon and limit the use of all capitals in briefs.[2]

---

[1]You can find a summary of and cites to scientific studies in Ruth Anne Robbins, *Painting with Print: Incorporating Concepts of Typographic and Layout Design into the Text of Legal Writing Documents*, 2 J. ALWD 108 (2004), and reproduced, by invitation, on the website of the United States Court of Appeals for the Seventh Circuit, http://www.ca7.uscourts.gov.

[2]Or. R. Sup. Ct. 5.05(4)(f) ("Briefs printed entirely or substantially in uppercase are not acceptable."); S.D. R. App. Ct. 15-26a-66(b)(1) ("The use of all-capitals text may be applied only for case captions and section names.").

Slowing readers down is no way to persuade them. Think of *italics*, underlining, and ALLCAPS as walking on a flight of stairs in which each stair is the wrong height or depth. Steps that are set too high will exhaust someone much faster than properly set stairs—and many people will prefer to skip it and wait for an elevator. A flight of stairs that is too shallow is just as difficult. Stair climbers have to watch their feet the whole time to make sure they don't trip.

As an alternative to ALLCAPS, graphic designers suggest we develop contrast by varying the look of the letters. There are two ways to optimize contrast on the black and white printed page: vary heavy/dark/boldface lettering with light lettering, and vary the style of the letters, or fonts. An easy way to do this is to use boldface for headings and unbolded text (called "Roman style") for the body of the material. To show different levels of the organization hierarchy, use a different font size for different levels of your outline headings.

This textbook uses the same font for headings and text, but uses boldface for the headings. The chapter titles are larger than the major point headings of each chapter, and those are larger than the next level of subheadings. The sample briefs in Appendices A through D use the same technique.

Another way to create contrast is to vary the font itself between heading and text, while still using the dark/light contrast. The shadow boxes of this textbook use a different font than the body of the text, as part of a

Off-black is the new black (for certain things)

Black and white documents are more than just black and white anymore. Word processing software gives you multiple options to decrease the depth of the black—just pull up your font color palette and look at the different shades available for black.

Text elements like bullet points do not need as much contrast as elements like headings. The bullet points themselves are not the focal point of the list—the information set off by the bullet points is. It takes only about three minutes to learn how to create and change bullet points (we timed it). And presto! all-black round bullets become gray square ones. The bullet points in this book, by the way, are a medium shade of off-black.

You can do the same thing with underlining and table rules: you may opt to use something other than pure, 100% black. On the other hand, sometimes you will have strategic reasons to make certain lines thicker or more decorative. The borders and shadings settings of tables allow you to change these things.

deliberate design to look different. Likewise, the shadowing sets off those boxes from the rest of the text. The two different fonts come from different font families—the text is set in a serif font ("with wings") and the shadow box material is set in a sans serif font ("without wings"). If you choose to vary the font as well as the size and weight, make sure the fonts come from different families so that there's enough contrast. Otherwise, the result can look something like wearing black pants with navy socks. A fashion faux pas. At the same time, the fonts from two different families should be in harmony—which can be hard to do. Things like the shapes of certain letters (a, e, g, and o) are things to look at.

B. Proximity: keep related items related with appropriate spacing

Proximity derives from the premise that when items are aligned on the page, they dance together as a cohesive unit and provide visual continuity. For example, a heading that is followed by too much space before reaching the text looks like it is unrelated to or floating away from the text. From a readability standpoint, it also causes a lowered retention rate of the information. From an organizational standpoint, the moving of things closer together demonstrates, visually, the relationship of the material.

Setting exact line spacing

In word processing programs, you can manually set the spacing by the exact number of points or by a multiple of the font size. In the line spacing options, choose the "exact" setting in the line spacing options and type in 14 or whatever other number you may want. Or, choose the "multiple" setting and type in 1.2 or any other number you may want.

Line spacing also affects the relative readability of a document. Look at any book, magazine, or newspaper. Do you see double spacing? It's doubtful. That's because educational psychologists and graphic design researchers have concluded that the most comfortable line spacing for reading is something approaching 20 percent larger than the size of the font. In word processing language, that translates to 14 points of space with a 12-point font (120 percent $\times$ 12 = 14.4 or 14 points of space). In practice, many print documents are slightly tighter than that. This textbook uses a line spacing that is slightly larger than a 1.2 multiple.

Here are the places in a brief where you should pay attention to spacing:

- *After headings and before the start of the text.* Close up that space to something small. We use spacing in the range of 3 to 6 points between headings and the start of the text. Over the course of several headings, that adds up quickly to several lines of recaptured space. When you are faced with a maximum page limit, those saved lines can be critical.

- *After a section ends and before the heading of the next section.* We use 12 to 24 points of spacing to show the chunking.
- *Between paragraphs.* This is typically set at the same size as the font. Just twice pushing the Enter key on your keyboard creates that space. A better way to do this is to set the "after" line spacing to the same size as your font size.
- *Line spacing between lines of a paragraph.* This textbook uses a multiple spacing of 1.2 (1.2 times the font size), which is the same multiple that the United States Supreme Court requires in briefs.
- *Line spacing in the headings.* Multiple-line headings still need to maintain their weight/darkness to effectively show contrast. For that reason, it is better to keep the space tighter than the text's line spacing. It is perfectly acceptable to use single spacing in headings.
- *Post-sentence spacing.* The rules about two spaces after periods derive from the days of typewriters. Think about the mechanics of typewriters. They worked like pianos. Every letter was individually set on its own piece of metal, which then hammered the paper through a ribbon loaded with ink. The effect was that the letter "i" used the same width of paper as the letter "w" even though an "i" is a much narrower character. Punctuation was set on the same individual pieces of a metal, which meant that there was no difference in width between a "w" and a period. For that reason, a typist had to use a second space to alert the reader to the ending of the sentence. But we have computers now, and individual characters take up only as much width as the shape of their character requires. There's no need to use that second space after sentences because we can all see the end of the sentence without it. The second space after periods can visually detract with "rivers of space." Moving to one space after periods might save you a line or two in a longer document.

C. Alignment: justification and tables

A frequent question about alignment is whether to use left or full justification. Unless you have professional desktop publishing software, left justification is the easiest to choose. The full justification setting changes the spacing between letters inside or between words to maintain the straight lines on the left and right margins. In legal writing, this causes some odd-looking and distracting spacing within citation sentences. The fix for that, called "kerning," can be problematic in common word processing software. It's not impossible, but it won't add to the document's readability either, at least according to the studies we have seen.

One alignment tip we offer now, to save you years of frustration later, is a better way to create a caption in a legal document. Figure 18-1 shows what a caption typically looks like. Rather than using tab stops to create this, use a table and then erase the borders of that table after it is completed. Figure 18-2 shows that same caption, with the table lines, revealed.

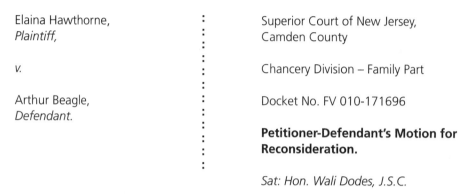

Elaina Hawthorne, *Plaintiff,*	:	Superior Court of New Jersey, Camden County
v.	:	Chancery Division – Family Part
Arthur Beagle, *Defendant.*	:	Docket No. FV 010-171696
	:	**Petitioner-Defendant's Motion for Reconsideration.**
	:	*Sat: Hon. Wali Dodes, J.S.C.*

Figure 18-1: Caption, set up using a three-column table, with no borders showing

Elaina Hawthorne, *Plaintiff,*	:	Superior Court of New Jersey, Camden County
v.	:	Chancery Division – Family Part
Arthur Beagle, *Defendant.*	:	Docket No. FV 010-171696
	:	**Petitioner-Defendant's Motion for Reconsideration.**
	:	*Sat: Hon. Wali Dodes, J.S.C.*

Figure 18-2: Three-column caption using center column for border

Elaina Hawthorne, *Plaintiff,*	Superior Court of New Jersey, Camden County
v.	Chancery Division – Family Part
Arthur Beagle, *Defendant.*	Docket No. FV 010-171696
	Petitioner-Defendant's Motion for Reconsideration.
	Sat: Hon. Wali Dodes, J.S.C.

Figure 18-3: Two-column caption showing internal table border as the divider

Another way to do it is by using a two-column table and erasing all but the middle line, which you can turn into a dashed line or just leave solid. Figure 18-3 shows this technique.

Hopefully you can see other immediate applications. For example, you can use tables to help create the "letterhead" of your resume. You will save some vertical space that way. The table lines are left in, but only to show you where they are. Omit them in your own resume:

Jane L. Student	**444 Cherry Tree Lane • Rutgersville, WY • 99999** **555-555-5555 • Janestudent@address.com**

D. Repetition and document consistency

The last principle of document design, repetition, is the easiest one to implement. Keep all formatting consistent. If the point headings are set in a size 14 boldface, then all point headings must be set in size 14 boldface. If the headings use a different font than the text, then every single heading must use that same different font—don't go back and forth.

Try this: document design and resumes

While you read this chapter, recall that one of the most important persuasive documents you will write is your resume. Document design principles are very relevant when you have only one page to convey information.

A quick Internet search will turn up many wonderful examples of well-designed legal resumes. Pay attention to techniques for designing elements such as columns, lists, and specialty text boxes. While we don't necessarily advocate using all techniques in all resumes, it's useful to see what's possible.

II. Application and limitations in legal documents

Chapter 17 noted that every jurisdiction has its own formatting rules. Those formatting rules govern briefs. As with any rule of law, they are susceptible to interpretation. And, like any other rule, they are subject to change.[3] Many courts' procedural rules will not allow you to use all of this chapter's design principles, particularly in appellate briefs. As nonsensical as it may seem, the longest of legal writing documents—the appellate brief—is often mandated to be the least readable. Many court rules are simply historical artifacts predating the computer. Court rules relating to formatting were first developed when lawyers no longer had to rely on professional printers to typeset their appellate briefs. Those professional printing days ended with the development of the mass-produced typewriter. Many court rules, even today, still reflect the typewriter era. If your jurisdiction is one that still speaks in characters per inch, pica, or requires a font like Courier or Courier New, you are working in a jurisdiction that has yet to fully embrace the advent of computers and word processing programs.[4]

Likewise, because the Word default font until 2007 was Times New Roman, many jurisdictions' court rules still reflect that as the best or only choice for appellate documents. If your jurisdiction's appellate rules require Times New Roman, then you must use it. That's a very different thing, however, than allowing appellate court guidelines to dictate the formatting of all documents you write. Times New Roman is a font that was designed for narrow newsprint columns in small font sizes. It was never intended for the types of documents we produce for courts. There are many better choices out there. Using a default font when it is isn't required is the same thing as abdicating choice, and typically signals to those in the know that the document's writer lacks a persuasive visual strategy.

Put another way, you should include document design in the list of persuasive techniques, but should also research the precise rules governing that document. If the court rules are silent on a particular point, or if the document you are writing is unbound by any court rules, then it is fine to design the document as you deem appropriate for the client's situation. For example, if no font rule is mentioned in trial court rules, then choose a

---

[3]As of the date of this book's publication, most of the court rules committees in the country would benefit from updating their formatting rules to reflect the science behind readability. Judges in the court systems, particularly at the appellate level, are spending more hours per week reading briefs than they would if the formatting rules were changed to allow optimized document design.

[4]Mass production of typewriters began in the 1880s. Mass production of computers began in the 1980s. The authors have faith that all of the courts in our country will eventually catch up.

What should your e-mail look like?

Because e-mail is projected on a computer screen, it is easier to read in a sans serif font. Which font depends completely on the tone you are trying to set. Some fonts look more informal than others.

Design experts advocate using more horizontal rather than vertical space for e-mail signature lines. The accepted industry standard is no longer than four lines. Career specialists also suggest including no more than two job titles (to include more apparently diminishes the sender's overall ethos). To accomplish these suggestions, the snail-mail address can be condensed to one line, separated by a symbol or bullet point or colon. If you have multiple titles, choose which ones to use depending on the situation.

font that brands your office (unless your office already has its own visual identity system, as many larger organizations already do). Or, as Professor Derek Kiernan-Johnson posits, choose one that sets the tone of the client's story.[5]

Remember that there are many other legal writing documents that could use your distinctive font.

- Trial-level briefs in some jurisdictions
- Pleadings
- Agreements
- Contracts
- Letters
- Intra-office memos
- Resumes
- E-mails
- Documents for presentations
- Public relations and publicity documents

Finally, branding is an important consideration. If your office has its own logo or icon, then it is fine to use it, miniaturized, as part of the signature block of the document. That includes e-mails and presentation handouts as well.

Turn to these resources for more information on the topic:

- Matthew Butterick, *Typography for Lawyers* (Jones McClure 2010), and http://www.typographyforlawyers.com.

---

[5]For much, much more about the tone of font and its use in legal writing, see Derek Kiernan-Johnson, *Telling with Type: Typography and Narrative in Legal Briefs*, 7 J. ALWD 87 (2010).

- Derek H. Kiernan-Johnson, *Telling with Type: Typography and Narrative in Legal Briefs,* 7 J. ALWD 87 (2010). Available at http://www.alwd.org/lc&r.html.
- Ruth Anne Robbins, *Conserving the Canvas: Reducing the Environmental Impact of Legal Briefs by Reimagining Court Rules and Document Design Strategies,* 7 J. ALWD 193 (2010). Available at http://www.alwd.org/lc&r.html.
- Ruth Anne Robbins, *Painting with Print: Incorporating Concepts of Typographic and Layout Design into the Text of Legal Writing Documents,* 2 J. ALWD 108 (2004). Appears, by invitation, at United States Court of Appeals, Seventh Circuit, http://www.ca7.uscourts.gov/.
- Robin Williams, *The Non-Designer's Design Book* 131 (2d ed., Peachpit Press 2003).

Part V

Oral argument

In some cases at the trial level, and in many cases at the appellate level, the written brief is the end of the process. The lawyers submit briefs, and the judge or judges use those briefs to make the decision. Approximately 74 percent of all federal appeals cases are resolved on the briefs, without the benefit of oral arguments. In a few jurisdictions, federal and state, the court rules permit oral argument only when lawyers specifically request it or the court itself orders it.

But, at both the trial and appellate levels, it is possible—and sometimes probable—that the reviewing court will want the opportunity to speak with the lawyers about the arguments contained in the briefs. Lawyers may be scheduled to attend a session of court in which the judge or judges ask the lawyers to present the arguments orally, and to engage in a discussion of the arguments and positions the lawyer has advanced for the client.

Part V of this book discusses effective oral presentation of the client's story in a formal oral argument to the court.

Chapter 19

Persuading in person: oral argument

Many judges rely on oral arguments to help them sort out the issues, think through the arguments, and make preliminary conclusions about how to rule. Although not all courts routinely grant oral arguments,[1] when they do, it likely means that something about your case has caught the eye of one or more judges. The case is likely a close one, so oral argument may be the key to winning or losing the appeal.

A recent textbook on the art of oral persuasion suggests four themes:

1. Good oral advocacy is "usually balanced, positive, factual, calm, clear," and logical.
2. The credibility of the advocate is hugely important. "Listeners value . . . demonstrations of judgment[ ] and a sense of fair play."
3. "Bitter, overstated, angry, sarcastic, biting, emotion-dominated rhetoric usually backfires."
4. Effective use of stories and visual images "transform the forgettable into the memorable."[2]

This chapter begins with an overview of the differences between oral arguments at the trial and

> ### Briefs are the coin of the realm
>
> It is probably true that the most important part of persuasion is the written brief. After all, it is the brief that will stay on the judge's desk as she writes the opinion in the case, serving as a reference outlining your client's reasons for winning. Moreover, in many appellate courts, oral argument is not routinely granted, and briefs are the only tool the lawyer has to persuade. However, in cases where oral argument is granted, the advocates are given an additional, and very important, opportunity to persuade.

---

[1]For example, in 2011 only 25.1 percent of federal court appeals were resolved after oral argument; the remaining 74.9 percent were resolved on the briefs alone. Administrative Office of the U.S. Courts, *2011 Annual Report of the Director: Judicial Business of the United States Courts* tbl. S-1, at 36 (Admin. Off. U.S. Cts. 2012). Comprehensive statistics for state court appeals are not readily available, but probably vary widely.

[2]Robert N. Sayler and Molly Bishop Shadel, *Tongue-Tied America: Reviving the Art of Verbal Persuasion* 4 (Wolters Kluwer L. & Bus. 2011).

appellate levels. It then offers some strategies that can help you persuade, regardless of what level of court you are appearing before, by employing the four themes suggested above.

I. Setting the stage: the purpose of oral argument

Because the functions of trial courts and appellate courts differ, both the structure and purpose of oral arguments at those levels differ too.

It is hard to generalize about the purpose of oral arguments, especially at the trial court level, since the variety and procedural posture of cases that judges hear vary widely. However, recall the discussion in Chapter 4 about the difference between the role of the trial court and the appellate court. Usually the trial judge is the first neutral person to hear all sides of a dispute and render a decision. Therefore, the trial judge may be particularly attuned to the facts of the case, more so than an appellate judge who may be more focused on the law. This is especially true when the trial judge sits as fact finder and must make decisions about credibility of witnesses and determine what really happened. Appellate courts, on the other hand, must accept the facts as found by the trial judge or the jury, so they have much less discretion in determining what happened.

You might be tempted to conclude that a trial court, which is more likely to be faced with a case in which the facts are not yet determined, is going to be more attuned to the story the lawyer tells in her brief. And to some extent, that may be true. But do not discount the power of story in appellate briefs. As one noted jurist once observed,

> There is a quaint notion out there that facts don't matter on appeal—that's where you argue about the law; facts are for sissies and trial courts. The truth is much different. The law doesn't matter a bit, except as it applies to a particular set of facts.[3]

Think about this for a moment. While every case requires a sound legal theory, the client is better served by the lawyer including an appealing theme as well. Give the judges a reason to feel good about ruling in the client's favor. Oral argument is another opportunity to showcase that theme.

Judges have jobs to do: they must decide the issues presented to them. They want to do their jobs well and reach decisions that they believe are

---

[3] Alex Kozinski, *The Wrong Stuff*, 1992 BYU L. Rev. 325, 330.

both fair to the parties and in full compliance with the existing law. This is often a difficult thing to do, so judges are looking for help from the lawyers. They read briefs carefully, and they ask questions that help them understand the immediate issues before them. Sometimes, especially in an appellate court, they ask questions to help them understand the future consequences of any decision they might make; that is, what kind of a precedent might they set with any possible ruling?

This suggests that a lawyer should approach oral argument as a discussion among professionals about the case. In fact, "oral argument" is an imprecise term at best. Instead, think of this experience as a conversation between the judges and the lawyers. Both the lawyer and the judge have important roles in the case, and an equal interest in doing a good job. Both are trained in the law and can learn from each other by engaging in a high-level, intelligent conversation about the law and how it applies in this specific case.

During oral arguments, judges will often want to discuss the law with you, especially in a situation where the law itself is unclear. When on that turf, judges and lawyers are on relatively equal analytical footing. Both have read the applicable statutes, cases, or other rules of law and can apply the tools of legal analysis to argue for—or reach—a particular conclusion. But when it comes to the facts of the case, lawyers are at a distinct advantage in oral argument. In most cases, lawyers have lived with the case from its inception. They have met the clients, interviewed the witnesses, taken the depositions, reviewed the documents, maybe even tried the case. In short, they know (or should know) the record of the case, cold. Judges know the facts of the case only from the briefs and perhaps from the record, if they have reviewed it. While most judges will have read the briefs before the argument, it is a very rare judge who will have read the entire record of the case. And even a reading of the paper record provides only a glimpse of the living controversy that the lawyers have been intimately involved with.

Thus, it is likely that when the law meets the facts in an oral argument (that is, when the court considers how the law applies), judges will ask the lawyers for help. And this creates opportunities for any advocate, at oral argument, either at the trial or appellate level, to tell the client's story.

There are three broad categories of things that you may try to accomplish during oral argument:

1. Emphasize the key arguments and facts of your client's case
2. Rebut arguments or claims made by the opposing party
3. Answer the questions and concerns of the court

Perhaps counterintuitively, the third thing is the most important: oral argument is all about satisfying the concerns of the judges who will decide the case. But lawyers cannot just walk up to the podium and ask the court, "Do you have any questions?" Rather, lawyers need to have something to start the conversation with, which could be either of the first two points on the list. At the same time, lawyers cannot try to do too much during oral argument; they simply don't have enough time. Planning and preparation are key.

II. Preparing for argument

The time needed to prepare for an argument is greatly disproportionate to the amount of time you will actually have to argue. Although you may have anywhere from 15 to 30 minutes to actually argue the case in court, you will need to spend many hours preparing for those few minutes.[4] Here is a checklist of things you should do to prepare for the argument:

☐ **Reread all briefs.**

Carefully review all of the briefs of all parties to the case, either supporting or opposing your position. Doing so will help you think about questions that the judge may need help with during oral argument.

☐ **Review the law.**

Review the key sections of any statute involved. Reread the key cases that you or other parties have cited. You might want to jot down a few lines of notes about each key case or statute, on an index card, that you can then affix to the inside of a manila folder to help you quickly find those authorities if you are asked about them in oral argument. (See the "Try this: using note cards" shadow box below for tips on how to do this.)

☐ **Review the record.**

As noted above, you likely know more about the record than the court does. For that reason, you are likely to get many questions from the court about what is, or is not, in the record. Again, keeping notes about the key parts of the record on $3'' \times 5''$ note cards may help you quickly locate those items during the argument.

---

[4]Sometimes lawyers are given no time limits or are given more than 30 minutes. The average time, however, falls within the 15 to 30 minute range.

☐ Determine your best arguments.

Once you have done all of the above, it is time to start planning how to use your limited time during oral argument. There is no way you will be able to restate, orally, all of the points you made in your brief; that would not be a good use of your time even if you could do it.

Remember that the court will always have your brief to review after the argument is over. You do not waive any issue or argument you make in your brief by failing to address it at oral argument.

☐ Think about your theme.

Ask yourself, why should the court want to rule in my client's favor? What is the emotional center of the case, and how can I bring it to life by telling my client's story? This should be easy; after all, you have intentionally chosen a theme while you were writing the brief. Remind yourself of that theme and think about the facts of your case that help you show that theme to the court. Then make a list of those facts for easy reference during the argument.

☐ Choose your strategy.

Use the three broad objectives you might have at oral argument (make your best points, rebut your opponent's points, answer questions from the court). You can't always anticipate questions, and you need to have a plan for how to start the argument, so think about the first two possibilities. Do you want to begin by making your own case as strongly as you can, or do you want to begin by attacking your opponent's case?

Don't be afraid to take on your opponent's best arguments directly. By the time you get to oral argument, you will have had ample opportunity to review all of the briefs in the case. If you are the appellant and did not anticipate an argument actually made by opposing counsel in appellee's brief, oral argument may be your best opportunity to refute the argument. But do so fairly. Don't present a caricature of what the opposing argument is, just so you can knock it down as a straw person argument. That will cost you credibility with the court. On the other hand, ignoring your opponent's actual arguments may signal that you are afraid of them or that you have no effective rebuttal.

Professors Robert Sayler and Molly Shadel suggest that audiences quickly tire of negative attacks, "particularly those that are personal or mean-spirited."[5]

---

[5]Sayler and Shadel, *supra* n. 2, at 141.

Thus, while it is important to address opposing arguments, it must be done respectfully.

☐ Outline your presentation.

Make a list of the major points you want to cover, in the order you want to cover them. You will want to decide which points to actively raise and which points to hold in reserve, ready to respond if your opponent or the court raises them. But while you should prioritize the major points, understand that you will almost never get to all of them or be able to take them up in the order you prefer.

You should plan to open strong and end strong. Just like in written advocacy, first impressions matter because they can engage the listener's attention; and the last thing you say will be the most easily remembered.[6] Thus, whether you plan to spend most of your time advancing your own presentation or attacking the other side, plan to make your strongest point clearly and succinctly both in your opening comments and in your planned closing.

☐ Prepare your notes.

Avoid the temptation to write a speech. You will never get to deliver it to the court (and you would be very ineffective even if the court allowed you to read your speech). A good oral argument involves lots of questions from the court, which will change the order of your presentation frequently. Rather than write down what you intend to say, make a list of the main points you intend to cover, filling in the broad outline you wrote in the previous step. Then be prepared to jump around in your outline as questions from the court direct you in different directions.

☐ Anticipate questions from the court.

This is both the hardest, and most important, part of preparation. As previously noted, the best use of your time during oral arguments is engaging the court in a conversation about the

---

Try this: using note cards and folders

Some advocates find it helpful to take notes about the important cases, or parts of the record, and write them on note cards. Then, take a blank file folder and affix these cards to the inside of the folder. Staple or tape only the tops of the cards; that way, you can flip them up and read what may be on the back of the card, or on the card underneath. Doing this can help prevent a disaster if, in your nervousness at approaching the podium, you accidentally drop your stack of papers or note cards.

Another tip, if you decide to type up your notes, is to staple or tape those notes to folders so that they cannot come loose or rustle in shaking hands. If you do decide to go strictly with papers, it is often easier to manipulate them by stapling them as a booklet rather than using one staple in a corner.

---

[6]*Id.* at 20.

case. But that conversation begins when the court asks a question. This often means that there is some aspect of your analysis that troubles or confuses the court. So, the more you can do in advance to anticipate those questions, and to plan out your answers to those questions, the better.

Even though many questions may seem to be challenging your position, that is not always the purpose. Sometimes, the judge agrees with your position and is merely seeking clarification—or perhaps even trying to help you state your position more clearly. Always listen to the question and think about why the judge asked it *before* you start your answer. The best time to think about your answers is when you are preparing, long before you actually enter the courtroom.

Probably the best source of potential questions comes from reading the opposing briefs. Those briefs were written by somebody with a different perspective than you, so they can be very instructive about what the weak points of your case may be. But the court will view briefs by all parties as equal and will want to find a way to reconcile what may appear to be conflicting interpretations of the law or the facts. Thus, courts frequently will pose questions that invite the lawyer to respond directly to the claims made by the other side.

Another way to anticipate questions is to think back to the struggles you may have had in writing the brief. Was there some issue that you felt unsure about or had a hard time understanding? If you had those thoughts when writing your brief, don't be surprised if the court has those same thoughts. The court may ask you for further explanation.

Try to put yourself in the shoes of the court. If you were a judge and had to decide this case, what would bother you about it? What would you find surprising about the arguments you have made? What concerns might the court have about setting future precedents? Think about the potential future consequences of the ruling you are seeking, and expect questions about those consequences.

Once you have come up with a list of potential questions, think about how you would answer them in a way that reassures the court that ruling in your client's favor is not only fair and just, but logical. Your answers should subtly invoke the theme you have chosen for your presentation. Jot them down on note cards too, if you like; but it is better to have these answers programmed in your head so that you don't have to fumble around during the argument looking for the right note card.

III. Conduct of oral argument

While the purpose of oral arguments in trial and appellate courts overlap in many ways, the form of the arguments can vary widely. Trial court arguments in particular take very different forms, depending on the preferences of the trial judge. In general, trial court arguments tend to be more informal and less structured than appellate arguments. Here is a brief table to help you think about the differences you may encounter between trial level and appellate arguments:

Trial court arguments	Appellate court arguments
Usually before a single judge	Almost always before a panel of three or more judges
Sometimes in judge's chambers, sitting down	Almost always in courtroom, at podium
Judge may direct order of presentations	Prescribed order for presentations
Often flexible as to time	Usually strict time limits enforced

The best advice we can give is to read the court rules for any court you will be arguing before. If the rules do not specify how oral argument is to be conducted, contact the court clerk's office or the judge's chambers (at the trial level) to find out what the judge's preferences are for oral argument. Or talk to other attorneys who have appeared before a particular judge.

Regardless of which level of court you are appearing in, here are a few tips on how to approach the argument:

☐ **Dress professionally.**

There are many different ideas about what "professionally" means, and there are undoubtedly regional differences about what is appropriate or not. "Appropriate" is different from "bland." The only universal guidance we can give here is that you want the judges to pay attention to your argument rather than your appearance. Lawyer attire signals respect for the seriousness of the occasion. Appropriate attire can go a long way in helping you establish credibility with the court, a key part of persuasion.

☐ **When arguing in a courtroom, take a minimum of stuff to the podium with you.**

You don't want to be fumbling through a lot of paper at the podium. If you must, you can take your brief to the podium, but preferably you will know it inside and out and can leave it at counsel table. If you did a folder with note cards attached inside, take that with you, along with any outline you have. You might also take a blank pad of paper and a pen with you in case you need to jot down some notes during the argument. The briefs and record should be in the courtroom, at counsel table, and perhaps tabbed for any point you anticipate or wish to make. But typically, these things stay behind, though at the ready.

☐ **Introduce yourself and state the party you are representing.**

Especially in a more formal appellate proceeding, it is unlikely that all of the judges on the panel know you. In law school moot court arguments, if you are arguing with a partner, the first person to speak should also introduce the partner. (Real appellate arguments rarely involve two attorneys speaking for the same client.)

☐ [Appellate arguments only] **Appellants: reserve time for rebuttal.**

Most appellate arguments have fairly strict time limitations. Since you, as counsel for the appellant, don't know what might come up during the appellee's argument, it is a good idea to always reserve a few minutes of your time to give a brief rebuttal to whatever came up during the appellee's argument. You can always waive rebuttal later if nothing happened during appellee's argument that you feel the need to rebut, but you cannot ask for additional time if you did not initially reserve a few minutes for rebuttal.

☐ **Give road map/introduction to argument.**

An informed listener is a good listener. Tell the court very briefly the main points you hope to cover (preferably no more than three). This is your chance to establish your main legal theories.

☐ **If you prefer, start with an ultra-abbreviated, boiled down, two-sentence version of the facts.**

Sometimes moot court competitors are given the coaching advice to begin by asking the court if it would like a brief recitation of the facts of the case. This is a moot court fiction and is very different from the actual practice of law. No advocate does that in a real oral argument.

That being said, the beginning of your argument is still a good opportunity to *tell* a piece of your client's story, to establish the case theme—unless there is some clear indication from the judges that they are uninterested. Yes, we did just say "tell" this time. But it must be brief! Judges typically are fine with a few sentences (i.e., less than a paragraph). If you open that way, use the few sentences to include those key facts that show both what the controversy is about and why a ruling in your client's favor would be fair and just.

☐ **Start from your outline (remember your objectives).**

If you have gotten this far without a question from the court, now is the time to begin making your legal arguments. Start with your first main point and keep going until you get a question from the court.

☐ **Avoid hyperbole or exaggeration.**

This doesn't work any better in oral argument than it does in written advocacy.

☐ **Answer all questions.**

Judges, particularly appellate judges, will tell you that the question and answer process is the most important part of oral argument. Judges don't ask questions just to harass attorneys; they ask questions because they want some help in doing their jobs properly. You actually want the court to ask questions. There is nothing worse during oral arguments than a silent bench, also called a "cold bench."

You should begin your answer, if you can, with a direct "yes" or "no." Then you should explain your answer fully. It is the explanation that the court really wants to hear.

Never, ever, say "I was planning to cover that later in my argument, Your Honor," and then go back to what you were saying before. The judge is interested in hearing about it now, and you should honor her request. On the other hand, do not attempt to butter up the judge by saying something like, "That's a really good question." Transparent attempts at flattery like that will cost you credibility.

If a question is based on an incorrect premise, correct it politely. As we said earlier, the judge wants to do his or her job well, and that can only happen if the judge correctly understands both the facts of the case and the legal arguments. If you don't fully understand the question asked, it is okay to ask the judge for a clarification, respectfully. For example, you could say something like, "Are you asking me whether . . ." and then rephrase the question in terms that you understand. But do not do this to avoid answering a perfectly clear question that you would prefer to ignore.

If you get a question you had not anticipated, do your best to think about it on the spot and come up with an answer. If the question is about the record or the facts of the case, use your theme to help you think about how to answer the question in a way that will help your client. If the question is about the law, think back to your basic legal theory and search for an answer there. If you are unable to come up with a satisfactory answer, do not try to guess the "right" answer; that will lead to disaster more often than not. Simply tell the court that you had not thought of that question before, and that you would be happy to file a supplemental brief answering that question if the court would like you to.

☐ **Stop talking when a judge begins speaking.**

As soon as a judge speaks, you should immediately stop whatever you are saying and listen. Let the judge control the direction of the conversation; by so doing, you can learn a lot about what the judge is thinking or might be troubled by. Do not interrupt the judge; let the judge finish asking the question before you speak again. If the question is a multipart question (which is fairly common), you may wish to jot a quick note on a pad of paper at the podium so that you can be sure to answer all parts of the question.

☐ **Go with the flow.**

Often, one question and answer will lead to another, and another. Just let it roll; keep answering the questions posed by the court. Once you complete an answer, however, if there is no follow-up question, you should steer back to wherever you were in your outline when the first question was posed. Or, better still, if the questioning has led you into another area that you had planned to cover anyway, it might be a good idea to jump into that portion of your argument since you now know that the court is very interested in that topic.

☐ **Accept all gifts.**

Remember that not every question posed by the court is a hand grenade. It may be an attempt by one judge to recruit another judge on the panel to a position you and the inquiring judge share. These are known as "softball" questions, where the judge asks you a question that he or she knows you will answer easily and forcefully in a way that might persuade that other judge down the bench. If you spot such a softball, don't hesitate to agree with the judge asking the question and make your point. (But make sure it really is a softball first; it is sometimes hard to know why a judge has asked such a seemingly easy question.)

☐ **Leave out issues or cases that were not briefed.**

But you may answer questions from bench even on topics not in your brief. Likewise, if you are the appellant, anything in your opposing counsel's brief that you had not anticipated when you filed your original brief is fair game.

☐ **You are not required to fill the time allotted.**

If you get through your entire outline of points you wanted to cover, and there are no more questions, it wastes the court's time by going back and repeating something you have already said. Instead, be willing to concede the extra time. Have a strong "sit-down" line prepared, telling the court exactly what you want it to do and why, then deliver the line and sit down. For example, it's perfectly acceptable to say "if your Honors have no further questions, [reiterate a key point and the requested relief] . . . Thank you."

IV. Tips on presentation

Many moot court competitions provide students with suggestions on how to make a good appearance at the podium. Some of this advice is useful; some is not so much. Primarily, we believe that if these "toastmaster tips" consume so much of the advocate's attention that he or she loses track of the substance of the argument, those tips can be more harmful than helpful. The substance of the argument is the most important thing. Most judges will forgive, or not even notice, minor tics or habits if what the advocate is saying is substantively compelling.

One of the most common "toastmaster tips" given to student advocates is to avoid using interjections like "um" or "uh." Aside from the point that those verbalizations are often very difficult to avoid, there is some evidence that these interruptions may actually serve several useful purposes in an oral presentation. As one attorney who has studied the subject puts it,

> Students are being told (through textbooks, public speaking classes, moot court feedback) that they should eliminate the use of *uh* and *um* in their oral arguments. This is consistent with generally accepted principles of public speaking and reflects the teachings of organizations like Toastmasters. Notably, however, it's not the advice given by judges who actually hear oral argument. Instead, those judges plead with lawyers to stop making speeches and to engage in a conversation with the Court. Most of all, judges just want lawyers to answer the Court's questions. Whether we use *uh* or *um* in those answers seems to be the furthest thing from the judges' minds.

Linguistic study has demonstrated that listeners typically are unaware of the *uh's* and *um's* that pepper our speech, at rates as high as 2% of every spoken word. It's only when we shine a light on *uh* and *um* that people become aware of these so-called "verbal fillers." And it may only be when we declare fillers to be "bad" that people form negative opinions about people who use them, which turns out to be virtually everyone. In fact, verbal fillers may actually increase our comprehension of speech. Studies have shown that verbal fillers function as low-level signals to listeners that can provide a range of valuable information. For example, saying *uh* may function as a warning that the speaker is encountering difficulty in word retrieval or sentence structure. But listeners don't discount what the speaker is about to say (unless they've been trained to do so). Instead, *uh* primes listeners to pay careful attention, because something new or complex is coming their way. Accordingly, listeners who hear *uh* or *um* grasp and remember complex information more quickly than listeners who hear an empty pause. *Uh* may also function as a turn holder, signaling that the speaker has not finished her thought and that the listener needs to remain patient.[7]

Another "toastmaster tip" that seems to have a lot of adherents is that the advocate should stand quite still at the podium and refrain from excessive hand motions or gestures. But if you are a person who commonly shows animation and engagement by "talking with your hands," trying to stop yourself from doing so may be overly distracting to you and cause you to feel stiff or unengaged. We doubt very many arguments have been lost because an advocate was animated; instead, that seems like a good way to signal to the court that you believe in what you are saying, and the court should, too.[8]

This is not to say you should start to intentionally inject "ums" and "uhs" into your presentation, since that can be very distracting and detract from your message. Nor do we suggest that you should start flailing about at the podium; too much gesturing will look phony and contrived, and therefore less persuasive. All we mean to say here is that you should not obsess about these minor quirks about your presentation. They may be serving you quite well, so long as they are natural and restrained.

---

[7]E-mail from Barbara Gotthelf, Esq., Litig. Partner, McCarter & English, Philadelphia, & Adjunct Prof., Leg. Writing Dept., Rutgers School of Law–Camden, to authors (July 28, 2012) (copy on file with authors).

[8]Michael J. Higdon, *Oral Argument and Impression Management: Harnessing the Power of Nonverbal Persuasion for a Judicial Audience*, 57 Kan. L. Rev. 631, 645(2009) (another excellent article to read; citing studies that show speakers who attempted to speak without such gestures were less persuasive to their audiences because their speech "lost its intonation, stress[,] and expressiveness; . . . there was a jerkiness to the speech, and a reduction of the number of words used.").

Having said that, evidence supports that coupling a strong substantive message with expressive nonverbal communication is more powerful than the substance standing alone. Just as a brief with both a sound legal theory and an appealing theme is more persuasive than a brief with just good logos, an argument with solid substance and good forensics will be more persuasive. The substance of the argument may help convince the court of the legal merit of your case (a very important aspect, indeed), but the nonverbal messages can help convey your feelings toward the case (i.e., the story).[9]

Here are a few forensic tips that we agree you should try (although, again, not at the expense of losing sight of the substance of what you are saying):

☐ **Speak clearly and at a normal conversational rate.**

This might be hard to do, if you are the kind of person who speaks quickly when nervous or under pressure. It takes some practice. If you have that problem, make an effort to slow down and enunciate clearly; but don't speak so slowly that you appear to be unsure of yourself. Find the happy medium. And don't stress out too much if you don't succeed at this. If the court has trouble understanding you, the judge will ask you to repeat your answer. That is never going to be a deal breaker about your argument.

☐ **Maintain eye contact.**

As we have mentioned before, judges want to have a conversation with the lawyers during arguments. In the United States, at least, it is more natural for people conversing to look at one another. Looking somebody in the eye when speaking to them shows sincerity; avoiding eye contact signals avoidance or insincerity.

☐ **Show confidence.**

This might be hard to do if you don't actually feel confident in the positions you are taking. But use the fact that you have researched and written a brief on the matter to believe in the legitimacy of your argument. Make it confidently, without apology. After all, if the court senses that you don't even believe in your argument, why should the court believe in it?

You can show confidence at the podium by maintaining an upright, but relaxed posture; by speaking clearly and directly in a normal tone of voice;

---

[9]*Id.* at 634.

by subtly varying the pitch and volume of your voice; and by maintaining good eye contact with the judges.[10]

☐ Speak conversationally rather than read your argument.

As noted above, you should internalize as much of your argument as you can. Don't plan to read a speech; you will not get a chance to do so. Besides, if your head is down, looking at your speech laying in front of you at the podium, you are not making eye contact with the court.

☐ Address the court, not opposing counsel.

This is easier to do when you are arguing in a courtroom, rather than in the judge's chambers, since opposing counsel will be seated at counsel table, outside of your line of sight. But in either setting (courtroom or judge's chambers), avoid the temptation to look at opposing counsel or speak to him. This is not a personal grudge match between you and opposing counsel. It is a professional discussion among colleagues. You need only to persuade the court; opposing counsel's job is to not be persuaded by you. Don't even try to persuade opposing counsel.

☐ The number one tip on oral argument: be yourself!

Everybody has different presentation styles, mannerisms, and quirks. That's okay. That's being human, and stories are all about humanity. If you take on airs or try to pretend you are somebody other than yourself, you will come off as phony. Per the principles of ethos, phoniness is the *last* thing you want to convey as an advocate.

---

[10]Sayler and Shadel point out that "audiences respond to confidence," but note also that "there is a difficult balance here—over-the-top delivery can backfire, but telegraphing, 'I'm just going through the motions because I get paid to do this' is worse." Sayler and Shadel, *supra* n. 2, at 140.

Epilogue

As we write this epilogue, the baseball season is winding down. The play-offs are well underway, and many stories are coming to their conclusions.

One stereotypical baseball story is that of the slugger who comes to the plate, bottom of the ninth inning, bases loaded, two outs. His team is down by three runs. In an epic battle with the other team's best relief pitcher, he fouls off pitch after pitch until he gets the pitch he wants: a fastball, low and away. With one mighty swing, he sends the ball over the fence for a game-winning grand slam. He is a hero! (A warrior hero, to be precise.)

But of course this imagined scene very rarely happens. In real life, most games are won by "small ball": a combination of singles, walks, and other seemingly minor events that allow one team to score enough runs to win the game. Even the slugger needed his teammates to get on base so he could send them home with his heroic swing. Most baseball games are won by every-player heros.

We opened this book with the legal equivalent of the baseball slugger who saves the team with one mighty swing: the story of Linda Brown, who against all odds challenged the status quo of "separate but equal" schools and ended up changing society. But even her victory would have been impossible without the many smaller wins by countless other litigants whose names are lost to history.

Linda Brown's story, representing as it did so many other schoolchildren in similar situations, had a powerful effect on the court. Big changes in the law only happen because a powerful story convinces a court that the pre-existing law is flawed in some significant way. But that does not mean that stories are only useful in the "big" cases that change the world. Every case is "big" to the litigants. We should use our most powerful persuasive tool, story, to help all of our clients.

The appendices that follow are typical of cases that lawyers handle every day, and that have great significance to the parties to those lawsuits. They were written by law students, and demonstrate capable representation of clients through brief writing. Read them and study how each writer made choices about how to tell the client's story. And think about how you, too, can become a client-centered legal storyteller.

We leave you now with our best wishes for many successes in your own legal writing endeavors.

Appendix A

Defendant Arthur Beagle's motion for reconsideration

(student brief)

217 North 5th Street
Camden, NJ 08102

Elaina Hawthorne,	)	Superior Court of New Jersey,
Plaintiff,	)	Camden County
	)	
	)	Chancery Division — Family Part
v.	)	
	)	
Arthur Beagle,	)	Docket No. FV 010-171696
Defendant.	)	
	)	**Petitioner-Defendant's**
	)	**Motion for Reconsideration.**
	)	
	)	*Sat: Hon. Wali Dodes, J.S.C.*

Preliminary statement

This brief is filed in support of Petitioner, Arthur Beagle's motion for reconsideration based on this Court's lack of subject-matter jurisdiction to hear Elaina Hawthorne's application for a restraining order pursuant to the New Jersey Prevention of Domestic Violence Act ("the Act"). Previously, Mr. Beagle filed a motion to dismiss the action, arguing that the online chats that these parties shared are far below the type of "family-like" relationships that the Legislative Declarations discusses in the Act, *N.J.S.A.* 2C:25-18. This Court denied that initial motion and has scheduled a date for a hearing on the merits of the final restraining order.[1]

---

[1]This brief uses New Jersey local rules of citation, which is what a New Jersey court would expect to see.

As a matter of law, however, this Court should have concluded that the parties' computer conversations were outside the category of "dating relationship" per Section 19(d) of the Act, *N.J.S.A.* 2C:25-19(d), and the Court had no legal jurisdiction over the parties in this matter. The parties were simply online "chat" friends, whose communications eventually soured. They have seen each other in person only on three occasions, and the sum total of their time in each other's physical presence adds up to perhaps ninety minutes, even though they live within an easy driving distance of each other. Ms. Hawthorne herself declined any opportunity to go on a date with Mr. Beagle. To construe those interactions as a "dating relationship" was in error, unsupported by the existing law.

Statement of the facts

Arthur Beagle is a student at the New Jersey State Police Academy. (R. at 22–23.) Mr. Beagle lives in Gloucester County, New Jersey, and has many friends in law enforcement there. (R. at 23.) Although he takes classes during the week and drives to and from Ocean County, he nevertheless enjoys a "moderate" social life. (R. at 23.)

As a way to improve his networking skills, and also to meet women, Mr. Beagle likes to spend time online in chat rooms related to novels. (R. at 23.) He also attends speed-dating events and singles events. (R. at 23.) At one of these speed-dating events in November 2009, Mr. Beagle met at least three women, one of whom was the Plaintiff, Elaina Hawthorne. Mr. Beagle went out on a number of dates with the other two women, and he also began to speak with Ms. Hawthorne over the Internet using a video chat program called "Skype." (R. at 24, 30.)

The parties spoke online two or three times a week for roughly six weeks. (R. at 29–30.) The conversations usually lasted for half an hour, but one or two of the conversations lasted for two hours. (R. at 15.) They talked about their jobs, common interests, and childhood memories, and they had inside jokes. (R. at 4, 18, 27.) The parties both know mutual acquaintances at the Gloucester County Prosecutor's Office, where Mr. Beagle spent a few weeks last summer and where Ms. Hawthorne is currently externing as a third-year law student. (R. at 5, 23, 30.) Mr. Beagle's "dream job" is to try to work for either the Sheriff's Office or the Prosecutor's Office as a detective, but he may become a member of a SWAT team. (R. at 23.) Ms. Hawthorne likewise hopes to work for the Gloucester County Prosecutor's Office after graduation. The parties thus had some stories to exchange about their experiences.

During one of their online conversations, because Ms. Hawthorne was wearing a scarf that made it difficult for Mr. Beagle to understand her, he asked her to take it off. (R. at 25.) She jokingly offered to take off more clothing, and so Mr. Beagle joked in turn that she should remove everything. (R. at 25.) Ms. Hawthorne began to remove her sweater, and so Mr. Beagle stated, "keep on going just as much as you want." (R. at 25.) Ms. Hawthorne then stopped removing clothing and put her sweater back on. (R. at 25.) Mr. Beagle joked about Ms. Hawthorne removing her clothes on a later occasion, but Ms. Hawthorne was unreceptive. (R. at 25.)

At some point a few weeks after they met, Ms. Hawthorne put a quote from *The Time Traveler's Wife* on her Facebook wall, which read, simply, "Why is love intensified by absence?" (R. at 6.) Mr. Beagle, who belongs to a Yahoo chat room devoted to that book, recognized the quote, and therefore clicked on the "like" indicator, which placed a thumbs' up symbol on her Facebook wall. (R. at 25.) When posting the quote, Ms. Hawthorne did not explicitly say that she meant absence from any particular person. Mr. Beagle did not understand the quote to have any personal meaning beyond its literary allusion. (R. at 24.)

During their online chat sessions, Ms. Hawthorne used the computer in her family's den. Plaintiff's sister, Sara, was frequently in the room during those chat sessions and sometimes sat in on them. (R. at 18.) Sara, when questioned at trial, was unable to say that the parties were in a dating relationship—only that they "seemed interested in one another." (R. at 18.)

In fact, Mr. Beagle was interested and for that reason, on at least three occasions, asked Ms. Hawthorne to go on a date: a dinner or a movie. (R. at 24.) She refused each of his three requests for a date—without ever offering to go out at another time. (R. at 24.) And so, the parties have never been out on a date together. (R. at 24.) Mr. Beagle's understanding was that Ms. Hawthorne was too busy to go out on a date with him but yet was puzzled that she happily flirted with him and engaged in "goodbye kisses" over the Internet as well as a long kiss or two. Mr. Beagle, however, thought that the kisses were "corny" and "weird," so he stopped that practice. (R. at 24.) He was also confused why she told him she had no time to go out on dates with him, yet had some other activities that she fit into her schedule, such as the occasional movie with friends and all-afternoon Sunday gym workouts. (R. at 26.) Eventually he assumed that she wasn't really interested in dating him, although he was happy to continue talking to her via Skype. (R. at 27.)

Having no other plans on New Year's Eve, Mr. Beagle attended a singles event with his friend, Al Gero. (R. at 26.) Ms. Hawthorne and her sister also attended the event. (R. at 26.) Although the parties had spoken during the week before New Year's Eve, neither mentioned the singles event to the other. Neither had they made any plans for what is traditionally a date night. (R. at 7.)

Mr. Beagle did not immediately register that Ms. Hawthorne was in the room, but instead first noticed her sister, Sara. "I saw a cute girl and I was about to introduce myself to her—and then realized she was standing next to Elaina and that this was Elaina's sister, Sara." Mr. Beagle guessed that Ms. Hawthorne might be upset by that and said to himself, "Self, this is NOT going to be your night for romance." (R. at 26.) Mr. Beagle guessed correctly: Ms. Hawthorne was upset with Mr. Beagle because she thought "it looked like maybe he was looking to meet other women," and so he attempted to calm her down by holding her hands and by saying "why do I need to look for anyone else when you are right here?" (R. at 8.) Ms. Hawthorne was not responsive to these attempts. (R. at 27.) Sara Hawthorne said that she saw Mr. Beagle nuzzle Ms. Hawthorne's neck while the parties were talking, but no one else, including Ms. Hawthorne, mentioned this in testimony. (R. at 22.) After Mr. Beagle was finished speaking with Ms. Hawthorne and Ms. Hawthorne left the singles event to have dinner with her family, Mr. Beagle and Mr. Gero met two other women and went out to dinner with them. (R. at 27.) The four spent the rest of the night together celebrating New Year's Eve. Mr. Gero testified that he did not believe the parties were in a dating relationship. (R. at 34.) He noted that even with a little bit of hand holding that he saw on New Year's Eve, he had concluded that Mr. Beagle "wasn't all that interested" in Ms. Hawthorne, especially because Mr. Beagle was so willing to go out with other women that same night. (R. at 34.)

Subsequently, Ms. Hawthorne called Mr. Beagle "weasely" on her Facebook account. (R. at 27.) Mr. Beagle had previously told Ms. Hawthorne that he connected being called any kind of animal name to memories of being routinely taunted and bullied as a child, both for his last name (a dog breed) and for his first name, Arthur (the name of a cartoon aardvark). He acknowledged the reaction as somewhat irrational, but nevertheless painful. (R. at 27.) As a result, he was upset by Ms. Hawthorne's comments. (R. at 27.)

More important, Ms. Hawthorne's comments were relayed to people at the Gloucester County Prosecutor's Office, and one person asked him how badly he had treated Ms. Hawthorne to warrant being called a weasel. (R. at 27.) Mr. Beagle also received comments on his own

Facebook wall that Ms. Hawthorne had been calling him a "scumbag" at her externship. (R. at 28.) Mr. Beagle had not previously realized that Plaintiff was "Facebook friends" with members of that office and felt that Plaintiff was deliberately trying to harm his professional standing in the very office where he hopes to work one day.

Distressed, and not wanting to have any more online communications but needing the negativity to cease, Mr. Beagle decided that it would be best to talk to Plaintiff in person. (R. at 28.) He bought flowers during his lunch hour because he wanted to handle the situation "in a nice manner." (R. at 28, 32.) Unfortunately, he left the flowers in the car for several hours and the January cold snap froze many flowers in the bouquet. By the time he arrived at Ms. Hawthorne's house that night, a few of the flower heads fell off and, in retrospect, "the bouquet was looking kind of sad and . . . [Mr. Beagle] probably should not have given them to her." (R. at 28.) When Mr. Beagle arrived at Ms. Hawthorne's door, he knocked loudly with his knuckles, "as per his training." (R. at 29.) Although Mr. Beagle was trying to explain how he felt about her ad hominem comments, "That can hurt a person's professional reputation. I am really good at what I do," the conversation devolved into a shouting match. (R. at 28.) Mr. Beagle ended up leaving after less than half an hour, and the parties have not spoken since that time.

Although the parties do not have the need to see or speak to each other again, Ms. Hawthorne decided to seek a restraining order in the Camden County family court, claiming that she was the victim of domestic violence between two parties in a dating relationship. The judge hearing Ms. Hawthorne's ex parte application for a Temporary Restraining Order ("TRO") granted it and set a hearing date for a Final Restraining Order.

Prior to that date Mr. Beagle filed a motion to dismiss the action, arguing that the parties had never been in a dating relationship, and that any dispute between them was outside the jurisdiction of the family court. Family courts may grant domestic violence restraining orders only when the parties' relationship is domestic or family-like enough to warrant the extraordinary relief permitted under the Act. *N.J.S.A.* 2C:25-18. After a hearing on the sole topic of the parties' relationship, Judge Dodes, in a written opinion, concluded that the parties did have enough of a relationship that Ms. Hawthorne could apply for a restraining order under the Act. Mr. Beagle has filed this motion for reconsideration of that ruling.

The total time that the parties have been in each other's physical presence is under ninety minutes, when one counts the speed-dating meeting, the chance encounter on New Year's Eve, and Mr. Beagle's visit to Ms. Hawthorne's home. Ms. Hawthorne herself has rejected the idea of the parties going on a date. And so, the parties have never been on a date. It seems illogical at best that Ms. Hawthorne can reject Mr. Beagle's offers of dates and then later claim that she was dating Mr. Beagle.

Legal argument

Section 19(d) of the New Jersey Prevention of Domestic Violence Act is designed for people in certain and very specific relationships under its definition of "victim of domestic violence." The statute provides that a victim of domestic violence includes any person who has been subjected to domestic violence by a person with whom the victim has had a "dating relationship." *N.J.S.A.* 2C:25-19(d). The statute leaves undefined "dating relationship," and so the courts have taken the responsibility of applying a commonsense definition of the term. *Smith v. Moore*, 298 *N.J. Super.* 121 (App. Div. 1997). Situations that stretch beyond that commonsense definition are ineligible for a hearing in a New Jersey family court. This case—two people conversing only with technology and not in person—represents one of those ineligible situations. As such, because this Court has overlooked or erred in its usage of the controlling law, Petitioner-Defendant, Arthur Beagle, requests that this Court grant his Motion for Reconsideration per *R.*4:49-2 and dismiss this case for a lack of subject-matter jurisdiction.

A. The court's decision went beyond the boundaries of "dating relationship" as interpreted by the precedent.

Because the Act is remedial in nature, the courts look beyond a literal interpretation of its provisions. *See Tribuzio v. Roder*, 356 *N.J. Super.* 590 (App. Div. 2003); *Cesare v. Cesare*, 154 *N.J.* 394 (1998). The statute's remedial purpose is to protect potential victims against abuse. *N.J.S.A.* 2C:25-18; *Cesare*, 154 *N.J.* 394; *Smith*, 298 *N.J. Super.* 121. Accordingly, the courts will construe the Act to grant subject-matter jurisdiction when there is a special need to protect the plaintiff against future violence. *Carfagno v. Carfagno*, 288 *N.J. Super.* 424 (Ch. Div. 1995).

Although the Act is remedial in nature, and otherwise carries broad interpretations, those broad remedies exist for people who qualify as victims under the definitions section, *N.J.S.A.* 2C:25-19(d). Its protections extend only to people who qualify as victims of "domestic" violence; the word "domestic" is a key threshold that first must be met before there is a broad construction of the Act's terms. The statute was never intended to protect against all violence in all contexts; it addresses violence only in a domestic setting. The Appellate Division has cautioned trial courts against stretching the jurisdictional limits to the point of absurdity. Smith, 298 *N.J. Super.* 121 (holding that two former renters of a summer shore house were not household members under the Act). Accordingly, the statute's ambit goes no further than the violence that takes place in a "family-like" domestic context. *N.J.S.A.* 2C:25-18. Those relationships covered under the Act might take on unusual forms in the case law, but courts will still avoid a construction that might "torture the English language" by extending the statute beyond its rational limits. *M.A. v. E.A.*, 388 *N.J. Super.* 612, 618 (App. Div. 2006) (holding that it was impossible to construe a stepfather's sexually abusive conduct as creating a "dating relationship" with his stepdaughter because there must be limits to the phrase "dating").

Instead, when discussing dating relationships in particular, the Chancery Division has established a number of factors that a plaintiff must demonstrate before a court can establish jurisdiction based on a "dating relationship" under the statute. *Andrews v. Rutherford*, 363 *N.J. Super.* 252 (Ch. Div. 2003). In addition, the appellate courts have refused to grant jurisdiction when the circumstances indicated that there was no potential for future abuse between the parties. *Tribuzio*, 356 *N.J. Super.* 590.

There are two reasons why the Court should once again refuse subject-matter jurisdiction over the present case. First, Ms. Hawthorne and Mr. Beagle were never in a dating relationship under Section 19(d) of the statute. Second, the facts of this case negate any reasonable possibility of future abuse.

B. The parties' online-only interactions never created a relationship beyond a mere friendship.

The courts have noted that the Act is not concerned with the individual words, neither "dating," nor "relationships"; rather, it is concerned with both words, i.e., "dating relationships." *See N.J.S.A.* 2C:25-19(d); *J.S. v. J.F.*, 410 *N.J. Super.* 611, 613 (App. Div. 2009); *Andrews*, 363 *N.J. Super.* at 382. To this end, the Chancery Court in *Andrews* settled on a factor test after conducting a survey of how other jurisdictions define a "dating relationship." *Andrews*, 363 *N.J. Super.* at 260. Subsequently, the Appellate

Division reused the *Andrews* test in *J.S. v. J.F.*, 410 *N.J. Super.* 611. The factors given in *Andrews* and *J.S.* are:

1. Whether the parties had a minimal social interpersonal bonding over and above a mere casual fraternization;
2. How long the parties' alleged dating activities continued prior to the acts of domestic violence alleged;
3. What the nature and frequency of the parties' interactions were;
4. What the parties' ongoing expectations were with respect to the relationship, either individually or jointly;
5. Whether the parties demonstrated an affirmation of their relationship before others by statement or conduct;
6. Whether there are any other reasons unique to the case that support or detract from a finding that a dating relationship existed.

Andrews, 363 *N.J. Super.* at 260. The *Andrews* court acknowledged that the factors it proposed were not necessarily exclusive, and the Appellate Division has noted that there may be other factors not mentioned in *Andrews* that may be relevant. *J.S.*, 410 *N.J. Super.* at 614; *Andrews,* 363 *N.J. Super.* at 260. The courts use these six factors to determine whether the totality of the circumstances justify labeling the relationship as a "dating relationship." Ibid.

In previous cases where the courts have held that the parties were in a dating relationship, there were a number of factual bases that, as a totality, justified the courts' holdings. In *Andrews*, the plaintiff and defendant were in a relationship for five months while the woman defendant had another boyfriend. 363 *N.J. Super.* 252. The parties held themselves out as a couple in front of the plaintiff's family, but because of the defendant's other boyfriend, they hid their relationship from the defendant's family. *Id.* at 261. They were seen kissing, hugging, and being affectionate, and they went out at least fifteen times over the course of a few months. Ibid. They would spend nights together, and they attended a number of social gatherings together. *Id.* at 261–62. The defendant argued that because she was in another relationship at the time, she could not be held to be in a dating relationship with the plaintiff. *Id.* Nevertheless, the court found that the sum of the circumstances sufficiently established that a dating relationship existed. *Id.*

Similarly, in *J.S. v. J.F.* the Appellate Division found that the facts were sufficient to affirm the trial court's conclusion that the parties were in a dating relationship. 410 *N.J. Super.* 611. The plaintiff in *J.S.* was an exotic dancer whom the defendant may or may not have paid as a hired escort to accompany him to a family Thanksgiving dinner. *Id.* at 616–17. The evidence also included testimony that the plaintiff had gone to the defendant's home and she was introduced to his parents. *Id.* at 617. They went out several times and would spend weekends together. Ibid. Additionally, they spent Thanksgiving together with the defendant's parents, and he had given her money "to help her out financially"; she believed that she was in a dating relationship with the defendant. Ibid. The Appellate Court determined that the defendant's attempts to characterize their relationship as a professional one would not prevent the court from granting jurisdiction. *Id.* at 617–18.

Previous cases have shown that there is usually a significant period of time, and frequent contact between the parties, before a dating relationship can be found. In *Andrews*, the parties dated for four months, went out on at least fifteen dates, were seen hugging and kissing, and on occasion spent nights together. 363 *N.J. Super.* 252. In *Tribuzio*, the parties dated for a year. 356 *N.J. Super.* 590. The parties in *Sperling v. Teplitsky* dated for two to three years. 294 *N.J. Super.* 312 (Ch. Div. 1996). In *D.C. v. F.R.*, the plaintiff and defendant dated for thirteen months. 286 *N.J. Super.* 589 (App. Div. 1996).

Since the parties in this case, Petitioner, Arthur Beagle, and Respondent, Elaina Hawthorne, only met briefly in person twice (once at a speed-dating event and a second time by chance at a New Years' Eve party a few weeks later) and were never physically intimate, Ms. Hawthorne is unable to establish that the parties were in a dating relationship. As such, this is a matter outside of the family court's jurisdiction.

1. There is an absence of a bond that goes beyond casual fraternization.

Jurisdiction is improper because Mr. Beagle and Ms. Hawthorne never formed the type of bond that is indicative of a dating relationship. All these parties ever did was talk online for six weeks while Ms. Hawthorne sat in her family's den, and with her sister often sitting in on the conversations. Unlike the parties in either the *J.S.* or the *Andrews* case, who each saw the other party in person on multiple occasions, Mr. Beagle and Ms. Hawthorne made no arrangements to spend time with one another outside of their online conversations. Nor did they ever physically manifest any emotional bond. There were no special occasions spent together, and they did not meet each other's family except in the case of Sara Hawthorne joining their online conversations. In these respects, the present case is wholly dissimilar to all cases where the courts have granted jurisdiction.

By her unwillingness to spend time with Mr. Beagle in person, Ms. Hawthorne has demonstrated that she was emotionally detached rather than emotionally invested in their relationship. Instead of spending time with Mr. Beagle, she went to a singles party with her sister on New Year's Eve. When people are in a dating relationship, as Ms. Hawthorne claims they were, they take time out of their schedules to go out together. Based on the frequency of their conversations, it is only reasonable to say that she had the time to meet Mr. Beagle in person, especially during her winter break. The only plausible conclusion from Ms. Hawthorne's conduct is that she wasn't willing to reserve the time to engage in a dating relationship with Mr. Beagle.

Additionally, they did not discuss anything that would indicate that a dating relationship existed. They talked about their jobs, common interests, childhood memories, and they had inside jokes. There is nothing about this that would show that they were anything but friends. It is true that they flirted, but this alone cannot amount to a dating relationship. Although the parties may have been interested in beginning a dating relationship, they never progressed to that point.

Their interactions were frequently marred by misunderstandings and unreciprocated attempts to advance the relationship. When Ms. Hawthorne's jokes about undressing for Mr. Beagle came to an abrupt end, it indicated that the parties were unprepared to engage in that sort of behavior. Additionally, when Mr. Beagle refused to continue giving "goodbye" kisses over the Internet, he demonstrated that he was uncomfortable with showing affection. Finally, the misunderstanding about the book quote that Ms. Hawthorne posted on her Facebook wall shows that the parties did not know how to be clear with one another about their feelings.

These few, awkward, and misunderstood encounters strongly suggest that there was an absence of the emotional bond that the courts of New Jersey have held is necessary to engage in a dating relationship.

2. The parties lacked a reasonable expectation of a committed dating relationship.

Mr. Beagle explicitly stated that he never believed the parties to be in a dating relationship. Although factor four of the *Andrews* test does not require that the parties agree on whether they were in a dating relationship, it is still important to note that one of the parties did not see a reason to believe that their online conversations amounted to a dating relationship.

Ms. Hawthorne here testified that she believed the parties were in a dating relationship. However, quite unlike the plaintiff's account in the *J.S.* case, in which her account of the parties' interactions reasonably demonstrated a dating relationship, Ms. Hawthorne's alleged belief that she and Mr. Beagle were in a dating relationship lacks a rational basis. For the reasons already discussed above, there is nothing on record to show that the parties were anything but friends, and that their intent was to be friends.

The parties had no expectation of an exclusive relationship. On New Year's Eve they separately, and without telling one another, went to a singles event. Mr. Beagle indicated that he was willing to meet new people and Ms. Hawthorne never indicated that she was not open to do the same. In fact, Mr. Beagle did end up meeting two women, and he and his friend, Mr. Al Gero, sat with them for some time after Ms. Hawthorne left the event to see her family. Although there may have been a mutual interest between the parties, their actions do not indicate that they expected to have a dating relationship.

Furthermore, Mr. Beagle's statements at the singles event indicate that he did not expect to foster any sort of dating relationship with Ms. Hawthorne. When Mr. Beagle saw Ms. Hawthorne at the event, he said to himself, "this isn't going to be a night for romance." When Mr. Beagle said that it wasn't a night for romance, he meant, in addition to other implications, that there would not be any romance between himself and Ms. Hawthorne. Furthermore, when Mr. Beagle tried to appease Ms. Hawthorne because she was upset with him, he may have demonstrated a desire to advance the relationship, but her rebuffs prevented him from believing that the nature of their friendship was changing.

Finally, Ms. Hawthorne's reaction to seeing Mr. Beagle at the singles event does nothing to indicate that the parties had an expectation of being in a relationship. Plaintiff herself never said at trial that she was angry that he was trying to cheat on her; she only said that she was "upset because it looked like maybe he was looking to meet other women." At most her statement reflects her desire to be the object of Mr. Beagle's affection.

3. *Their friends and family never considered the parties in a dating relationship.*

Both the *J.S.* and *Andrews* courts spent some time reviewing the evidence that family and friends knew about the parties' romantic dating relationship. There was testimony about family events, and photographs and videos of the parties together in romantic poses. In contrast, the evidence in this case is very thin or nonexistent about the parties holding themselves out as anything other than online chatters. No one besides Ms. Hawthorne has stated that the parties were in a dating relationship. Mr. Beagle's friend, Mr. Gero, testified that he had no belief that the parties were ever in a dating relationship, although he was aware of their conversations and the general nature of their interactions. He noted that Mr. Beagle "wasn't all that interested" in Ms. Hawthorne.

Even Sara Hawthorne, who witnessed more of the parties' interactions than anyone else, would say only that they were interested in each other. Additionally, she stated that she never saw the parties being affectionate during their conversations. She further noted that she might have seen the parties holding hands at the singles event. However, "holding hands" conjures an image that runs counter to the actual occurrence. Mr. Beagle held Ms. Hawthorne's hand to help calm her down, but he received only a mild response and Ms. Hawthorne remained "standoffish." Sara Hawthorne also said that Mr. Beagle "nuzzled" Ms. Hawthorne's neck when they saw each other at the singles event. The veracity of this testimony is suspect, however, because no other witness mentioned this when describing the same event. It appears most likely that Mr. Beagle was leaning in to speak to Ms. Hawthorne and it appeared from a distance to be a display of affection.

Without affirmation from the people who are close to the parties here, it would be unreasonable to accept Ms. Hawthorne's characterization of her relationship with Mr. Beagle.

4. To find that a purely online relationship is a dating relationship would be a significant and unjustified break with established law.

The facts of this case are without precedent with respect to the online nature of the friendship. In all of the past cases that have dealt with the present issue, the parties' interactions were primarily in person.

A brief examination of the present state of online relationships shows that relationships conducted online are not "dating" relationships. A recent study demonstrated that younger members of society are less likely to view online relationships as being serious. Trent Parker, How Bad is It? Perceptions of the Relationship Impact of Different Types of Internet Sexual Activities, 25 Contemp. Fam. Therapy 415, 419–20 (2003). This is probably attributable to the ubiquity and anonymity of online interactions that younger Internet users are more accustomed to. In contrast, older members of society are more likely to believe online relationships are serious, which helps to explain why marriages are occasionally harmed by sexual interactions online. Ibid. Thus Ms. Hawthorne's thorough reliance on the "generational factors" mentioned in *J.S. v. J.F.* is unsupported by the evidence: Ms. Hawthorne's argument would be more appropriate if the parties were twice as old as they are. 410 *N.J. Super.* 611.

Online "dating" is not an end in and of itself. The purpose of online dating websites is to meet a person online, develop a rapport, and eventually start an in-person relationship. Match.com's and eHarmony's "success stories" webpages feature lists of couples who met through their services. eHarmony Success Stories, http://www.eharmony.com/success/stories (last visited Apr. 18, 2010); Match.com, Success@Match, http://success.match.com (last visited Apr. 18, 2010).[2] Importantly, the pictures of the successful couples show the couples together in person. The "success stories" are not lists of people who continue to happily talk online; they are lists of people who are happily dating, engaged, and married. The online aspect of the relationships was merely a stepping-stone for the real intimacy that comes with in-person interaction. The parties here have remained on the hypothetical "first stone."

It would be an unprecedented and harmful change in law to apply the Prevention of Domestic Violence Act to the present circumstances. It would allow the courts to call a series of online conversations a "dating relationship" despite the absence of anything that could reasonably be called a "date" and where the situation completely lacks the domestic context that the statute necessarily requires. Extending the statute in this manner would wholly disregard the statute's intended purpose: to protect victims of violence in a family-like setting.

Consideration for the factors set forth in *Andrews* shows that there is an absence of any interaction that would justify finding that the parties were in a dating relationship. The jurisdictional limitations and considerations set forth by the Appellate Division are important to effectuate the true intent of the Act. As this Court is surely cognizant, there are no gradations of remedies permitted under the Act: the same nonexpiring restraints and indefinite limitations are imposed on a defendant regardless of whether the alleged abuse was a serious assault or, as was the situation between these parties, merely a mutual verbal argument between two people disagreeing about the professional impropriety of Facebook postings. Thus, courts must dismiss when there is no evidence of a relationship between

---

[2]N.B.: date left in place from date student author last checked.

the parties. In light of the extraordinary and permanent implications of a restraining order, as well as the minimal nature of the parties' acquaintanceship, this Court should grant this Motion for Reconsideration and dismiss this case for lack of subject-matter jurisdiction.

Conclusion

For the foregoing reasons, it is respectfully submitted that this Honorable Court committed an error in denying jurisdiction, and the Court should thus grant Mr. Beagle's Motion for Reconsideration and dismiss this case.

Respectfully Submitted,

1L Student Intern
On the brief
For Petitioner-Defendant, Arthur Beagle

Appendix B

Plaintiff Elaina Hawthorne's brief in opposition to motion for reconsideration

(student brief)

Elaina Hawthorne,	:	Superior Court of New Jersey,
	:	Camden County
Plaintiff,	:	Chancery Division – Family Part
	:	
	:	
v.	:	Docket No. FV010-171696
	:	
Arthur Beagle,	:	**Plaintiff-Respondent's brief in**
	:	**opposition to motion for**
	:	**reconsideration**
Defendant	:	
	:	Sat: Hon. Wali Dodes, J.S.C.

Preliminary statement

Plaintiff-Respondent, Ms. Elaina Hawthorne, began this domestic violence case in January 2010, seeking a Temporary Restraining Order (TRO) against Defendant-Petitioner, Arthur Beagle. The TRO was granted, and, per standard procedures, the date for a full hearing on the merits of a Final Restraining Order (FRO) was set for two weeks later. Ms. Hawthorne sought this protection based on Defendant-Petitioner Arthur Beagle's threatening and harassing conduct toward her just after the parties' breakup. Prior to the scheduled FRO hearing date, Defendant-Petitioner filed a motion to dismiss, challenging this Court's jurisdiction to hear the matter. This Court held a hearing on the sole issue of whether the parties' relationship falls under the jurisdictional category of "dating." At the end of that proceeding, and after hearing testimony from the parties, plus two other witnesses, this Court issued a written opinion, concluding that the parties did, in fact, have the requisite dating relationship, pursuant to *N.J.S.A.*

2C:25-19(d), and that Ms. Hawthorne was entitled to a hearing on the merits of an FRO.[1]

Nevertheless, Defendant-Petitioner has filed, also at the family, trial level, this Motion for Reconsideration of this Court's written opinion finding jurisdiction. This response brief, thus, is filed on behalf of Plaintiff-Respondent, Elaina Hawthorne, in opposition to that Motion for Reconsideration. By liberally construing the Prevention of Domestic Violence Act, this Court's opinion properly gave effect to the Legislature's intent and followed the guidance prior appellate case law. Accordingly, Ms. Hawthorne respectfully requests that this Court deny Defendant-Petitioner's Motion for Reconsideration and move forward with the scheduled hearing on the merits of her application for an FRO.

Statement of the case

Plaintiff-Respondent, Elaina Hawthorne, is a third-year law student at Rutgers School of Law in Camden, New Jersey. (R. at 4.) In November, at a local speed-dating event, Ms. Hawthorne met the Defendant, Mr. Arthur Beagle, a student at the New Jersey State Police Academy. (R. at 4.) The two bonded at the event after finding that they had much in common. For example, both are interested in working for the Gloucester County criminal justice system after each graduates from his or her respective program. In addition to being a student carrying a sixteen-credit load, Ms. Hawthorne spends twenty hours each week (four academic credits) externing with the Gloucester County Prosecutor's Office and hopes to be offered a job in that office after graduating and passing the bar exam. *Id.* Likewise, after graduation, Beagle aspires to work in either "the Sheriff's Office or as a detective in the Prosecutor's Office" of Gloucester County. (R. at 23.)

Recognizing their shared interests, the two developed their relationship using, with increasing frequency, telephone calls, Skype video phone calls, Facebook, and Yahoo chat rooms. Of those several methods, the parties opted more and more for Skype: within a short time after the parties met they were using Skype several times a week in order to have real-time and face-to-face calls. Skype allowed them to chat with each other in a very personal and one-on-one manner. (R. at 4.) These meet-ups took place over the course of months and occurred up to three times a week, often lasting two hours at a time. (R. at 14, 15.) During their

---

[1]This brief uses New Jersey local rules of citation, which is what a New Jersey court would expect to see.

conversations, Ms. Hawthorne and Mr. Beagle talked about common interests, flirted, and traded quotes about love. (R. at 5, 31.) They would also "blow kisses to each other," and once or twice Ms. Hawthorne and Mr. Beagle even went so far as to fully kiss their respective video cameras as if they were "making out." (R. at 6, 20, 24.) During other, more casual conversations, Ms. Hawthorne's sister, Sara Hawthorne, was occasionally present and spoke to Mr. Beagle a few times. She understood that the parties had a "romantic interest in each other." (R. at 18.) At one point during the relationship, Ms. Hawthorne told her sister that she "might be able to fall in love with [Mr. Beagle]." Ibid.

Although the parties spoke and interacted quite frequently each week, Ms. Hawthorne and Mr. Beagle each were also balancing their busy end-of-semester studying schedules and had little time for a lot of social activity. (R. at 24.) Ms. Hawthorne testified that grades were very important to her because of her goal to become a prosecutor and that she studies and prepares for classes at least two or three hours each day. (R. at 4.) In November and December, students at Rutgers Law are busy preparing outlines for final exams. Her fall semester course schedule kept her at school from early afternoon until 8 or 9 p.m. two days each week,[2] and her fieldwork externship at the Gloucester County Prosecutor's Office meant that she was working in a law office two or three other weekdays. Ms. Hawthorne also holds a part-time waitressing job with hours on some weekend nights and some weekend mornings. (R. at 5.) Mr. Beagle was likewise in class during the week, commuting over an hour each way to school (R. at 24), and Ms. Hawthorne, in addition to attending her regular classes and externship, was working on law school outlines and final exams. Additionally, numerous serious snowstorms occurred during the same period of time. As the newspaper reports demonstrate, 2009 was the "Snowiest Winter in History" in Philadelphia.[3] Given all that was happening at that point in the academic year, the parties were unable to schedule more traditional dates during November and December. Thus, Skype became a very easy and efficient way for the parties to nurture their relationship.

Ms. Hawthorne and Mr. Beagle also engaged each other through Facebook, even though Ms. Hawthorne was new to it. (R. at 17.) On one

---

[2]RUTGERS SCHOOL OF LAW, Camden Academic Calendar 2009–10, http://camlaw.rutgers.edu/cgi-bin/academic-calendar.cgi (last visited Apr. 18, 2010) (N.B.: last-visit date left intact from student's brief).
[3]Vince Lattanzio, It's Officially the Snowiest Winter in History, NBC PHILA., Feb. 11, 2010, available at http://www.nbcphiladelphia.com/news/breaking/Its-Officially-the-Snowiest-Winter-in-History-84065947.html.

occasion, Ms. Hawthorne posted her status as "why is love intensified by absence," which she testified referred to her absence from Mr. Beagle. He responded on Facebook that he "liked" it. (R. at 6.) Nevertheless, Ms. Hawthorne remained listed as "single" on Facebook during her relationship with Mr. Beagle. (R. at 17.) When asked why she was listed as "single" despite the fact that she believed she was in a dating relationship with Mr. Beagle, Ms. Hawthorne noted that she had been advised by others, "it is better to say single no matter what" on Facebook. (Ibid.)

It was after seeing this particular status that Mr. Beagle asked Ms. Hawthorne to undress in front of the camera during a Skype session. (R. at 6, 21, 25.) She agreed to wear a tank top for their next video phone call, but would not go further. Ms. Hawthorne was reluctant and uncomfortable, she explained, for two reasons. First, the video camera was located in a common area of her house. (R. at 6.) Second, Ms. Hawthorne's personal belief system involves a pledge of chastity before marriage. Mr. Beagle was aware that Ms. Hawthorne is a member of the Facebook group "Purity." (R. at 25.)

Ms. Hawthorne and Mr. Beagle saw each other in person during a New Year's Eve party at T.G.I. Friday's. (R. at 7, 26.) Ms. Hawthorne attended the party because Sara Hawthorne, her sister, asked for company. (R. at 7.) Mr. Beagle attended with his friend, Al Gero, as a "wingman." (Ibid.) Ms. Hawthorne testified that she was "unhappy" to see Mr. Beagle at the event, particularly because this was only a few days after the conversation in which he asked her to take off her clothes. (Ibid.) Mr. Beagle, however, seemed happy to see her and immediately asked his friend to please let Mr. Beagle and Ms. Hawthorne have some alone time. (R. at 33.)

Both parties testified that they sat down next to each other—side by side—in a booth. They began talking and holding hands. (R. at 8, 21, 27.) Ms. Hawthorne's sister testified that she saw the parties "being kind of cuddly" and that Mr. Beagle "nuzzled her neck once." (R. at 20, 22.) Later, both of the Hawthorne women needed to leave for a family dinner. (R. at 7.)

Although Mr. Beagle told her that he was at that New Year's Eve event only as a "wingman" for his friend, Ms. Hawthorne was somewhat upset that she saw him at the event. (R. at 9, 7.) Nevertheless, the parties continued their relationship via Skype just as they did before. (R. at 9.) During one such Skype session, Mr. Beagle again asked Ms. Hawthorne to undress. (Ibid.) It was then that Ms. Hawthorne began to become skeptical of Mr. Beagle and posted on her Facebook wall "Arthur is really Weasely," which, she testified, was an obvious, joking reference to

Harry Potter. (R. at 1.) Both parties are readers and belong to online chat rooms about popular books. (R. at 8.) Mr. Beagle was angry about the post, however, because he had previously told her about being teased for his name earlier in his life. (R. at 23.) He called Ms. Hawthorne, admonishing her for that, and also for not being "more physical" in their relationship. (R. at 27, 10.) In response, Ms. Hawthorne then told Mr. Beagle "we should just be friends," to which Mr. Beagle responded "sure, OK." (R. at 10.) Ms. Hawthorne viewed this conversation as "that's when we broke up." (R. at 10.)

The next day at her externship, Ms. Hawthorne expressed frustration to her co-workers that Mr. Beagle did not understand a simple joke. (R. at 10.) Mr. Beagle became aware of Ms. Hawthorne's comments through mutual friends and, the very next night, appeared, uninvited, at Ms. Hawthorne's house. He had never been to her house prior to that time. (R. at 11.) Mr. Beagle banged on Ms. Hawthorne's door so loudly that it appeared to Ms. Hawthorne and her sister that he was using his nightstick, although Mr. Beagle denies this. (R. at 10, 20, 29.) Ms. Hawthorne answered the door and found Mr. Beagle "so mad that he was shaking." (R. at 11.) He screamed "don't you dare call me stupid to my friends! And don't post things about me on Facebook! That can hurt a person's professional reputation! I am really good at what I do, you know!" (Ibid.) Ms. Hawthorne testified that this particular statement worried her because "he is a very good marksman. So I knew what he was suggesting—that he might hurt me. Because he is such a good marksman." (Ibid.) In his testimony, Mr. Beagle has agreed that he "takes great pride in his ability to shoot guns accurately." (R. at 19.)

Adding to Ms. Hawthorne's unease at the scene, Mr. Beagle presented her with a bouquet of dead, headless flowers. (Ibid.) Trying to defuse the situation, Ms. Hawthorne said she was "sorry that it had not worked out between us." Mr. Beagle was upset and responded, "no, this is not working and it is just too bad." (R. at 12.) After he left her house, Ms. Hawthorne called the police and sought the restraining order. Although admitting that their relationship was nontraditional, Ms. Hawthorne testified:

> This thing I had with Arthur was not just friends. It was definitely much more than that. We were in a relationship. And now I am scared about what he might do to me—we could very well end up seeing each other all the time because of the line of work we are both in.
>
> [(R. at 12).]

Despite the Defendant's challenge to this Court's jurisdiction, the Honorable Wali Dodes ruled that this matter can be adjudicated under the New

Jersey Prevention of Domestic Violence Act. Specifically, Judge Dodes reviewed the applicable case law interpreting the "dating relationship" language in the Act, before he held that "plaintiff and defendant showed affection through words and actions, they outwardly demonstrated their relationship, and they spoke regularly for long periods of time (albeit on the Internet). These actions undoubtedly reflect typical behavior in a dating relationship as outlined by our statute and by prior decisions." (Tr. Op. at 2.) Because Judge Dodes's ruling accurately reflects the state of the law, this Court should likewise deny Defendant-Petitioner, Arthur Beagle's current motion to the same court for reconsideration of that jurisdictional ruling.

Legal argument

A. The Defendant-Petitioner is unable to show any sort of error in this Court's previous ruling that would give rise to an appropriate reconsideration under *R.* 4:49-2.

Defendant-Petitioner's Motion for Reconsideration is premised upon a narrow view of modern dating trends. This Court, on the other hand, has already properly concluded that under the expansive reach of the Prevention of Domestic Violence Act ("the Act"), these parties were dating.

The standard for Motions for Reconsideration are codified by New Jersey Rule 4:49-2, which states:

> [T]he motion shall state with specificity the basis on which it is made, including a statement of the matters or controlling decisions which counsel believes the court has overlooked or as to which it has erred.
>
> [(*R.* 4:49-2).]

There was neither an overlooked fact nor a legal error in this Court's ruling on Defendant's Motion to Dismiss. Rather, the parties' relationship satisfies several of the factors approved by the Appellate Division in *J.S. v. J.F.,* 410 *N.J. Super.* 611 (App. Div. 2009). Because this Court's prior holding correctly applied the germane case law, this Motion for Reconsideration should be denied and Ms. Hawthorne should receive a hearing to argue the merits of a FRO.

B. This Court has already properly effectuated the broad intent of the Act's scope and the courts' expansive interpretation of "dating relationship" when it took jurisdiction over the case.

This Court can comfortably deny Defendant-Petitioner's Motion for Reconsideration because its initial ruling was well within the purview of what the Legislature intended. The pertinent law indicates that a "victim of domestic violence" includes "any person who is 18 years of age or older or who is an emancipated minor who has been subjected to domestic violence by a spouse, former spouse, or any other person who is a present or former household member." *N.J.S.A.* 2C:25-19(d). The New Jersey Legislature amended this provision in 1994 to include protection for individuals who have "been subjected to domestic violence by a person with whom the victim has had a dating relationship." Ibid.

The pertinent section of the statute does not provide a definition of what constitutes a "dating relationship." Interpreting courts have rejected the notion of an absolute or plain meaning to the phrase. Instead, courts will interpret it in light of the policy set out by the New Jersey Supreme Court to look at the Act through a broad lens. *Cesare v. Cesare*, 154 *N.J.* 394 (1998). The New Jersey Supreme Court has stressed the importance of a liberal interpretation "to achieve its salutary purposes" so as to "assure the victims of domestic violence the maximum protection from abuse the law can provide." *Id.* at 399.

Because the Legislature has called for a liberal construction, courts have developed and use an expansive and liberally construed factor test to determine when parties are in a dating relationship. There are relatively few opinions that look at the specific issue of what is or isn't a dating relationship in New Jersey. Each of the cases, however, has agreed that a broad factor test is the appropriate analysis vehicle. The most often cited opinion, though trial level, outlined a series of factors after considering the various tests used in other states. *Andrews v. Rutherford*, 363 *N.J. Super.* 252, 260 (Ch. Div. 2003). Those factors, though broken out into six separate parts, really boil down to some sort of romantic attachment between the parties beyond that of "mere casual fraternization." Ibid.

1. Was there a minimal social interpersonal bonding of the parties over and above mere casual fraternization?

2. How long did the alleged dating activities continue prior to the acts of domestic violence alleged?

3. What were the nature and frequency of the parties' interactions?

4. What were the parties' ongoing expectations with respect to the relationship, either individually or jointly?

5. Did the parties demonstrate an affirmation of their relationship before others by statement or conduct?

6. Are there any other reasons unique to the case that support or detract from a finding that a "dating relationship" exists? Ibid.

A recent Appellate Division opinion, covering some of the same ground, found the *Andrews'* decision factors "useful" though not mandatory. *J.S. v. J.F.*, 410 *N.J. Super.* 611, 616 (App. Div. 2009). The appellate court, reminded that the Act calls for liberal construction, declined to adopt any exclusive formula, because it worried that doing so would potentially fall short of embracing a broad enough category of people covered by the Act's protections. Rather, the Appellate Division encouraged courts to combine a factor analysis with an examination of "the parties' own understanding of their relationship as colored by socio-economic and generational influences" in order to best achieve the broad relief that the Legislature intends. *Id.* at 616; *see also Andrews*, 363 *N.J. Super.* at 260 ("in the interest of interpreting the Act broadly as required by Cesare and the statute itself, these factors should also be liberally construed.").

Those relationships covered under the Act might take on unusual forms but, so long as they still demonstrate some romantic connection, can provide a jurisdictional basis for the family court to consider a restraining order. For example, the Appellate Division in *J.S. v. J.F.* easily affirmed the family court's finding of jurisdiction, regardless of the defendant's claim that the nature of the relationship—and the physical affirmations—were based in finances rather than romance. 410 *N.J. Super.* 611. The defendant in *J.S.* claimed that the plaintiff, an exotic dancer by profession, was his paid escort at his family's Thanksgiving dinner. Even if he had paid for her Thanksgiving company, the Appellate Division reasoned, "the fact that a person receives monetary benefit from engaging in a relationship does not automatically disqualify that person from the Act's benefits." Indeed, the Appellate Division opined, in dicta, that *au pairs* should be considered household members under the Act even when the relationship's foundation was financial. *Id.*

Instead, the Appellate Division focused on the relationship's other qualities that tended to weigh in favor of calling this a dating situation. *Id.* at 615. Enough of the other factors were present to merit the family court taking jurisdiction. The parties admittedly had a romantic and physical relationship. They shared time together and spent a holiday together in the presence of the defendant's family—the Thanksgiving dinner for which he allegedly paid her to attend with him. *Id.* at 617. The court, without much pause, affirmed the family court's finding that these facts amounted to a dating relationship.

Similarly, a couple may still be in a legally defined dating relationship even when one of the partners has multiple other dating partners and no real expectations of permanency or exclusivity with the other party. *Andrews*, 363 *N.J. Super.* at 265. A court in that situation will still look at the overall romantic nature of the parties' relationship. In *Andrews*, the defendant denied dating the plaintiff because she had another, publicly acknowledged boyfriend. The plaintiff, according to the defendant, was just someone whom she spent time with and had physical relations with. When the *Andrews* court set aside the existence of the defendant's other boyfriend, the relationship between the parties met other factors. The parties sustained a relationship over the course of several months that included "the typical conduct of young people who are exploring the limits of each other's feelings for one another." *Id.* at 265. The family court found that the parties demonstrated an interpersonal bonding over and above a mere fraternization by the fact that they "saw each other regularly" in a noncasual fashion and had physical affirmations of their romantic attraction to each other, evidenced, by way of example, in a video of the parties enjoying themselves in a hotel room during a late night New Year's Eve party. *Id.* at 264. The evidence also demonstrated other examples of romantic and physical attraction to each other. Ibid. The plaintiff had introduced the defendant to his friends and family, even though she had not reciprocated with her friends or family. The family court used the commonsense reasoning that these parties were dating because the presence of the other factors counterbalanced the nonexclusivity of the relationship, and ultimately controlled the legal conclusion. *Id.* at 260, 265.

Moreover, in one of the very few unpublished opinions on point, the Appellate Division recently held that a dating relationship was present in a case in which the only factor that was considered was the sixth "catch-all" factor outlined by the *Andrews* court. *Jensen v. Baratta*, No. A-3805-07T3, 2009 LEXIS 3185 (N.J. Super. Ct. App. Div.). In Jensen, the parties met at a five-day real estate class and had several lunches together in the company of other attendees. *Id.* at *2. The parties also went out to dinner once, though the relationship fizzled after this meeting. Ibid. Six years later, the defendant was seen in his car outside the plaintiff's house with a loaded gun, $10,000 in cash, and a notebook that said "real-estate girl." *Id.* at *3. The Appellate Division agreed with the family judge, who "gave great weight to number six of the *Andrews* factors, that is, other reasons unique to the case that supported the finding that a 'dating relationship' existed." *Id.* at *6. Thus, a court's discretion is broad enough to find a dating relationship solely under just one of the factors, if the circumstances warrant it.

The only limitation that a court has ever mentioned with respect to dating relationships are those situations, far different from the romantic situations our parties are in, where the ruling would be "absurd." *M.A. v. E.A.,* 388 *N.J. Super.* 612 (App. Div. 2006). The appellate judge in that case was speaking about a very different set of circumstances—a sad situation in which a mother was trying to obtain a restraining order for her teenage child, who was being sexually abused under circumstances not covered by the New Jersey child abuse statute. Although recognizing that the facts fell into a gap between the two statutes, and although reluctant to leave the child with no recourse, the appellate panel was forced to agree that sexual molestation could not, nor could it ever, be considered a "dating relationship" because such a finding would "unacceptably torture the English language and euphemize the hostile nature of defendant's alleged behavior." *Id.* at 618. The M.A. case, therefore, is typically considered outside of the dating relationship panoply of decisions.

Under the courts' holistic and liberal examination of dating relationships, this Court properly concluded that these parties had a dating relationship. From the first meeting of the parties at the speed-dating event—an event whose very purpose was to further the attendees' goal of finding someone with whom to have a dating relationship—these parties moved beyond a mere casual fraternization. The courts have already determined that they will disregard one unusual factor if the overall tone of the relationship is romantic. That is exactly what characterizes this relationship.

First, the parties interacted frequently over the course of their months together. Given the limited amount of free time that either party had during November and December, they chose to spend quite a lot of it with each other. They were in each other's company for numerous hours, juggling their individual time constraints and their obligation–restrictions in order to be with each other. The parties were stymied by school, studies, and unexpectedly bad weather. Throughout their relationship, Ms. Hawthorne was a busy third-year law student, taking evening courses, studying, waitressing, and working twenty hours each week at the very office where she hopes to work after graduation. She was also studying for her finals during many of those weeks. The Defendant-Petitioner spent several hours of his week with Ms. Hawthorne even with his own studies and three hours of commuting time each day. The level of commitment the parties demonstrated to each other was at least as serious, if not more so, than the dating relationships in the *J.S.* and *Andrews* cases.

The nature of the parties' frequent interactions also bears the hallmarks of a dating relationship, even if some of their dates were not the traditional dinner-and-a-movie. There was just as much, if not more, alone time for this fledgling couple. In addition to other means of communication such as traditional phone calls and Facebook, the parties Skyped with each other quite often—typically three times a week for almost two months, with some sessions even lasting as long as two hours. During that time, the parties demonstrated the type of "clear romantic attraction to each other" noted as important in the *Andrews* case. Mr. Beagle and Ms. Hawthorne talked about each other's interests, flirted, and even traded love quotes. Moreover, they kissed each other albeit via a computer screen and camera. The video calls were intimate enough that Mr. Beagle asked Ms. Hawthorne several times to undress in front of the camera. People do not kiss casual acquaintances on the lips; nor do they ask them to undress.

Both Ms. Hawthorne's sister and Mr. Beagle's friend testified that they were aware of the parties' frequent communications. Ms. Hawthorne's sister had personal knowledge of the communications because she had been invited into some of them. Likewise, just as the holidays in the two reported cases played a role in demonstrating the dating relationships, the New Year's Eve event at T.G.I. Friday's similarly demonstrated to friends and family that their romantic interest in each other was beyond "mere casual fraternization." Both Mr. Beagle's friend, Al Gero, and Ms. Hawthorne's sister concur in their testimony that the parties were sitting alone together, holding hands, cuddling, and "nuzzling necks." Defendant-Petitioner himself asked Mr. Gero if he could have some time alone with Ms. Hawthorne, forsaking his promised role as "wingman" for Mr. Gero, helping him meet women.

Courts must continue to broadly define "dating relationships" and recognize that technology will play an increasingly significant role in dating practices. To do otherwise will soon render the Act largely irrelevant to the modern world. This case is a perfect example of why the court must continue to construe "dating relationship" broadly. The presence of technology in this relationship is merely a sign of modern times. In every other way the bond looks like a traditional dating relationship. The Legislature, in leaving "dating relationship" undefined, purposely deferred to future courts to refine the contours of the term to reflect future understanding of dating. As the appellate court in *J.S.* has signaled, modern relationships should be understood and colored by "generational influences." Skype was just a vehicle to let the parties be in the same room with each other in real time.

Even if these parties fall under the category of "online dating," that is still within the new boundaries of this era and this Court has plenty of discretion to include online dating as falling within the jurisdiction of the Act. That is why the sixth "catchall" factor in the *Andrews* case exists. Online dating is a growing trend that shapes the structure of dating relationships. The New York Times has reported,

> Since the current recession began, the popularity of online dating has surged—memberships are up and new matchmaking portals have emerged to take advantage of the demand—industry growth of up to 30 percent is expected in the next year or two, according to the tracking site DatingService.com.

> [Scott James, In Calculations of Online Dating, Love Can Be Cruel, N.Y. Times, Feb. 12, 2010, at A25A.]

In 2007, the online dating industry was estimated to have generated $900 million in revenue.[4] This number is estimated to grow to over $1.9 billion by 2012.[5] The practice has become so common that to provide protection for online daters, the New Jersey Legislature passed the Internet Dating Safety Act in May 2007.[6] Just as the Legislature did, the Judiciary should act to provide protection for online daters.

Thus, this Court had sufficient legal justification to conclude that this relationship is covered by the New Jersey Prevention of Domestic Violence Act. There is nothing in either the law or in the facts of this case that would warrant a ruling in favor of Defendant-Petitioner's Motion for Reconsideration. Rather, this case should proceed to the hearing on the merits of granting a Final Restraining Order.

---

[4]Businesswire.com, JupiterResearch Sees Steady Growth for Online Personals, Despite Explosion of Social Networking (Feb. 11, 2008), http://www.businesswire.com/portal/site/home/permalink/?ndmViewId=news_view&newsId=20080211005037&newsLang=en.
[5]Ibid.
[6]The Internet Dating Safety Act requires that online dating sites tell customers whether they do background checks on their members.

Conclusion

For the foregoing reasons, Respondent, Elaina Hawthorne, respectfully requests that this Honorable Court deny this Motion for Reconsideration and reschedule the remainder of the Final Restraining Order hearing.

Respectfully submitted,

1L Law Student Intern
On the brief
for Plaintiff-Respondent, Elaina Hawthorne

Plaintiff's brief in support of plaintiff's motion for summary judgment and in opposition to defendant's motion for summary judgment

(student brief)

**In the Superior Court of
Marion County, Indiana**

The Gloucester Hotel of Indiana polis, a Delaware corporation	))	
Plaintiff	))	
v.	)))	No. 1531-GD-2012
Save Our Forest Trees, Inc., a California nonprofit corporation,	)))	
Defendant	)	

Plaintiff's brief in support of plaintiff's motion
for summary judgment and in opposition
to defendant's motion for summary judgment

I. Preliminary statement

The Gloucester Indianapolis Hotel is a relatively new luxury hotel in downtown Indianapolis, with a growing reputation in hosting meetings for nonprofit and business organizations. In summer 2011, it agreed to be the host hotel for a two-day conference of 75 to 100 members of the organization Save Our Forest Trees, Inc. The Hotel entered a contract to hold 150 room nights open for the organization's members, thereby forgoing the opportunity to book other organizations for that same time period. The contract included a provision that required SOFT to sell 90% of the reserved block to its members. If it failed to do so, SOFT would be responsible for the difference between 90% of the reserved block (or 135 room nights) and the actual number of room nights sold to SOFT guests, at the contracted room rate (a discount from the hotel's normal rate).

SOFT guests in fact reserved only 82 room nights, far less than the contractually required 135 room nights. Accordingly, the Hotel invoiced SOFT for the 53 room nights it had promised to sell but failed to use. When SOFT refused to pay the invoice, this litigation ensued.

Since these essential facts are all undisputed, both parties have moved for summary judgment.

II. The facts of the case

The Gloucester Indianapolis Hotel is part of the Gloucester Worldwide hotel group, a growing chain of luxury hotels and resorts. The Indianapolis hotel, which opened in 2007, achieved an 82.3% occupancy rate in 2012, the second highest in the entire Gloucester Worldwide chain and well above the Indianapolis average rate of 68.2%. Mason Dep. 5:11–6:19, Aug. 20, 2013.

Sometime in August 2011, Julius Mason, the General Manager of the Gloucester Indianapolis, received a call from a representative of a nonprofit organization known as Save Our Forest Trees, Inc., headquartered in California. *Id.* at 10:1–14. The organization wished to host a conference on the campus of Indiana University Purdue University Indianapolis (IUPUI) in July 2012 and wished to reserve a block of rooms for up to 75 out-of-town participants who were expected to attend (a total of 150 room nights for the two-day conference). Since this was well within Gloucester Indianapolis' capacity of 250 rooms, Mr. Mason negotiated a group rate of $159 per night, a discount from the normal summer rate of $189 per night. He prepared the standard hotel contract for a group reservation and mailed it to SOFT's headquarters in Eureka, California. *Id.* at 11:10–14. It was returned by mail about ten days later, and the reserved block was entered into the hotel's reservation system. *Id.* at 12:3–6.

The contract signed by SOFT included this paragraph:

Reservation Deadline: June 1, 2012

In order to qualify for the guaranteed room rate, individuals must reserve rooms on or before the Reservation Deadline specified above, and must specify the Group Name. After the Reservation Deadline, rooms not reserved in the Group Name will be returned to the Hotel's general inventory and may be sold by the Hotel to any guest at normal Hotel rates. Group acknowledges that it may forgo the opportunity to reserve those rooms for other guests prior to the Reservation Deadline, and that the Hotel will incur costs in reselling rooms, and that these damages are difficult to ascertain. In the event that the Group fails to reserve 90 % of the Room Block Reservation specified above by the Reservation Deadline, Group agrees to pay as liquidated damages, and not as a penalty, the difference between the actual number of rooms reserved by Group guests and 90 % of the Room Block specified above, at the Guaranteed Room Rate, such payment to be due 15 days after the Reservation Deadline.

Contract for Room Reservations, Aug. 15, 2011, attached to Freebird Dep. Ex. 1, Aug. 20, 2013.

Less than a month later, Mr. Mason received a call from the Hoosier Club, an organization of Indiana small- to mid-size business leaders interested in promoting Indiana businesses to global markets. Mason Dep. 15:6–19. The Hoosier Club met annually, usually in Indianapolis, and usually drew as many as 200 participants to its summer meetings. It wanted to schedule its 2012 conference at the hotel, on the same weekend previously booked by SOFT. However, due to the preexisting commitment to SOFT and a few other contractual obligations, Mr. Mason could offer only 125 rooms per night to the Hoosier Club, so the group elected to book rooms at another nearby hotel. *Id.* at 17:2–21.

Shortly after June 1, 2012, Mr. Mason checked the pickup report for the SOFT conference and learned that only 82 rooms had been reserved from the SOFT block, far fewer than the total of 150 reserved by SOFT. *Id.* at 22:17–23:4. Per the contract, Mr. Mason instructed his staff to invoice SOFT for the shortfall, but for reasons that he cannot explain, that invoice was not sent until July 27, 2012. *Id.* The invoice was for $9480.38, representing room charges and tax for a shortfall of 53 rooms (90% of the block of 150, less the 82 rooms actually reserved by SOFT guests). Freebird Dep. Ex. 3.

Luckily for the Gloucester Hotel, the Hoosier Club meeting that weekend was larger than usual. Gloucester was able to accommodate many of the overflow guests attending the Hoosier Club meeting, at the hotel's normal room rate of $189 per night. Mason Dep. 26:5–16.

SOFT has paid no part of the July 27 invoice and has indicated verbally to Gloucester that it does not intend to pay any part of it. Freebird Dep. 42:17–24. Gloucester therefore filed this action to collect the amount due under the contract provision. After the completion of discovery, both parties agreed that the basic facts are undisputed, and both parties have filed Motions for Summary Judgment that are now before the Court for resolution.

III. Issues

A. Is a liquidated damages clause enforceable on its face when it was freely bargained for and when the hotel would be unable, at the time the contract was signed, to predict how much it would be damaged if the booking party breached its promise to generate stated room revenue?

B. Is the amount of the liquidated damages stipulated in the contract reasonable since it is proportional to the extent of the breach by the booking party?

IV. Argument

Summary judgment should be granted where there is no genuine issue of material fact, and where the moving party is entitled to judgment as a matter of law. Ind. Trial Rule 56(C). Construction of a written contract is generally a question of law for the court, and summary judgment is a particularly appropriate means for resolving such cases. *Ancich v. Mobil Oil Corp.*, 422 N.E.2d 1320, 1322 (Ind. Ct. App. 1981). It is undisputed that SOFT signed the Group Contract for a conference to be held July 13 and 14, 2012, at the Gloucester Hotel, and that it failed to sell 90% of the rooms reserved to its guests, so summary judgment is appropriate in this case.

Liquidated damages provisions are enforceable when, if a breach occurs, the resulting damages are uncertain and difficult to ascertain, and the sum stipulated as liquidated damages may fairly be allowed as compensation for the breach. *Gershin v. Demming*, 685 N.E.2d 1125, 1127–28 (Ind. Ct. App. 1997). The designation in a contract of a sum as "liquidated damages" in the event of a breach indicates the parties' intention to limit their recovery to only the amount of the stated damages. *Beck v. Mason*, 580 N.E.2d 290, 293 (Ind. Ct. App. 1991). Where the sum stipulated in the agreement is not greatly disproportionate to the loss likely to occur, the provision is valid. *Nylen v. Park Doral Apts.*, 535 N.E.2d 178, 184 (Ind. Ct. App. 1989).

In this case, the damages that the Gloucester Hotel might have suffered if SOFT did not sell the required block of rooms was uncertain and difficult to ascertain. The liquidated damages clause in the contract was intended by the parties to be the exclusive remedy in the event of a breach, and the sum specified is directly proportional to what the actual damages likely would have been. The clause is therefore enforceable.

A. The liquidated damages clause in this contract is valid and enforceable

Whether a contractual provision stipulating damages in the event of a breach is a valid liquidated damages clause or a penalty is a question of law for the court. *Mandle v. Owens*, 164 Ind. App. 607, 330 N.E.2d 362, 364 (1975). In determining whether a stipulated sum payable on breach of a contract constitutes liquidated damages or a penalty, the court will consider the facts, the intention of the parties, and the reasonableness of the stipulation under the circumstances of the case. *Nylen*, 535 N.E.2d at 184.

In this case, the parties freely entered into a contract knowing that it contained a liquidated damages clause, not a penalty. Because the amount of actual damages in the event of a breach were, at the time the contract was negotiated, difficult or impossible to ascertain, and because the contract provides for no other remedy besides payment of liquidated damages, the clause is valid.

1. The clause was freely bargained for and is unambiguous

Indiana courts presume that contracts represent the freely bargained agreement of the parties. *Grott v. Jim Barna Log Sys.–Midwest, Inc.*, 794 N.E.2d 1098, 1102 (Ind. Ct. App. 2003). Nothing in this record suggests that this contract was not freely bargained.

Absent ambiguity, courts need only examine the contract itself to determine the intention of the parties. *Kincaid v. Lazar*, 405 N.E.2d 615, 620 (Ind. Ct. App. 1980). Here, the contract unambiguously includes a liquidated damages clause, specifying the amount of damages that SOFT should pay in the event that SOFT attendees did not reserve 135 rooms (90% of the block of 150).

The Executive Director of SOFT testified that she did not read the entire contract before signing it, Freebird Dep. 9:2–10:14, but that is not a defense to enforcement of the unambiguous provisions of the contract. In *Sanford v. Castleton Health Care Center*, 813 N.E.2d 411 (Ind. Ct. App. 2004), the plaintiff sought to avoid enforcement of an unambiguous provision of a contract with a health care institution for the care of her mother. The plaintiff brought her mother to the Castleton Health Care Center for treatment. During the admission process, her mother, who suffered from Alzheimer's, became agitated and aggressive; in addition, the plaintiff had to care for her own children who were with her as she completed the form. As a result, she signed the health care contract without reading it, although she admitted that nobody at the care facility prevented her from doing so. *Id.* at 415. The court held the contract enforceable on its terms.

Here, SOFT has even less reason to avoid the unambiguous contract language than did the plaintiff in *Sanford.* Ms. Pat Freebird, the SOFT Executive Director, testified that she received the contract in the mail in her office in Eureka, California, and that she had enough time to review its provisions to be sure they conformed to her understanding of the reservation she wanted to make. Freebird Dep. 9:2–10:14. There was no chaos or confusion, or really any sort of time pressure; the contract was returned to the hotel ten days after it was sent. Mason Dep. at 12:3–6. Accordingly, the contract is enforceable on its own terms.

2. At the time the contract was negotiated, actual damages for a possible breach were difficult to ascertain

A liquidated damages clause provides for the payment of a stated sum of money upon breach without proof of damages. *Gen. Bargain Ctr. v. Am. Alarm Co.*, 430 N.E.2d 407, 411 (Ind. Ct. App. 1982). Courts hold such clauses to be appropriate where, in the event of a breach, the resulting damages would be uncertain and difficult to ascertain. *Id.* For example, a provision in a residential lease requiring the tenant to pay a late fee of 1% of the monthly rent per day a rent payment was overdue was held to be an enforceable liquidated damage provision because it fairly compensated the landlord "for the administrative expense and inconvenience associated with untimely rent, including late payment notices and additional bookkeeping, and for the loss of use of rental income," all of which are uncertain and difficult to ascertain. *Gershin v. Demming*, 685 N.E.2d 1125, 1130 (Ind. Ct. App. 1997).

Likewise, the administrative expenses and inconvenience occasioned by SOFT's breach in this case were uncertain and difficult to ascertain. Gloucester had no way of knowing, at the time the contract was signed in August 2011, how many rooms short SOFT might be in June 2012. It could not predict what advertising costs or expenses it might incur to find additional guests to purchase the unsold rooms in an effort to mitigate damages. Nor could it know in advance what room rate the hotel might get for reselling those rooms; in fact, common sense suggests that finding substitute guests at the last minute might require the hotel to deeply discount its rooms in order to sell them. In addition, most guests at Gloucester also purchase meals and other services during their stay, all of which generate revenue for the hotel. It is impossible to determine how much revenue was lost from those ancillary sources as a result of SOFT's breach. Mason Dep. 22:2–23:19.

It is true that another organization, the Hoosier Club, was hosting a very popular event in a nearby hotel at the same time as the SOFT meeting, and that Gloucester was able to sell rooms to overflow guests from the host hotel for that meeting. *Id.* at 31:12–18. But this lucky circumstance does not save SOFT. For one thing, it should be noted that SOFT's pre-existing contract for rooms at Gloucester prevented the hotel from contracting with the Hoosier Club to be the host hotel for that meeting. *Id.* For another, the relevant time period for determining the foreseeability of actual damages is the date of signing the contract, not the date of breach. In *Zalewski v. Simpson*, 435 N.E.2d 74 (Ind. Ct. App. 1982), the court upheld a liquidated damages provision where it determined "[t]he purpose of the provision was not to force compliance with the contract, but rather to compensate in the event of breach for damages which were uncertain and difficult to ascertain *at the time the contract was executed.*" *Id.* at 77 (emphasis supplied). In August 2011, when this contract was signed, Gloucester had no knowledge that the Hoosier Club was going to host a meeting on the same weekend, and therefore could not have predicted whether it would be able to resell any rooms in the event SOFT breached its contract. Mason Dep. 31:12–18.

3. The parties intended the liquidated damages clause to be the exclusive remedy

In some cases, a dispute has arisen as to whether a liquidated damages provision is the exclusive remedy or whether a nonbreaching party may seek relief in addition to liquidated damages. *See, e.g., Beck v. Mason*, 580 N.E.2d 290, 293 (Ind. Ct. App. 1991) (holding that describing an earnest money deposit in a real estate sales contract as "liquidated damages" was sufficient proof that the parties intended to limit their remedies to that clause); *accord, Rogers v. Lockard*, 767 N.E.2d 982 (Ind. Ct. App. 2002). In our case, however, Gloucester seeks no remedy other than payment of liquidated damages. Pl.'s Compl. ¶ 21, Apr. 17, 2013, and *ad damnum* clause.

Accordingly, since the parties intended to create a liquidated damages clause, and since damages in the event were uncertain and difficult to ascertain, this Court should enforce the liquidated damages clause.

B. The sum specified as liquidated damages is proportional to the actual damages

SOFT, in its First Affirmative Defense, alleges that Gloucester was fully sold out on the nights of the SOFT conference and that therefore it has suffered no damage. Def.'s Answer, May 10, 2013, First Affirmative Defense. But this is not a sufficient defense.

First, as noted above, the purpose of liquidated damages clauses is to fix the amount of damage in the event of breach. *Gershin*, 685 N.E.2d at 1127 ("[a] typical liquidated damages provision provides for the forfeiture of a stated sum of money upon breach *without proof of damages*.") (emphasis supplied). The amount of actual damages incurred therefore is irrelevant, when the court determines that the liquidated damages clause is enforceable.

The most common argument made by those seeking to avoid application of the agreed-upon liquidated damage clause is that the amount of the specified damages is disproportionate to the amount of the actual damage that may occur. *See, e.g., id.* at 1128; *Czeck v. Van Helsland*, 143 Ind. App. 460, 241 N.E.2d 272 (1968). But it is important to remember that this determination is evaluated as of the time of the signing of the contract, not at the time of breach. *Rogers*, 767 N.E.2d at 991 (liquidated damages clauses are unenforceable where the payment specified "is grossly disproportionate to the loss *which may result* from breach") (emphasis supplied); *Gershin*, 685 N.E.2d at 1128 (liquidated damages clauses are enforceable where the payment specified "is not greatly disproportionate to the loss *likely to occur*") (emphasis supplied). Both of those formulations of the rule use predictive language, proving that the relevant inquiry is from the time the clause is agreed to by the parties.

As noted in section A-2 of this brief, *supra*, in August 2011 the amount of damages that Gloucester might suffer as a result of SOFT's brief was difficult or impossible to predict. When Gloucester entered into the contract, it gave up the opportunity to sell those rooms to other groups (like the Hoosier Club) that may have been planning meetings in Indianapolis over the same weekend. It had no way of determining in advance how many rooms SOFT members might fail to book, nor whether it would be able to resell those rooms to anybody, or at what rate. But, rather than arbitrarily specify a flat amount as liquidated damages, it agreed to a formula that directly proportioned the amount of damages to the amount of the shortfall in room sales. Thus, rather than being "grossly disproportionate" to the possible future loss of revenue, it was directly proportionate.

The formula specified in the contract is not, however, a measure of actual damages. As noted previously, it was impossible for Gloucester to know in advance how much advertising or other work it would need to do in order to resell the rooms, or how much ancillary revenue (food service and similar revenue) it would lose from having vacant rooms. Setting the amount of liquidated damages at the contract room rate times the number of unsold rooms was a reasonable estimate of the actual loss that would be occasioned if SOFT breached the agreement. Therefore, the contract provision is reasonable and should be enforced as a valid liquidated damages provision.

V. Conclusion

SOFT freely entered into a contract in which it reserved the exclusive right to book a specific number of rooms at the Gloucester Indianapolis Hotel for its guests. The Gloucester Hotel, relying on that promise, gave up other business opportunities, in exchange for a reasonable liquidated damages provision expressly proportioned to estimate the actual loss that might occur if SOFT failed to sell the number of rooms it promised to sell. The mere fact that SOFT may now regret its agreement is not a sufficient reason to avoid the contract. This Court should enforce the liquidated damages clause and enter judgment in favor of the Gloucester Hotel in the amount of $9480.38.

Respectfully Submitted

Sara Bellum, Esq.
4321 East Broad Street
Indianapolis, IN

Appendix D

Defendant's brief in opposition to plaintiff's motion for summary judgment and in support of defendant's motion for summary judgment

(student brief)

In the Superior Court of
Marion County, Indiana

Gloucester Hotel of Indianapolis, Inc., a Delaware corporation
   Plaintiff
 	
                v.
 	
Save Our Forest Trees, Inc., a California nonprofit corporation,
   Defendant
	)
	)
	)
	)
	)
	) No. 1531-GD-2012
	)
	)
	)
	)
	)

Defendant's brief in opposition to plaintiff's motion
for summary judgment and in support of defendant's
motion for summary judgment

I. Preliminary statement

Save Our Forest Trees, Inc., is a small nonprofit organization devoted to raising public awareness about the effects of deforestation on global warming, as well as facilitating scientific exchanges of research on this topic. It sponsored a conference in Indianapolis in summer 2012 at the Gloucester Hotel Indianapolis, part of the Gloucester Worldwide chain of hotels. The Hotel is seeking $9,480.38 from SOFT under a Group Contract for guest rooms it claims SOFT reserved but did not use; it claims that amount pursuant to a liquidated damages clause in the contract. However, the Hotel has admitted that it was sold out on the nights of the conference; as a consequence, numerous attendees of the SOFT conference had to find rooms elsewhere. The Hotel in fact suffered no loss of revenue.

Both parties have filed Motions for Summary Judgment, which are now before the Court for decision. The facts giving rise to this dispute are described in more detail below.

II. Statement of the facts

Global climate change has been the subject of a great deal of scientific inquiry and discussion in recent years. Many scientists have explored possible causes of the phenomenon and possible steps that society might take to slow or reverse the trend. One theory is that deforestation contributes to the problem by removing large numbers of trees that could otherwise convert a notorious greenhouse gas, carbon dioxide, into oxygen. One nonprofit organization, Save Our Forest Trees, Inc. ("SOFT") has devoted its existence to promoting an exchange of ideas and information among climate scientists working on this issue.

In summer 2012, SOFT hosted a two-day conference at the Gloucester Hotel Indianapolis. However, because Gloucester had booked other events at the same time and sold out the entire hotel on the nights of the conference, SOFT conference attendees were not able to purchase the number of hotel rooms specified in the contract between SOFT and the Gloucester Hotel. Gloucester's attempt to charge SOFT for the rooms its members could not buy has led to this lawsuit.

A. Save Our Forest Trees

Ms. Pat Freebird, now thirty-two years old, formed SOFT shortly after being awarded a bachelor's degree in biology and volunteering her time with other nonprofits and environmental advocacy groups. While her title is Executive Director for SOFT, in fact she is the organization's only employee, working long hours to realize its mission of connecting scientists and environmentalists to share their research findings and discuss ways to bring awareness to the problem of deforestation and climate change. Freebird Dep. 2:14–3:9, Aug. 20, 2013.

SOFT's headquarters are in Ms. Freebird's home, although she charges no rent to SOFT. Operating costs are kept to a bare minimum by communicating and advertising primarily over the Internet and through e-mail. Ms. Freebird herself earns only $30,000 in income, although she is a full-time employee. *Id.*

In 2011 SOFT had nearly $160,000 in total revenue. Freebird Dep. Ex. 1. Nearly $100,000 of that revenue came from the registration fees at four national conferences, usually held at universities where space is donated. About $30,000 of the revenue came from membership dues of $25 per member; the remainder of SOFT's income came from charitable donations. *Id.* Over the ten years it has been in existence, SOFT has accumulated a fund balance of only $25,000; in most years, its income and expenses have balanced out. Freebird Dep. 15:6–16:10. The organization currently has about 1200 dues-paying members. Membership benefits include access to one another's contact information and publications, quarterly newsletters by e-mail, and invitations to SOFT's national conferences. Def.'s Answer to Interrog. ¶ 5, Aug. 8, 2013.

To date, SOFT has held more than twenty successful national conferences. In 2012, conferences took place in four major cities: Miami Beach, Portland, New York City, and Indianapolis. *Id.* ¶ 7. A typical conference will draw around 200 registered participants. In a given year, usually at least half of SOFT's members, currently around 1500 people, attend one or more of these conferences. Freebird Dep. 12:6–21. Most conferences generate revenue of between $10,000 and $15,000 in excess of conference expenses, although some have generated net income as high as $18,000. Def.'s Answer to Interrog. ¶ 8. Participants are expected to make their own arrangements for hotel accommodations, but Ms. Freebird always arranges for a nearby hotel that offers a discounted rate to registrants. The main cost to SOFT is the cost of the opening reception where participants network and share ideas. Freebird Dep. 13:2–8.

Ms. Freebird has frequently arranged for hotel rooms through the Gloucester chain for group discounts, partly because it has hotels in most major cities, but also because it has a corporate policy of being "green." For example, it gives its guests the option of not washing linens and towels, serves only Fair Trade coffee, and offers a wide selection of fully organic meals, mostly from local farms, in many of its restaurants. *Id.* at 8:3–9:16.

B. The Indianapolis conference at the Gloucester Hotel

In summer 2011, SOFT selected Indianapolis as the site for a conference. Ms. Freebird called the Hotel to inquire about conference dates in July

2012. She requested a block of 150 rooms to be held over for July 13 and 14, 2012 (approximately 75 per night). *Id.* at 7:13–8:9. Based upon that number and the dates requested, the reservation agent for Gloucester told Ms. Freebird that the Hotel could offer a rate of $159 per night, which represented a significant discount from the hotel's normal rate of $189 per night. *Id.* at 8:1–6. Shortly after that phone call, a form contract arrived in the mail entitled "Group Contract," dated August 15, 2011 ("the Agreement"). Ms. Freebird checked the form to ensure that the room rate and block were accurate, and then signed it and returned it in the mail. *Id.* at 9:2–10:14.

Ms. Freebird did not read the contract in detail before signing it but testified at her deposition that "most of those contracts are all the same; just a bunch of legalese." *Id.* Based upon past arrangements with other hotels in the Gloucester chain and in the hotel industry generally, Ms. Freebird believed that the Agreement was meant to be simply a confirmation of the earlier conversation with the person she spoke to on the telephone. She believed that a signature was necessary to ensure that her group would get the discounted rate. *Id.*

In late June 2012, several SOFT members contacted Ms. Freebird to tell her that Gloucester was already sold out. *Id.* at 21:13–19. Ms. Freebird assumed from this information that the block of rooms under the Agreement had all been reserved by other members. She then recommended to the callers that they seek accommodations at another nearby hotel. *Id.* at 22:2–18.

When Ms. Freebird and the other participants arrived at the Hotel for the July conference, many SOFT guests were unable to check in on time. *Id.* at 26:1–27:16. Guests Carla Johnson and Milton Jones were both told by a clerk at the registration desk that the Hotel was "completely sold out." Johnson Aff. ¶ 4, Aug. 7, 2013. Many conference attendees were told that their rooms were not ready for the 4:00 p.m. check-in time they were promised; in fact, many participants did not get into their rooms until after 6:00 p.m. Freebird Dep. 19:2–14. On account of the "chaos," many of the out-of-town guests staying there missed the conference's opening reception and the catered refreshments. *Id.*

C. Pat Freebird returns to Eureka

Attendance at the conference turned out to be lower than Ms. Freebird had expected. Instead of 200 registrations, there had been only 152; and several of those were from Indiana residents who did not stay overnight at the Hotel. Because of the lower-than-expected attendance, the conference generated only about $5800 of income over expenses. Def.'s Answer to Interrog. ¶ 11 and Ex. 2 thereto.

A week or so after the Indianapolis event, SOFT received an invoice from the hotel charging $9480.38 for "attrition for unused guest rooms." The invoice claimed that there were 53 "unused" rooms. Freebird Dep. Ex. 3. Ms. Freebird was unsure how there could have been a shortfall if the hotel was turning away guests and claiming that it had been full, so she called the Hotel for an explanation. Nobody provided her with any information. *Id.* at 29:14-30:2.

Ms. Freebird then spoke with some of the people who had registered for the conference and found that several of them had been charged $189 per night rather than the discounted conference rate for their rooms; she assumed this was because the reserved block had sold out and that the guests then bought rooms at the regular Hotel rate. *Id.* at 31:15–23. She also discovered that at least a dozen SOFT members had been unable to book rooms at Gloucester during the conference and had to stay in other nearby hotels. *Id.* at 32:16–20.

Since she had not gotten a satisfactory answer on the phone, Ms. Freebird wrote a letter to the Hotel requesting a list of the participants who had reserved rooms, including how many were counted as part of the group. *Id.* Ex. 4. She hoped she would be able to determine from that list whether everybody who should have been counted toward the room block was in fact counted. *Id.* at 32:3–7. But instead of the guest list, about a month later, an attorney for the Hotel sent a letter insisting upon full payment of the entire amount within one week. *Id.* at 32:17–21 and Ex. 5. The attorney claimed that the amount sought represented liquidated damages for unused rooms ("attrition"), based on this clause in the contract:

Reservation Deadline: June 1, 2012

> In order to qualify for the guaranteed room rate, individuals must reserve rooms on or before the Reservation Deadline specified above, and must specify the Group Name. After the Reservation Deadline, rooms not reserved in the Group Name will be returned to the Hotel's general inventory and may be sold by the Hotel to any guest at normal Hotel rates. Group acknowledges that it may forgo the opportunity to reserve those rooms for other guests prior to the Reservation Deadline, and that the Hotel will incur costs in reselling rooms, and that these damages are difficult to ascertain. In the event that the Group fails to reserve 90% of the Room Block Reservation specified above by the Reservation Deadline, Group agrees to pay as liquidated damages, and not as a penalty, the difference between the actual number of rooms reserved by Group guests and 90% of the Room Block specified above, at the Guaranteed Room Rate, such payment to be due 15 days after the Reservation Deadline.

Contract for Room Reservations, Aug. 15, 2011, attached to Freebird Dep. Ex. 1. The Hotel then instituted this action when SOFT refused to pay for the allegedly unused guest rooms. Pl.'s Compl., Apr. 17, 2013.

During discovery in this case, the Hotel admitted that it was in fact sold out on both of the nights in question. Pl.'s Answer to Req. for Produc. of Doc. ¶ 6, July 18, 2013. It claimed, however, that it had turned down another conference for the same dates shortly after SOFT had signed its contract. Pl.'s Answer to Interrog. ¶ 13, July 18, 2013. It also claims that SOFT guests purchased only 82 room nights, rather than the 135 required by the contract (calculated as 90% of the 150 rooms in the original contract block). *Id.* at ¶ 15. While SOFT disputes both of those claims, even if the jury resolves both claims in favor of the Hotel, the Hotel cannot recover, and thus those disputes of fact are not material to the resolution of SOFT's Motion for Summary Judgment.

III. Issues

1. Is Gloucester's claim for additional payment from SOFT a penalty, and therefore not a valid liquidated damages clause? *Suggested answer:* Yes.

2. Since Gloucester sold all of its available rooms on the nights of the SOFT conference, has it been damaged at all? *Suggested answer:* No.

3. Did the sale by Gloucester of all available rooms on the nights of the SOFT conference make it impossible for SOFT to perform its obligations under the contract? *Suggested answer:* Yes.

IV. Argument

The attrition clause in the contract is a penalty rather than a liquidated damages clause; it is therefore unenforceable. Payment of the invoice by SOFT would be grossly disproportionate to damages (if any) suffered by the Hotel as a result of the shortfall in bookings by SOFT and result in a windfall to the Hotel. Moreover, the Hotel was not damaged because it was able to resell any rooms not reserved by SOFT guests, presumably at a higher price, and was therefore likely put in a better position than it would have been if SOFT's guests had filled the 53 "unused" guest rooms at the contract rate. In addition, by selling all of the rooms not reserved by SOFT, the Hotel made it impossible for SOFT to perform the contract.

A. The hotel seeks to enforce a penalty because the amount claimed is disproportionate to the actual damages and is easily calculable

To recover for a breach of contract, a plaintiff must prove that (1) a contract existed, (2) the defendant breached the contract, and (3) the plaintiff suffered damage as a result of the defendant's breach. *Collins v. McKinney*, 871 N.E.2d 363 (Ind. Ct. App. 2007). The plaintiff bears the burden of proof as to the amount loss resulting from a defendant's breach. The parties to a contract, however, may stipulate a sum in advance to be recoverable for a breach of contract where the loss suffered would be uncertain or difficult to ascertain. A liquidated damages provision "provides for the forfeiture of a stated sum of money without proof of damages." *Harbours Condo. Ass'n v. Hudson*, 852 N.E.2d 985, 993 (Ind. Ct. App. 2006).

However, a contract provision that claims to be a liquidated damages clause will not be enforced if it is in reality a penalty for nonperformance. This determination is made on a case-by-case basis, without the benefit of strict guidelines. *Gershin v. Demming*, 685 N.E.2d 1125, 1127–28 (Ind. Ct. App. 1997) ("In determining whether a stipulated sum payable on a breach of contract constitutes liquidated damages or a penalty, the facts, the intention of the parties and the reasonableness of the stipulation under the circumstances of the case are all to be considered.").

Here, the "attrition clause" sought to be enforced by the Hotel bears all the hallmarks of an unenforceable penalty. "[W]here the sum named is declared to be fixed as liquidated damages, is not greatly disproportioned to the loss that may result from a breach, and the damages are not measurable by any exact pecuniary standard, the sum designated will be deemed to be stipulated damages." *Jaqua v. Headington*, 16 N.E. 527, 528 (Ind. 1888). Further, there must be some nexus between the amount claimed and the damages flowing from a breach: a "stipulated sum will not be allowed as liquidated damages unless it may fairly be allowed as compensation for the breach." *Sterne v. Fletcher Am. Co.*, 204 Ind. 35, 49–50, 181 N.E. 37 (1932).

In one case, a hotel was required to refund the plaintiff's deposit because of the otherwise disproportionate loss that the plaintiff would have suffered. *2625 Bldg. Corp. v. Deutsch*, 179 Ind. App. 425, 385 N.E.2d 1189 (1979). In that case, the plaintiff reserved six hotel rooms during the weekend of the Indianapolis 500 race and, upon doing so, paid $1008.00 to the hotel, representing the full cost of the rooms. Two months prior to the reservation dates, the plaintiff cancelled the reservations and requested a refund. The hotel refused to return any of the advance payment. *Id.* at 1190.

Although the contract in that case was oral and thus included no express liquidated damages clause, the court held that allowing the hotel "to retain damages representing payment for use of all the rooms, regardless of the fact that damages could be ascertained, would be to enforce a penalty or forfeiture." *Id.* at 1192. Moreover, "assessing Deutsch for the full amount of his room payments would cause him to suffer a loss which was wholly disproportionate to any injury sustained by [the hotel]." *Id.* at 1193. The court therefore ruled that the defendant hotel was required to refund the plaintiff's deposit.

In the recent case of *Corvee, Inc. v. French*, 943 N.E.2d 844 (Ind. Ct. App. 2010), a collection company obtained a default judgment for an unpaid $8500 hospital bill and further sought to recover $3400 in attorney fees under a liquidated damages provision. The hospital admission form imposed responsibility on the patient for forty percent (40%) of the outstanding balance in connection with any attempt to collect the money due. The trial court awarded only $1000 in attorney fees to the collection agency as the reasonable fee for the default judgment collection action. Determining that the contract unambiguously required payment of the $3500, designated as attorney fees, the court of appeals considered whether the provision was an enforceable liquidated damages clause.

The Court of Appeals considered three factors relevant to the determination as to whether the liquidated damages provision was valid or an unenforceable penalty: (1) the difficulty of ascertaining damages resulting from a breach; (2) whether the stipulated sum can be "fairly allowed as compensation for the breach"; and (3) whether the party seeking enforcement of the liquidated damages clause has shown a correlation between the liquidated damages and actual damages, which is necessary "to assure that a sum charged may fairly be attributed to the breach." Reasoning that the calculation of attorney fees incurred during litigation should not be considered difficult to ascertain, and that the amount must be reasonable (even under a contractual provision), the court of appeals upheld the award of reasonable attorney fees. The court further stated that to allow the attorney pursuing the default judgment to recover the stipulated amount—in the absence of evidence that the fees were actually incurred—"gives rise to the possibility that [the attorney] will enjoy a windfall at [the defendant's] expense." *Id.* at 848.

In this case, the liquidated damages claimed by the Hotel fail to meet the legal requirements of an enforceable liquidated damages provision and should therefore be considered an unenforceable penalty provision. Just as the court in *2625 Building Corp.* found that damages in the event of a breach were easily ascertainable, damages in this case are easily ascertainable: the Hotel sent an invoice to SOFT for exactly 53 unused guest rooms. Freebird Dep. Ex. 3. More important, however, just as the court in *2625 Building Corp.* held that charging the patron who reserved the rooms but did not use them for the full value of those rooms was wholly disproportionate to any injury sustained by the hotel, charging SOFT with the full value of the rooms its members did not use is grossly disproportionate to any loss the Hotel might suffer. This is because the Hotel admittedly resold the rooms not reserved by members of SOFT. Pl.'s Answer to Req. for Produc. of Doc. ¶ 6. When reselling those rooms, the Hotel was no longer obligated to offer them at the lower rate called for in the SOFT contract; instead, it was free to sell the rooms at its standard rates. The Hotel therefore stood to make more money by reselling the rooms than by seeking liquidated damages. Any damages awarded to the Hotel would therefore likely result in a windfall to the hotel.

But even if the Hotel had been forced to sell the rooms at rates lower than those specified in the SOFT contract, they were not given away for free. Thus, the Hotel's damages, if any, were less (and likely far less) than the total cost of the rooms that the Hotel now seeks to recover from SOFT. Thus, the damages claimed are grossly disproportionate with the actual damages suffered, and therefore this liquidated damages clause is unenforceable.

B. The Hotel has not been damaged because it sold all of the rooms in the SOFT reservation block to other guests

To maintain a cause of action for breach of contract, a plaintiff must prove that it has been damaged. *Collins v. McKinney*, 871 N.E.2d 363 (Ind. Ct. App. 2007).

As noted in the previous section, the Hotel has admitted that it was sold out on the nights of the SOFT conference; in all likelihood, it sold the rooms at a rate higher than the contract rate. (There is in fact some evidence that several SOFT guests paid the higher rate of $189; *see, e.g.,* Johnson Aff. ¶ 6.) The Hotel has not claimed in any of the discovery materials in this case, nor in any of its pleadings or briefs, that it was forced to sell rooms at a rate lower than the contract rate in order to fill the hotel on the nights in question.

Since there is no evidence that the Hotel suffered any damage at all, its cause of action for breach of contract must fail.

C. The Hotel made it impossible for SOFT to perform by selling all of the rooms in SOFT's block to other guests

Where, after a contract is entered into, something happens that is not the defendant's fault but that renders defendant's performance of the contract "absolutely impossible," the defendant is excused from performing. *Krause v. Bd. of Trustees*, 162 Ind. 278, 283, 70 N.E. 264 (1904); *Kruse, Kruse & Miklosko, Inc. v. Beedy*, 170 Ind. App. 373, 394, 353 N.E.2d 514 (1976).

Most of the cases dealing with impossibility of performance deal with acts of God or other unforeseen events that are the fault of neither party to the contract. *See, e.g., Krause*, 162 Ind. at 265 (fire caused by lightning strike made it impossible for building renovation contract to be completed). However, the rule should apply with even greater force when one contracting party, by its own actions, renders it impossible for the other party to perform the contract. Stated another way, if one party to a contract engages in conduct that makes it impossible for the other party to perform the contract, the party creating the impossibility should not be allowed to recover for the breach it caused. *Cf. Prather v. Latshaw*, 188 Ind. 204, 122 N.E. 721, 722 (1919) (apparently accepting the proposition that a party to a contract is not bound to perform it where performance is rendered impossible by the act of God, by the law, or by the act of the other party to the contract).

Here, Gloucester admits that it sold all of the hotel rooms it had on the nights of the SOFT conference to non-SOFT guests. Pl.'s Answer to Req. for Produc. of Doc. ¶ 6. Since the contract did not prohibit SOFT members from purchasing rooms after the reservation deadline, Gloucester's sale of those rooms made it impossible for SOFT to sell rooms to its own guests. Accordingly, Gloucester should not be allowed to charge SOFT with a breach of contract consisting of a failure to sell those rooms.

D. Conclusion

The Hotel's admission that it was sold out on the nights of the SOFT conference is fatal to its claim in this case, for a number of reasons. First, the contract language in this case does not create a valid liquidated damages clause since any damages would be easily calculable. Instead of liquidated damages, therefore, the Hotel is limited to any actual damages that it can prove. But it cannot prove any damages at all since it was able to resell all of the rooms originally reserved for SOFT guests. Second, the Hotel's act of selling all of the available rooms rendered it impossible for SOFT to perform its obligation under the contract. The Hotel should not be allowed to profit from its actions by demanding that SOFT pay it a second time for rooms that it has already been paid for by other guests.

This Court should grant SOFT's Motion for Summary Judgment, deny the Hotel's Motion for Summary Judgment, and dismiss this action with prejudice.

Respectfully Submitted

_____

Amanda Reckonwith, Esq.
1234 West Main Street
Indianapolis, IN

Index

(Figures, notes, and tables are indicated by f, n, and t following page numbers.)

About the authors

Ruth Anne Robbins, *Clinical Professor of Law and Director of Lawyering Programs, Rutgers School of Law–Camden.* Professor Robbins teaches first year and advanced legal writing courses and the law school's internal moot court program. She also founded and still teaches in the law school's Domestic Violence Clinic. She is a past president of the Legal Writing Institute and is the co-Editor in Chief of *Legal Communication & Rhetoric: JALWD.* Professor Robbins co-founded and organizes the Applied Legal Storytelling international conference series. Her glasses (not pictured: please visualize them as ultra-hip) have interchangeable stems, and it amuses her to matchy-match them to her outfits.

Steve Johansen, *Professor and Director of Legal Analysis and Writing, Lewis & Clark Law School.* Professor Johansen teaches 1L legal writing, contract drafting, and professional responsibility. He is a past president of the Legal Writing Institute and a co-founder and organizer of the Applied Legal Storytelling conference series. In 2009, he received the Thomas Blackwell Memorial Award from the Legal Writing Institute and the Association of Legal Writing Directors. He shares his office with his dog Quigley and likes his Sox red and his beer black.

Ken Chestek, *Assistant Professor of Law and Assistant Director of the Center for the Study of Written Advocacy, University of Wyoming College of Law.* Professor Chestek was a trial lawyer in Pennsylvania for 21 years before teaching at the University of Michigan, Indiana University McKinney School of Law, and the University of Wyoming. He served as President of the Legal Writing Institute from 2010–2012 and has published several articles studying the impact of stories on judicial decision making. He has 12 states left to complete his lifetime quest of running a marathon in all 50 states, but isn't sure whether completing the quest will make him a hero or some other type of character.